International Organizations in World Politics

SAGE was founded in 1965 by Sara Miller McCune to support the dissemination of usable knowledge by publishing innovative and high-quality research and teaching content. Today, we publish over 900 journals, including those of more than 400 learned societies, more than 800 new books per year, and a growing range of library products including archives, data, case studies, reports, and video. SAGE remains majority-owned by our founder, and after Sara's lifetime will become owned by a charitable trust that secures our continued independence.

Los Angeles | London | New Delhi | Singapore | Washington DC | Melbourne

International Organizations in World Politics

Tamar Gutner
American University

Los Angeles | London | New Delhi
Singapore | Washington DC | Melbourne

FOR INFORMATION:

CQ Press
An Imprint of SAGE Publications, Inc.
2455 Teller Road
Thousand Oaks, California 91320
E-mail: order@sagepub.com

SAGE Publications Ltd.
1 Oliver's Yard
55 City Road
London EC1Y 1SP
United Kingdom

SAGE Publications India Pvt. Ltd.
B 1/I 1 Mohan Cooperative Industrial Area
Mathura Road, New Delhi 110 044
India

SAGE Publications Asia-Pacific Pte. Ltd.
3 Church Street
#10-04 Samsung Hub
Singapore 049483

Acquisitions Editor: Michael Kerns
Editorial Assistant: Zachary Hoskins
Production Editor: Laura Barrett
Copy Editor: Elizabeth Swearngin
Typesetter: Hurix Systems Pvt. Ltd.
Proofreader: Dennis W. Webb
Indexer: Nancy Fulton
Cover Designer: Karine Hovsepian
Marketing Manager: Amy Whitaker

Printed in the United States of America

ISBN 978-1-5680-2924-5

This book is printed on acid-free paper.

SFI Certified Sourcing
www.sfiprogram.org
SFI-00453

16 17 18 19 20 10 9 8 7 6 5 4 3 2 1

Table of Contents

Preface

As this book was going to press, 195 countries met in Paris under the auspices of the United Nations (UN) to discuss climate change. There, they reached an agreement to work together to slow the increase in the global average temperature, in order to minimize or avoid potentially catastrophic consequences for the planet: severe droughts, rising sea levels, destructive storms, and associated challenges to food and water security. UN Secretary-General Ban Ki-moon hailed the agreement as "a monumental triumph for people and our planet." Laurent Fabius, the French foreign minister presiding over the conference, called the agreement a "historical turning point." The deal commits every country to take action to address climate change. But the agreement is also voluntary and unenforceable, which means it remains up to the states, supported by other stakeholders, to keep their promises and implement measures that will make a difference. Skeptics immediately expressed concern that the agreement will not go far enough to stop temperatures from rising more than 2 degrees Celsius, which scientists estimate as the point of no return.

The simultaneous expressions of euphoria and concern in the aftermath of the UN-sponsored climate negotiations mirror the general consensus about international organizations (IOs). Some people view IOs as essential actors that make a difference by bringing states together to address problems that do not respect national borders. Others view IOs as lacking the necessary power, support, tools, or incentives to make a difference, perhaps even setting the world up for failure.

Are IOs saviors, irrelevant, or even harmful? There is no single answer to this question. There is great variation among IOs and even within a single IO over time or with respect to different issues. There are examples of successful actions and costly mistakes for each IO. The UN may be praised for getting states to negotiate on a number of topics, and it has produced new norms of behavior and even averted conflict. But there are many instances where it failed to act and the cost was human lives and enormous suffering. It is also case that IO failures tend to make global headlines, whereas the many successes, often small in scope, are likely to go unnoticed beyond the local population. There are also different ways of defining success and failure, as the Paris agreement underscores. Many would argue that the mere fact the UN brought so many countries together, and that they agreed on something in principle, is success in and of itself. Others would claim that success has only one measure: if the accord paves the way for the world to avoid the catastrophic changes that will result from excessive warming.

Approach and Organization of the Book

The book is premised on the belief that IOs play a critical role in global governance, even if their performance is mixed across institutions, issues, and time. IOs offer fora for cooperation, provide expertise, initiate ideas and agendas, disseminate knowledge, encourage collaboration, and implement policies, programs, and projects. They can be found working to avert or end a conflict; vaccinating children; helping farmers with their crops; stopping the contagion of a financial crisis or a virus; bringing clean water to a village or saving tigers. They are involved in all the pressing issues of our time: the global environment, trade, terrorism, health, security, development, education, human rights, conflict resolution, agriculture, migration, crime, and more. Indeed, it is difficult to find a transboundary issue that that some IO somewhere is *not* engaged in. Nonetheless IO involvement does not necessarily mean the problem is solved, or is even properly addressed.

How can we understand the role of IOs in global governance? The purpose of the book is to give the reader a nuanced and comprehensive understanding of major IOs and their evolving role in international politics and global governance. It does so by first, in chapters 1 and 2, looking at the big picture—how to conceptualize IOs and their roles in the world, and different ways scholars, mainly in international relations, have thought about and debated the importance of IOs. IOs operate in a broader and more complex institutional landscape of global governance, constantly interacting with states, other IOs, civil society, business groups, philanthropists, networks of national officials, and other actors to confront the problems facing the world. States remain the most powerful actors in international politics, although a number of scholars and others are questioning whether this is changing. While the most powerful states remain critically important to the success or failure of an IO, they do not always get what they want and they are not always the most influential players among the many stakeholders that may converge around a specific issue. IOs also have different degrees of flexibility as actors in their own right.

Chapters 3-10 focus on the most influential IOs: the United Nations, World Bank, International Monetary Fund (IMF), and World Trade Organization (WTO). Each IO is covered in a pair of chapters. The first chapter contains the "nuts and bolts" of the IO, beginning with the circumstances surrounding its origin. What prompted states to create the IO? How is it structured and governed? What does it actually do, and has its work changed over time? How has the IO performed? What are some different perspectives on its actions and effectiveness? The chapters show how this diverse set of organizations share several common challenges, including how to adapt to a changing world and how to remain relevant and legitimate while doing so.

The second chapter in each pair presents a case study that explores an important but difficult issue that IO has faced. The case studies cover a wide range of topics and help the reader to understand how complicated the issues, politics, and IO responses are in situations where there are no easy answers. Chapter 4 is a case study of the UN's failure to act in the Rwandan genocide of the mid-1990s, where tens of thousands of people were massacred in 100 days. Why did the UN, and the world, do so little? Chapter 6 examines the World Bank's zigzag performance in addressing major environmental issues. The World Bank has been a leader in global environmental governance while simultaneously it has been accused of causing environmental destruction. Chapter 8 reviews the IMF's role in the 2008 global financial crisis. Before the crisis erupted, the IMF was allegedly losing credibility and relevance. The crisis dramatically changed the IMF, infusing it with fresh life and importance as the centerpiece of global economic governance. How well did it perform? Chapter 10 examines the WTO's actions in the area where intellectual property rights, trade, and access to medicine interact. Balancing intellectual property rights with human health can literally be a matter of life and death.

Regional organizations are a category of IOs that deserve their own attention. Chapter 11 looks broadly at regional organizations, their roles in global governance, and the debates about them. The chapter focuses on the European Union (EU), the most innovative and powerful organization among the regionals. To illuminate a major challenge the EU is facing today, the chapter examines the euro crisis. Chapter 12 offers a case study of the peace operations of the African Union (AU). The AU moved away from its predecessor's emphasis on the principle of *non-interference* in member states, adopting instead the principle of *non-indifference*. The chapter describes and evaluates how successful the AU's peace operations have been in managing conflict in the region while pursuing a new commitment to democracy and the rule of law.

As long as we need global cooperation to work toward global solutions, IOs have a vital role to play. IOs will never exist in a vacuum, and their successes and failures are inextricably linked to the political will of their member states, and increasingly influenced by actions from other actors as well. Over a half century ago, the pioneer IO scholar Inis Claude, Jr. observed that IOs are a response "to the challenging problems and terrible dangers of international life in an era of increasing interdependence." His words still hold true today.[1]

ACKNOWLEDGEMENTS

The world of people who study international organizations, work in them, or interact with them in other ways, often finds itself divided into communities or networks that focus on the smaller picture—an individual organization, region, or issue area—rather than a more holistic view across a range of organizations. This is especially true in the scholarly world. I want to thank CQ Press, consequently, for giving me the opportunity to write a book that allowed me to take more of a bird's eye view, while simultaneously exploring some of the most important IOs more in-depth. Special thanks to Charisse Kiino at SAGE, who supported this project at every step of the way. I also want to express my gratitude to Martha Finnemore for connecting me with SAGE/CQ Press, and to the editorial and production staff at SAGE/CQ Press who have been so helpful over the years, especially Elise Frasier.

A number of colleagues and friends provided substantive advice on the overall project, as well as individual chapters. Special thanks to the participants in my "book incubator": David Bosco, Randy Henning, Miles Kahler, Rachel Sullivan Robinson, Mike Schroeder, and Susan Sell. Their comments made a significant difference on the design and content of the book, and their own scholarly work is always an inspiration. Amitav Acharya, Bill Belding, Chuck Call, Michelle Egan, Sikina Jinnah, Carl Levan, and Nina Yamanis were also generous in sharing their expertise; I am fortunate to be part of such a supportive, multi-disciplinary intellectual environment at American University's School of International Service. The SIS dean, Jim Goldgeier, made sure there was time for my research and writing during my stint as Associate Dean for Faculty Affairs and Graduate Education. His predecessor, Lou Goodman, encouraged me to take on this project and has always been a mentor. I was also privileged to work with supportive staff at SIS, who were amusingly diligent in protecting my research hours when I could easily have spent that time on administrative work. Thank you to Brittany Stewart, Jenny Napolitano, and Lee Schwentker. Thanks, too, to Holly Christensen, and Shannon Looney, for helping with the book incubator. I also benefited from excellent research assistance provided by Jason Rancatore, Marcy Babicz, Shawn Trumbo, Rachel Nadelman, Jyahyun Albert Lee, and Elise Voorhis. I also want to thank the anonymous reviewers for their excellent feedback on the book. Elizabeth Swearngin was a patient and thorough copyeditor.

Heartfelt thanks are due to Mike Berrisford, Debra Marks, Melissa Moye, Elena Georgieva, Bruce Rich, Neil Shenai, and other friends outside of academia who are experts on issues covered in the book and offered so many helpful suggestions. My conversations with the late Luca Barbone on the World Bank are now special memories. Margel Highet, Joyce Erony, Dalia Dassa Kaye, Sharon Weiner, and Alexa Robertson were always there for moral support and encouragement.

Finally, I would like to thank my family, especially my husband, Max Holland, who is the most patient person and thorough researcher I know. He was always available to listen, to brainstorm, to read, to ask questions, and to help with issues large and small. This book is dedicated to him.

1 Introduction

Men and nations want the benefits of international organization, but they also want to retain the privileges of sovereignty, which are inseparable from international disorganization. The development of international organization has been plagued by the failure of human beings to think logically and realistically about the inexorable relationships between the purchase and the price, between the having and the eating of the cake.

–Inis Claude Jr. (1956)[1]

International organizations (IOs) are essential, but controversial, actors in world politics today. They are expected to rebuild war-torn societies, help to stop the spread of the Ebola virus and other diseases, assist countries in avoiding or overcoming financial crises, adjudicate disputes between states, reduce extreme poverty and malnutrition, push countries to cooperate on major global environmental problems, make trade more free and fair, promote gender equality, reform legal systems, reduce corruption, and tackle terrorism. These examples are only a drop in the bucket, since IOs find themselves working in almost every imaginable international issue area that states cannot easily address individually, issues that former United Nations Secretary-General Kofi Annan famously called "problems without passports." All IOs have seen their mandates expand over time, and they all struggle to balance so many goals and tasks as they are expected to constantly adapt to a changing global context. The work of IOs directly affects the lives of billions of people. But instead of being praised for their contributions, IOs face relentless attacks from critics who believe IOs cause or enhance the same set of problems they are supposed to solve. IOs are also part of a complex global institutional landscape today that includes states, nongovernmental organizations (NGOs), multinational corporations, private foundations, and a host of other players that impact how decisions and policies are made, and whether and how problems are solved. Many global policy issues today impact multiple IOs, as well as local and regional actors. In this complex and sometimes confusing topography of governance, cooperation across levels and effective institutions are necessary to make a meaningful dent in addressing the "problems without passports." Therefore, it is important that IOs remain relevant actors even as the institutional landscape evolves.

Whether and how to reform IOs is a topic of lively debate. For each major IO there is a spectrum of opinions, ranging from why we should abolish it to why we should help it to grow larger and do even more. The debates are rich and sometimes raucous. The only agreements are that the world has changed dramatically since most major IOs were established at the end of World War II, that the architecture of global governance from that era is ill-equipped to address the global and regional challenges of today, and that this change requires some type of shift in what IOs are expected and able to do.

The purpose of this book is to provide a comprehensive understanding of major IOs and their changing role in world politics and global governance. It presents the tools and knowledge useful for navigating the cacophony of opinions about IOs, which allow for an informed view of IO principles, practices, and performance. The tools of navigation are developed by first grounding the study of IOs in an intellectual setting that surveys different approaches to analyze the importance and impact of IOs found in the IO literature (Chapter 2). The remaining chapters examine the historical development, governance, activities, structure, and performance of a set of major IOs. The book focuses on the United Nations (UN), World Bank, International Monetary Fund (IMF), and World Trade Organization (WTO), which are the most powerful, important, and influential IOs in the world. The UN is the leading IO created to try to maintain peace in the world. The World Bank, IMF, and WTO are the IOs that have most influenced the phenomenon of *globalization*, a process by which sharply lower communication and transportation costs and fewer barriers to transboundary flows of trade, knowledge, and people have created more integration among states, markets, people, and technologies.[2] The European Union is also an important player in global politics and is addressed as part of a chapter that examines regional organizations more broadly. Regional organizations play important roles in international politics today, and their ability to successfully address problems is also contested.

A second chapter on each of the major IOs presents a case study designed to illuminate a major challenge or issue confronting the organization in order to help understand both its ability to help solve global problems and the factors that influence its activities, responses, and evolution. The UN case study examines why the UN and the entire international community failed to act in the Rwandan genocide of the mid-1990s, where over half a million people were massacred in 100 days. The World Bank case study focuses on the institution's environmental behavior and performance. The bank's environmental behavior in the 1980s prompted the first major campaign by environmental NGOs against it and resulted in decades of uneven reform. This case provides insight into how such a large organization struggles with its growing number of mandates. The IMF case reviews the IMF's actions before, during, and after the 2008 global financial crisis. Before the crisis, the IMF was struggling with its legitimacy. Lending was down, staff were let go. During the crisis, the G20 leaders turned to the IMF to be a financial firefighter, and suddenly the IMF was once again at the center of global economic governance. The WTO case study looks at the role of the organization in the area of intellectual property rights, trade, and access to medicine. The issue of poor country access to medication raises big questions on how to balance intellectual property rights with saving lives. The case study on regional organizations examines the evolving role of the African Union with a focus on its ability to reduce conflict in Africa.

Understanding the role of IOs in global politics has become even more important in recent years as policymakers and scholars grapple with the concept of *global governance*—what it means, what has changed, and why it matters. The idea behind the term is that states, international organizations, NGOs, corporations, and a variety of other actors must interact to help address global problems that no actor can solve alone. The verb *to govern* has a wide variety of meanings that includes "to exercise sovereignty over" (like a government has inside a state), "to exercise authority," "to rule without sovereign power and usually without having authority to determine basic policy," and to "have decisive influence."[3] *Governance*, in turn, has to do with administering, ruling, exercising authority, and exerting leadership. As the former Director-General of the WTO Pascal Lamy noted, governance also has to provide legitimacy, leadership, and coherence.[4]

It should be no surprise, then, that in the scholarly and policy worlds, there are a number of definitions for *global governance*. Some are simple and straightforward. The US National Intelligence Council and EU institute of Security Studies, in a report entitled "Global Governance 2025: At a Critical Juncture," defined global governance as "the collective management of common problems at the international level."[5] Rapid globalization, they argued, means that problems and threats that states used to be able to manage at the local level are not only more global, but may also be threats to global security and peace. Examples include food and water scarcity, ethnic conflict, terrorism, and infectious diseases. Scholars Thomas Weiss and Ramesh Thakur, by contrast, have a much broader definition of global governance. Global governance, they stated, is "the sum of laws, norms, policies, and institutions that define, constitute, and mediate relations among citizens, society, markets, and the state in the international arena—the wielders and objects of international public power."[6] They made two important points. Their first point echoes the global governance report noted above: Collective arrangements can help to address transboundary problems, even though there is no overarching global authority. Their second point is that global governance does not necessarily produce positive outcomes. It "can be good, bad, or indifferent."[7] It is important to remember that the fact that a global problem is on the radar of many different types of actors does not mean the problem will be solved, or even reduced. The different involved actors often disagree on how best to solve a particular problem. It is safe to say that global governance may often be a messy process.

Compounding the challenge of getting different types of actors to work together to address global problems is the vagueness of *who* is doing the governing. As Deborah Avant, Martha Finnemore, and Susan Sell pointed out, policymakers and academics often treat global governance as a process that happens, but they do not ask themselves who are the global *governors*.[8] Governors, the authors argued, may be states, IOs, corporations, advocacy groups, and other actors, all of whom are involved in a dynamic political process in which they are exercising power across borders to have an impact on policy and policy outcomes. The authors argued that the "character of the relationship" between the governors and the governed is important to understanding global politics.[9]

The remainder of this chapter returns to the focus on IOs by offering basic definitions and concepts on IOs, what they do, when and why they were born, and a brief history of their evolution.

WHAT IS AN IO?

What is an international organization? There is no simple, straightforward definition, because there are differences between how scholars define IOs and what the term means in everyday use. The general definition of an international organization is *a formal organization with members from three or more states that pursues a specific set of goals*.[10] Technically, there are two main categories of IOs. The first is an intergovernmental organization (IGO) whose members are states represented by their governments. IGOs are established by inter-governmental agreement. Examples include the UN, the World Bank, and regional organiza-tions, such as the North Atlantic Treaty Organization (NATO). The second category is an international NGO whose members are individuals, groups, or associations. Amnesty International and World Wildlife Fund are well-known examples.[11] Today, there are thou-sands of international NGOs operating around the world, and they are interacting in com-plex ways with other more traditional actors. What distinguishes traditional NGOs from IGOs is that members of the former do not officially represent governments. To complicate matters, there are also *hybrid* organizations, with members from both inside and outside of government.[12] An example is the International Labour Organization, the first specialized agency of the UN, with a Governing Body that consists of government, employer, and employee members. In practice, when most people refer to IOs, they mean the first cate-gory, IGOs. They are mostly referring to the global organizations rather than regional ones. When referring to the second category, people use the term NGOs. This book will use the terms IO and IGO synonymously and use NGO and regional organization for those latter categories.

Another difference between scholarly and every-day language can be found in the term *international institutions*. For most people, the term international institution is synonymous with international organization. The UN, IMF, and WTO, for example, are commonly referred to as either. In this book, the terms are also used interchangeably. But in the scholarly world, *institution* also has meanings that are broader than the term *organization*. International insti-tutions have been defined by political scientists as "persistent and connected sets of rules and practices that prescribe behavioral roles, constrain activity, and shape expectations."[13] These are the rules that help to govern world politics. They may include international law and international norms, for example, that may or may not be the responsibility of a particu-lar organization. In other words, in the scholarly world, an international institution may include both "the rules that govern elements of world politics and the organizations that help to implement those rules."[14]

Many scholars have also used the term *institutions* synonymously with *regimes*, defined as "sets of implicit or explicit principles, norms, rules, and decision-making procedures around which actors' expectations converge in a given area of international relations."[15] This broad definition was especially popular during the 1980s, as scholars sought to examine issues such as trade regimes or security regimes that consisted of broader governing arrange-ments that may or may not encompass formal organizations. One way to make the distinc-tion between institution/regime and organization is to think of organizations as institutions with walls and bureaucrats, or as one scholar quipped, "palpable entities with headquarters and letterheads, voting procedures, and generous pension plans."[16] To illustrate, the Bretton Woods system was set up in 1944 as a regime to govern international monetary relations by pegging currencies to the dollar and the dollar to gold, but at its center was an international organization—the IMF.[17] The distinction may sound like a trivial one, but it is analytically important when there is a need to separate a particular organization from the broader issues to which it is linked. In other words, there are reasons to look at the trees rather than the forest when trying to understand how IOs themselves impact international problems and policy for better or for worse.

BRIEF HISTORY AND EVOLUTION

The modern IO has its roots in the mid-nineteenth century, when states set up a handful of organizations to cooperate on a focused set of issues such as health and trade.[18] Many of the IOs created in the 19th century were born in Europe, and in the wake of major outbreaks of violence, such as the Napoleonic wars, Franco-Prussian War, and Crimean War.[19]

One of the first modern IOs (which still exists) was the Central Commission for Navigation of the Rhine, established in 1815 by the Final Act of the Congress of Vienna to promote free navigation on the Rhine River.[20] The Superior Council of Health was created in 1838 in Constantinople with Ottoman and European delegates to control outbreaks of cholera and other diseases, in part, by promoting new sanitary measures and calling for quarantines.[21] The European Commission for the Control of the Danube was set up in 1856 to improve navigation on the Danube, as part of the Treaty of Paris signed at the end of Crimean War.

The *diplomacy by conference* that was firmly established in the 19th century was also a precursor to the modern IO, as was the development of international law.[22] For example, the Congress of Vienna—itself created by the victors of the Napoleonic Wars—provided opportunities for its members to consult periodically as a means to balance power and deter aggression. While the Congress of Vienna did not succeed in creating the regular consultations envisioned, as Inis Claude, Jr. noted, "the techniques of diplomacy had been irrevocably changed."[23] The subsequent Concert of Europe consisted of the Great Powers (Russia, Prussia, Austria, Great Britain, and later joined by France), and met on occasion for the rest of the century to try and collaborate on issues of concern. It has been credited with opening up diplomatic channels as well as laying the foundation of an executive council that some saw as a prototype for the UN Security Council.[24] The process of consultation and coordination, and the dominating role of the most powerful states, contributed to norms about multilateral diplomacy and negotiation, and also reflected a growing awareness that international cooperation could help states achieve outcomes they might be unable to achieve unilaterally. All this was occurring as communication and transport links continued to draw people closer together, enhancing opportunities for both conflict and cooperation.[25]

The 19th century developments were mixed in terms of their success. Collaboration often failed, the conference system functioned sporadically, and it did not produce permanent institutions. "The Concert of Europe was rather inappropriately named," wrote Claude. "It was an orchestra without a conductor or regular rehearsals, whose members played with so little respect for the score that they produced cacophony more often than harmony."[26] In the aftermath of World War I (1914–1918), a number of IOs and NGOs were born amid renewed efforts to create a more peaceful world and avoid a return to the horror and destruction caused by what was known as the Great War. The most important of these was the League of Nations, the forerunner of the UN. The League was established in 1920 out of the Versailles Peace Conference negotiating an end to World War I. Based in Geneva, Switzerland, its mandate was to achieve international peace and security in part by having member states agree to submit disputes with members or nonmembers for arbitration or judicial settlement, and agree "in no case to resort to war until three months" after attempts at such settlement or decision occurred.[27] Articles 12–16 reflected an attempt at a collective security provision, in calling for members to respond against a member resorting to war by severing trade or financial relationships, and, if necessary, using military, naval, or air force.

The creation of the League had its immediate roots in a number of private and public efforts to help design a post-war order. Groups such as the League of Nations Society (Britain) and League to Enforce Peace (United States) were vocal. Government officials in France, Britain, South Africa, and elsewhere were also actively drafting proposals for the organization of the post-war era.[28] US President Woodrow Wilson ardently backed the notion of a League of Nations as early as 1916, and most famously called for "a general association of nations . . . formed . . . for the purpose of affording mutual guarantees of political independence and territorial integrity to great and small states alike" as the last point of his "Fourteen Points" speech presented to the US Congress in January 8, 1918.

While the League was a novel and dramatic experiment at the time, an embodiment of liberal views dating back at least to Immanuel Kant's *Perpetual Peace* (1795), it was also burdened by a number of weaknesses that ultimately led to its failure and collapse in 1939. The League was unable to check the aggressive behavior of Japan (which quit the League in 1931), Italy (which withdrew in 1937), and Germany (which joined in 1926 and exited in 1933), and therefore slow or halt the inevitable steps leading toward World War II. Ambiguity about the specific roles of the League's Council and Assembly and the requirement of unanimity on voting on important issues also all contributed to the League's downfall.[29] And while Wilson "dominated the ideological scene" surrounding the League's development, the United States in the end did not join, and the absence of a major international power also hurt the League deeply.[30] It was formally disbanded in April 1946.[31]

Today's most powerful IOs were born in the waning days and aftermath of World War II. The UN, World Bank, IMF, General Agreement on Tariff and Trade (later to evolve into the WTO), and the European Coal and Steel Community (later to evolve into the European Union) were founded between 1944 and 1951. Their histories, governance, activities, and challenges are discussed in subsequent chapters. Like the League of Nations, they were created above all as grand, dramatic experiments to help avoid future world wars, even though individual countries may have had additional reasons for participating.

The number of IOs has also grown dramatically since the end of World War II. In some ways it is even difficult to know how many there are. According to the *Yearbook of International Organizations* 2014–2015, there are at least 260 "conventional" intergovernmental international organizations today, of which almost three-quarters have regionally-based membership. These organizations vary enormously in size, scope, goals, and influence. By contrast, there are over 8,500 international NGOs. The *Yearbook* adds additional categories that show even more variety, including "organizations emanating from places, persons, bodies"; "organizations of special form"; and "autonomous conference series" to name a few.[32] But there is no consensus on numbers, with other sources listing fewer or more.

In terms of size, the entire UN family, for example, consists of 193 nations and employs around 45,000 people. The UN once put the seemingly large numbers of employees into perspective by pointing out that Disneyland and Disney World together employed more people than the UN.[33] Its core budget for 2014–2015 was $5.7 billion.[34] Its peacekeeping budget, which can fluctuate substantially as missions change, was around $8 billion.[35] By contrast, the Geneva-based WTO has a small staff of 635 and a budget of less than 200 million Swiss francs in 2013–2014.[36]

RANGE OF IO GOALS

IO goals also range from the very narrow to the very broad. The small, Paris-based International Institute of Refrigeration, with a membership of 38 countries, has the specific mandate of expanding knowledge of refrigeration technology and applications. Compare that to the World Bank, which works in poor countries to reduce poverty, combat HIV/AIDS, promote sustainable development, support private sector development, modernize judicial and legal systems, build educational systems, and promote gender equality and justice. When organizations have huge, broad goals, it is also difficult to measure their performance. The UN Security Council, for example, is tasked with "maintaining international peace and security." Does that mean it is unsuccessful every time there is a conflict or that we can realistically expect it to reduce all conflict?

Regional organizations also come in all shapes and sizes from the very large (European Union) to the much smaller Asian and Pacific Coconut Community. Like their global relations, their goals cover a broad range of sectors and activities. IOs, global and regional, operate in areas that include security, development, education, telecommunications, health, environment, human rights, trade, agriculture, labor, migration, tourism, and so on—just about every imaginable issue that crosses borders.

WHY DO STATES CREATE IOs?

States create IOs to pursue a variety of common interests and to serve a variety of functions that states cannot achieve individually. At the most basic level, an IO provides a forum where states can meet regularly to accomplish whatever goals they have set for it. This regular communication makes it easier for states to share information and to pursue common interests, which results, ideally, in greater cooperation through specific actions that help to achieve shared goals. IOs bring together experts and decision makers to create and disseminate new knowledge, policies, and rules. They also help to implement and monitor the outcomes of these actions. Therefore, IOs help to coordinate global responses and the global rules themselves, and they monitor and enforce actors' compliance with those rules. The small United Nations Environment Programme, for example, has played a critical role facilitating interstate agreement on a variety of international environmental treaties, such as ozone depletion and persistent organic pollutants. It also works to promote state compliance with international environmental agreements.

IOs also provide states the ability to coordinate their actions by pooling financial, technological, and analytical resources to accomplish common goals. For example, the World Bank and its regional relatives get financial resources from member states and then raise their own money on international capital markets, so they can lend billions of dollars a year to poor countries. The International Food Policy Research Institute, likewise, organizes analytical resources on a smaller scale, as it conducts research and works with developing countries to help them create policies to reduce hunger and malnutrition.

States ask IOs to draft laws, build scientific networks, rebuild war-torn states, and help to create new democracies. In this sense, states are delegating authority and power to IOs to carry out the states' interests.[37] At the same time, states are not keen to lose their sovereignty, so often the result has a contradictory quality. Jessica Mathews described this as a process by which states "hand international organizations sweeping new responsibilities and then rein them in with circumscribed mandates or inadequate funding."[38]

States are often attracted to IOs for their strategic value or as another path to pursue foreign policy objectives. For instance, the United States has sought UN approval to offer international legitimacy for its actions. One of the most famous examples of this was when the Truman administration sought and received UN Security Council approval for its decision to defend South Korea after communist North Korea attacked it in 1950. Although this was a Cold War conflict (with North Korea backed by China and the Soviet Union), the United States was able to get around the Soviet veto on the Security Council because at the time the Soviets were boycotting the Security Council, protesting that Communist China was excluded from holding a permanent seat (which was held by the exiled government in Taiwan until 1971). In fact, for some time now, almost all of the United States' interventions received endorsements from either the UN Security Council, or NATO.[39]

Scholar G. John Ikenberry has argued that states winning major wars in the 19th and 20th century created international institutions as a way to "lock in" their victory by creating a "favorable and durable post-war order" even though there is a cost to such a strategy—that new institutions ultimately restrain the victors' ability to exercise their power.[40] For realists and neorealists, the strategic component is even starker—that powerful states create IOs as a means to pursue their self-interest in maintaining or increasing their share of world power.[41]

IOs also have important symbolic value for states. Many former Soviet bloc countries were passionate about joining NATO after the end of the Cold War, in part because NATO symbolized the "West" that they wanted to be part of. While NATO's *raison d'être*, deterring Soviet aggression in Western Europe, was in flux after the Soviet Union had collapsed, its symbolic importance never waned.[42]

States also join IOs to show they are in favor of the IO goals, even if they really are pursuing policies that clearly clash with those goals. As Susan Strange put it, the symbolic value of an IO allows "everybody to declare themselves in favor of truth, beauty, goodness, and world community, while leaving governments free to pursue national self-interests and do exactly what they wish."[43] The former UN Commission on Human Rights was abolished in 2006 because its members included states that were clearly abusing the human rights of their citizens.

There are also other domestic political reasons that make IO membership attractive to states, reasons that have little to do with broader issues of international cooperation. For example, Jon Pevehouse has argued that new democracies may seek membership in some IOs whose members are mainly democracies, as a means to show that they, too, are committed to democratic reform.[44] The domestic determinants of IO memberships can also reveal the inner workings of domestic politics, particularly how some domestic actors use IOs to gain leverage over other domestic actors.

States also find it useful to use IOs as scapegoats for difficult policy decisions taken or not taken. Developing country governments often enter into economically painful agreements with the IMF as a way to push through unpopular policies. Countries regularly blame the UN as an organization for its inaction, even when such inaction may also reflect decisions made by its powerful member states. Former UN Under-Secretary Sir Brian Urquhart pointed out that the UN has been the "fall guy" for governments ever since its birth. A classic case, he recalled, was when the United States decided that it would not go to war with the Soviet Union over its 1956 invasion of Hungary, then passed the issue to the UN "and had a lovely time saying the UN was absolutely useless because they hadn't thrown the Soviet Union out of Hungary."[45]

IOs play many other roles for states. IOs are increasingly involved in broad agenda setting exercises that bring together diverse groups of actors to create policy networks, and develop soft law, action plans, or other guiding documents aimed at addressing specific international problems. These activities give IOs the ability to create and spread norms, ideas, and standards of behavior in a growing number of issue areas. One example is the World Bank's involvement, along with the International Union for Conservation of Nature, in creating the World Commission on Dams in 1998, which brought together a variety of stakeholders to evaluate the role and impact of large dams on development. Another example is the Millennium Development Goals (MDGs), a set of ambitious development goals that IOs helped to develop and states signed onto, as a means to halve extreme poverty and improve the welfare of the world's poorest people by 2015, now replaced by the new and equally ambitious Sustainable Development Goals, which run to 2030.[46]

States have created IOs to adjudicate their disputes. The International Court of Justice (ICJ), the main judicial organ of the UN, was set up to resolve disputes between member states, as well as to offer advisory opinions on questions of international law. While the ICJ had little, if any, impact on major disputes before the end of the Cold War, since then it has become fairly active. The WTO's Dispute Settlement Mechanism is one of the more powerful international judicial bodies, given that member states must submit to it and accept its rulings. States have also created international law organizations to try individuals accused of war crimes and other grave crimes against humanity, as well as to promote reconciliation and bring justice to victims. Examples include the international criminal tribunals for Rwanda and the former Yugoslavia, as well as the newer International Criminal Court.

States have also created IOs as a means to pool their sovereignty. This is evident in the grand experiment taking place in Europe: the European Union (EU). The EU and its institutions are a unique mix with characteristics of traditional IOs, plus something more. The EU has been called a transnational polity, a post-sovereign system, and a *supranational* system, among other descriptions. Member state sovereignty and borders are sacrosanct in some areas, but not others. For example, the European Court of Justice can override member state law and create new law, while the European Central Bank manages member state monetary policy.

Whatever we call the EU, it is clearly one of the most powerful examples of a regional organization. Organizations like NATO, Association of Southeast Asian Nations, Asia-Pacific Economic Cooperation, and Mercosur are often in the news as they tackle issues of great importance to their regions. Regional organizations have complex relationships with international organizations. Sometimes they cooperate, sometimes they clash. Depending on the issue area and region, regional organizations may enhance or undermine an international organization's legitimacy and authority.

CONCLUSION

The remaining chapters not only aim to provide readers with the nuts and bolts about what exactly specific IOs do and why they were created, but also seek to bring to life the many different perspectives and contentious debates concerning what IOs *should* be doing, and whether they are working effectively. Underneath many of the debates are fundamental, irresolvable philosophical differences, especially when it comes to issues such as whether IOs should or do infringe on sovereignty. There is real and deep disagreement over issues such as whether IOs should intercede to stop genocide and other human rights violations, whether IOs should force countries to change specific policies (economic and environmental, for example), and how much power and authority states should give to IOs. The implications of these debates are very tangible because they affect individual lives. It is also the case that, between the extreme views of IOs as scoundrels or saviors and IOs as creatures of powerful states or the foundation of future global government, there is a vibrant middle-ground where there is more nuanced analysis of these important actors in world politics. This is important because we cannot make sweeping pronouncements about the role or utility of IOs. There is so much variation in what they do, why they do it, and how well they do it. All IOs are working on complex, multifaceted problems that are difficult to solve. With so many member states in each IO, consensus can be difficult and made more complex by all the other actors involved in a given issue area. Dag Hammarskjöld, the United Nations Secretary-General from 1953 until his death in a plane crash in 1961, is reported to have said that the UN was "not created in order to bring us to heaven, but in order to save us from hell."[47] This view seems appropriate to a range of IOs, which may be imperfect, but have clearly made some contributions to reducing "problems without passports."

BIBLIOGRAPHY

Avant, Deborah D., Martha Finnemore, and Susan K. Sell, eds. *Who Governs the Globe*. New York: Cambridge University Press, 2010.

"Cholera at Mecca." *The New York Times*, November 13, 1881.

Claude, Inis L. *Swords into Plowshares: The Problems and Progress of International Organization*. New York: Random House, 1956.

Europa Publications Limited. *The Europa Directory of International Organizations 2005* (7th ed.). London, UK: Routledge, 2005.

Haas, Peter M., Robert O. Keohane, and Marc A. Levy. *Institutions for the Earth: Sources of Effective International Environmental Protection*. Cambridge: MIT Press, 1993.

Ikenberry, G. John. *After Victory: Institutions, Strategic Restraint, and the Rebuilding of Order after Major Wars*. Princeton, NJ: Princeton University Press, 2001.

Iriye, Akira. *Global Community: The Role of International Organizations in the Making of the Contemporary World*. Berkeley: University of California Press, 2002.

Jacobson, Harold K. *Networks of Interdependence: International Organizations and the Global Political System*. 1st ed. New York: Knopf, 1979.

Kennedy, Paul. *The Parliament of Man: The Past, Present, and Future of the United Nations*. New York: Random House, 2006.

Keohane, Robert O. "International Institutions: Can Interdependence Work?" *Foreign Policy*, no. 110 (Spring 1998): 82.

Krasner, Stephen D. "Structural Causes and Regime Consequences: Regimes as Intervening Variables." In *International Regimes*, edited by Stephen D. Krasner, 1–21. Ithaca: Cornell University Press, 1983.

Lamy, Pascal. "Global Governance: Getting us Where we all Want to go and Getting us There Together." *Global Policy* 1, no. 3 (October, 2010): 312–14.

Mathews, Jessica T. "Power Shift." *Foreign Affairs* 76, no. 1 (Jan/Feb 1997): 50.

Mearsheimer, John J. "The False Promise of International Institutions." *International Security* 19, no. 3 (Winter 1994): 5–49.

National Intelligence Council and EU Institute of Security Studies. "Global Governance 2025: At a Critical Juncture." Washington, DC: Office of the Director of National Intelligence, 2010.

Pevehouse, Jon C. "Democratization, Credible Commitments, and Joining International Organizations." In *Locating the Proper Authorities: The Interaction of Domestic and International Institutions*, edited by Daniel W. Drezner, 25–48. Ann Arbor: The University of Michigan Press, 2003.

Pollack, Mark A. *The Engines of European Integration: Delegation, Agency, and Agenda Setting in the EU*. New York: Oxford University Press, 2003.

Ruggie, John Gerard. *Multilateralism Matters: The Theory and Praxis of an Institutional Form*. New Directions in World Politics. New York: Columbia University Press, 1993.

"Sanitary Reform at Last in Arabia's Holy Places." *The New York Times*, 1895.

Stiglitz, Joseph E. *Globalization and Its Discontents*. 1st ed. New York: W. W. Norton, 2002.

Strange, Susan. "Cave! Hic Dragones: A Critique of Regime Analysis." *International Organization* 36, no. 2 (Spring 1982): 479–96.

Thompson, Alexander. "Coercion Through IOs: The Security Council and the Logic of Information Transmission." *International Organization* 60, no. 1 (2006): 1–34.

Union of International Associations, ed. *Yearbook of International Organizations 2014–2015*. Brussels, Belgium: Brill, 2014.

United Nations. "Peacekeeping Fact Sheet: Fact Sheet as of 31 March 2015." http://www.un.org/en/peacekeeping/resources/statistics/factsheet.shtml.

United Nations General Assembly. "Programme Budget for the Biennium 2014–2015, A/C.5/69/17."

Urquhart, Brian. *Hammarskjold*. 1st ed. New York: Knopf, 1972. http://www.un.org/en/ga/search/view_doc.asp?symbol = A/C.5/69/17.

———. Interview by Harry Kreisler. "The United Nations After 9/11: Conversation with Sir Brian Urquhart." University of California Berkeley, 23 February 2004. http://globetrotter.berkeley.edu/people4/Urquhart/urquhart04-con0.html.

Wallace, Michael, and J. David Singer. "Intergovernmental Organization in the Global System, 1815–1964: A Quantitative Description." *International Organization* 24, no. 2 (Spring 1970): 239–87.

Weindling, Paul. *International Health Organisations and Movements, 1918–1939*. New York: Cambridge University Press, 1995.

Weiss, Thomas G., David P. Forsythe, and Roger A. Coate. *The United Nations and Changing World Politics*. 4th ed. Boulder, CO.: Westview Press, 2004.

Weiss, Thomas G., and Ramesh Thakur. *Global Governance and the UN: An Unfinished Journey*. United Nations Intellectual History Project. Bloomington: Indiana University Press, 2010.

World Trade Organization. "WTO Secretariat Budget for 2013–2014." https://http://www.wto .org/english/thewto_e/secre_e/budget_e.htm.

2 Intellectual Context
The Evolution of IO Theory

Theories provide a way of packaging patterns from the past in such a way as to make them usable in the present as guides to the future.

–John Lewis Gaddis[1]

Academic conventions divide up the seamless web of the real social world into separate spheres, each with its own theorizing; this is a necessary and practical way of gaining understanding. Contemplation of undivided totality may lead to profound abstractions or mystical revelations, but practical knowledge . . . is always partial or fragmentary in origin . . . Whether the parts remain as limited, separated objects of knowledge, or become the basis for constructing a structured and dynamic view of larger wholes, is a major question of method and purpose. Either way, the starting point is some initial subdivision of reality, usually dictated by convention. It is wise to bear in mind that such conventional cutting up of reality is at best just a convenience of the mind.

–Robert W. Cox[2]

Scholars and researchers study organizations from many different disciplines, including political science, economics, sociology, history, and law. Some fields cross disciplinary boundaries, such as the field of organizational studies, which draws from economics, political science, sociology, psychology, and anthropology. The range of research on organizations is enormous, which is unsurprising since organizations are ubiquitous, infusing and impacting all aspects of our lives, from the community level to the international level. Academics are interested in why organizations exist, how they are designed, what kinds of influence they have, why they succeed or fail, why and how they change, and whether they are legitimate. Obviously, these issues are not just important to academics. They are directly relevant to policymakers seeking to create, design, use, and improve organizations for a variety of purposes. They are relevant to the broader public, for example, where there is concern IOs may be tools of powerful states or concern the work of IOs has caused or encouraged some type of harm. The famous German sociologist Max Weber recognized in the 19th century that society was bureaucratized, and that trend has continued to deepen, particularly in the international realm. As Inis Claude Jr., author of a seminal study of international organizations, noted more than fifty years ago, "The growing complexity of international relations has already produced international organizations; the world is engaged in the process of organizing."[3] More recent debates about the complex effects of globalization on the dominance of the nation-state and its monopoly on governance and how we conceptualize global governance itself has further increased scrutiny of IOs and the roles that they do or should play in the global political and economic system.[4]

This chapter focuses on the major debates and approaches within the field of international relations (a subfield of political science) that shape our understanding of IOs, but it will also draw on theories and other approaches found in other fields that have influenced IO theory. The borders between fields are fluid, and many scholars straddle more than one. For example, a number of scholars within the field of comparative politics specialize in regional politics and institutions, such as the European Union, and they regularly contribute to broader theoretical and empirical work on IOs. IO scholars in the field of international relations also commonly borrow and build upon ideas with roots in other disciplines, such as economics and sociology, which explains some of the fault lines running through the IO literature.

Many scholars have pointed out that the field's emphasis is often shaped by events and by their own political orientation.[5] It is no surprise that the field is largely populated by scholars who think IOs matter and have an impact on world politics; the vast majority of those who disagree do not choose to devote their scholarly career to studying IOs, but may dip a toe in now and then with a strong argument about why IOs are largely irrelevant. In fact, in the study of IOs, one of the perennial debates is whether IOs have an influence on political and other outcomes as independent actors with some degree of autonomy, or whether they are merely stages at the margins of world politics where states, as the "real" and most important actors, meet to pursue their self-interests.

The chapter proceeds with a brief history of the field of IO, highlighting some of the factors, events, thinkers, and strands of research that have influenced the field over the years. It then turns to the major debates that have shaped the contemporary field, as well as how different ways of organizing theoretical approaches, methodologies, and research programs offer insights about the types of questions scholars ask and the answers they offer. It concludes by discussing several of the cutting edge issues of today to give readers a sense of some of the directions in which the field is heading. IO scholarship is eclectic but there are also a handful of key research questions that keep popping up. In addition to whether IOs are actors or stages, these include why states create IOs, whether and how IOs help states to cooperate, why IOs perform poorly, why and how IOs change, whether and how IOs exert power and influence, and what role IOs do or should play in global governance. It is also the case that scholars and practitioners still lack easy or conclusive answers for some of the basic issues. Many of the debates found in this and subsequent chapters are alive, incomplete, and unresolved, leaving plenty of room for future generations of IO scholars and practitioners to contribute to deepening our understanding of what makes these organizations tick.

1930s–1970s

Some of the early scholarship on IOs pre-World War II appeared within the fields of diplomatic history and international law, inspired in part by the Wilsonian idealism embodied in the ill-fated League of Nations. International lawyers analyzed the multilateral treaties underlying the international organizations. Political scientists studying comparative governmental organizations tended to compare institutional structures and procedures with each other and with platonic forms. Generally, these studies were more descriptive than theoretical, and many did not look closely at questions of politics, power, and performance. Claude compared the early studies of IOs to learning about an automobile by looking at the blueprints and under the hood, rather than by seeing how the automobile actually works while driven in traffic.[6]

In the 1940s and 1950s, the field of international relations took shape in the post-World War II world, amidst an enormous reconstruction effort and the creation of a handful of major IOs designed to help protect the world from future world wars. These profound changes sparked a flurry of studies examining the new institutions and analyzing the appropriateness of their design, their possible impact, and their ability to influence domestic politics, among other issues.[7] A new journal, *International Organization*, was founded in 1947 by the World Peace Foundation with these issues in mind and is today the leading journal in the field of IOs.[8] Many of the major themes about politics, design, behavior, and performance discussed and analyzed in the 1950s are still visible in today's scholarship. The difference is that the literature today is more explicitly social scientific and theoretical in nature and less descriptive and policy oriented. Some scholars believe that the earlier insights did not resonate over the years because they lacked a "theoretical hook" on which to hang their conclusions.[9]

As *behavioralism* became the dominant approach in American political science by the 1960s, its more explicitly social scientific methodology influenced the study of IOs. Behavioralists tended to focus on the political behavior of actors and institutions, with an emphasis on verifying testable propositions through quantitative methods.[10] It was a reaction against, as Gabriel Almond and Stephen Genco noted, "a tradition of ideographic, descriptive, noncumulative, and institutional case studies that had dominated much of the discipline."[11] A good deal of work on IOs in the 1960s focused on the United Nations, emphasizing topics such as the statistical analysis of voting behavior in the General Assembly and various national attitudes toward the UN.[12] Over time, these issues seemed to border on irrelevance in light of important events and trends in world politics, and scholarly attention turned elsewhere. For example, given that the General Assembly lacks power, sophisticated analysis of its voting behavior was not terribly insightful in explaining the factors shaping world politics. As the Cold War unfolded, the UN itself was revealed to be "usually little more than a sideshow" on the geopolitical stage.[13] Meanwhile, the United States grew increasingly disillusioned with the anti-Western bent of a General Assembly that, by the early 1970s, was dominated by newly-independent members who held the majority of votes and often voted in ways that conflicted with US interests.[14]

Another active strand of research on IOs between the 1960s and early 1970s was taking place among scholars seeking to make sense of the novel and exciting experiment in economic integration taking place in Europe and understand what impact integration would have on the nation-state. Steps toward European integration posed a challenge to the realist theories that dominated international relations in the 1950s, which could not account for attempts by states to pool sovereignty. Early scholars of *integration theory* were interested in how the political processes of integration helped to shape political actors, their interests, and their strategies. Ernst Haas, for example, argued that once an integration process was underway, it would also have unintended consequences that would reinforce the process. This would happen as interest groups realized the benefits of integration in one area and pushed to see it in other areas. Haas called this "spillover."[15] Karl Deutsch, in turn, was interested in how shared values, effective communication channels, and other related factors could create "security communities" that were political communities with an ability to eliminate war.[16]

Some of the more optimistic assumptions about economic integration in Europe made in the 1950s and 1960s ran into trouble when the process appeared to stagnate given French President Charles de Gaulle's opposition to supranationality and his demand that member states comprising the Council of Ministers have the right to veto European Community (EC) activities. The resulting informal agreement that required member state unanimity on questions seen as important to national interest dampened the pace of integration.[17] Optimism about Haasian "spillover" effects were replaced by discussion of "spillback," "spillaround," and even "muddle-about."[18] Unsurprisingly, when the pace of European integration picked up in the late 1980s, fresh attention was given to these early theories.

1970S–1990S: REALISM, NEOREALISM

Attention to the study of formal international organizations waned by the early 1970s, as gaps between major international issues and the activities of international organizations seemed to widen. The Vietnam War, the collapse of the Bretton Woods system of international exchange rate management, and the 1973 oil crisis are some examples of major events that either took place outside of traditional IOs or showed how impotent IOs were in managing or solving global problems.[19] In the US-based scholarly world, both liberals and realists became more interested in how international institutional structures that were broader than formal organizations interacted with power politics and capabilities.[20] The result was scholarly interest in analyzing *regimes*, or the broad rules, norms, and principles that defined the "rules of the game" helping to shape international politics.[21] Regimes might encompass, but also go beyond, traditional IOs. For example, the international trade regime included the General Agreement of Tariff and Trade (GATT) treaty and the regular meetings of the GATT contracting parties, who negotiated tariff reductions and other measures to encourage free trade. Another example from the 1970s is the international norms and rules regarding how to safeguard nuclear materials.[22] Scholars examined how regimes were formed; how they influenced the abilities of states to cooperate; and what their other effects were on power, norms, and specific policy issues.[23]

As with any new academic fashion, there were critics. One of the best-known critics of regime theory was Susan Strange, who famously called the concept "woolly" since it had been used to mean a number of different things, from the very narrow to the overly broad.[24] She also felt that existing global structures reflected the United States' position as the system's hegemon and argued that power politics shouldn't disappear in the haze of regime analysis. For example, she argued that the international security regime is not something based on the United Nations Charter, "which remains as unchanged as it is irrelevant," but rather on "the balance of power between superpowers."[25]

This critique dovetailed with neorealist Kenneth Waltz's seminal 1979 book *Theory of International Politics*, which had a major impact on the academic field of international relations. Realists, and their more social-scientific descendants, *neorealists*, view the state as the main unit of analysis in a world characterized by anarchy (in the sense that there is no power above the state) and assume that states seek power in order to ensure their survival. It is a pessimistic view of world politics that has been around for thousands of years.[26] Cooperation between states may exist, but it is constrained by the larger issues of competition for security and power. For Waltz, the anarchic structure of the international system was its defining feature, and has a very important impact on shaping state behavior.[27] He was critical of the idea that domestic politics determine a state's behavior at the international level, instead arguing that state decisions are "shaped by the very presence of other states as well as by interactions with them."[28] In his view, domestic politics were essentially unimportant.

The contemporary realist and neorealist view of world politics had a significant impact on the study of IOs, because it assumed IOs function at the margins of international politics and as such, were also unimportant. As neorealist John Mearsheimer put it, powerful states may create IOs as a way to "maintain their share of world politics, or even increase it."[29] Realist Hans Morgenthau, writing in 1948 in the aftermath of World War II, looked askance at the liberal views heard at the time that organizations like the United Nations could do away with power politics, arguing instead that "the struggle for power is universal in time and space and is an undeniable fact of experience."[30] This debate on whether or not IOs matter or have any significance or autonomy in world politics was a central one in the field for many years, usually pitting the realists against everyone else. Many of the most important scholarly contributions to the IO field have been attempts to show that IOs *do* matter, and how they matter.

FLAVORS OF INSTITUTIONALISM

Beginning in the mid-1980s, academics began a fresh effort to chip away at the pessimistic arguments made by realists. The ideas that hegemony was necessary for cooperation via regimes and that cooperation in a "realist" world was hard to come by were challenged by Robert Keohane, who developed in the mid-1980s a functional theory of regimes.[31] The argument was simple but counterintuitive; even in the face of (what appeared to be at the time) a decline in the United States' role as hegemon, regimes remained viable and useful.[32] Regimes, according to Keohane, fill a variety of functions, such as providing information, reducing the cost of bargaining, and increasing opportunities for reciprocity. The result is a reduction in uncertainty and more occasions for cooperation. Keohane's views were initially labeled as *modified structural realist*, given the fact that he shared many of the same basic assumptions as realists regarding state as the main units of analysis in an anarchic world. Over time, this functionalist argument became known as *neoliberal institutionalist*, as Keohane and others argued that IOs were able to exert a much greater impact on state behavior than realists believed to be the case. States are still the most powerful actors in this perspective, IOs are still stages and not actors, but the formal and informal rules found in formal organizations and regimes help states to define their interests, to make commitments that are credible, and to monitor one another.[33] IOs enable states to cooperate in the neoliberal institutionalist view, in contrast with the realist assumption that IOs may constrain state behavior.[34]

Neoliberal institutionalism was nested in the broader research agenda of rational choice institutionalism, which in turn was one of several strands of *institutionalist* theorizing that took shape in the 1970s and 1980s. In fact, each form of institutionalism—*rationalist choice institutionalism, sociological institutionalism,* and *historical institutionalism*—gave rise to rich families of research that continue to resonate through the field of IO. They all shared the view that, in some way or another, institutions mattered in terms of influencing political, economic, and social outcomes. But, they all differed in terms of *how* institutions mattered; for instance, whether or not they have any independence and which methodologies and theoretical orientations were most useful for explaining their roles. This scholarship was responding to realist views of IOs, but it also tapped into a deeper reaction to the behavioralist approaches that argued formal institutions defined more broadly as political and economic structures were epiphenomenal.

This renewed attention to institutions, dubbed *new institutionalism*, extended well beyond the field of IO, since it was rippling across the social sciences with a lively degree of interdisciplinary interaction between political scientists, economists, sociologists, and organizational theorists.[35] As sociologists Paul DiMaggio and Walter Powell noted, "there are as many 'new institutionalisms' as there are social science disciplines."[36]

The branch of new institutionalism known as rational choice institutionalism evolved as an effort by scholars to extend and critique neoclassical economic theories. Rational choice institutionalism is based on the assumption that individuals are self-interested, rational actors who pursue strategies to maximize their well being. Their preferences are assumed to be stable and "given" (or exogenous). The "new institutionalists" in this strand of scholarship were interested in how institutional features matter—that is, how they provide a "strategic context" that shapes individual choice.[37] In the field of American politics, many scholars applied these insights to the study of the US Congress and how its rules and procedures arise, how they influence the behavior of legislators, and how Congress interacts with other regulatory agencies. In the field of IO, some of the assumptions of this work can be found in Keohane's functionalist theory of regimes, discussed above, and other work in the neoliberal institutionalist vein.

One strand of rational choice institutionalism that emerged from the economics field was labeled the *new institutional economics*. It responded to neoclassical theories treating the firm as a black box (or a collection of possible production choices) by developing organizational theories to explain why firms behave in particular ways and how they are organized. One of the roots of this literature was the work of Ronald Coase, who argued that efforts by rational agents to reduce transaction costs, or the costs of doing business, will influence a firm's size and the type of market or nonmarket arrangement chosen.[38] Research in this area modified some of the standard assumptions of microeconomic theory, especially the ways in which individual actors are able to maximize their behavior. The new institutional economists studied issues such as problems of incomplete information, the challenges of enforcement, decision-makers' cognitive limits, and other factors influencing organizational design and behavior.

Another strand of rational choice institutionalism, also coming out of the economics field, was *agency theory*. Its modern roots grew out of economic studies in the 1970s seeking to explain and improve the performance of firms.[39] Agency theory was premised on the assumption that performance problems within firms naturally arise when one actor (the principal) delegates to another actor (the agent) the authority to act in the former's interest. Economists recognized that inherent in this relationship of delegation is the fact that the two parties have different interests, and this may result in the agent's actions differing from the principal's expectations. Much of the literature assumes the central problem to be solved is how to induce the agent to maximize the principal's welfare, and it also recognizes that there are costs to the various control mechanisms. Think of the employee who is spending part of the day shopping on the Internet rather than doing his job. What steps should the employer take to ensure the employee is doing his job? One of the key issues that interested agency theorists was how a contract might be structured to provide the sticks and carrots necessary to encourage employees to put in their best performance, and therefore do what the principals expected.[40]

The common solutions include screening and selection mechanisms to help principals avoid selecting an incompetent, corrupt, or otherwise unattractive agent; mechanisms to control agency discretion; financial incentives linked to performance; and different forms of oversight and monitoring mechanisms linked to positive benefits or negative sanctions, so that the principal can keep an eye on what the agent is doing.[41]

Agency theory migrated into political science via studies of the behavior of Congress, with the principal-agent (P-A) relationship generally viewed as a political principal (such as Congress) delegating some degree of policymaking authority to an implementing bureaucratic agent. Scholars applying P-A models to political institutions were well aware of the differences between the behavior of firms and public organizations, but found that the model itself was a useful way to look at issues arising when delegation takes place. For example, government agencies often have numerous tasks to accomplish that are often difficult to measure, and they are often agents to multiple, competing principals. And real-world politicians, unsurprisingly, often do not make delegation decisions based on notions of efficiency.[42]

In the past decade or so, agency theory has appeared in the study of IOs. For example, Europeanists have applied P-A models to analyze when and how European Union (EU) institutions may gain autonomy from their member states, why states delegate to supranational institutions, and how EU institutions impact P-A relationships at the member state level.[43] Development economists, meanwhile, have long used P-A models to study organizations like the World Bank and International Monetary Fund to examine why the conditionality attached to their loans is so often ineffective.[44] Conditionality is, by definition, a P-A issue, because it is the primary means that donors (the principals, in this case, the institution) use to induce policy change in recipient countries (the agents) in return for aid.

Public choice theory is a third strand of rational choice institutionalism and is closely related to new institutional economics and agency theory, given that it focuses on how individuals make decisions and interact with one another in different institutional settings.[45] It uses tools of neoclassical economic analysis to examine political processes and shares many of the basic assumptions of the other forms of rational choice institutionalism, such as the "rational" individual (in this case, politicians and bureaucrats) as the unit of analysis. Scholars in this area asked questions like why countries join IOs, how international bargaining impacts the benefits from international agreements, and whether and how IOs provide public goods.[46]

In the field of sociology, scholars were interested in how shared systems of rules found in institutions both structured and constrained actors and influenced their interests. The sociological institutionalists were critical of the rational choice assumptions that institutional design somehow reflected ideas of efficiency or functionality. Instead, they argued that culturally specific practices influenced institutional forms and procedures.[47] This work defined *institutions* more broadly and somewhat differently than rational choice and historical institutionalists. For sociologists, institutions not only consisted of formal rules, norms, and organizations, but also included "symbol systems, cognitive scripts, and moral templates."[48] Some sociological institutionalists were also more interested in the social features of institutions than the structural features of concern to other institutionalists.[49] Focusing on a wide range of institutions, including industry, states, markets, and government ministries, sociological institutionalists studied issues such as why institutions take on particular shapes or symbols; how their practices are diffused across time, space, and sectors; and how their behavior is shaped by factors such as external cultural legitimation, rather than functional demands.[50]

While most of the work done by sociological institutionalists is not international, many of the ideas overlap with a sociological approach to the study of international organizations that is now commonly labeled *constructivism*.[51] Constructivist theorists in the field of international relations are interested in the ways that ideas, norms, culture, and other aspects of social life influence politics, issues that had been neglected by liberals and realists. They argue that ideational factors are the key in shaping human interaction, that some of these are widely shared, or *intersubjective*, beliefs, and that these shared beliefs help to shape political actors' interests and identities.[52] Identities, norms, and interests, are then seen as mutually constitutive. As Finnemore and Sikkink state, "Understanding the constitution of things is essential in explaining how they behave and what causes political outcomes."[53]

Within the field of IO, a number of different research strands within the constructivist approach had developed by the mid-1990s. Some scholars looked at how international norms are created and diffused, and were especially interested in the role that transnational advocacy networks played in influencing states' behavior[54] Michael Barnett and Martha Finnemore analyzed how IO bureaucracies gain autonomy, exercise power, and often exhibit dysfunctional performance.[55] John Ruggie focused more broadly on regime theory by developing the concept of *embedded liberalism* to argue that the post World War II economic order does not simply reflect power politics, but also state-society relations that "express shared social purposes regarding the role of authority vis-à-vis the market." By this he meant that the emphasis on open markets that characterized the regime was balanced by a "social bargain," whereby governments would contain some of the negative costs, such as pollution that such open markets produced.[56]

Historical institutionalism, meanwhile, blossomed in the field of comparative politics, where scholars sought to determine how the institutional setting of a country's economy or polity influenced political struggles and outcomes. Historical institutionalists defined institutions as including formal organizations and informal rules and procedures that shape how individuals and "units of the polity and economy" interact.[57] They studied how institutions shaped issues such as health care, organized labor, tax policies, and economic crises.[58] Rather than accepting preference formation as a given, as rational choice institutionalists tended to do, historical institutionalists shared the sociological institutionalists' concern with how institutional contexts shape not only strategies, but also actor interests and goals. Historical institutionalists, as their name suggests, were especially interested in the historical processes by which coalitions are formed, policies are packaged, and institutions functioned. These ideas have been applied to the study of international organizations by scholars such as Paul Pierson, who examined how and why EU institutions may evolve in unanticipated ways, and exhibit "sticky behavior," given gaps in member states' imperfect ability to tightly control the institutions' day-to-day life and activities.[59]

1990s–PRESENT: CONTEMPORARY ISSUES AND DEBATES

The three forms of institutionalism played an important role in shaping scholarship in the field of IO, as scholarship continued to evolve and change. The contemporary field of IO within international relations (IR) can be divided by theoretical approaches, methodologies, specific research programs, issue areas, and institutions studied. Individual scholars are likely to work within a specific theoretical tradition and on either a specific IO or broader issues of global governance. The most common approach within the field of international relations for several decades was to divide the IO literature among the main traditions found in the broader IR field. Within the realist/neorealist, liberal/neoliberal, and constructivist perspectives are scholars who focus specifically on IOs.[60] This division by grand perspective then pitted those who argue IOs are marginal (the realists/neorealists) against those who think IOs may be powerful actors in global politics (constructivists, neoliberal institutionalists, some parts of the principal-agent literature). The previous discussion on realism versus the different types of institutionalism highlighted some of the differences between grand perspectives.

Rationalist vs. Rationalist

There are also other ways of lining up debates in the field that go beyond the "division by grand perspective." Sometimes scholars who share a basic methodological predilection may still violently disagree on the role of IOs in global governance. This shows some of the richness even the same approaches to theorizing can produce. An excellent example of this is the debate between neorealists and neoliberal institutionalists who share a rationalist approach to the study of IOs but reach very different conclusions about whether and how IOs influence states and international issues.[61] To illustrate, Kenneth Waltz's theory of neorealism is built on microeconomic theory, given his view that international political systems are analogous to economic markets because both are "individualist in origin, spontaneously generated, and unintended."[62] Waltz's view that states are the major actors who "set the scene in which the others must act" is also analogous to the way oligopolist sectors work in the economic sphere.[63] IOs do not play an important role in such a self-help perspective, other than as an instrument to help powerful states pursue their interests. Neorealist John Mearsheimer went further, in the mid-1990s in an article entitled *The False Promise of International Institutions*, arguing that not only do international institutions "have minimal influence on state behavior" but that liberal institutionalist and other institutionalist theories were logically flawed and lacked "little support in the historical record."[64] He argued that liberal institutionalists could not explain cases where state interests were conflictual to begin with, where states did assume they might gain through cooperation. This, he said, was more characteristic of security issues, compared with economic issues.[65]

Rationalist neoliberal institutionalists fought back. In a direct response to Mearsheimer, Keohane and Martin replied that the realists' narrow account of why states create institutions is "incomplete and logically unsound," for why would states "act rationally" when they create new institutions, if they believe that the institutions "will have no impact on patterns of cooperation?"[66] Mearsheimer's argument that institutionalists divide security and economic issues, they said, is "illusory," given that there is no clear division between the two, and institutionalist theory's focus on the role of institutions in providing information adds to the significance of these institutions in security-related issues.[67]

Economics vs. Sociology

Another major fault line in the scholarly field of IO, alluded to above, divides rationalists, who draw from the field of economics, from the constructivists, who draw from sociology.

The constructivist research agenda in IR began to take shape in the 1980s and then grew quickly at the end of the Cold War. Its growth reflected scholarly interest in the role that ideas, values, identities, and norms play in influencing world politics. The major IR theories at the time failed to predict the end to the Cold War, one of the most stunning and significant events in the late twentieth century.[68] Scholars were also grappling to make sense of the phenomenon of globalization and its impact on power and politics.

Constructivists often work in areas that are ignored by rationalists—such as the factors shaping the interests and identity of states and the important roles the social rules and culture play in why IOs are created, as well as what IOs do. As a result, constructivist research has sought to bring the *organization* back into the study of IOs, by analyzing IOs as actors and not just stages and, as important, analyzing how IOs behave and what they do. A notable example of this is work by Barnett and Finnemore that called for bringing back an analysis of IOs as bureaucracies that are "social creatures" that have independent sources of power and authority, in part because they make rules, create actors, form new interests, and disseminate advice and practices that may have a profound impact on the world.[69] Examples included the ways that IOs help define terms like *human rights* and *refugees* and help to transfer political models such as democracy. More importantly, Barnett and Finnemore's analysis also suggested that a focus on IOs as bureaucratic actors can help explain the many instances where IO behavior is dysfunctional. According to Barnett and Finnemore, echoing Max Weber's insights from the 19th century, it is often the very same features that give IOs authority that also make them prone to dysfunctional behavior. In other words, "virtues" such as bureaucracies' ability to create and use knowledge to solve problems and their standardized rules of action may create biases and specific processes that in the end create pathological behavior.[70] One example, they argued, is UN officials emphasizing rules for peacekeeping that espoused neutrality, which ultimately allowed the UN to legitimize standing on the sidelines when 800,000 people were massacred in the Rwandan genocide of 1994.[71]

Rationalists and others critique this constructivist line of thinking for focusing too closely on the bureaucracy and not enough on the interests of an IO's powerful member states that may influence the organization's actions and performance. For example, much has been written attributing the failure of the international community to stop the genocide in Rwanda to the lack of political will of the United States and other members of the United Nation's Security Council.[72] Rationalists have also been adapting principal-agent models to explain poor or mixed IO performance in ways that both capture the actions and interests of member states (principals), as well as the bureaucracy (agent). Some have used a P-A model to show how powerful member states rein in the behavior of IO bureaucrats when there is a gap between how the IO is behaving and how its shareholders would like it to behave.[73] Others use a P-A model to show precisely the opposite: that some of the sources of poor IO performance are not due to agency slack, but rather problems on the principal side of the equation, such as antinomic delegation, where principals are delegating conflicting or complex tasks to the IO agent that are extremely difficult to implement. As a result, without more political will and clarity of goals, the usual tools used by principals to shape agents' behavior may not work very well.[74] Rationalism, then, can be applied to explain dysfunctional IO behavior, as well as to explain why reform efforts may proceed unevenly and with imperfect results.

Ultimately, neither rationalism nor constructivism is actually a substantive theory of world politics or international organizations. They both offer frameworks for thinking about politics and behavior, but do not come with content attached. Agency theory, in fact, is misnamed, given that it offers a *model*, not a theory, of delegation. James Fearon and Alexander Wendt have argued that framing rationalism and constructivism as a debate is not terribly useful, given that the philosophical underpinnings and ontological commitments attached to each are "not likely to be settled soon, if ever, and almost certainly not by IR scholars."[75] They also believe that there are areas where the two approaches are in agreement. For example, while the two approaches disagree on *how* ideas matter, they do not disagree that ideas do matter, given their assumptions that actors make choices "based on their beliefs."[76]

One useful result of this debate is that it has turned more attention to issues such as how to analyze IO behavior and performance, why some ideas get captured by IOs and others do not, and what exactly we mean by the power of IOs. Another useful result is a growing awareness in the field that IO autonomy is not necessarily a black and white issue, but rather one seeped in shades of gray that requires more exploration and explanation.

Stages or Actors

A final major fault line that provides a way to understand the IO field divides scholars who are more interested in looking from the outside in at IOs versus those who focus on an inside out approach. Scholars looking *outside in* are interested in how politics shape state behavior toward organizations, why states create and delegate authority to institutions, and whether institutions have an impact on cooperation among states. This puts the neorealists and liberals back on the same side since both groups are interested in answering these types of questions and assume IOs are stages or instruments of the powerful, rather than actors in their own right.

Inside out approaches, by contrast, are more interested in the IO as actor and what it *does*—that is how organizational structure, bureaucratic politics and culture, and staff expertise and power may shape the organization's actions, outcomes, and effectiveness. Scholars who see the IO as an actor tend to be more interested in issues of organizational performance, while those viewing the IO as a stage focus more on member state behavior. Some seek to combine the two, such as work by Fang and Stone that examines the conditions under which IOs are able to persuade governments to adopt their policy recommendations.[77] Analysis of the IO as an actor highlights some common interests among constructivists, organizational theorists, sociologists, and historical institutionalists. Agency theorists, who are rationalists, are also aligned with these perspectives, because by definition, the *agent* in the principal-agent relationship is an actor pursuing its own interests. Therefore, while constructivists and agency theorists may disagree about many things, they agree that it is important to bring the IO bureaucracy back in and look at issues such as IO behavior and performance. Scholars studying IO bureaucracy often drill down deeper and examine how the characteristics of individual staff members or leaders inside of the organization can influence how it behaves.[78] Many of the contemporary theorists already mentioned in this chapter can easily be placed into the actors or stages camp. The view that IOs are *both* actors *and* stages is more common among policy analysts and journalists who write about IOs.[79]

One additional example of the outside-in approach is the argument G. John Ikenberry made in *After Victory*. Ikenberry examined how states build international order after major wars, which are dramatic times of upheaval. Leading states, he argued, have created new IOs in such times not just to solve a specific set of problems or create new opportunities for cooperation, but also to allow the leading state to "lock in" a "favorable order." But in a twist to a traditional realist argument, he also noted that leading states realize that this strategy also restrains their own exercise of power. Yet, they choose such self-binding strategies because they create stable institutional structures that will persist and serve their long-term interests. One obvious example is the United States choosing to "institutionalize its power" after World War II by creating an unprecedented number of new IOs to lock in favorable arrangements.

Neorealists, Ikenberry argued, cannot explain why we have not seen more efforts by Europe or Japan to "balance against" American power since the end of the Cold War. And liberal theories are also incomplete, he posited, because they have not addressed why and how powerful states may use IOs to "restrain themselves."[80] This argument as to why institutions exist, versus how they actually perform, has interesting, unexplored implications. For example, if the United States is more interested in the role of IOs like the World Bank and International Monetary Fund in locking in a particular order, it may more easily turn a blind eye to their mixed or poor performance. Even IOs that face performance problems may still be successful to the United States if they are serving a larger role.

Some New Directions

As noted in Chapter 1, scholars are thinking conceptually about definitions of global governance, and the related issues about who the governing actors are and how they interact in specific issue areas. There are also pockets of research that do not always neatly fit into one of the institutionalist categories above. These scholars explore issues such as the influence of domestic politics on IOs and regime formation,[81] whether and how IOs are accountable (and to whom),[82] whether or not power is shifting away from states to IOs and nongovernmental organizations (NGOs),[83] what the role of NGOs themselves is in influencing IOs and states,[84] whether and how IOs can "learn,"[85] how we may better understand IO performance, and the role of IOs in broader issues of global governance and as global governors.[86]

The strands relating to the changing role of domestic and international NGOs reflect the increased access these organizations have had to IOs. Scholars often use the term NGOs interchangeably with *transnational actors*, *transnational advocacy networks*, or *nongovernmental policy networks*. The terms may be defined somewhat differently, but generally involve civil society actors who are advocating on issues that may include the environment, corruption, and human rights, among others. These organizations have become involved with IOs in a wide range of ways that include partners, watchdogs, advisors, and service providers. Do these changing roles matter? There seems to be great variation, depending on the type of access, the point of access, and the type of institution. There are examples of where access matters and where it does not. One example of the latter is the case of the World Bank, when civil society actors were involved in an unprecedented review of the bank's extractive industry policy, but the bank rejected many of the recommendations.[87]

One newer strand in the IO literature looks at institutional overlap and interplay, regime complexity, regime shifting, forum shopping, and/or forum shifting. This work reflects the fact that in many policy issues there are multiple institutions and levels of institutions that may impact how the issue is addressed and potentially solved (or not solved). Institutional overlap, for example, has to do with how institutions interact with one another. After all, institutions hardly ever act in isolation. Quite often they are overlapping in terms of part of their mandate. IOs regularly cooperate on specific issues, or find themselves acting in the same issue area as a variety of other actors. Of course IOs often share members. Regional institutions such as NATO (26 members) and the European Security and Defense Policy (27 members) share 21 of the same members. The overlap between the institutions studied in this book is obviously quite large.

Oran Young pointed out that "institutional arrangements regularly interact with one another," even though scholars often separate them for analytical purposes. An example is how environmental regimes interact with trade regimes on issues like the transboundary movement of hazardous waste.[88] Other scholars have highlighted the role of *interplay* as when one institution directly impacts another institution's development or performance. With the environment/trade issue, an example would be how trade rules have hurt the ability of states to design environmental agreements that allow for trade restrictions.[89] Chapter 10 in this book highlights the intersection of trade and health regimes. Sometimes overlapping issues or mandates can lead to inefficient outcomes because accountability mechanisms are weak or an IO is poorly equipped to contribute to the common issue states ask it to take on.[90]

A branch of the interplay literature has taken a fresh look at regimes, as well as complexes and clusters. Kal Raustiala and David Victor argued that institutions have become denser and define *regime complex* as "a collective of partially overlapping and nonhierarchical regimes."[91] Examples occur where different fora involving different actors create and maintain a set of common legal agreements. This can get confusing when it is unclear who resolves conflicts where there are different interpretations of the rules.

David Fidler has a slightly different take on this, positing that complexity may actually consist of overlapping *regime clusters* characterized by "multiple players (that) address specific problems through different processes by applying various principles." He argued that the global health governance regime complex is an example of such a cluster given that different issue areas involve a range of global, national, private, and nonprofit organizations. Global health issues by their very nature need different types of responses. As he noted, the global response to HIV/AIDS would simply not work as a guide for how we respond to an influenza pandemic.[92] Daniel Drezner has argued that we still lack clear answers as to how regime complexity may influence the strategies of different types of actors. On one hand, when actors have choices about which governance arrangements or bodies they can use to purse their interests, the result may be that institutions compete or act strategically to be the more attractive option. But on the other hand, regime complexity does not always result in better outcomes. Drezner found evidence of contradictory outcomes as well as examples where a regime has undermined the role of an individual institution.[93] Too many cooks may spoil the broth.

One final strand of this newer literature has to do with *shifting* and *shopping*, terms that come out of the legal literature. This is a different approach to the idea that when institutions overlap (or regimes are complex), states can shop around for (or shift to) the one that best suits their interest. If states are unhappy with how an issue is being played out in one institution or set of institutions, they may seek to move the issue elsewhere. An example is when US unhappiness by WIPO's (World Intellectual Property Organization) "one-state, one-vote rule" prompted it to move the discussion of intellectual property to the GATT during the Uruguay Round of negotiations in the mid-1980s. In the GATT, the more powerful states had more influence.[94] This is an example of horizontal forum shifting. But states can also shift vertically, from multilateral organizations to bilateral or domestic ones. States may also shift if they think they have a better chance of getting what they want elsewhere. Marc Busch has shown that states have many options about where to address their trade disputes. For example, when Mexico wanted to challenge a US trade rule, it could have filed the case with the World Trade Organization's dispute settlement mechanism, which seemed a better fit given the issues, but instead chose to go through the North American Free Trade Agreement. As noted in the introduction, it is increasingly clear that policy issues interface with IOs and larger regime complexes in challenging ways. The important underlying questions running through this newer area of research is how the richer institutional fabric of global politics impacts the ability of states and other actors to get what they want and the ability of various groupings of actors and organizations to address global problems.

The issues of IO legitimacy and performance may be among the most powerful underlying themes in the contemporary literature. After all, what good are IOs if they do not help to solve global problems, or if they make matters worse? Can geopolitical tensions or actions, such as China's increasing assertiveness in East Asia, weaken IO legitimacy? The study of performance remains a tricky issue. First, there are many ways to define performance. An IO's annual report may take an overly narrow or broad definition, which may be different from how NGOs, scholars, local communities, or IO staff view performance. IOs face powerful "eye of the beholder" problems.[95] For example, powerful countries may be satisfied when the IO reflects their interests, while the impacted public may be protesting. Leaders of coal power plants may have a different view than environmentalists on IO work relating to climate change. Who defines how we understand an IO's performance? If IOs are perceived to lack transparency in their decisionmaking or be too removed from individual citizens, their ability to be effective becomes even more important.[96]

Efficiency is a concept that ties in with performance. The efficiency of peace operations is very important if a slow response makes it easier for conflict to resurface. One scholar has argued that institutions with more informal institutional cultures typically react more efficiently in providing peace operations than institutions that have more formal institutional cultures. Stated differently, since informality is tied to personal relationships and socialization, one can say that institutional friendships can ultimately facilitate faster decisionmaking in times where speedy actions can have life and death repercussions.[97] Individual interactions, not just state interests or interactions, and bureaucratic expertise and authority, may matter too. That said, efficiency is not the same as effectiveness, since "minimizing input of time to maximize productivity" is not necessarily equal to how well an activity was accomplished.[98]

International organizations themselves regularly engage in monitoring and evaluation exercises at different levels of their work. Monitoring is defined as the ongoing collection of data that can be used to track the performance of an activity, such as a program or project. Evaluation is the assessment of performance.[99] IOs want to be able to measure their results so they can learn from success and correct failures, and show that they are accountable for their actions. Evaluation can also help IOs recognize new problems, rethink how they handle particular activities, and determine how they use resources. As two World Bank evaluation experts noted, "evaluation is emerging as a key way in which to systematically address and answer the question, 'so what?' It is not enough to document that one is busy, it is now a requirement to document that one is (or is not) effective."[100]

CONCLUSION

This chapter has laid out some of the main debates and strands of literature addressing IOs spanning almost an entire century. While there are some perennial questions, the changing international context and changing directions in scholarship have inspired newer areas of research as well. Scholars have done well in answering some questions, but still struggle with other questions and regularly confront new ones. One trend that is likely to continue to deepen is the interaction of the literature in political science with those of other disciplines on questions of the role and effectiveness of international organizations in global governance. Political scientists, sociologists, economists, anthropologists, legal scholars, and others certainly have a great deal they can learn from one another. The following chapters will also discuss the literature specific to individual IOs or groups of IOs. Some of those literatures resonate with the broader studies discussed here. Other debates are more narrow and institution specific.

BIBLIOGRAPHY

Adler, Emanuel. "Constructivism and International Relations." In *Handbook of International Relations*, edited by Walter Carlsnaes, Thomas Risse, and Beth A. Simmons, 95–118. London: Sage, 2002.

Alchian, Armen A., and Harold Demsetz. "Production, Information Costs, and Economic Organization." *The American Economic Review* 62, no. 5 (1972): 777–95.

Almond, Gabriel A., and Stephen J. Genco. "Clouds, Clocks, and the Study of Politics." *World Politics* 29, no. 4 (July 1977): 489–522.

Ashley, Richard K. "The Poverty of Neorealism." *International Organization* 38, no. 2 (1984): 225–86.

Avant, Deborah D., Martha Finnemore, and Susan K. Sell, eds. *Who Governs the Globe?* New York: Cambridge University Press, 2010.

Axelrod, Robert M. *The Evolution of Cooperation*. New York: Basic Books, 1984.

Baldwin, David A. *Neorealism and Neoliberalism: The Contemporary Debate*. New York: Columbia University Press, 1993.

Barnett, Michael N. *Eyewitness to a Genocide: The United Nations and Rwanda*. Ithaca, NY: Cornell University Press, 2002.

Barnett, Michael N., and Martha Finnemore. *Rules for the World: International Organizations in Global Politics*. Ithaca, NY: Cornell University Press, 2004.

———. "The Politics, Power, and Pathologies of International Organizations." *International Organization* 53, no. 4 (Autumn 1999): 699–732.

Barnett, Michael N., and Raymond Duvall. *Power in Global Governance*. New York: Cambridge University Press, 2005.

Bawn, Kathleen. "Political Control Versus Expertise: Congressional Choice About Administrative Procedures." *American Political Science Review* 89, no. 1 (1995): 62–73.

Bergman, Torbjörn. "Delegation and Accountability in European Integration: Introduction." *Journal of Legislative Studies* 6, no. 1 (2000): 1–14.

Betsill, Michelle M., and Elisabeth Correll, eds. *NGO Diplomacy: The Influence of Nongovernmental Organizations in International Environmental Negotiations.* Cambridge: MIT Press, 2007.

Bob, Clifford. *The Marketing of Rebellion: Insurgents, Media, and International Activism.* New York: Cambridge University Press, 2005.

Börzel, Tanja A. *States and Regions in the European Union.* New York: Cambridge University Press, 2002.

Buchanan, Allen, and Robert O. Keohane. "The Legitimacy of Global Governance Institutions." *Ethics and International Affairs* 20, no. 4 (2006): 405–37.

Buchanan, James M., and Gordon Tullock. *The Calculus of Consent: Logical Foundations of Constitutional Democracy.* Indianapolis, IN: Liberty Fund Inc., 1957.

Bundy, Harvey H. "An Introductory Note." *International Organization* 1, no. 1 (Feb. 1947): 1–2.

Claude, Inis L. *Swords into Plowshares: The Problems and Progress of International Organization.* New York: Random House, 1956.

Coase, Ronald H. "The Nature of the Firm." *Economica* 16 (1937): 1–44.

Conybeare, John A. C. "International Organization and the Theory of Property Rights." *International Organization* 34, no. 3 (Summer 1980): 307–34.

Cox, Robert W. "Social Forces, States and World Orders: Beyond International Relations Theory." In *Neorealism and Its Critics*, edited by Robert O. Keohane, 204–54. New York: Columbia University Press, 1986.

Deutsch, Karl W. *Political Community and the North Atlantic Area: International Organization in the Light of Historical Experience.* Publications of the Center for Research on World Political Institutions. Princeton, NJ: Princeton University Press, 1957.

DiMaggio, Paul, and Walter W. Powell. "Introduction." In *The New Institutionalism in Organizational Analysis*, edited by Walter W. Powell and Paul DiMaggio, 1–38. Chicago, IL: University of Chicago Press, 1991.

Downs, Anthony. *An Economic Theory of Democracy.* New York: Harper, 1957.

Drezner, Daniel W. *Locating the Proper Authorities: The Interaction of Domestic and International Institutions.* Ann Arbor: The University of Michigan Press, 2003.

———. "The Power and Peril of International Regime Complexity." *Perspectives on Politics* 7, no. 1 (2009): 65–70.

Easton, David. "Introduction: The Current Meaning of Behavioralism in Political Science." In *The Limits of Behavioralism in Political Science: A Symposium Sponsored by the American Academy of Political and Social Science*, edited by James Clyde Charlesworth. Philadelphia, PA: American Academy of Political and Social Science, 1962.

Evans, Peter B., Harold K. Jacobson, and Robert D. Putnam. *Double-Edged Diplomacy: International Bargaining and Domestic Politics.* Berkeley: University of California Press, 1993.

Fang, Songying, and Randall W. Stone. "International Organizations as Policy Advisors." *International Organization* 66, no. 4 (2012): 537–69.

Fearon, James, and Alexander Wendt. "Rationalism v. Constructivism: A Skeptical View." In *Handbook of International Relations*, edited by Walter Carlsnaes, Thomas Risse and Beth A. Simmons, 52–72. London: Sage, 2005.

Fidler, David P. "The Challenges of Global Health Governance." In *International Institutions and Global Governance Program*. New York: Council on Foreign Relations, 2010.

Finnemore, Martha. "Norms, Culture, and World Politics: Insights from Sociology's Institutionalism." *International Organization* 50, no. 2 (Spring 1996): 325–47.

Finnemore, Martha, and Kathryn Sikkink. "Taking Stock: The Constructivist Research Program in International Relations and Comparative Politics." *Annual Review of Political Science* 4 (2001): 391–416.

Friedman, Thomas L. *The World Is Flat: A Brief History of the Twenty-First Century*. 1st ed. New York: Farrar, Straus and Giroux, 2005.

Gaddis, John Lewis. "International Relations Theory and the End of the Cold War." *International Security* 17, no. 3 (Winter 1992/93): 5–58.

Grant, Ruth, and Robert O. Keohane. "Accountability and Abuses of Power in World Politics." *American Political Science Review* 99, no. 1 (2005): 29–43.

Grieco, Joseph M. "Anarchy and the Limits of Cooperation: A Realist Critique of the Newest Liberal Institutionalism." *International Organization* 42, no. 3 (1988): 498–500.

Gruber, Lloyd. *Ruling the World: Power Politics and the Rise of Supranational Institutions*. Princeton, NJ: Princeton University Press, 2000.

Gutner, Tamar. "Explaining the Gaps between Mandate and Performance: Agency Theory and World Bank Environmental Reform." *Global Environmental Politics* 5, no. 2 (2005): 10–37.

———. "When 'Doing Good' Does Not: the IMF and the Millennium Development Goals." In *Who Governs the Globe?*, edited by Deborah D. Avant, Martha Finnemore, and Susan K. Sell, 266–91. New York: Cambridge University Press, 2010.

———. "World Bank Environmental Reform: Revisiting Lessons from Agency Theory." *International Organization* 59 (Summer 2005): 773–83.

Gutner, Tamar, and Alexander Thompson. "The Politics of IO Performance: A Framework." *Review of International Organizations* 5, no. 3 (2010): 227–48.

Haas, Ernst B. *The Uniting of Europe: Political, Social, and Economic Forces, 1950–1957*. Stanford, CA: Stanford University Press, 1958.

———. *When Knowledge Is Power: Three Models of Change in International Organizations*. Berkeley: University of California Press, 1990.

Hall, Peter A. *Governing the Economy: The Politics of State Intervention in Britain and France*. New York: Oxford University Press, 1986.

Hall, Peter A., and Rosemary C.R. Taylor. "Political Science and the Three New Institutionalisms." *Political Studies* 4, no. 4 (December 1996): 936–57.

Hannan, Carolyn. "Feminist Strategies in International Organizations: The United Nations Context." In *Feminist Strategies in International Governance*, edited by Gülay Caglar, Elisabeth Prügl, and Susanne Zwingel, 74–91. London: Routledge, 2013.

Hardt, Heidi. *Time to React: The Efficiency of International Organizations in Crisis Response*. New York: Oxford University Press, 2014.

Heclo, Hugh. *Modern Social Policies in Britain and Sweden*. Cambridge, UK: Cambridge University Press, 1974.

Ikenberry, G. John. *After Victory: Institutions, Strategic Restraint, and the Rebuilding of Order after Major Wars*. Princeton, NJ: Princeton University Press, 2001.

Jain, Devaki. *Women, Development, and the UN: A Sixty-Year Question for Equality and Justice*. Bloomington: Indiana University Press, 2005.

Jensen, Michael C., and William H. Meckling. "Theory of the Firm: Managerial Behavior, Agency Costs and Ownership Structure." *Journal of Financial Economics* 3, no. 4 (1976): 305–60.

Jervis, Robert. "Realism in the Study of World Politics." *International Organization* 52, no. 4 (Autumn 1998): 971–91.

Kahler, Miles. "Rationality in International Relations." *International Organization* 52, no. 4, International Organization at Fifty: Exploration and Contestation in the Study of World Politics (Autumn 1998): 919–41.

Kahler, Miles, and David A. Lake. *Governance in a Global Economy: Political Authority in Transition*. Princeton, NJ: Princeton University Press, 2003.

Kahn, Mohsin S., and Suni Sharma. "IMF Conditionality and Country Ownership of Adjustment Programs." *World Bank Research Observer* 18, no. 2 (2003): 227–48.

Keck, Margaret E., and Kathryn Sikkink. *Activists Beyond Borders: Advocacy Networks in International Politics*. Ithaca, NY: Cornell University Press, 1998.

Keohane, Robert O. *After Hegemony: Cooperation and Discord in the World Political Economy*. Princeton, NJ: Princeton University Press, 1984.

———. *International Institutions and State Power: Essays in International Relations Theory*. Boulder, CO: Westview Press, 1989.

Keohane, Robert O., and Lisa L. Martin. "The Promise of Institutionalist Theory." *International Security* 20, no. 1 (1995): 39–51.

Kiewiet, D. Roderick, and Mathew D. McCubbins. *The Logic of Delegation: Congressional Parties and the Appropriations Process*. Chicago, IL: University of Chicago Press, 1991.

Killick, Tony. "Principals, Agents and the Failings of Conditionality." *Journal of International Development* 9, no. 4 (1997): 483–95.

Krasner, Stephen D. *International Regimes*. Ithaca, NY: Cornell University Press, 1983.

Kratochwil, Friedrich V. *Rules, Norms, and Decisions: On the Conditions of Practical and Legal Reasoning in International Relations and Domestic Affairs*. New York: Cambridge University Press, 1989.

Martin, Lisa L., and Beth A. Simmons. "Theories and Empirical Studies of International Institutions." *International Organization* 52, no. 4 (Autumn 1998): 729–57.

Mathews, Jessica T. "Power Shift." *Foreign Affairs* 76, no. 1 (Jan/Feb 1997): 50–66.

McCubbins, Mathew D., Roger G. Noll, and Barry R. Weingast. "Administrative Procedures as Instruments of Political Control." *Journal of Law, Economics, and Organizations* 3, no. 2 (1987): 243–79.

———. "Structure and Process, Politics and Policy: Administrative Arrangements and the Political Control of Agencies." *Virginia Law Review* 75 (1989): 431–82.

Mearsheimer, John J. "The False Promise of International Institutions." *International Security* 19, no. 3 (Winter 1994): 5–49.

Meyer, John W., and Brian Rowan. "Institutionalized Organizations: Formal Structure as Myth and Ceremony." *American Journal of Sociology* 83, no. 2 (Sep. 1977): 340–63.

Miles, Edward L. *Environmental Regime Effectiveness: Confronting Theory with Evidence*. Cambridge: MIT Press, 2002.

Milgrom, Paul, and John Roberts. "Bargaining Costs, Influence Costs and the Organization of Economic Activity." In *Perspectives on Positive Political Economy*, edited by James E. Alt and Kenneth A. Shepsle, 57–89. Cambridge, UK: Cambridge University Press, 1990.

Milner, Helen V. *Interests, Institutions, and Information: Domestic Politics and International Relations*. Princeton, NJ: Princeton University Press, 1997.

Moe, Terry. "The New Economics of Organization." *American Journal of Political Science* 28, no. 4 (1984): 739–77.

——. "The Politics of Structural Choice: Toward a Theory of Public Bureaucracy." In *Organization Theory: From Chester Barnard to the Present and Beyond*, edited by Oliver E. Williamson, 116–53. New York: Oxford University Press, 1990.

Morgenthau, Hans J., Kenneth W. Thompson, and W. David Clinton. *Politics among Nations: The Struggle for Power and Peace*. 7th ed. Boston: McGraw-Hill Higher Education, 2006.

Morra Imas, Linda G., and Ray C. Rist. *The Road to Results: Designing and Conducting Effective Development Evaluations*. Washington, DC: The World Bank, 2009.

Nielson, Daniel L., and Michael J. Tierney. "Delegation to International Organizations: Agency Theory and World Bank Environmental Reform." *International Organization* 57, no. 2 (2003): 241–76.

North, Douglass C. *Institutions, Institutional Change, and Economic Performance*. The Political Economy of Institutions and Decisions. New York: Cambridge University Press, 1990.

——. *Structure and Change in Economic History*. 1st ed. New York: Norton, 1981.

Oestreich, Joel E. *International Organizations as Self-Directed Actors: A Framework for Analysis*. Routledge Global Institutions Series. New York: Routledge, 2012.

Olson, Mancur. *The Logic of Collective Action: Public Goods and the Theory of Groups*. Cambridge, MA: Harvard University Press, 1971.

Onuf, Nicholas G. *World of Our Making: Rules and Rule in Social Theory and International Relations*. Columbia: University of South Carolina Press, 1989.

Oye, Kenneth A. *Cooperation Under Anarchy*. Princeton, NJ: Princeton University Press, 1986.

Pierson, Paul. "The Path to European Integration: A Historical Institutionalist Perspective." *Comparative Political Studies* 29, no. 2 (1996): 123–63.

Pollack, Mark A. *The Engines of European Integration: Delegation, Agency, and Agenda Setting in the EU*. New York: Oxford University Press, 2003.

Powell, Walter W., and Paul DiMaggio. *The New Institutionalism in Organizational Analysis*. Chicago, IL: University of Chicago Press, 1991.

Power, Samantha. *A Problem from Hell: America and the Age of Genocide*. New York: Basic Books, 2002.

Raustiala, Kal, and David G. Victor. "The Regime Complex for Plant Genetic Resources." *International Organization* 58 (2004): 277–309.

Rich, Bruce. *Foreclosing the Future: The World Bank and the Politics of Environmental Destruction*. Washington, DC: Island Press, 2013.

——. *Mortgaging the Earth: The World Bank, Environmental Impoverishment, and the Crisis of Development*. Boston, MA: Beacon Press, 1994.

Riggs, Robert E., Karen Feste Hanson, Mary Heinz, Barry B. Hughes, and Thomas J. Volgy. "Behavioralism in the Study of the United Nations." *World Politics: A Quarterly Journal of International Relations* 22, no. 2 (Jan. 1970): 197–236.

Ruggie, John Gerard. *Constructing the World Polity: Essays on International Institutionalization.* New York: Routledge, 1998.

———. "International Responses to Technology: Concepts and Trends." *International Organization* 29, no. 3 (Summer 1975): 557–83.

Schmitter, Philippe. "A Revised Theory of European Integration." In *Regional Integration: Theory and Research,* edited by Leon N. Lindberg and Stuart A. Scheingold. Cambridge, MA: Harvard University Press, 1971.

Schweller, Randall L., and David Priess. "A Tale of Two Realisms: Expanding the Institutions Debate." *Mershon International Studies Review* 41 (1997): 1–32.

Sell, Susan K. "TRIPS Was Never Enough: Vertical Forum Shifting, FTAS, ACTA, and TPP." *Journal of Intellectual Property Law* 18, no. 447 (2011): 447–78.

Shepsle, Kenneth A. "Studying Institutions: Some Lessons from the Rational Choice Approach." *Journal of Theoretical Politics* 1 (1989): 131–49.

Skocpol, Theda. *States and Social Revolutions: A Comparative Analysis of France, Russia, and China.* New York: Cambridge University Press, 1979.

Smith, Adam. *An Inquiry into the Nature and Causes of the Wealth of Nations.* London: Printed for W. Strahan and T. Cadell, 1776.

Stokke, Olav Schram, and Sebastian Oberthür. "Introduction: International Interaction in Global Environmental Change." In *Managing Institutional Complexity: Regime Interplay and Global Environmental Change,* edited by Sebastian Oberthür and Olav Schram Stokke, 1–23. Cambridge: MIT Press.

Strange, Susan. "Cave! Hic Dragones: A Critique of Regime Analysis." *International Organization* 36, no. 2 (Spring 1982): 479–96.

Talberg, Jonas. "Delegation to Supranational Institutions: Why, How, and with What Consequences." *West European Politics* 25, no. 1 (2002): 23–46.

Tharoor, Shashi. "Why America Still Needs the United Nations." *Foreign Affairs* 82, no. 5 (Sep/Oct 2003): 67–80.

Tirole, Jean. "The Internal Organisation of Government." *Oxford Economic Papers* 46, no. 1 (1994): 1–29.

Urquhart, Brian. "Looking for the Sheriff." *New York Review of Books* (July 16, 1998).

Vaubel, Roland, and Thomas D. Willett. *The Political Economy of International Organizations: A Public Choice Approach.* The Political Economy of Global Interdependence. Boulder, CO: Westview Press, 1991.

Waltz, Kenneth N. "Theory and International Politics." By Harry Kreisler. *Conversations with History.* Institute of International Studies, UC Berkeley. February 10, 2003. globetrotter.berkeley.edu/people3/Waltz/waltz-con1.html (Accessed March 20, 2013).

———. *Theory of International Politics.* 1st ed. Boston, MA: McGraw-Hill, 1979.

Wapner, Paul Kevin. *Environmental Activism and World Civic Politics.* Suny Series in International Environmental Policy and Theory. Albany: State University of New York Press, 1996.

Weiss, Thomas G., David P. Forsythe, and Roger A. Coate. *The United Nations and Changing World Politics*. 4th ed. Boulder, CO: Westview Press, 2004.

Wendt, Alexander. *Social Theory of International Politics*. New York: Cambridge University Press, 1999.

Williamson, Oliver E. *Markets and Hierarchies, Analysis and Antitrust Implications: A Study in the Economics of Internal Organization*. New York: Free Press, 1975.

———. *The Economic Institutions of Capitalism: Firms, Markets, Relational Contracting*. New York: Free Press, 1985.

Woods, Ngaire. "Good Governance in International Organizations." *Global Governance* 5, no. 1 (January-March 1999): 39–61.

Young, Oran R. *Governance in World Affairs*. Ithaca, NY: Cornell University Press, 1999.

———. *The Effectiveness of International Environmental Regimes: Causal Connections and Behavioral Mechanisms*. Cambridge: MIT Press, 1999.

———. *The Institutional Dimensions of Environmental Change: Fit, Interplay, and Scale*. Cambridge: MIT Press, 2002.

3 United Nations

The United Nations itself is but a cross section of the world's peoples. It reflects, therefore, the typical fears, suspicions and prejudices which bedevil human relations throughout the world.

–Ralph Bunche[1]

The United Nations is actually a family of organizations, consisting of six *principal organs*, but also a panoply of agencies, programs, commissions, and more with a veritable alphabet soup of acronyms. The United Nations family today addresses virtually every imaginable international issue, from the major issues of international peace and security, to more specialized issues such as improving the safety of international shipping, developing networks for meteorological observations, raising countries' levels of nutrition, and reducing the spread of infectious diseases. At the heart of the UN is the Security Council, which is responsible for maintaining international peace and security.[2] While the Security Council receives more attention (and criticism) than other parts of the UN, its work can be far removed from the other activities going on elsewhere within the broader UN family.

Given the variety of organizations and activities that the UN encompasses, it is not easy to make blanket statements about the UN's effectiveness or define it as either an actor or stage. There is no single answer, since some parts of the UN are more effective than others, and at different times, and the UN has acted as both actor and stage, depending on which part of it you are looking at, which issue, and which time period. The UN's parts are perhaps greater than the sum of its whole, and ultimately, need to be analyzed separately. The story of the Security Council may be intertwined with that of the General Assembly, but in the end the Security Council has much more clout in international relations than the General Assembly. Laboring steadily, but out of the headlines, is the International Court of Justice, which has become an influential actor in adjudicating disputes between mid-sized states. States remain the dominant actors at the UN, and their political will is the foundation upon which the UN will succeed or fail, but civil society and private sector actors are also becoming more visible and involved.[3] As former US Ambassador to the UN Nancy Soderberg once noted, "There is no such single thing as the UN."[4] It is a group of 193 member states, many of which have different agendas, which are supported by a large body of civil servants.

This chapter discusses the UN's birth, describes its structure and major activities, highlights the major ways in which the organization has evolved over its 70 years of existence, and lays out some of the most pressing issues and debates confronting the organization today.

BIRTH OF THE UN

The League of Nations' inability to forestall Japanese, Italian, and German expansionism, and the subsequent outbreak of World War II, inspired many to begin thinking, well before the end of World War II, about how a new organization might work better. President Franklin D. Roosevelt is widely seen as the driving force behind the establishment of the UN, and by 1939, two years before the US entered World War II, the US State Department was already developing plans for such an organization.[5] Roosevelt was disillusioned with the League and felt that any successor should be designed to reflect the realist nature of world politics. He envisioned an organization where the four major powers—the United States, Britain, Soviet Union, and China—would act as "Four Policemen" to provide security for the world.[6] His idea was that if an aggressive country "started to run amok and seeks to grab territory or invade its neighbors," a new global institution would "stop them before they got started."[7] When Roosevelt said, "An attack on one is an attack on all," he was voicing what political scientists call the concept of *collective security*, or the idea that states in a collective security arrangement agree to respond together to an attack on one of their members in hopes that such an arrangement will deter potential aggressors.

British Prime Minister Winston Churchill was also very much involved in working with Roosevelt to produce a common strategy on a postwar order. It was Churchill who wrote the first draft of the August 1941 Atlantic Charter, which laid out the two leaders' vision for a postwar order. One of the draft principles suggested by Churchill was the creation of an "effective international organization." Roosevelt finally agreed on a principle that called for, more broadly, "the establishment of a wider and permanent system of general security," linked to the belief he shared with Churchill that "all of the nations of the world . . . must come to the abandonment of the use of force."[8]

Five months after the Atlantic Charter was signed, 26 nations signed in Washington, DC, the "Declaration of United Nations" to pledge unity in their war against the Axis powers.[9] Roosevelt himself coined the term "United Nations," apparently gaining Churchill's approval by barging into his bedroom at the White House while the Prime Minister was taking a bath.[10] Unfortunately, Roosevelt would never live to see the realization of his dream of creating a new world body, since he died on April 12, 1945, a mere two months before the UN Charter was approved.[11]

MAJOR DATES SURROUNDING THE BIRTH OF THE UNITED NATIONS

September 1, 1939, Germany invades Poland, starting WWII in Europe

December 8, 1941, United States enters WWII after Japan bombs Pearl Harbor on December 7

June 6, 1944, D-Day invasion opens second front in Europe

January 27, 1945, Auschwitz concentration camp liberated by Soviet Red Army

May 8, 1945, VE Day

June 25, 1945, UN Charter approved, San Francisco

August 15, 1945, VJ Day

October 24, 1945, UN Charter becomes effective

The United States played a leading role in the design and establishment of the UN. Six weeks after the United Nations Declaration was signed, Secretary of State Cordell Hull created a new "Advisory Committee on Postwar Foreign Policy" that, in turn, created a number of subcommittees to examine a host of issues. In June 1942, Undersecretary of State Sumner Welles set up a subcommittee to focus on international organization. A little-known State Department official, Leo Pasvolsky, who was Hull's personal assistant, played a seminal role in organizing and influencing a number of draft charters, the latest of which was the "basic frame of reference" for the negotiations of what became the UN Charter.[12]

The main negotiations that crafted the UN Charter took place in two international conferences that seem surprisingly long from today's vantage point.[13] The first, a conference at the Washington, DC, estate Dumbarton Oaks, began August 21, 1944, and ran for more than a month. The estate, bequeathed to Harvard University by a former US Ambassador to Sweden and Argentina, was chosen because its buildings and many acres of spacious gardens offered some escape from the harsh Washington heat and humidity. (This same Washington heat is what drove the negotiators of the World Bank and the International Monetary Fund to escape up to cooler Bretton Woods, New Hampshire, a month earlier.) At Dumbarton Oaks, the United States, Great Britain, the Soviet Union, and China negotiated the basic framework, structure, and functions of the UN. The British delegation arrived a week early to work with the Americans on a common set of ideas. The Soviets arrived next so the three most important Allied powers could negotiate.[14] Because Roosevelt insisted that China should be included as a great power, the Chinese met with the Americans and British after the Soviets left. According to David L. Bosco, the British and Soviet diplomats did not take seriously the idea of China as a great power, given the precarious position of its leader, Chiang Kai-shek. As British diplomat Gladwyn Jebb, put it

> We in the Foreign Office generally, I think, never thought that China had any chance of being a real world power for a very long time . . . but we had to imagine that it was a world power in order to please President Roosevelt.[15]

One reason the conference ran so long is the number of important issues that were difficult to resolve, usually pitting the Soviets against the Americans and British. In fact, a number of issues were not resolved at Dumbarton Oaks, including the absolute veto, who would be invited to join the United Nations, and the role of the General Assembly.[16]

The following year representatives of 46 governments met in San Francisco for nine weeks, from late April to late June, to finish negotiating, and then ratifying the UN Charter.[17] Notably excluded were delegates from the Axis countries—Germany, Japan, and Italy. The conference was enormous, as Stephen C. Schlesinger described it, with

> a fluctuating populace of some 5,000 people. . . . There were some 850 delegates and advisors; 2,600 media; over 1,000 workers at the UN Secretariat; 300 or so security people; 120 interpreters translating the five main languages—English, French, Spanish, Russian, and Chinese; 37 foreign ministers; and 5 prime ministers. Untold numbers of local San Franciscans also attended sessions.[18]

The Granger Collection, New York

This cartoon appeared with a June 24, 1945 article in *The New York Times* applauding the negotiations over the UN Charter.

The three biggest powers—the United States, Great Britain, and the Soviet Union—had the most clout in shaping the outcome. That outcome was by no means certain, given that there were plenty of debates and obstacles along the path to the Charter. Despite the challenges, in the midst of the negotiating there was still great hope that a new organization could be created that might possibly be able to end future wars.[19] It is hard to imagine today how great these hopes were at the time, as the incredibly devastating war in Europe was winding down, with an official end on May 8, while Japan had not yet surrendered (and would do so on August 15).

The Charter was signed with great fanfare on June 26, 1945, by 50 governments (as four more were added to the official roster before the end) and entered into force on October 24, a day still celebrated each year as UN Day. Instead of following the usual method of voting by hand, Lord Halifax, who presided over the plenary session, asked delegates to vote by standing given "the world importance of the vote."[20] As the delegates stood, the audience of more than 3,000 "jumped to its feet to cheer and applaud for a full minute." "The Charter," said *The New York Times*, "was a gift to a world ravaged by war." The actual signing of the documents had to be delayed until the following morning, since the task of printing enough copies of the Charter and its related documents in the five official languages of the conference was too much for San Francisco's printing shops to manage.[21]

Although Roosevelt had earlier thought the UN might be located in different places—with the Security Council on an island, such as the Azores, or Hawaii, and the General Assembly held around the world at different times,[22] the UN's General Assembly at its first session in February 1946 (in London) voted to locate the UN's headquarters near New York City. No one anticipated that appropriate space could be found in crowded Manhattan, but a gift of $8.5 million by John D. Rockefeller, Jr., made possible the purchase of an area populated by slaughterhouses and light industry. The US Government then approved a $65 million interest free loan for building construction (which was not fully repaid until 1982), and the four, interconnected main buildings were completed by 1950.[23] The headquarters are considered to be international, and not US, territory.

THE UN CHARTER AND MAIN ORGANS

The UN Charter is an international treaty that is the UN's constituting agreement. It establishes the various organs of the UN, lays out how they will operate, and also sets out the duties and rights of member states. The main purposes of the UN are set out in Article 1: "to maintain international peace and security"; "to develop friendly relations among nations based on respect for the principle of equal rights and self-determination of peoples"; "to achieve international cooperation in solving international problems of an economic, social, cultural, and humanitarian character, and . . . [promote and encourage] respect for human rights and for fundamental freedoms for all without distinction as to race, sex, language, or religion"; and "to be a centre for harmonizing the actions of nations in attaining these common ends."[24]

The signatories agreed to the following principles: the UN is "based on the sovereign equality of all its members"; that members will settle international disputes "by peaceful means and without endangering international peace and security and justice"; that members "are to refrain from the threat or use of force against any other state"; and that "nothing in the Charter is to authorize the United Nations to intervene in matters which are essentially within the domestic jurisdiction of any state."[25]

The United Nations consists of six major organs, described in this section:

The Security Council

The General Assembly

The Economic and Social Council (ECOSOC)

The Secretariat

The International Court of Justice (ICJ)

The Trusteeship Council

The Security Council

The Security Council is the realist heart of an organization with a liberal mission. It is in the Security Council where the five most powerful countries after WWII—Roosevelt's Four Policemen, plus France, have the right to veto any proposed resolution, which gives them more power than any other members. Without this veto power, the form of which was debated at great length at Dumbarton Oaks and in San Francisco, the powerful states would never have agreed to create the United Nations. After such a terrible war against fascism, the negotiators realized how important it was to pool state power to help manage global problems. As Thomas Weiss, David Forsythe, and Roger Coate put it, "This was hardly wild-eyed idealism run amok."[26] This right for five major countries to veto is one of the main design features that distinguish the UN's Security Council from the League's—for the League's Council and Assembly most decisions required a unanimous vote, which essentially meant that any country could veto.[27]

As to the composition of the Security Council, France was added since it was the most powerful country in continental Europe after Germany was defeated. China was soon overwhelmed by political upheaval, given the 1949 Communist revolution and takeover. The Republic of China (Taiwan) managed to hang onto its seat until 1971, when the communist People's Republic secured it. Upon the Soviet Union's dissolution in 1991, Russia inherited the old Soviet seat. The permanent five, known as P-5, were joined at first, by six, and by 1966, ten, additional nonpermanent members that rotate every two years, and are chosen along geographical lines.[28] Each member of the Security Council has one vote, and most resolutions require nine affirmative votes and no veto.

The Security Council can meet at any time, and as a result, each member always has a representative at UN headquarters. If a complaint about a threat to peace is brought before it, the Security Council has a number of options for responding. It will usually begin by bringing the parties involved together to try and reach a peaceful agreement. It can also propose principles for dispute resolution, or mediate the dispute itself. It can request that the Secretary-General try to help the parties reach a peaceful agreement. In all of the above examples, it is playing an advisory or moderating role. These are laid out in Chapter VI of the Charter, titled "the Pacific Settlement of Disputes."

What gives the Security Council some teeth is Chapter VII, which allows it to use coercive power to enforce peace. Under Chapter VII, the Security Council may call upon UN members to sanction the offending state through economic sanctions or by completely or partially interrupting transportation linkages and communication linkages, as well as cutting off diplomatic relations. If these actions don't work, Article 52 allows the Security Council to "take such action by air, sea, or land forces as may be necessary to maintain or restore international peace and security." These latter actions can include "demonstrations, blockades, and other operations by air, sea, or land forces of the Members of the United Nations."

While the Security Council therefore has a number of tools it can use to try to prevent, reduce, or end conflict, and to keep the peace once conflict has ended, perhaps the most visible activity that takes place under its auspices is peacekeeping. UN peacekeepers, or "Blue Helmets" as they are often called (because they wear light blue helmets and berets), were first used in 1948 to supervise the truce between Israel and its Arab neighbors, and in fact this group—the United Nations Truce Supervision Organization (UNTSO)—remains in the region today.[29] Peacekeeping has grown rapidly since the end of the Cold War, with over 50 new missions deployed, compared with only 13 during the UN's first 40 years. But while peacekeeping operations are central to the Security Council's efforts to secure international peace, the term *peacekeeping* is not mentioned at all in the UN's Charter. Former UN Secretary-General, Dag Hammarskjöld famously referred to peacekeeping as "Chapter six and a half," of the UN's Charter, since it takes place in the grey area between the mediation and fact-finding actions called for in Chapter VI, and the embargoes and military interventions referred to in Chapter VII.[30]

The General Assembly

The UN's General Assembly (GA) is the one place on Earth where the world's governments can all meet together to deliberate, and where each member has one vote. Every September, shortly after the GA begins its official year, a large number of heads of state flock to New York to address it. The GA has a number of responsibilities and activities: it can bring issues to the attention of the Security Council; it can often make recommendations to UN member states and the Security Council (SC); it can initiate studies that seek to promote international coop-eration in a variety of fields; it approves the UN's budget; it elects the rotating members of the Security Council; and together with the Security Council, it elects the International Court of Justice's judges and appoints the UN's Secretary-General. A two-thirds majority of member states present and voting is necessary for decisions on important issues, including the admis-sion of new members, the budget, and issues related to peace and security. Other decisions require a simple majority.

Given that the tiny Seychelles Islands (population of around 90,000) has the same one vote as the United States, it should be no surprise that the GA is hardly considered to be a powerful component of the UN. Indeed, its resolutions are not legally binding, and therefore, the GA's importance lies in raising global consciousness on particular issues, and expressing the gen-eral opinion of the "world community." Many people recognize the importance of having such a forum for states to discuss virtually any issue related to international peace and security. Supporters of the GA hope that one day it will evolve into a global parliament, while others argue that such a progressive outcome is unlikely.

The GA was given a somewhat larger role in the big issue of maintaining international peace and security in its November 3, 1950, resolution, "Uniting for Peace." Under this resolution, if the Security Council failed to act (i.e., because one of the P-5 used its veto), but a majority of its members wanted to act, the GA could consider an act of aggression or other breach of peace and directly make recommendations to member states on ways of restoring peace. This resolu-tion was sponsored by the United States and six other countries as a way to get around the Soviet veto during the Korean War.[31]

It was first officially used twice in the beginning of November 1956, a harrowing week where the Security Council was stymied in attempting to respond to the Israeli-Franco-British attacks on Egypt and occupation of the Suez Canal (in response to Egypt's nationalization of the strategically important canal) and the Soviet invasion of Hungary. In the first case, the "Uniting for Peace" resolution was used not to get around a Soviet veto, but rather a French and British veto of a United States/Soviet Union-sponsored resolution calling for an Israeli-Egyptian ceasefire. The General Assembly held an emergency session November 2 to pass a resolution calling for "all parties" involved in the hostilities "to agree to an immediate cease-fire" and to halt "the movement of military forces and arms into the area."[32] A withdrawal of British, French, and Israeli troops occurred soon after, facilitated by the first deployment of what became known as UN "peacekeepers" to separate the warring forces and create a buffer zone between Israel and Egypt.[33]

Two days later on November 4, after the Soviets vetoed a United States' Security Council resolution deploring the use of force in Hungary (in a 5 a.m. session), another special session of the Assembly was convened, and the Assembly promptly called on the Soviet government to withdraw its forces from Hungary "without delay."[34] This was in response to Soviet forces invading Budapest and other parts of Hungary earlier that day to crush a nationwide revolt against the Soviet-supported government and policies.

While the General Assembly was respected and taken seriously in these heady early years, over the decades its influence has waned. Granted, its ability to speak up on international issues gives it a voice on the global stage, but more recently the General Assembly has been criticized for an "inability to break from a mind-numbing routine of adopting resolutions on nearly all of the more than 150 items on its agenda each year," which only serves to deepen "its obscurity."[35] It is often criticized for being overly bureaucratic and inefficient in its desire to be fair and inclusive. Its president is elected each year at the beginning of the new session, which means there is no continuity in leadership. And under the president, there are a whopping twenty-one vice presidents and six main committees. The General Assembly's culture favors consensus, which is difficult to achieve, given that each of the United Nation's 193 members has a seat at the table.[36]

Former UN Secretary-General, Kofi Annan, in his seminal 2005 report, *In Larger Freedom*, recognized that UN member states were concerned about the General Assembly's declining prestige and contributions. Its goal of achieving consensus on a growing number of resolutions has

> not proved an effective way of reconciling the interests of Member States. Rather, it prompts the Assembly to retreat into generalities, abandoning any serious effort to take action. Such real debates . . . tend to focus on process rather than substance and many so-called decisions simply reflect the lowest common denominator of widely held opinions."

The solution he called for was for the General Assembly to narrow its agenda, procedures, and committee structures, to "concentrate on the major substantive issues of the day." The political will, he argued, needed to come from member states.[37]

These suggestions have not been acted upon. The agenda for the 69th session of the General Assembly in 2014, for example, included over 170 topics that addressed virtually every imaginable international issue, including "harmony with nature," "international strategy for disaster reduction," "globalization and interdependence," "sport for development and peace," "effects of atomic radiation," and "the role of diamonds in fuelling conflict," among others.[38]

The Economic and Social Council (ECOSOC)

The Economic and Social Council, known as ECOSOC, was set up by the UN Charter to take the lead on discussing, studying, and researching issues that went beyond security—or "international economic, social, cultural, educational, health, and related matters." It can make recommendations on these issues as well as "promoting respect for, and observance of, human rights," to the General Assembly, the UN's specialized agencies, and individual member states. It is also able to compose draft conventions or call for and prepare international conferences. Finally, it receives reports from the UN's eleven funds and programs, and acts to coordinate their work, although it does not control them. Today, ECOSOC consists of 54 member states, with overlapping three-year terms that are elected by the General Assembly with seats divvied up by region.[39] It holds its main four-week session in July, alternating between Geneva and New York.

ECOSOC is essentially a deliberative forum, which gives it the ability to discuss, research, initiate, and deepen dialogue with a variety of actors, including civil society and academics, but no power. It makes suggestions, issues recommendations, manifestos, and declarations.

Unsurprisingly, it has a reputation of lacking a clear public profile and being largely irrelevant.[40] It may also be the case that ECOSOC is under-appreciated. Some of its functions are no doubt useful, but they generally occur behind the scenes. For example, it is the main UN body that negotiates the agreements governing the ways NGOs can interact with the UN. Today there are over 4,000 NGOs with consultative status with ECOSOC, which gives the NGOs the ability to participate in a variety of ECOSOC and other UN meetings, and to make statements and present reports.

The Secretariat; Secretary-General

The Secretariat consists of the international civil servants working at the United Nations, which today totals over 43,000 people from 186 different countries. These are the people who administer the UN's peacekeeping operations, prepare studies on a variety of issues, translate documents, organize conferences, and work with the international media, among other things. They work in departments/offices, on regional commissions, tribunals, or in field operations. The largest single number (over 6,000) is based on New York. The second and third top locations are Sudan and Switzerland.[41] The UN staff, as international civil servants, take an oath that says they do "not seek or receive instructions from any Government or any other authority," outside the UN.[42]

Heading the Secretariat is the UN's Secretary-General (SG). This position is described very simply in the UN's charter, as the organization's "chief administrative officer" (Article 97). The SG's official duties are to run the organization; to carry out unspecified "functions" entrusted to him by the Security Council, General Assembly, Trusteeship Council, and ECOSOC (Article 98); and to bring to the Security Council's attention any matter which "in his opinion may threaten the maintenance of international peace and security" (Article 99).

Scholars and practitioners agree that the SG's job is complex and extremely demanding, with the SG facing high international expectations. As longtime UN official Shashi Tharoor said,

> Over the years, observers have both granted various attributes to the Secretary-General and challenged his fulfillment of them. He has been variously described as the personification of the collective interests of humanity, the custodian of the aspirations of the Charter, the guardian of the world's conscience (if not the symbol of

UN SECRETARIES-GENERAL

Trygve Lie (Norway)	1946–52	Javier Perez de Cuellar (Peru)	1982–91
Dag Hammarskjöld (Sweden)	1953–61	Boutros Boutros-Ghali (Egypt)	1992–96
U Thant (Burma)	1961–71	Kofi Annan (Ghana)	1997–2007
Kurt Waldheim (Austria)	1972–81	Ban Ki-moon (South Korea)	2007–2016

the conscience itself), and more prosaically as the globe's chief diplomat and its premier civil servant.[43]

The first Secretary-General, Trygve Lie, told his successor, Dag Hammarskjöld, it was "the most impossible job on this earth."[44] One reason this was the case was that the advent of the Cold War sidetracked the UN from visions of global importance, as Brian Urquhart noted "the new organization became occupied with preventing a cataclysmic nuclear confrontation between its key members."[45] It did this by trying to address regional conflicts that could blow up into dangerous US-Soviet confrontations. A key side effect was that the Cold War forced the UN to improvise ways to maintaining international peace and security that resulted in expanding the secretary-general's role.[46]

Hammarskjöld, who had been Sweden's deputy foreign affairs minister, was only 45 when he took the post. Urquhart, who was Under-Secretary-General of the UN from 1972–1986, praised Hammarskjöld for being an unusually skilled diplomat with a keen intellect, who was able to diffuse superpower tensions more than once. His efforts helped to expand the SG's position beyond its administrative mission to a more flexible diplomatic one, and he was awarded the Nobel Peace Prize in 1961.[47] Hammarskjöld's work, in the end, cost him his life; he was killed in a suspicious September 1961 plane crash, on his way to peace talks in Northern Rhodesia (now Zambia) to end a messy conflict that included fighting between secessionist forces and UN troops in the former Belgian Congo (now the Democratic Republic of Congo).[48]

The end of the Cold War put a new set of demands on the SG, as intrastate conflict escalated, severely straining UN peacekeeping abilities. Boutros Boutros-Ghali, an Egyptian scholar-diplomat, faced the debacles of peacekeeping in Somalia, Bosnia, and Rwanda, discussed below. He was known as a brilliant intellectual with an authoritarian leadership style, who often spoke his mind to member states and the press in ways that sometimes got him into trouble. He also had a tense relationship with the United States (particularly its permanent representative, Madeleine Albright), which ultimately resulted in the United States making clear it would refuse his bid for a second term.

Kofi Annan, in turn, is often likened to Hammarskjöld in terms of his negotiating skills (and like his predecessor, Annan was awarded the Nobel Peace Prize—in 2001). He was the first SG to emerge from the UN bureaucracy, after a 30-year career through the ranks. He was the head of UN peacekeeping during the "two defining genocidal crimes of the second half of the twentieth century," Rwanda and Srebrenica.[49] But despite these failures and others while he was SG, Annan was known as affable, calm, and possessing a certain moral authority.[50] As SG, he ran into trouble with the United States over its 2003 invasion of Iraq, which Annan said was illegal from the "Charter point of view."[51] (Annan also joked that the acronym, SG, stood for "scape goat."[52]) During his tenure, Annan also had to cope with some damaging UN reports that found "widespread" evidence that UN peacekeepers and staff had sexually abused or exploited war refugees in West Africa, and in individual countries such as the Democratic Republic of Congo.[53] Finally, in 2004, the UN was also charged with mismanagement in the UN oil-for-food program in Iraq, which in the end almost ended his leadership of the UN. The program started up in 1996 to allow proceeds from the sale of Iraqi oil to be used to help buy food and other necessities for Iraqi citizens who were hurt by international sanctions. Instead, Saddam Hussein figured out how to use the program to receive over $1 billion in kickbacks from companies getting lucrative contracts, while smuggling over $10 billion in oil into Iraq.

An independent inquiry charged by Annan and the Security Council to review management of this program also found plenty of evidence of mismanagement and unethical conduct.[54]

When Ban Ki-moon took over the Secretary-General position in 2007, he acknowledged that the institution was under the strain of scandal and criticism of weak management. "You could say that I am a man on a mission, and my mission could be dubbed 'Operation Restore Trust,'" he said, "I hope this mission is not 'Mission: Impossible.'"[55] Ban, a former South Korean foreign minister, has a quiet leadership style, which initially generated criticism that he was making changes to the UN bureaucracy without sufficient transparency or consultation.[56] His priorities have included increasing awareness of climate change as a major global problem; consolidating the UN's work with women into a new agency, UN Women; creating a mediation support unit for peacekeeping conflicts; strengthening the UN's response to major disasters and crises, like the devastating cyclone in Myanmar (2008), the earthquake in Haiti (2010), the flooding in Pakistan (2010), and the exodus of refugees from Syria (2015); and improving the UN's ability to act quickly to safeguard human rights. He has also been keen to strengthen UN peacekeeping, especially by prioritizing prevention and mediation, making missions more responsive and ending the problem of peacekeepers engaging in sexual abuse and exploitation.[57]

Perhaps the greatest challenge facing a UN Secretary-General is how to maneuver between being an independent voice and diplomat and being an agent of the states that appoint him/her. As Simon Chesterman noted, unsurprisingly, member states are "most enthusiastic about the independence of the Secretary-General . . . when his decisions have coincided with their national interests."[58] Secretary-Generals have used what wiggle room they have in a variety of ways. In addition to negotiating an end to conflict, they also may mobilize international support for a variety of issues; and they may suggest normative changes in how states think about maintaining peace and security. For example, Annan played a leading role in pushing states to embrace a norm of *responsibility to protect* people against genocide, ethnic cleansing, and other crimes against humanity, and that norm has certainly spread over time, even if it is not always followed.

The International Court of Justice (ICJ)

The International Court of Justice (also known as the ICJ or the World Court) is the UN's main judicial body and is based in The Hague, Netherlands. It is the only one of the UN's six main organs that is not located in New York City. The ICJ has two primary duties: to settle disputes between member states and to offer advisory opinions to the UN and its specialized agencies. In a way, it embodies a revolutionary idea in a world of *realpolitik*—that states with a dispute can go to a "neutral" body to adjudicate. Many people mistakenly assume that the ICJ can try individuals, but it cannot. Also, states, and not individuals, bring cases to the ICJ. Rulings are made by the 15 judges who are elected by the General Assembly and the Security Council for 9-year terms. Judges are distributed by region, and must be "persons of high moral character," widely recognized as experts in international law or as qualified to be appointed to their own country's "highest judicial offices."[59] The judges make a declaration in the court that they do not represent any country, but rather will act "impartially and conscientiously."[60] Only states that are members of the UN (and/or are parties to the Court's Statute) can bring cases to the Court; it is therefore not open to cases from individuals or private institutions or other international institutions. (This is in contrast, for example, to the relatively new International Criminal Court, which was created in 1998 to punish individuals guilty of crimes against humanity.)

The ICJ had its roots in the Permanent Court of International Justice (PCIJ), which was set up in 1920 under the old League of Nations along similar lines as the ICJ. The ICJ essentially replaced the PCIJ, incorporating the latter's doctrine, procedures, even staff, but it is also different in several ways. One is that while the PCIJ was a parallel institution to the League, the ICJ has equal standing to the Security Council, General Assembly, and other primary UN bodies. Second, Axis countries and their allies, who were not invited to join the UN, were also not invited to be members of the new court. When the new court was created, the old one was formally dissolved, and its archives were handed over to the new ICJ, which was located in the same Peace Palace in The Hague. In another sign of continuity, the last president of the PCIJ, Judge José Gustavo Guerrero (El Salvador), was elected as the first president of the ICJ in April 1946.[61]

In adjudicating disputes, the court uses several sources of international law, including treaties, international custom, general legal principles, and judicial decisions or teachings of well-known legal scholars. If the parties agree (and none have done so to date), the ICJ can even make a decision *ex aequo et bono*, which means based on what is considered to be fair and equitable, rather than existing international law.

Throughout most of its life, the ICJ has not been at the forefront of solving interstate disputes. ICJ judgments were certainly not requested in most of the serious conflicts that came before the UN during the Cold War, including Korea and Vietnam. Powerful states prefer to solve their problems on their own, and not entrust them to a body of impartial third parties. In fact, during the Cold War, the Court sometimes had little in its docket. In the 44 years between 1947 and 1991, the Court had 66 contentious cases, or an average of 0.6 a year. It also had 22 advisory cases. Between 1963 and 1966, it did not take on any new cases. Since the end of the Cold War, the ICJ's caseload has increased but not to impressive heights; between 1992 and 2014 it considered 68 contentious cases, or an average of 3 a year.

One reason behind the Court's light docket is that under international law, there is no *compulsory jurisdiction*. That means that here is nothing to force a state to be part of a case at the court. That being said, if a state agrees to submit a case, then under the ICJ's rules, that state has to abide by the Court's decision. Nonetheless, the Court has no way to enforce compliance. The ICJ's statute tried to get around the problem of lack of compulsory jurisdiction through Article 36, paragraph 2, known as the *optional clause*. It says that states can declare in advance that they accept compulsory jurisdiction. Ideally, this makes it harder for states to cherry pick the cases they will accept (i.e., never accepting cases where they are the defendant). To date, however, only 72 states out of the UN's 193 members have accepted this clause. Some states that accepted the clause in the past set time limits on their acceptance, which have since lapsed or been terminated.[62] Today, only one member of the P-5 that accepts the Court's compulsory jurisdiction is the United Kingdom; the United States and France had accepted the clause in the past, but subsequently withdrew, and China and Russia have never agreed to it.[63]

States have, however, indirectly agreed to accept the Court's jurisdiction when they sign treaties that contain clauses that say disputes will be submitted to the Court. Several hundred of such treaties exist today. When a case comes before the Court, the state submitting the case is called the "applicant" and the other state is the "respondent." There is a written stage (which can range from months to several years) and an oral stage (which can last up to six weeks), the latter of which usually takes place in the Court's Great Hall of Justice in the Peace Palace. The judges' deliberations are secret, but their final judgment is issued in public. States do not have the possibility of appeal.

Many of the Court's cases have involved disputes over land or maritime boundaries, but it has also ruled a variety of issues that include disputes over dam projects, international criminal law, and military activities.[64] The number of these cases has picked up since the end of the Cold War, in part because such disputes between developing nations can no longer quickly escalate up to a superpower confrontation. In other words, the removal of the lid of superpower rivalry has allowed long simmering disputes between smaller countries to bubble up to the surface. Since the end of the Cold War, the Court has become a key institution for solving border and boundary disputes, mostly between developing countries. Examples include the land and maritime boundary between Cameroon and Nigeria, the ownership of islands between Bahrain and Qatar, and the ownership of islands between Benin and Niger. But big states are involved, too, and sometimes bring cases against each other. One example is *Germany vs. the United States* (2001), where Germany wanted to overturn a capital punishment conviction of two German brothers sentenced to death in Arizona for stabbing a man to death in 1982 in a failed bank robbery.[65]

Trusteeship Council

The Trusteeship Council is somewhat of an oddity, because since November 1994, it only exists on paper, mainly because it completed its job. In fact, this is a rare instance of an international institution fulfilling its mission and going out of business. The Trusteeship Council's job was to administer "Trust Territories" placed under its care, and to help these territories move toward self-government or independence. The Trust Territories were territories (mainly colonies) "detached from enemy states" following WWII, or "held under mandate," since the League of Nations era. There were 11 such territories. The last one was the Trust Territory of the Pacific Islands (Palau), which became independent in 1994.

One reason the Trusteeship Council still exists is because removing it requires amending the UN Charter to delete Chapter XIII, which lays out the Trusteeship's role. Moves to amend the Charter, in turn, quickly get bogged down by contentious politics, since there are many other aspects of the Charter that some states would like to see changed, and others would like to see remain the same. It is also worth pointing out that the activities undertaken by the Trusteeship Council still exist, but not under its auspices. For example, the UN was involved in administrative functions in Cambodia and Somalia in the early and mid-1990s, respectively, in East Timor (1999–2002) and in Kosovo, since 1999.[66]

THE LARGER UN FAMILY

Beyond the UN's six main organs is a rich panoply of agencies, programs, funds, and other organizations, some of which predate the UN itself (see figure 3.1). Some of these are well-known, such as the World Health Organization (WHO), one of the specialized agencies; United

Figure 3.1 United Nations Organogoram

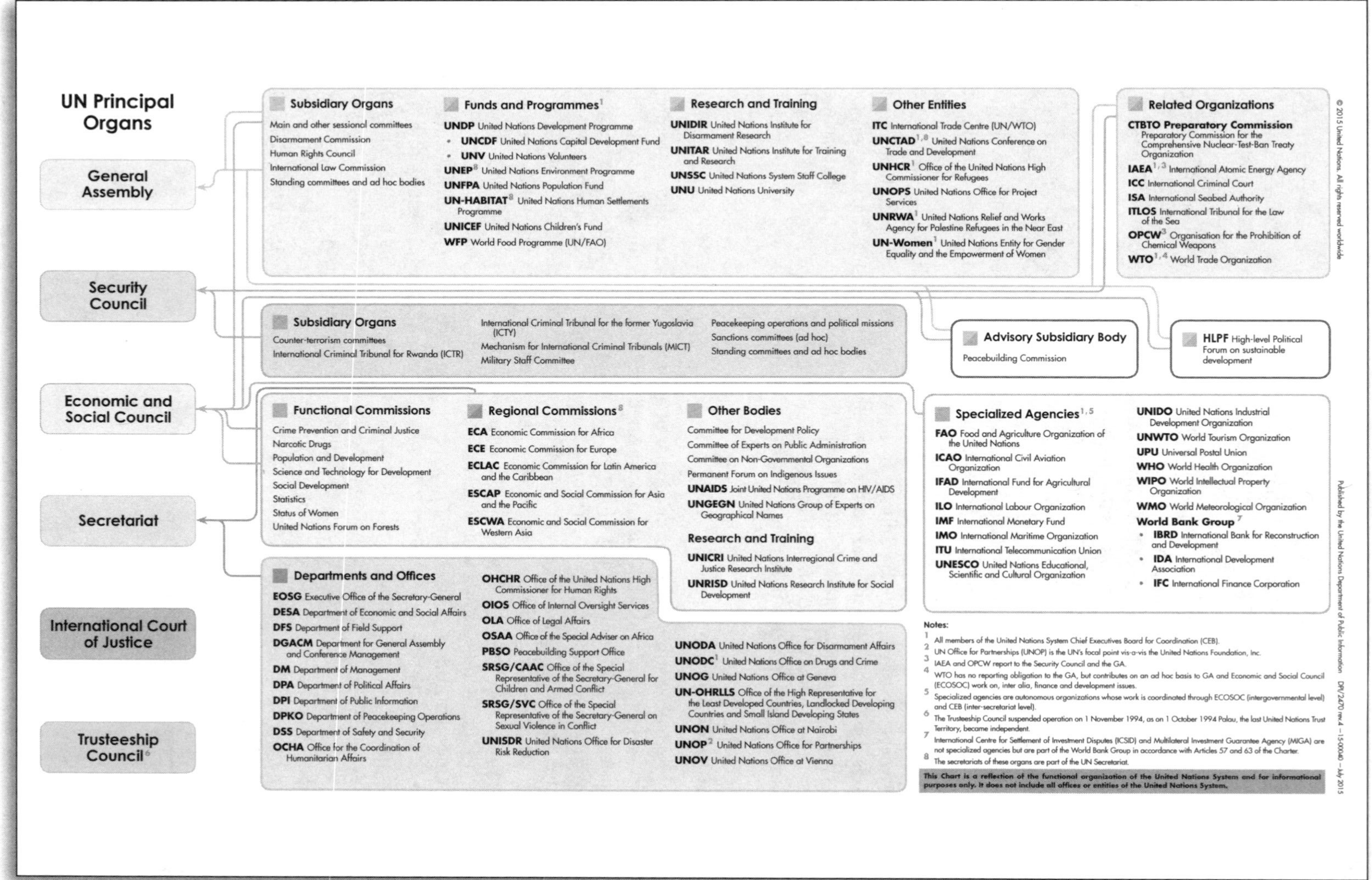

Published by the United Nations Department of Public Information   DPI/2470 rev.4 – 15-00040 – July 2015

UN Principal Organs

General Assembly

Subsidiary Organs
- Main and other sessional committees
- Disarmament Commission
- Human Rights Council
- International Law Commission
- Standing committees and ad hoc bodies

Funds and Programmes[1]
- **UNDP** United Nations Development Programme
  - **UNCDF** United Nations Capital Development Fund
  - **UNV** United Nations Volunteers
- **UNEP**[1] United Nations Environment Programme
- **UNFPA** United Nations Population Fund
- **UN-HABITAT**[1] United Nations Human Settlements Programme
- **UNICEF** United Nations Children's Fund
- **WFP** World Food Programme (UN/FAO)

Research and Training
- **UNIDIR** United Nations Institute for Disarmament Research
- **UNITAR** United Nations Institute for Training and Research
- **UNSSC** United Nations System Staff College
- **UNU** United Nations University

Other Entities
- **ITC** International Trade Centre (UN/WTO)
- **UNCTAD**[1,8] United Nations Conference on Trade and Development
- **UNHCR**[1] Office of the United Nations High Commissioner for Refugees
- **UNOPS** United Nations Office for Project Services
- **UNRWA**[1] United Nations Relief and Works Agency for Palestine Refugees in the Near East
- **UN-Women**[1] United Nations Entity for Gender Equality and the Empowerment of Women

Related Organizations
- **CTBTO Preparatory Commission** Preparatory Commission for the Comprehensive Nuclear-Test-Ban Treaty Organization
- **IAEA**[1,3] International Atomic Energy Agency
- **ICC** International Criminal Court
- **ISA** International Seabed Authority
- **ITLOS** International Tribunal for the Law of the Sea
- **OPCW**[3] Organization for the Prohibition of Chemical Weapons
- **WTO**[3,4] World Trade Organization

Security Council

Subsidiary Organs
- Counter-terrorism committees
- International Criminal Tribunal for Rwanda (ICTR)
- International Criminal Tribunal for the former Yugoslavia (ICTY)
- Mechanism for International Criminal Tribunals (MICT)
- Military Staff Committee
- Peacekeeping operations and political missions
- Sanctions committees (ad hoc)
- Standing committees and ad hoc bodies

Advisory Subsidiary Body
- Peacebuilding Commission

Economic and Social Council

Functional Commissions
- Crime Prevention and Criminal Justice
- Narcotic Drugs
- Population and Development
- Science and Technology for Development
- Social Development
- Statistics
- Status of Women
- United Nations Forum on Forests

Regional Commissions[8]
- **ECA** Economic Commission for Africa
- **ECE** Economic Commission for Europe
- **ECLAC** Economic Commission for Latin America and the Caribbean
- **ESCAP** Economic and Social Commission for Asia and the Pacific
- **ESCWA** Economic and Social Commission for Western Asia

Other Bodies
- Committee for Development Policy
- Committee of Experts on Public Administration
- Committee on Non-Governmental Organizations
- Permanent Forum on Indigenous Issues
- **UNAIDS** Joint United Nations Programme on HIV/AIDS
- **UNGEGN** United Nations Group of Experts on Geographical Names

Research and Training
- **UNICRI** United Nations Interregional Crime and Justice Research Institute
- **UNRISD** United Nations Research Institute for Social Development

Specialized Agencies[1,5]
- **FAO** Food and Agriculture Organization of the United Nations
- **ICAO** International Civil Aviation Organization
- **IFAD** International Fund for Agricultural Development
- **ILO** International Labour Organization
- **IMF** International Monetary Fund
- **IMO** International Maritime Organization
- **ITU** International Telecommunication Union
- **UNESCO** United Nations Educational, Scientific and Cultural Organization
- **UNIDO** United Nations Industrial Development Organization
- **UNWTO** World Tourism Organization
- **UPU** Universal Postal Union
- **WHO** World Health Organization
- **WIPO** World Intellectual Property Organization
- **WMO** World Meteorological Organization
- **World Bank Group**[7]
  - **IBRD** International Bank for Reconstruction and Development
  - **IDA** International Development Association
  - **IFC** International Finance Corporation

Secretariat

Departments and Offices
- **EOSG** Executive Office of the Secretary-General
- **DESA** Department of Economic and Social Affairs
- **DFS** Department of Field Support
- **DGACM** Department for General Assembly and Conference Management
- **DM** Department of Management
- **DPA** Department of Political Affairs
- **DPI** Department of Public Information
- **DPKO** Department of Peacekeeping Operations
- **DSS** Department of Safety and Security
- **OCHA** Office for the Coordination of Humanitarian Affairs
- **OHCHR** Office of the United Nations High Commissioner for Human Rights
- **OIOS** Office of Internal Oversight Services
- **OLA** Office of Legal Affairs
- **OSAA** Office of the Special Adviser on Africa
- **PBSO** Peacebuilding Support Office
- **SRSG/CAAC** Office of the Special Representative of the Secretary-General for Children and Armed Conflict
- **SRSG/SVC** Office of the Special Representative of the Secretary-General on Sexual Violence in Conflict
- **UNISDR** United Nations Office for Disaster Risk Reduction
- **UNODA** United Nations Office for Disarmament Affairs
- **UNODC** United Nations Office on Drugs and Crime
- **UNOG** United Nations Office at Geneva
- **UN-OHRLLS** Office of the High Representative for the Least Developed Countries, Landlocked Developing Countries and Small Island Developing States
- **UNON** United Nations Office at Nairobi
- **UNOP**[2] United Nations Office for Partnerships
- **UNOV** United Nations Office at Vienna

International Court of Justice

Trusteeship Council[6]

HLPF High-level Political Forum on sustainable development

Notes:

1. All members of the United Nations System Chief Executives Board for Coordination (CEB).
2. UN Office for Partnerships (UNOP) is the UN's focal point vis-à-vis the United Nations Foundation, Inc.
3. IAEA and OPCW report to the Security Council and the GA.
4. WTO has no reporting obligation to the GA, but contributes on an ad hoc basis to GA and Economic and Social Council (ECOSOC) work on, inter alia, finance and development issues.
5. Specialized agencies are autonomous organizations whose work is coordinated through ECOSOC (intergovernmental level) and CEB (inter-secretariat level).
6. The Trusteeship Council suspended operation on 1 November 1994, as on 1 October 1994 Palau, the last United Nations Trust Territory, became independent.
7. International Centre for Settlement of Investment Disputes (ICSID) and Multilateral Investment Guarantee Agency (MIGA) are not specialized agencies but are part of the World Bank Group in accordance with Articles 57 and 63 of the Charter.
8. The secretariats of these organs are part of the UN Secretariat.

This Chart is a reflection of the functional organization of the United Nations System and for informational purposes only. It does not include all offices or entities of the United Nations System.

Nations Children's Fund (UNICEF), and UN Environment Programme (UNEP). Others do important work, but rarely make it to the headlines, such as the International Maritime Organization (IMO).

These various other bodies are involved in just about every imaginable issue area in international politics, including human rights, humanitarian aid, women and children, nutrition, minorities and indigenous people, sustainable development, agriculture, and the prevention of terrorism and organized crime, among others. They have a wide range of tasks as well, which include bringing states together to recognize issues and sign treaties; monitoring compliance of treaties; education; distributing specific forms of aid (vaccines, seeds, blankets, shelter, food); training; coordinating other states and non-state actors; developing standards and formulating rules on specific issues; gathering, disseminating, and manipulating information; and building networks in specific issue areas. Their activities may be judged individually, given that each body has its own history, rules, management, and so on; but they may also be evaluated by issue area, since often multiple UN bodies are working on the same area and have different degrees of success at coordinating their activities. There is a rich literature, for example, describing and evaluating the UN's activities in human rights, the environment and sustainable development, and global health.[67]

UN EVOLUTION

The Cold War began soon after the UN was created, and it lasted for 40 years, from the late 1940s until the Soviet Union imploded in 1991. The Four Policemen that Roosevelt envisioned would maintain international peace and security were replaced by two superpowers, armed with nuclear weapons, facing each other with suspicion in a newly bipolar system.[68] The Soviets used their veto power regularly against other members of the Security Council in the early years, often to kill proposed membership from other countries, including Ireland, Italy, Nepal, Libya, Spain, and Jordan, since the United States would not approve the Soviet republics' separate memberships. The Soviets wielded their veto 71 times in the UN's first decade, for example, compared with France (3), China (1), the UK (2), and the United States (0). The United States did not wield its veto until 1970, highlighting that it was comfortable with the Council's direction during the earlier period.

While Cold War tensions shrunk the UN's ability to be a major power in the world, its role was far from unimportant. For example, the UN acted as a safety valve when it kept regional conflicts from exploding into broader and more dangerous East-West confrontations. This was important in parts of the Middle East, Cyprus, and Africa. There were several important peacekeeping initiatives during the Cold War, including the disastrous example in the former Belgian Congo between 1960 and 1964. The Republic of Congo declared independence on June 30, 1960, after which its former colonial power, Belgium, launched a military intervention. UN peacekeepers were to help facilitate the withdrawal of the Belgian troops, to help set up the post-colonial government, and to maintain Congo's political independence. Around 20,000 peacekeepers were there at the peak of the operation. Meanwhile, the rich Katango province seceded, and the superpowers lined up on opposite sides of the domestic political conflict. (The Soviets supported the prime minister, and the West and UN supported the president, and at one point the president and prime minister fired each other before the prime minister was murdered.) At some point government infrastructure collapsed and no one was the authority. This case was infamous because the UN was embroiled in a domestic conflict, and it ended up not being neutral. This is also where Dag Hammarskjöld lost his life.[69]

And, while the UN was not able to act decisively in many serious Cold War matters, it did give states a way to protest loudly to show their indignation. One example was the Soviet invasion of Czechoslovakia in 1968. While the United States was not willing to intervene directly, it made its displeasure known in the Security Council, where its ambassador called the invasion "an affront to all civilized sensibilities."[70]

Finally, the UN actively encouraged decolonization (supported by the United States), which in turn contributed to the rapid growth of newly independent countries as members of the United Nations after India's independence in 1947. UN membership jumped from 51 countries in 1945 to 144 by 1975, with the biggest increase taking place in Africa, where membership jumped from 3 to 47 countries.[71]

Table 3.1   List of UN Peacekeeping Operations 1948–2014

Acronym	Mission Name	Start Date	End Date
UNTSO	United Nations Truce Supervision Organization	May 1948	Present
UNMOGIP	United Nations Military Observer Group in India and Pakistan	January 1949	Present
UNEF I	First United Nations Emergency Force	November 1956	June 1967
UNOGIL	United Nations Observation Group in Lebanon	June 1958	December 1958
ONUC	United Nations Operation in the Congo	July 1960	June 1964
UNSF	United Nations Security Force in West New Guinea	October 1962	April 1963
UNYOM	United Nations Yemen Observation Mission	July 1963	September 1964
UNFICYP	United Nations Peacekeeping Force in Cyprus	March 1964	Present
DOMREP	Mission of the Representative of the Secretary-General in the Dominican Republic	May 1965	October 1966
UNIPOM	United Nations India-Pakistan Observation Mission	September 1965	March 1966
UNEF II	Second United Nations Emergency Force	October 1973	July 1979
UNDOF	United Nations Disengagement Observer Force	June 1974	Present
UNIFIL	United Nations Interim Force in Lebanon	March 1978	Present
UNGOMAP	United Nations Good Offices Mission in Afghanistan and Pakistan	May 1988	March 1990
UNIIMOG	United Nations Iran-Iraq Military Observer Group	August 1988	February 1991
UNAVEM I	United Nations Angola Verification Mission I	January 1989	June 1991

Acronym	Mission Name	Start Date	End Date
UNTAG	United Nations Transition Assistance Group	April 1989	March 1990
ONUCA	United Nations Observer Group in Central America	November 1989	January 1992
UNIKOM	United Nations Iraq-Kuwait Observation Mission	April 1991	October 2003
MINURSO	United Nations Mission for the Referendum in Western Sahara	April 1991	Present
UNAVEM II	United Nations Angola Verification Mission II	June 1991	February 1995
ONUSAL	United Nations Observer Mission in El Salvador	July 1991	April 1995
UNAMIC	United Nations Advance Mission in Cambodia	October 1991	March 1992
UNPROFOR	United Nations Protection Force	February 1992	March 1995
UNTAC	United Nations Transitional Authority in Cambodia	March 1992	September 1993
UNOSOM I	United Nations Operation in Somalia I	April 1992	March 1993
ONUMOZ	United Nations Operation in Mozambique	December 1992	December 1994
UNOSOM II	United Nations Operation in Somalia II	March 1993	March 1995
UNOMUR	United Nations Observer Mission Uganda-Rwanda	June 1993	September 1994
UNOMIG	United Nations Observer Mission in Georgia	August 1993	June 2009
UNOMIL	United Nations Observer Mission in Liberia	September 1993	September 1997
UNIMIH	United Nations Mission in Haiti	September 1993	June 1996
UNAMIR	United Nations Assistance Mission for Rwanda	October 1993	March 1996
UNASOG	United Nations Aouzou Strip Observer Group	May 1994	June 1994
UNMOT	United Nations Mission of Observers in Tajikistan	December 1994	May 2000
UNAVEM III	United Nations Angola Verification Mission III	February 1995	June 1997
UNCRO	United Nations Confidence Restoration Operation in Croatia	May 1995	February 1999
UNPREDEP	United Nations Preventive Deployment Force	March 1995	February 1999
UNMIBH	United Nations Mission in Bosnia and Herzegovina	December 1995	December 2002
UNTAES	United Nations Transitional Administration for Eastern Slavonia, Baranja, and Western Sirmium	January 1996	January 1998
UNMOP	United Nations Mission of Observers in Prevlaka	January 1996	December 2002
UNSMIH	United Nations Support Mission in Haiti	July 1996	July 1997
MINUGUA	United Nations Verification Mission in Guatemala	January 1997	May 1997
MONUA	United Nations Observer Mission in Angola	June 1997	February 1999

(Continued)

Table 3.1 Continued

Acronym	Mission Name	Start Date	End Date
UNTMIH	United Nations Transition Mission in Haiti	August 1997	December 1997
MIPONUH	United Nations Civilian Police Mission in Haiti	December 1997	March 2000
UNCPSG	UN Civilian Police Support Group	January 1998	October 1998
MINURCA	United Nations Mission in the Central African Republic	April 1998	February 2000
UNOMSIL	United Nations Observer Mission in Sierra Leone	July 1998	October 1999
UNIMIK	United Nations Interim Administration Mission in Kosovo	June 1999	Present
UNAMSIL	United Nations Mission in Sierra Leone	October 1999	December 2005
UNTAET	United Nations Transitional Administration in East Timor	October 1999	May 2002
MONUC	United Nations Organization Mission in the Democratic Republic of the Congo	November 1999	June 2010
UNIMEE	United Nations Mission in Ethiopia and Eritrea	July 2000	July 2008
UNMISET	United Nations Mission of Support in East Timor	May 2002	May 2005
UNMIL	United Nations Mission in Liberia	September 2003	Present
UNOCI	United Nations Operation in Côte d'Ivoire	April 2004	Present
MINUSTAH	United Nations Stabilization Mission in Haiti	June 2004	Present
ONUB	United Nations Operation in Burundi	June 2004	December 2006
UNMIS	United Nations Mission in the Sudan	March 2005	July 2011
UNMIT	United Nations Integrated Mission in Timor-Leste	August 2006	December 2012
UNAMID	African Union-United Nations Hybrid Operation in Darfur	July 2007	Present
MINURCAT	United Nations Mission in the Central African Republic and Chad	September 2007	December 2010
MONUSCO	United Nations Organization Stabilization Mission in the Democratic Republic of the Congo	July 2010	Present
UNISFA	United Nations Organization Interim Security Force for Abyei	June 2011	Present
UNMISS	United Nations Mission in the Republic of South Sudan	July 2011	Present
UNSMIS	United Nations Supervision Mission in Syria	April 2012	August 2012
MINUSMA	United Nations Multidimensional Integrated Stabilization Mission in Mali	April 2013	Present
MINUSCA	United Nations Multidimensional Integrated Stabilization Mission in the Central African Republic	April 2014	Present

Source: http://www.un.org/en/peacekeeping/documents/operationslist.pdf.

One unintended consequence of this growth in membership, from the view of the United States, was that the General Assembly went from being dominated by Western opinion comfortably beyond the Soviet veto (or being what John Foster Dulles called the "town meetings of the world," that "served to enlighten world opinion about the nature of Soviet leadership") to a body that began to challenge American views and interests.[72] By the 1960s, the developing world had achieved an automatic majority in the General Assembly, and was not shy to use it. The developing world often voted along with the Soviet bloc and against the wishes of the United States. As Edward Luck put it, "Ironically, by getting its way in supporting the decolonization struggle, the United States helped to transform the General Assembly into a far more diverse and contentious place."[73]

The result was that US policymakers became alienated from the General Assembly. In 1971, the General Assembly voted to have Beijing take the place of Taipei in the Chinese seat on the Security Council (and several delegates danced in the General Assembly's aisles to celebrate the vote). This move put two Communist powers among the P-5, and removed a US ally. US President Gerald Ford, in a 1974 speech to the General Assembly, reminded its representatives to be "alert to the danger of the 'tyranny of the majority.'"[74] The following year, the General Assembly stepped up the heat in criticizing Israel, by passing a resolution equating Zionism with racism. This move angered US policymakers and resulted in both the Senate and House passing resolutions to reassess the United States' continuing participation in the General Assembly. The US Ambassador Daniel Patrick Moynihan famously responded that the United States "does not acknowledge, it will not abide by it, it will never acquiesce in this infamous act," which he said gave anti-Semitism "the appearance of international sanction."[75] While the United States remained in the General Assembly, it did pull out of the International Labour Organization in 1977, accusing it of being too politicized (among other things, it had granted observer status to the Palestinian Liberation Organization, which the United States accused of being a terrorist group). The United States and Great Britain also pulled out of UNESCO in the 1980s for similar reasons.[76]

POST-COLD WAR AND BEYOND

The end of the Cold War, and years leading up to it, saw a dramatic change in the role of the UN as a more prominent actor in global governance. The Soviet leader, Mikhail Gorbachev, is widely credited with initiating a dramatic thaw in the Security Council relations, by calling on the UN to play a more prominent role in world politics in 1987. Cooperation between the superpowers and other members of the Security Council further deepened in 1990 and 1991 as the diplomatic process aimed at getting Iraq out of Kuwait (after Iraq's August 1990 invasion) led to Security Council approval of the use of force against Iraq. The resulting, successful, campaign against Iraq was led by the United States, with a number of other countries, such as Great Britain and Saudi Arabia, also contributing troops.

According to one UN observer, this was a period of "euphoria" in the Security Council, as a number of complex UN peace operations were launched in places like Cambodia, Namibia, Somalia, and the former Yugoslavia. Indeed, UN peacekeeping activities expanded dramatically between 1988 and 1994, with more than 20 new operations approved in a six-year period, compared with 13 in the forty years between the UN's birth and 1988. The number of peacekeepers rose from 11,000 to 75,000.[77]

In the decades since the Cold War ended, the UN's activities have continued to expand and deepen in areas such as the global environment, development, health, and human rights, among others. This has happened along with growing understanding that the UN's central mandate of promoting international peace and security intersects with issues such as poverty reduction and human rights. The UN popularized the term *human security* in the early 1990s to highlight the fact that individual security goes beyond the absence of conflict. As Boutros Boutros-Ghali noted in *An Agenda for Peace*, "a porous ozone shield could pose a greater threat to an exposed population than a hostile army. Drought and disease can decimate no less mercilessly than the weapons of war."[78]

In the area of environment, for example, the UN hosted treaty-making conferences on issues that include sustainable development, climate change, ozone depletion, biodiversity, and dangerous chemicals. There is great variation in the success of these treaties, with UN efforts on ozone depletion among the more successful and efforts on biodiversity much less so. The UN has played a leadership role in organizing science and negotiations around climate change. The Intergovernmental Panel on Climate Change, for example, is a scientific body that brings together research on climate change related issues, including its impact and policy options for addressing its consequences. It shared the 2007 Nobel Peace Prize with former US Vice President Al Gore. Bodies of the UN that work on global environmental issues include UNEP, World Meteorological Organization, Food and Agriculture Organization, and UN Development Programme (UNDP).

The UN's activities in the area of development are equally extensive. The UN launched the Millennium Development Goals (MDGs) in 2000 as a way for relevant countries and donor organizations to cooperate to tackle eight major development goals with 18 specific targets by the end of 2015, including the eradication of extreme poverty and hunger, the reduction in child mortality, improvements in maternal health, and the promotion of sustainable development.

It is true that there have been improvements in some of the issue areas and in some parts of the world. The world met the goal of halving the number of people living in extreme poverty (compared with the baseline year of 1990), and it also reached the goal of halving the number of people who lack access to reliable sources of clean water. There have also been sharp declines in the rates of maternal and infant mortality and more people have access to water and better sanitation services. But other goals were not met, sometimes because they were unrealistic. For example, Goal 2 was to achieve universal primary education. Around 10 percent of children still remain out of school, although that percentage has been shrinking over the past 15 years. UN Secretary-General Ban Ki-moon admitted that even where the MDGs have been successful progress has been uneven with "the poorest of the poor" still left behind.[79] The most progress occurred in Asia, and the least in sub-Saharan Africa. But even inside individual countries and regions, trends were often uneven.

After three years of negotiations, UN member states agreed in August 2015 on a new set of ambitious goals, called the Sustainable Development Goals to succeed the MDGs and run to 2030. There are 17 goals, with 169 targets. The new goals, adopted by world leaders in a September 2015 Sustainable Development Summit at the United Nations, also are aimed at eradicating poverty. But they are also more explicit about bringing in the economic, social, and environmental dimensions of sustainable development.

UN AND HUMAN RIGHTS

The area of human rights has seen a great deal of evolution over the years. The term *human rights* is built into the UN Charter, which makes seven different references to human rights as a basic purpose of the organization. That said, the Charter did not define human rights. It just noted that states should respect them and that the UN should promote and encourage

Figure 3.2   Progress in Implementation of MDGs

O
2015
TIME FOR
GLOBAL ACTION
FOR PEOPLE AND PLANET

Goals and Targets	Africa		Asia				Oceania	Latin America and the Caribbean	Caucasus and Central Asia
	Northern	Sub-Saharan	Eastern	South-Eastern	Southern	Western			
GOAL 1 | Eradicate extreme poverty and hunger									
Reduce extreme poverty by half	A	C	A	A	A	B	M	A	A
Productive and decent employment	C	B	A	B	B	D	C	C	D
Reduce hunger by half	A	C	A	A	B	D	D	A	A
GOAL 2 | Achieve universal primary education									
Universal primary schooling	A	C	A	B	B	B	B	C	C
GOAL 3 | Promote gender equality and empower women									
Equal girls' enrolment in primary school	B	B	A	A	A	B	C	A	A
Women's share of paid employment	D	B	A	C	B	C	C	A	A
Women's equal representation in national parliaments	B	B	D	C	B	B	D	B	B
GOAL 4 | Reduce child mortality									
Reduce mortality of under-five-year-olds by two thirds	A	B	A	B	B	B	C	A	B
GOAL 5 | Improve maternal health									
Reduce maternal mortality by three quarters	B	B	A	B	B	C	B	C	A
Access to reproductive health	B	C	B	B	B	B	C	B	C
GOAL 6 | Combat HIV/AIDS, malaria and other diseases									
Halt and begin to reverse the spread of HIV/AIDS	D	A	D	B	A	D	A	B	A
Halt and reverse the spread of tuberculosis	C	B	A	A	B	A	D	A	C
GOAL 7 | Ensure environmental sustainability									
Halve proportion of population without improved drinking water	B	B	A	A	A	A	D	A	D
Halve proportion of population without sanitation	A	D	A	B	C	A	D	B	A
Improve the lives	A	C	B	B	B	D	M	B	M
GOAL 8 | Develop a global partnership for development									
Internet users	A	B	A	A	B	A	B	A	A

The progress chart operates on two levels. The text in each box indicates the present level of development. The colours show progress made towards the target according to the legend below:

■ Target met or excellent progress, A

■ Poor progress or deterioration, D

■ Good progress, B

■ Missing or insufficient data, M

■ Fair progress, C

For the regional groupings and country data, see *mdgs.un.org*. Country experiences in each region may differ significantly from the regional average. Due to new data and revised methodologies, this Progress Chart is not comparable with previous versions.

Source: http://mdgs.un.org/unsd/mdg/Resources/Static/Products/Progress2015/Progress_E.pdf

them. There is no language that the UN should protect them. Given that Article II of Chapter 1 states that the UN should not meddle in any member's domestic affairs, the role of the UN in helping to spread human rights norms has been an important one.

Human rights, as the UN defines them today, are

rights inherent to all human beings, whatever our nationality, place of residence, sex, national or ethnic origin, colour, religion, language, or any other status. We are all equally entitled to our human rights without discrimination. These rights are all inter-related, interdependent and indivisible.[80]

As scholars Weiss, Forsythe, Coate, and Kelly-Kate Pease have noted, the UN has been at the center of the development of human rights law. One of the foundational documents was the 1948 Universal Declaration on Human Rights, which as a *declaration* was not a binding treaty.

SUSTAINABLE DEVELOPMENT GOALS

Goal 1:   End poverty in all its forms everywhere

Goal 2:   End hunger, achieve food security and improved nutrition, and promote sustainable agriculture

Goal 3:   Ensure healthy lives and promote well-being for all at all ages

Goal 4:   Ensure inclusive and equitable quality education and promote lifelong learning opportunities for all

Goal 5:   Achieve gender equality and empower all women and girls

Goal 6:   Ensure availability and sustainable management of water and sanitation for all

Goal 7:   Ensure access to affordable, reliable, sustainable and modern energy for all

Goal 8:   Promote sustained, inclusive and sustainable economic growth, full and productive employment and decent work for all

Goal 9:   Build resilient infrastructure, promote inclusive and sustainable industrialization, and foster innovation

Goal 10: Reduce inequality within and among countries

Goal 11: Make cities and human settlements inclusive, safe, resilient, and sustainable

Goal 12: Ensure sustainable consumption and production patterns

Goal 13: Take urgent action to combat climate change and its impacts

Goal 14: Conserve and sustainably use the oceans, seas, and marine resources for sustainable development

Goal 15: Protect, restore, and promote sustainable use of terrestrial ecosystems, sustainably manage forests, combat desertification, and halt and reverse land degradation and halt biodiversity loss

Goal 16: Promote peaceful and inclusive societies for sustainable development; provide access to justice for all; and build effective, accountable, and inclusive institutions at all levels

Goal 17: Strengthen the means of implementation and revitalize the Global Partnership for Sustainable Development

---

Source: United Nations General Assembly, "Draft outcome document of the United Nations summit for the adoption of the post-2015 development agenda," p. 14.

This was the first attempt by states to specify what the Charter meant by human rights. Its 30 principles were a mix of those important to both democratic/capitalist and Marxist ideals, and reflected an incredible level of compromise in the negotiation process. The Soviet Union pushed for the abolition of the death penalty, designed to annoy the United States, especially as Stalin was slaughtering civilians at the same time. (In the end, the Soviets abstained.) Saudi Arabia was not comfortable with the "religious freedom" clause, and South Africa, heading into a system of apartheid, was not happy about Article 21 (1) "Everyone has the right to take part in the government of his country, directly or through freely chosen representatives."[81]

The *negative rights* were actions that a government should not take against a person. Governments should allow freedom of speech, freedom from slavery, freedom from torture. *Positive rights* were actions that a government is obligated to provide a person. These include the right to food, clothing, and housing, and the right to rest and leisure. Another way to view the negative and positive rights is to see them in terms of government obligations: what governments are obligated not to do, and obligated to do. Soon after the Declaration was signed, members moved to build the principles into legally binding treaties. Today there are over 25 UN human rights conventions, which include treaties on the elimination of slavery, on refugee status, on genocide, the rights of the child, and against torture. Many norms have spread, often with the help of NGOs, such as Amnesty International and Human Rights Watch. As scholar Anne Marie Clark has noted

> Numerous treaties and monitoring mechanisms are in place. Every year, UN bodies receive reports from states and nongovernmental organizations on human rights conditions in scores of states. . . . Human rights standards are now built into peacekeeping agreements and many types of multilateral treaties.[82]

Scholars evaluating the UN's human rights machinery agree that as impressive as it is, the results are mixed to poor. As Weiss et al. have noted, "UN activity concerning human rights often displays an enormous gap between the law on the books and the law in action."[83] States regularly oppose stronger action on human rights or (as the following chapter notes) have engaged in abusing human rights.

Human rights are addressed in many parts of the UN. There is the Security Council, which can link a human rights problem to a breach of international peace and security. For example, in 1991 the Security Council called Iraq's attacks on its Kurdish people a threat to international peace and security. This opened the way for "implicit approval" of the use of force in Iraq by the United States and others. The UN created the position of the High Commission for Human Rights in 1993, for a person who would act as the UN's "principal human rights official" by supporting the work of other parts of the UN and working with states to uphold human rights. There was also the former UN Commission on Human Rights, which existed between 1946 and 2006. In its later years, it was considered to be a joke of the UN system, since its members included countries known for abusing human rights. Libya, for example, was well-known for its systematic violations of human rights, yet it was nominated to preside over the Commission in 2002. At one point, the Commission's membership included Sudan, during the time in which its government was slaughtering people in Darfur. The Commission was replaced by the United Nations Human Rights Council (HRC), designed to have 47 member states elected by the UN General Assembly with three-year terms, with no option for immediate re-election after two consecutive terms. In some years the member states continued to include countries that were not widely seen as prioritizing human rights, including China, Russia, Egypt, Saudi Arabia, and Cuba. Former UN Secretary-General Kofi Annan, current Secretary-General Ban Ki-moon, and others questioned the HRC's early focus on condemning Israel nine times but saying nothing about countries like North Korea, Sudan, and Myanmar.[84] The United States refused to join at first, worried that the Council would be packed with human rights abusers. But US President Barack Obama decided to join given his emphasis on the importance of multilateral institutions, and some have argued the HRC has become more effective as a result.[85]

PEACEKEEPING AND PEACE OPERATIONS

The UN's actions in peacekeeping have been one of the most visible and contentious areas of its work in the past few decades, mainly because of a set of highly criticized failures, especially in Bosnia, Somalia, and Rwanda, that prompted so much soul searching and analysis seeking to explain what went wrong and why.

As noted earlier, the demand for peacekeeping rose exponentially in the early and mid-1990s. Nineteen ninety-two was a banner year for the start of huge operations, including Cambodia (20,000 troops); Croatia (12,000); El Salvador (several hundred); and Mozambique (several thousand). There were more conflicts, to be sure, but at least initially, there was also a positive feeling that the UN could help resolve them, given positive public opinion on the success of the US-led intervention in the Gulf War.

The nature of peacekeeping also evolved. Traditional peacekeeping operations during the Cold War had certain common criteria: the conflicts were *interstate*, and not *intrastate*; the peacekeepers went in after fighting was over and with the consent of all parties. The peacekeepers monitored ceasefires and were unarmed, or lightly armed, and neutral in the sense that they were not to interfere. Force was only allowed for self-defense (The UN's actions in Korea and Congo were exceptions). The idea was that peacekeepers could help monitor a truce that would allow diplomats to negotiate a peace. This type of arrangement still exists on the border between Kuwait and Iraq, in the Golan Heights between Israel and Syria, and in Cyprus. Some scholars argue that these operations may only have succeeded in delaying conflict, not resolving it.[86] In fact, the three basic principles still exist today: consent of the parties, impartiality, and no force except in cases of self-defense or where it's necessary to defend the mandate. Yet, not all peacekeeping missions have followed all of these principles.

After the Cold War, many peacekeeping missions became more complex, and multidimensional, such as the cases in Cambodia (1991–1993), El Salvador (1991–1995), and Namibia (1989–1990), Mozambique (1992–1994), and Eastern Slavonia (Croatia, 1996–1998). These are sometimes called *second-generation peacekeeping*. In these cases peacekeeping operations had more objectives, although they were still based on consent of parties, and involved interstate disputes. These operations included civilian experts as well as soldiers, and their missions might include collecting arms, reintegrating former combatants, drafting and helping to implement peace treaties, reforming the police, and monitoring elections. The overarching idea is that the missions are not only maintaining peace and security, but they are protecting civilians and human rights, and helping the countries restore the rule of law.

This change coincided with Boutros-Ghali's landmark report, *Agenda for Peace* (1992) and its 1995 supplement. In *Agenda for Peace*, Boutros-Ghali noted that the 100 conflicts that have taken place since the UN's birth left around 20 million people dead. He admitted that the UN had little power to address these conflicts, pointing out that 279 vetoes were cast in the Security Council during this period. The goal of the report was to revisit how the UN reacted to conflicts on ways that went beyond peacekeeping. The report presented the additional processes of *preventive diplomacy*, *peacemaking*, and *post-conflict peacebuilding*. The idea behind preventive diplomacy was to try to avert disputes or prevent them from escalating into broader conflict. Peacemaking was "action to bring hostile parties to agreement." Parties would end their conflict and negotiate a peaceful settlement. Post-conflict peace building was seen as helping to "avoid a relapse into conflict" by using a variety of diplomatic, political, military, social, and economic development means to help to sustain peace. The report also called for "peace-enforcement" units that would be more heavily armed than peacekeeping units and could be authorized to use force.[87]

Third generation operations, or what Boutros-Ghali called "peace-enforcing" are the most contentious and the most different from traditional peacekeeping. In these cases, the UN may go in without consent of all parties. The disputes have been intrastate, which directly contradicts the UN's Charter, Article 2, about not intervening in matters within a state's domestic jurisdiction. And, finally, the peacekeeping forces have used force to implement a peace (that not all the parties agreed to) when there was no peace to keep. The parties to the conflict did not adhere to peace agreements and/or the peacekeepers did not have enough political or logistical support to succeed. The failed peacekeeping examples of Bosnia, Somalia, and Rwanda were all examples of third generation peacekeeping. Many analysts have argued that these specific cases deeply damaged the UN, showing it to be ineffective, or worse. A key dilemma for the UN in these cases has been whether or not to remain impartial and neutral.

Bosnia

The UN struggled with one of its largest and most expensive peacekeeping operations in history in the former Yugoslavia between 1992 and 1995. This was a case of UN peacekeepers entering a full-blown war, where the United States and leading European powers were simply not willing to intervene more forcefully. Over 250,000 people ultimately died, with millions more made homeless. This conflict grew out of the dissolution of Yugoslavia, which ultimately triggered great violence and ethnic cleansing. Yugoslav leader Josip Broz Tito held the country and its major ethnic groups together from 1953 until his death in 1980. The country splintered after his death, and a rotating presidency failed by June 1991, when Slovenia and Croatia declared their independence while ethnic Serbs sought to form a "Greater Serbia" by seizing land in Croatia and Bosnia. Croatian forces fought against the mainly Serb forces in the Yugoslav People's Army and Croatian Serb militias. The war began in April 1992. Within two months, a million people were displaced, and "several tens of thousands," primarily Bosnian Muslims, were killed.[88] The literature on the war in former Yugoslavia contains numerous explanations of the conflict. These include the role of domestic elites and animosity between poor and wealthy republics.[89]

While there was killing on all sides, the ethnic cleansing in this case was primarily a campaign controlled by the Bosnian Serb army aimed at killing, raping, torturing, and expelling Bosnian Muslims and Bosnian Croats. A special horror was the 1995 slaughter of more than 8,000 Bosnian Muslim men and boys in Srebrenica, a city deemed to be a "safe area" by the United Nations, which was unable to protect these people in the end. Indeed, none of the six safe areas the UN created for Muslim enclaves inside Bosnia had enough troops to make them safe. Over 100 members of the United Nations Protection Force (UNPROFOR) also died in or near the safe areas.[90] The Serbs even chained UN peacekeepers to bridges and other strategic targets to prevent NATO from fighting via air raids. The slaughter at Srebrenica has been labeled "genocide" by the International Criminal Tribunal for the Former Yugoslavia and others. The UN's involvement was insufficient by all measures. The 1991 UN arms embargo mainly helped the Serbs, who already had the former Yugoslav army's military equipment. The United States did not see the conflict as a threat to US strategic interests. Boutros–Ghali said in June 1993 that he estimated 34,000 troops would be necessary to protect the safe areas, but knowing he would not get that number from member states, asked for 7,600. He only received 5,000, which deployed nine months later.[91] Prospects for peaceful settlement only became possible after heavy NATO bombing of strategic Bosnian Serb positions, which brought the various parties to an air force base in Dayton, Ohio, in 1995, to negotiate a political settlement, the Dayton Peace Accord. As Weiss, Forsythe, Coate, and Pease have noted, the subsequent deployment of a huge, 60,000-person NATO-led peacekeeping mission post-Dayton created another set of problems for the United Nations. Bosnia-Herzegovina became a center of sex-trafficking into Western Europe, and a number of UN peacekeeping officials were accused of being involved in this.[92]

Somalia

In the case of Somalia, the UN was entering a failed state beset by conflict between warring groups and a ballooning humanitarian crisis where people were dying of starvation and sickness. There were no legitimate leaders to consent to UN peacekeeping involvement. General Mohamed Siad Barre had led a repressive regime for twenty one years and had alienated other political factions (clans) from government positions. These other clans eventually rose up against his rule. Unlike the case of Bosnia, Somalia is a country of one religion and even one language. Barre was ousted in 1991 by General Mohamed Farrah Aideed, who led a militia against Barre. Power struggles between the clans resulted in thousands of civilians being killed or wounded. In the midst of the conflict, by early 1992, people were starving. Boutros-Ghali was especially upset that the Security Council was focused more on Bosnia than on Somalia.[93] The United States responded with humanitarian aid, much of which disappeared to looting and corruption in the country. Media coverage of the humanitarian horror (including television images of emaciated children) fueled public opinion in the United States and elsewhere that the United States and United Nations needed to act. Of the three different peacekeeping missions in Somalia between 1992 and 1995, one was a small, traditional peacekeeping force (UNOSOM I), one was a US-led multinational force, and one was a "peace-enforcement" mission, which replaced the previous two.[94] While the UN acted in the name of a threat to international peace and security, this was clearly an intrastate conflict and humanitarian disaster.

The subsequent debacle of the UN in Somalia has been widely analyzed in the literature, and the main explanations for the failure focus on the fact that the UN missions were vague, relations between Aideed and UN negotiators were poor, and UNOSOM II was poorly run (and indeed many Somalis thought the UN itself was about to invade the country).[95] Analysts also note that the humanitarian aid did save lives. At the peak of UN involvement, more than 38,000 were involved in peacekeeping in Somalia, with the bulk coming from the United States. A traumatic moment for the United States occurred in 1993, when US Army Rangers were killed and one Ranger's naked corpse was dragged through the streets of Mogadishu, amid shouting and laughter, after militias shot down two US Black Hawk helicopters. The photos of the body dragged through the streets, taken by Canadian photographer Paul Watson, horrified the American public, which was not used to US soldiers dying in a country the US had no strategic interest in, in a mission that was seen as humanitarian. Subsequently, the US formally ended its mission in Somalia in 1994. While the US initially blamed the UN for the fiasco, in fact the US soldiers were under a US chain of command, with the decision to send them in coming from Special Operations in Florida.[96] The rest of the peacekeepers left a year later.

Today, Somalia continues to be unstable. Its first parliament in over 20 years was elected in August 2012. The country has been challenged with Islamic extremism, famine, pirating, and continued poverty. Chapter 12 discusses the African Union's peace operations in Somalia.

Are There Any Successful Cases?

While this set of horrific peacekeeping cases hurt the UN's legitimacy, there have also been successful cases of peacekeeping. Two examples are United Nations Transition Assistance Group (UNTAG) in Namibia, and United Nations Observer Mission in El Salvador (ONUSAL) in El Salvador. The purpose of UNTAG was to help Namibia prepare for independence, which it achieved in 1990. UNTAG's job was to supervise elections to ensure they were fair, to make sure South African troops withdrew from Namibia, ensure that Namibian refugees could return home, and that political prisoners were released. Scholar Lise Morjé-Howard argued that this case was the UN's first major success because UNTAG was well run, not micromanaged from New York, and especially good at responding to local political forces at important moments in the process.[97] In El Salvador, ONUSAL was created in 1991 to help mediate the negotiations that ended the civil war, to broker a peace agreement, to monitor compliance by both sides, to monitor and promote human rights, and to help promote democratization. The mission was created six months before a ceasefire ended a civil war that had lasted more than a decade. There was no guarantee this mission would be a success. Scholar Tommie Sue Montgomery attributes the success to factors that include the fact that both warring parties were on board with having the UN there as a mediator, the skill of the UN negotiating team, the quality of the ONUSAL staff, and support from people across the political spectrum.[98]

Despite disillusionment in the UN, peacekeeping missions continued on, and after a lull in peacekeeping from 1996 to 1998, there was a surge in the number of missions and troops sent at the end of the decade, including the 1999 launch of missions to Kosovo, Sierra Leone, East Timor, and the Democrat Republic of Congo. These were also complex, multi-dimensional missions in places where governance was not functioning well or at all. The Security Council's practice of authorizing coalitions of member states to engage in using force has also increased in recent decades, including the cases of the 1994 US intervention in Haiti, NATO's intervention in Bosnia in the mid-1990s, and the 1999 Australian-led intervention in East Timor.[99] The disastrous cases of the mid-1990s also prompted the UN to assess and revise its peacekeeping strategy. UN Secretary-General Kofi Annan created a group of experts to make recommendations for how to improve peacekeeping. The group, led by UN Under-Secretary-General Lakhdar Brahimi, produced *Report of the Panel on United Nations Peace Operations* (the "Brahimi Report") in August 2000.[100] The report made numerous recommendations. These included arguments that peacekeepers needed "clear, credible and achievable mandates," as well as "solid commitments from Member States" for forces. If those were not forthcoming, the Security Council should not send in peacekeepers. Part of having clear mandates is that, according to the report, "The Secretariat must tell the Security Council what it needs to know, not what it wants to hear, when formulating or changing mission mandates."[101] It was a blunt, straightforward report. It also adopted the terminology that has been becoming more prevalent since the 1990s of *peace operations* as including peacekeeping, conflict prevention, mediation, and peacebuilding. For example, peace operations today also include what are called "special political missions," which are run out of the UN's Department of Political Affairs (DPA) and focus on preventive diplomacy, mediation, and longer term post-conflict peacebuilding. The DPA, set up in 1992, has seen its stature grow in recent years given more support for alternatives to a militarized approach. Some, but not all, of the Brahimi Report's recommendations have been implemented. According to William Durch et al., the UN has done better implementing the more concrete recommendations than those aimed at changing strategy or member state actions.[102]

R2P and More Recent Peace Operations

One major response to the UN's inability to prevent widespread civilian death in the three cases mentioned above, as well as Kosovo, was the appearance of a new norm to encourage the world to act in such horrific situations. The *Responsibility to Protect* norm (R2P) was first promulgated by the International Commission on Intervention and State Sovereignty in a 2001 report.[103] The idea is that sovereign states have a responsibility to protect their citizens from "avoidable catastrophe—from mass murder and rape, from starvation," and if they are "unwilling or unable" to act, then other states should bear that responsibility. It is a view concerning under what circumstances the international community has the responsibility to violate a state's sovereignty, and what "humanitarian intervention" may mean in practice. The report was written in response to Secretary-General Kofi Annan's call for some way to have international unity around this difficult question. And while the report was written before the terrorist attacks in the United States on September 11, 2001, the authors argued that their ideas can extend to a response to terrorism as well. "Military power," they argued, "should always be exercised in a principled way, and the principles of last resort, proportional means and reasonable prospects . . . are . . . all applicable to such action."[104]

The report laid out a number of ways that the international community can have leverage over a situation where there is a strong need for human protection, such as political, economic, and judicial actions. It argued that military intervention may be considered as a possibility in extreme cases where a number of criteria are satisfied, including situations where people are faced "with the threat of serious and irreparable harm," such as large-scale loss of life due to actions, neglect, or failure by the state and large-scale ethnic cleansing.[105] Annan endorsed the principles and urged governments to embrace them as a means to protect victims of atrocities, and the General Assembly and Security Council both affirmed the principles in 2005 and 2006, respectively.[106]

While many agree that the R2P offers a strong moral framework for intervention, the fact is that it does not yet have the political traction needed to be translated into notable action. It has been applied in cases that many find dubious, such as Russia's unilateral use of force in Georgia. It has not been applied in cases where it would seem highly relevant, such as Afghanistan and Iraq, and where it has been used to justify action, it has not succeeded. R2P was not used to mobilize an international response to the Burmese government's refusal to allow outsiders to deliver promised aid following the 2008 Cyclone Nargis, which killed tens of thousands of people and doomed thousands more to suffering. It has not been used in Syria, where war and atrocities prompted more than half of the country's population of 22 million to leave their homes, creating a refugee crisis.

Darfur is a case where the international community was slow to stop what is widely considered to be genocide, despite invoking R2P. Darfur is a region in Western Sudan where conflict broke out in 2003. The Sudanese government responded to an attack by rebel groups by sending troops and militia groups to bomb and burn villages and commit rape and other atrocities. By the end of 2006, hundreds of thousands of people had died, and over two million (a third of the Darfur population) had been displaced.[107] Former US Secretary of State Colin Powell publicly labeled the conflict as a genocide in September 2004 (but was also advised that this did not mean the United States had to be involved with a military intervention).[108] The UN was in an uncomfortable position for a variety of reasons, including China's resistance to Security Council resolutions to condemn Sudan and Kofi Annan's worries that member states would force the UN to act without giving it necessary resources to do so, and as a result moved slowly to take action.[109] Nonetheless, the Security Council did take actions such as authorizing an arms embargo and a ban on Sudanese military flights. A peace agreement between the Sudanese government, one faction of rebels, and the government of Nigeria, was signed in May 2006. The Security Council later reaffirmed R2P in an April 2007 resolution on Darfur, and subsequently it authorized the deployment of a 26,000 person hybrid UN and African Union (AU) force to Darfur (UNAMID) to support the implementation of the peace agreement and to protect civilians. The mission faced many challenges, including violent attacks on peacekeepers and the Sudanese government's confrontational behavior. What seemed like a case study of how R2P could work in practice has not been a clear success. As an influential report to the UN noted, "the hybrid African Union-United Nations mission is a mere shadow of its original purpose, restricted to the delivering on the narrow objectives of monitoring conflict, patrolling camps and stimulating local efforts to build dialogue."[110]

The case of the UN in Libya is an example of a UN Security Council Resolution that sought to apply the principle of R2P and did not involve UN peacekeepers. The Libyan crisis began in

February 2011, when a demonstration protesting the arrest of a human rights activist resulted in Libyan government security forces firing at the crowds and killing over 100 people. The protests were seen as part of the Arab Spring, a wave of protests, riots, and rebellions against undemocratic regimes that began in Tunisia in December 2010. As protests spread throughout Libya, amid calls for democracy, political reform, and justice, the government response was violent and brutal. The UN Security Council adopted Resolution 1973 in March 2011 that condemned the government's use of violence and violation of human rights and authorized (under Chapter VII) member states to "take all means necessary" other than a "foreign occupation force" to protect civilians under threat of attack. It also authorized a no-fly zone, banned travel, and froze assets of relevant officials.[111] The resolution provided the legal basis for intervention by the US, France, and UK, soon followed by NATO. NATO took the lead in operations against Libyan forces, which lasted seven months until Libya's dictator, Col. Mummar el-Qaddafi was captured and killed by Libyan opposition forces. The subsequent mission in Libya, the United Nations Support Mission in Libya, was a peacebuilding mission run by the DPA, not a peacekeeping mission run by the Department of UN Peacekeeping Operations. While the UN has worked to bring warring coalitions together to end conflict in the country and create one government, the country remains unstable and its infrastructure is in bad shape.

We can see from these cases that R2P is no panacea. Writer and activist Alex de Waal has argued that if the international community pursued humanitarian intervention in Darfur under the R2P banner, the results could be disastrous, with the government closing down humanitarian efforts, and the rebels gaining heart to fight harder and longer. He posited that R2P "should be seen less as a normative vocabulary that can catalyze action, and more as a policy agenda in need of implementation."[112]

In terms of how to improve overall UN peace operations, in June 2015, the High Level Independent Panel on United Nations Peace Operations, chaired by Jose Ramos-Horta, presented its report to Secretary-General Ban Ki-moon. Horta is a former president of East Timor, co-recipient of the 1996 Nobel Peace Prize, and head of the United Nations Integrated Peacebuilding Office in Guinea-Bissau. The report made four main recommendations that reflected the growing importance of the DPA's approach. The first called for putting political solutions ahead of military engagements in the design and implementation of peace operations. Second, it calls for a more flexible use of the "full spectrum of UN peace operations," arguing for smoother transitions between the special political missions and peacekeeping operations. Third, it argues for more collaboration and consultation throughout the UN system and with relevant partners. And finally, it calls for more "field-focused" and "people-centered" peace operations.

More than 120,000 people currently serve in UN peace operations around the world, which is a record level of deployment. The budget for current peacekeeping operations is around $8.5 billion. Since the birth of peacekeeping, over 3,000 UN peacekeepers have lost their lives. Refer to Table 3.1 for all peacekeeping operations since the founding of the UN. Peacekeeping and other peace operations are increasingly taking place in more difficult environments, where often there is no peace to keep and peacekeepers are operating in the midst of conflict, often facing attacks from extremist groups. As the 2015 Report noted,

> Today a growing number of missions operate in remote and austere environments where no political agreement exists, or where efforts to establish or re-establish one have

faltered. They face ongoing hostilities and parties who are unwilling to negotiate or otherwise undermine the presence of a mission by condoning or inflicting restrictions on its ability to operate. The challenge is multiplied in large, infrastructure-poor countries where it is harder for UN missions to make their presence felt. Logistical supply lines in vast, landlocked and often insecure operating environments are often stretched thin and left vulnerable to disruption.[113]

SCHOLARLY EVALUATION OF PEACEKEEPING

There are many strands of literature on the UN today. One strand focuses on the UN's history and evolution, often with an emphasis on the Security Council. Some scholars focus on individual UN bodies, such as UNDP or UNEP, or specific issues areas, such as human rights, development, refugees, the environment, and humanitarian assistance to name a few. There is also a literature on the UN and its role in international law and specific analysis of the various Ad Hoc Tribunals created under the Security Council auspices. Indeed, the literature on the UN spans disciplines beyond political science, including international law, sociology, public health, and development economics.

To give readers a taste of the literature on the UN, it is worth examining the category of research that asks whether peacekeeping has been effective.[114] One example is the work of Morjé-Howard, who argued that variation between success and failure in peacekeeping in civil wars can be explained by how three conditions play out. The first is how favorable "situational factors" are. These include factors such as whether the warring parties have consented to having peacekeepers in the country. The second is the degree of Security Council interest in the conflict. She argues that very high levels of Security Council interest can actually undermine the ability of peacekeepers to carry out their mandates, as can very low levels of interest. Moderate interest, she concluded, is necessary but not sufficient for success. Finally, the degree of organizational learning matters as a factor distinguishing success from failure. While she outlined a number of indicators of learning, the message is that peacekeeping missions that were able to adapt and adjust to their conditions were likely to be more successful.[115] From a different perspective, Virginia Page Fortna argued that not only should one compare cases of peacekeeping, but also look at cases where peacekeeping was not used. If peacekeepers are only sent to easy places, she argues, we are likely to see a strong effective impact. In fact, peacekeepers tend to be deployed in difficult situations. She concluded that peacekeeping does have significant and positive impact on the stability of peace, by changing the incentives for war versus peace, reducing uncertainty about what each side intends, and helping to reduce the likelihood of "accidents" that may lead to war.[116]

Michael Lipson presented a very different view of peacekeeping. Instead of focusing on mandate fulfillment, he examined organizational or process performance. In these areas, he argued that it is very difficult to evaluate the UN's performance in peacekeeping because of the ambiguity inherent to them. Ambiguity, for example, can occur in a lack of agreement about what a type of conflict (is it civil war or genocide?), or about who has authority over a mission within the UN, or about the goals of the mission. Today's multidimensional peacekeeping operations include the Department of Peacekeeping Operations as well as various other UN agencies, funds, and programs, all of which may have different mandates and cultures.[117] Heidi Hardt explored why some organizations make peace operations decisions more efficiently than others, and argued that "informal institutionalization" is key to speeding up decisionmaking when it counts. In particular, informal norms of working method, communications, and personal politics seem to matter in security-related negotiations involved in setting up peace operations.

CONCLUSION

In 1996, the late US Republican Senator Jesse Helms wrote an article in *Foreign Affairs* arguing that if the UN could not get its proliferating bureaucracy under control, it should be abolished. At the time, Helms was chairman of the powerful US Senate Committee on Foreign Relations. He was concerned that the UN was taking sovereignty away from states as a "power hungry and dysfunctional organization," and criticized the UN for making every problem in the world its own.[118] That criticism echoes similar views from people who want to abolish the World Bank or the International Monetary Fund and represents one end of the political spectrum. The UN responded, in part to this type of criticism, with some reforms to its bureaucracy. But Helms's views still resonate today in some quarters. Most of the more mainstream accounts today begin with the assumption that we need the United Nations even with its flaws. As Madeline Albright, former US permanent representative to the United Nations and former US Secretary of State, wrote a decade ago, "for $1.25 billion a year—roughly what the Pentagon spends every 32 hours—the United Nations is still the best investment the world can make in stopping AIDS and SARS, feeding the poor, helping refugees, and fighting global crime and the spread of nuclear weapons."[119] Ultimately the ability of the UN to remain effective in global politics depends on the political will of its members, the quality of its staff, the institution's resources, and its ability to respond as nimbly as possible to global problems. As the UN has now celebrated its 70th birthday, this likely means that while we should not expect any miracles, we are likely to continue to see variation across UN bodies, and we can hope that ongoing debates about the best ways to reform the UN and its parts result in some positive steps.

BIBLIOGRAPHY

Albright, Madeline K. "United Nations." *Foreign Policy* (September/October 2003): 16–24.
Annan, Kofi. "In Larger Freedom: Toward Security, Development and Human Rights for All." New York: United Nations, 2005.
———. "Report of the Secretary-General Pursuant to General Assembly Resolution 53/35: The Fall of Srebrenica." New York: United Nations, 1999.
Ban, Ki-moon. "'Poorest of the Poor' Lagging Amid 'Uneven' Progress on Millennium Development Goals, Secretary-General Tells Economic and Social Council Launch of Report." news release, July 7, 2011, http://www.un.org/press/en/2011/sgsm13694.doc.htm.
Bellamy, Alex J. "The Responsibility to Protect—Five Years On." *Ethics & International Affairs* 24, no. 2 (2010): 143–69.

Bosco, David L. *Five to Rule Them All: The UN Security Council and the Making of the Modern World*. New York: Oxford University Press, 2009.

Boutros-Ghali, Boutros. "An Agenda for Peace: Preventive Diplomacy, Peacemaking and Peace-Keeping." United Nations, 1992.

Brahimi, Lakhdar. "Report of the Panel on United Nations Peace Operations." New York: United Nations, 2000.

Bunche, Ralph. Nobel Lecture. University of Oslo. Oslo, Norway: December 11, 1950.

Charter of the United Nations. "Chapter XV, Article 100, 1." 1945.

Chesterman, Simon. "Introduction: Secretary or General?" In *Secretary or General? The UN Secretary-General in World Politics*, edited by Simon Chesterman, 1–11. New York: Cambridge University Press, 2007.

Clark, Anne Marie. *Diplomacy of Conscience*. Princeton, NJ: Princeton University Press, 2001.

Cohen, Roger. "U.S. Execution of German Stirs Anger." *The New York Times*, March 5, 1999.

Crawford, James, and Tom Grant. "International Court of Justice." In *The Oxford Handbook on the United Nations*, edited by Thomas G. Weiss and Sam Daws, 193–213. New York: Oxford University Press, 2007.

Davies, Lawrence E. "Historic Plenary Session Approves World Charter." *The New York Times*, June 26, 1945, 1, 10.

Diehl, Paul F. *International Peacekeeping* (Perspectives on Security). Baltimore, MD: Johns Hopkins University Press, 1993.

Doyle, Michael W., and Nicholas Sambanis. *Making War and Building Peace: United Nations Peace Operations*. Princeton, NJ: Princeton University Press, 2006.

Durch, William J., Victoria K. Holt, Caroline R. Earle, and Moira K. Shanahan. "The Brahimi Report and the Future of UN Peace Operations." Washington, DC: The Henry L. Stimson Center, 2003.

Evans, Gareth, and Mohamed Sahnoun et al. "Responsibility to Protect: Report of the International Commission on Intervention and State Sovereignty." Ottawa, Canada: International Development Research Centre, 2001.

"Excerpts from the Debate in the U.N. Security Council." *The New York Times*, August 22, 1968, 21.

Fasulo, Linda M. *An Insider's Guide to the UN*. New Haven, CT: Yale University Press, 2004.

Ford, Gerald R. "President Gerald R. Ford's Address to the 29th Session of the General Assembly of the United Nations." September 18, 1974.

Fortna, Virginia Page. *Does Peacekeeping Work? Shaping Belligerents' Choices after Civil War*. Princeton, NJ: Princeton University Press, 2008.

Helms, Jesse. "Saving the U.N.: A Challenge to the Next Secretary-General." *Foreign Affairs* 75, no. 5 (1996): 2–7.

High-Level Independent Panel on Peace Operations. "Uniting Our Strengths for Peace - Politics, Partnership and People." New York: United Nations, June 2015.

Hoge, Warren. "Panel Says Annan Didn't Intervene in Iraq Contract." *The New York Times*, March 30, 2005.

——. "U.N. Chief Is Assuaging Doubts About Leadership." *The New York Times*, February 19, 2007.

Hoopes, Townsend, and Douglas Brinkley. *FDR and the Creation of the U.N.* New Haven, CT: Yale University Press, 1997.

Ignatieff, Michael. "The Confessions of Kofi Annan." *The New York Review of Books* LIX, no. 19 (December 6, 2012): 4, 6.

International Court of Justice. "The Lagrand Case (Germany v. United States of America): Summary of Order." International Court of Justice, 1999.

——. "Members of the Court." http://www.icj-cij.org/court/index.php?p1 = 1&p2 = 2&PHPS ESSID = 8ab362b09042424317d7145e2ace59ac.

"Iraq War Illegal, Says Annan." *BBC News*, September 16, 2004.

Kennedy, Paul. *The Parliament of Man: The Past, Present, and Future of the United Nations.* New York: Random House, 2006.

Kluckhohn, Frank L. "War Pact Is Signed." *The New York Times*, January 3, 1942, 1.

Lipson, Michael. "Performance under Ambiguity: International Organization Performance in UN Peacekeeping." *Review of International Organizations* 5, no. 3 (2010): 249–84.

Loconte, Joseph. "The U.N. Sex Scandal." *The Weekly Standard*, January 3, 2005.

Luck, Edward C. *Mixed Messages: American Politics and International Organization, 1919–1999.* Washington, DC: Brookings Institution Press, 1999.

Mastanduno, Michael. "Economics and Security in Statecraft and Scholarship." *International Organization* 52, no. 4, International Organization at Fifty: Exploration and Contestation in the Study of World Politics (Autumn 1998): 825–54.

Meisler, Stanley. *United Nations: The First Fifty Years.* 1st ed. New York: Atlantic Monthly Press, 1995.

Mertus, Julie. *The United Nations and Human Rights: A Guide for a New Era.* New York: Routledge, 2005.

Meyer, Howard N. *The World Court in Action: Judging Among the Nations.* Lanham, MD: Rowman & Littlefield Publishers, 2002.

Montgomery, Tommie Sue. "Getting to Peace in El Salvador: The Roles of the United Nations Secretariat and ONUSAL." *Journal of Interamerican Studies and World Affairs* 37, no. 4 (Winter 1995): 139–72.

Morjé Howard, Lise. *UN Peacekeeping in Civil Wars.* New York: Cambridge University Press, 2008.

Murphy, John Francis. *The United States and the Rule of Law in International Affairs.* Cambridge, UK: Cambridge University Press, 2004.

Newmann, Maria. "Ban Ki-Moon." *The New York Times*, September 26, 2007.

Oestreich, Joel E. *Power and Principle: Human Rights Programming in International Organizations.* Washington, DC: Georgetown University Press, 2007.

Office of the High Commissioner for Human Rights. "United Nations Human Rights." United Nations. http://www.ohchr.org/en/issues/pages/whatarehumanrights.aspx.

Paris, Roland. *At War's End: Building Peace after Civil Conflict.* Cambridge, UK: Cambridge University Press, 2004.

Parrott, Lindesay. "U.N. Body Orders Study in Hungary." *The New York Times*, November 5, 1956, 1.

Petersen, Keith S. "The Uses of the Uniting for Peace Resolution." *International Organization* 13, no. 2 (Spring 1959): 219–32.

Peterson, M. J. *The UN General Assembly.* New York: Routledge, 2006.

Power, Samantha. *Chasing the Flame: Sergio Vieira De Mello and the Fight to Save the World.* New York: Penguin, 2008.

Prunier, Gerard. *Darfur: The Ambiguous Genocide.* Ithaca, NY: Cornell University Press, 2005.

Rutherford, Ken. *Humanitarianism under Fire: The US and UN Intervention in Somalia.* Sterling, VA: Kumarian Press, 2008.

Schlesinger, Stephen C. *Act of Creation: The Founding of the United Nations.* Boulder, CO: Westview Press, 2003.

Tharoor, Shashi. "'The Most Impossible Job' Description." In *Secretary or General? The UN Secretary-General in World Politics*, edited by Simon Chesterman, 33–46. New York: Cambridge University Press, 2007.

The Atlantic Charter. August, 1941.

Thompson, Alexander. *Channels of Power: The UN Security Council and U.S. Statecraft in Iraq.* Ithaca, NY: Cornell University Press, 2009.

Traub, James. *The Best Intentions: Kofi Annan and the UN in the Era of American World Power.* 1st ed. New York: Farrar, Straus and Giroux, 2006.

———. "U.N. Human Rights Council Condemns Actual Human Rights Abusers!" *Foreign Policy*, June 1, 2012. foreignpolicy.com/2012/06/01/u-n-human-rights-council-condemns-actual-human-rights-abusers/.

United Nations Department of Public Information. "The International Court of Justice." New York: United Nations, 2000.

———. "UNTSO: United Nations Truce Supervision Organization." New York: United Nations. http://www.un.org/en/peacekeeping/missions/untso/background.shtml.

United Nations General Assembly. "Agenda of the Sixty-Ninth Session of the General Assembly." New York: United Nations, September 19, 2014.

———. "Composition of the Secretariat: Staff Demographics." New York: United Nations, 2012.

———. "Resolution 997 (Es-I)." 1956.

———. "Rules of Procedure." http://www.un.org/ga/ropga_delegt.shtml.

United Nations Information Service. "Looking Back/Moving Forward." http://www.unis.unvienna.org/unis/en/60yearsPK/index.html.

United Nations Peacekeeping. "Post Cold-War Surge." United Nations. http://www.un.org/en/peacekeeping/operations/surge.shtml.

United States Government Accountability Office. "Darfur Crisis: Death Estimates Demonstrate Severity of Crisis, but Their Accuracy and Credibility Could Be Enhanced." US Government Accountability Office. http://purl.access.gpo.gov/GPO/LPS77420.

UN News Centre. "In New Report, Ban Outlines Measures to Strengthen UN Peace Operations, Tackle Abuse." New York: United Nations, September 11, 2015.

UN Visitor's Centre. "Fact Sheet: History of the United Nations Headquarters." http://www.un.org/wcm/webdav/site/visitors/shared/documents/pdfs/FS_UN%20Headquarters_History_English_Feb%202013.pdf.

Urquhart, Brian. "The Evolution of the Secretary-General." In *Secretary or General? The UN Secretary-General in World Politics*, edited by Simon Chesterman, 15–32. New York: Cambridge University Press, 2007.

———. "How to Fill a Job with No Description." *Foreign Affairs* 85, no. 5 (September/October 2006): 15–22.

———. "Looking for the Sheriff." *New York Review of Books* (July 16, 1998).

Volker, Paul A, Richard J. Goldstone, and Mark Pieth. "Independent Inquiry Committee into the United Nations Oil-for-Food Programme." United Nations, 2005.

Weiss, Thomas G. *What's Wrong with the United Nations and How to Fix It.* 2nd ed. Malden, MA: Polity, 2012.

Weiss, Thomas G., David P. Forsythe, and Roger A. Coate. *The United Nations and Changing World Politics.* 4th ed. Boulder, CO: Westview Press, 2004.

Weiss, Thomas G., David P. Forsythe, Roger A. Coate, and Kelly-Kate Pease. *The United Nations and Changing World Politics.* 6th ed. Boulder, CO: Westview Press, 2010.

——. *The United Nations and Changing World Politics.* 7th ed. Boulder, CO: Westview Press, 2014.

Weiss, Thomas G., Tatiana Carayannis, Louis Emmerij, and Richard Jolly. *UN Voices: The Struggle for Development and Social Justice.* Bloomington: Indiana University Press, 2005.

Wilde, Ralph. "Trusteeship Council." In *The Oxford Handbook on the United Nations*, edited by Thomas G. Weiss and Sam Daws, 149–60. New York: Oxford University Press, 2007.

4 United Nations Case Study
Rwanda/Genocide

It has been over twenty years since one of the worst acts of genocide in the twentieth century. In April 1994, approximately 800,000 people were massacred in 100 days in the tiny, land-locked country of Rwanda in central Africa. As Michael Barnett made vividly clear, that is equivalent to five and a half deaths a minute, or 333 and one-third deaths an hour.[1] The international community, including the UN, essentially stood aside and did little to nothing to stop the genocide, although heroic individuals managed as best they could on the ground. In fact, in the midst of the genocide, the UN Security Council called for most of the UN troops in the country to be withdrawn. Not only did members of the Security Council exhibit a lack of political will to take action, but the UN Secretariat also did not speak up loudly and clearly for any type of meaningful action.

How could such a "nonresponse" be possible, given the existence of an international genocide convention that enjoins states to take action, as well as changing norms on humanitarian intervention? Numerous reports, books, and articles have been written on the subject, each seeking to figure out who was to blame or why things went wrong. There is much hand-wringing and finger-pointing, but little consensus, even more than twenty years after the genocide. Rwanda stands with Somalia and Bosnia as three prominent places in the post-Cold War era where the UN failed dramatically to save lives.

This case study is an important one in examining how the international community stood by and did little amid so much carnage. It raises questions about what the role of the UN and international community should be in addressing genocide and other crimes against humanity. This chapter will describe the events leading up to the Rwandan genocide, the genocide itself, and some of its aftermath, with special attention paid to the role of the UN and its Security Council member states. It then examines some of the most prominent arguments about what went wrong in the genocide and shows when and how they relate to different theoretical perspectives of IO behavior.

WHAT HAPPENED

Rwanda is the most densely populated country in Africa, with a population today of almost 10 million. The majority of its people are Hutu (at around 84%), followed by the Tutsi (at around 15%), and then the Twa (at 1%).[2] During the colonial era, first under Germany, and later Belgium, the minority Tutsis solidified their positions of power. The Belgians, in particular, adopted and institutionalized the racist idea that the Tutsis were superior because they were perceived to have more Caucasian features than the Hutu. As Rwanda headed toward independence in the late 1950s, ethnic violence broke out as the Hutus challenged Tutsi rule, demanding power and revenge. Rwanda achieved independence in 1962, with the Hutu formally winning power in elections the previous year. Ethnic violence continued, with the Hutu government retaliating against attacks by Tutsi refugees, driving out the Tutsi elite, and leaving a death toll of around 10,000–20,000 Tutsis.[3] The country was stable for around 15 years under the dictatorship of Juvénal Habyarimana, a Hutu. Over time, the Rwandan Patriotic Front (RPF) emerged out of the Tutsi diaspora based in Uganda and in 1990 it invaded Northern Rwanda. Eventually, inroads by the rebels, along with international pressure, pushed Habyarimana to share power with the Tutsis in a peace agreement signed in Tanzania in August 1993, which was expected to result in free, multiethnic elections. UN peacekeepers arrived in October to help implement the accords. The Security Council authorized just over 2,500 personnel to cover a variety of tasks. It is important to remember that United Nations Assistance Mission for Rwanda (UNAMIR) had a rather simple mandate: addressing issues like contributing to the security of Kigali, monitoring observance of the ceasefire agreement, and assisting in the coordination of humanitarian relief.[4] By February 1994, Belgian diplomats were concerned that there might be a "new bloodbath" in Rwanda. The Belgian Ambassador to the United Nations, Paul Noterdaeme, told Brussels that, in fact, the United States and United Kingdom did not want to strengthen UNAMIR's mandate. He also wrote that the United Nations Secretary-General, Boutros Boutros-Ghali, also was against any changes to UNAMIR's work.[5]

Two months later, six months into the shaky peace, an event occurred that triggered the genocide. On April 6, 1994, a plane carrying Rwandan president Habyarimana, Burundian president Cyprien Ntarymira, and members of their entourage, was shot down as it approached the Kigali airport. Everyone on board was killed. Within hours of the crash, the extremist militia, the Presidential guard, and members of the Rwandan armed forces began to slaughter Tutsi politicians and moderate Hutus in what was obviously a well-organized plan to remove Rwanda's moderate leadership. High on the list of targets was the opposition's Prime Minister and her husband, the president of the constitutional court, other major political leaders, and even the negotiator of the Arusha Accords. By the second day, ordinary Tutsis and moderate Hutus were being slaughtered, and the killings continued to escalate at a rapid pace. The government-run radio station and the extremists' Radio-Television Libre des Mille Collines (RTLM) urged Hutus to take revenge on Tutsis, who they claimed were behind the murder of President Habyarimana. Many Tutsis left their homes and sought safety in places they felt were safe, such as churches, stadiums, and schools. This strategy protected them for some days until better armed Hutus from the army, national police, and Presidential Guard, began to arrive at these sites. Thousands upon thousands of Tutsi who sought safety at such gathering places were ultimately killed by gunfire, grenades, hacked to death by machetes, or beaten to death with clubs.[6] Women and girls were raped and tortured before being slaughtered, and young children were often slaughtered in front of their parents, with the Interahamwe, the Hutu extremist group, cutting off one arm and then the other, allowing the child to bleed slowly to death.[7]

The onset of the killings put UNAMIR in an impossible situation of addressing the growing violence with a relatively small number of lightly armed peacekeepers, who were told by New York headquarters shortly after the plane crash to avoid conflict.[8] Romeo Dallaire, then a major general in the Canadian army who commanded UNAMIR, had already known plans were afoot by the Hutu extremists to slaughter Tutsis. A Hutu informant, who had been an officer in the Presidential Guard and then became the chief trainer for the Interahamwe, warned Dallaire's second-in-command in January 1994 that he suspected the extremists were planning to create death squads that could "kill a thousand Tutsis in Kigali within twenty minutes of receiving an order."[9] He described these plans in great detail and also revealed the extremists' intention to kill some Belgian peacekeepers. The Belgians were the "backbone" of UNAMIR, and if Belgium pulled out, this might precipitate the collapse of UNAMIR. Dallaire then sent a fax to UN headquarters on January 11 relaying this information, along with his intent to raid a major weapons cache the informant said Interhamwe had organized to distribute weapons throughout Kigali.[10]

This fax became famous as evidence that the UN was flagged about the risk of genocide well before the genocide began. The reply, by Iqbal Riza, deputy to Kofi Annan, then the head of peacekeeping, said Dallaire must immediately suspend this operation. A second reply from headquarters (again signed by Riza for Annan) added that the operation proposed by Dallaire went beyond UNAMIR's mandate. Instead, Dallaire and Jacques-Roger Booh Booh, Annan's Special Representative in Rwanda, were to request an urgent meeting with President Habyarimana to share with him the information they had about threats to the peace process.[11]

Once the killings began, Dallaire sent peacekeepers to protect the prime minister, Agathe Uwilingiyimana. The 10 Belgian peacekeepers among them were surrounded by Rwandan soldiers, told to surrender their weapons, and then tortured, mutilated, and killed. The prime minister and her husband were also shot and killed. As the extremists had predicted, this deliberate act resulted in Belgium withdrawing its troops a week later and ultimately prompted the UN to pull the majority of its troops out as well.[12]

Members of the UN Security Council first responded to the killings by sending planes to Kigali to evacuate their citizens to safety, a move many say further encouraged the genocidaires. Dallaire thought that the well-trained and equipped elite forces helping with the evacuation might "possibly bring an end to the killings. But such an option wasn't even being considered."[13] In New York, when the Security Council discussed what to do about the chaos and killing in Rwanda, one group, led by the United States and United Kingdom, pushed for withdrawing UNAMIR. The Clinton administration felt UN peacekeeping operations in general were too bloated, but more importantly did not want a repeat of the failures of peacekeepers and US soldiers in Somalia, and finally, Rwanda was of no strategic importance to the United States. More importantly, the firefight in Mogadishu discussed in Chapter 12 occurred six months before the Rwandan genocide. After US Rangers were shot down in Mogadishu, US policymakers were more determined than ever to keep US troops out of wars in countries that did not involve US strategic interests. Commentators often refer to how the failure in Somalia played an important role in how the United States, and also the UN, perceived Rwanda. In the United States, the issue of genocide in Rwanda "did not even merit high-level attention," and the Clinton administration favored a complete pullout.[14] The lesson for the broader UN, in turn, was to avoid peace enforcement activities while internal conflicts were taking place in states. The idea was to reduce rather than increase the risks to peacekeeping operations. Belgium also argued for withdrawing UNAMIR since it didn't want to withdraw alone.[15] A group led by Nigeria, New Zealand, and the Czech Republic argued for intervention.

The UN Security Council stopped considering intervention by mid-April. According to Barnett, the "last gasp from the intervention camp" occurred on April 13, when Nigeria circulated among nonpermanent council members the written record of its oral presentations calling for intervention. But Nigeria never distributed its paper to the entire council, given pressure on everyone to achieve consensus.[16]

On April 21, the UN Security Council voted unanimously to reduce UNAMIR's forces to 270 men. The decision came after Secretary-General Boutros Boutros-Ghali argued that the two choices were either reducing the force to a symbolic size or strengthening it significantly. Among the factors the Security Council members used to justify their decision were the facts that it was unclear whether a ceasefire would occur; the UN troops had no mandate to fight the Hutu; and the Belgian government's withdrawal of its peacekeepers, the strongest and most fully equipped contingent in Rwanda. Coincidentally, Rwanda's genocidal government was a member of the Security Council at the time, and there was no call for its UN representative to be expelled. The UNAMIR officials were furious and dejected. Dallaire's assistant, Major Brent Beardsley, later expressed his frustration,

> The world just didn't care and it made no difference what you said or how you said it to them. . . . We could have packed up dead bodies, put them on a HERC, flown to New York, walked in the Security Council and dumped them on the floor in front of the Security Council, and all that would have happened was we would have been charged for illegally using a UN aircraft.[17]

By the end of April, UN Secretary-General Boutros-Ghali recommended a reversal of the Security Council's decision to reduce UNAMIR's forces. He sent a letter to the Security Council arguing that UNAMIR lacked the power to take effective action against the slaughter and asked the Council to consider actions, "including forceful action," that would "restore law and order." Acknowledging the fact that members of the Security Council had so far done little, he noted that he was aware "such action would require a commitment of human and material resources on a scale which Member States have so far proved reluctant to contemplate."[18] The Security Council continued its inconclusive debate in the days that followed.

By early May, a few weeks after the Security Council vote, at least a quarter-million Tutsi and moderate Hutu were dead. Analysts estimated that more than 75 percent of the Tutsi population of Rwanda were killed during the genocide.[19] Dallaire managed to keep around 500 troops, and he and his men did their best to save as many lives as they could. Mbaye Daigne, a Senegalese captain, saved around 100 lives by himself, before being killed by a mortar shell.[20] Ten UN peacekeepers and four UN military observers protected several hundred people who sought their protection at a Kigali hotel, the Hotel des Mille Collines. UN peacekeepers also managed to protect around 10,000 Rwandans seeking shelter at a Kigali stadium.[21] But the peacekeepers also failed to protect other lives. In one case at the beginning of the genocide, 2,000 people sought refuge at the Ecole Technique Officielee (ETO) in a suburb of Kigali, in hopes that UNAMIR troops there would protect them. But after the expatriates at ETO were removed, the remaining Belgian peacekeepers left the school and the waiting militia and soldiers then proceeded to move in and massacre those men, women, and children left behind.[22]

On May 17, the Security Council adopted a resolution to increase UNAMIR's troop levels and to impose an arms embargo on Rwanda. Unsurprisingly, the Rwandan representative on the Security Council voted against the embargo. Deployment of UNAMIR II was unlikely to take place before July because very few countries were willing to commit troops to it.

In June, the French government sent 2,500 soldiers to Rwanda "to assure the security and protection of displaced persons and civilians at risk in Rwanda."[23] The French said this "Operation Turquoise," would be a bridge until UNAMIR II arrived. Many were critical of the French move, arguing that France, which had close ties with the Hutu regime, was motivated by its foreign policy interests in Rwanda and the region. As Barnett noted:

> Few on the Security Council believed that France was motivated by strictly humanitarian concerns and with good reason. This was the same France that only the year before had intervened in Rwanda to save its allies, the very same individuals who were now closely associated with the genocide. Therefore, the council's general opinion was that it was virtually unimaginable that France had had a crisis of conscience and much more believable that it was about to use the cover of the UN's seal of approval to rescue its Rwandan allies and perhaps to even confront the RPF. If so, then the council might very well be providing support to the genocidaires. To complicate matters, the RPF announced that it opposed the French intervention.[24]

On June 22, the council reluctantly approved the French plan. While the French humanitarian zone no doubt contributed to saving lives, it was also evident that Rwandan troops and genocidaires were among those the French protected.[25] The French even helped some of the genocidal authorities leave the country after the RPF victory.[26] Unsurprisingly, the RPF was upset by news of the French intervention and reacted with hostility toward UNAMIR, given the UN's support of the French intervention. Rebels even "robbed, insulted, and roughed up" some of UNAMIR's Franco-African troops as a retaliation, according to Dallaire.[27]

Ultimately, the genocide was halted not by the international community, but by the victory of the RPF under the command of Paul Kagame. The rebel strategy was to sweep across the eastern part of Rwanda, slowly isolating the capital. They captured Kigali's airport in May. By June the RPF was successfully battling the Presidential Guard, civil defense forces, and militia in Kigali. The RPF was victorious, and a ceasefire was declared July 18. As Dallaire noted, the ceasefire was just "another name for a total RPF victory," but despite an end to the horror and the killing, "there were no crowds cheering the peace in the streets of Kigali."[28] Human Rights Watch accused the RPF of also "committing grave violations of international humanitarian law," because even after the combat had ended, its soldiers killed unarmed citizens believed to be participants in the genocide.[29] Kagame was soon sworn in as vice president and minister of defense along with the new president, moderate Hutu Pasteur Bizimungu. In 2000, Kagame became president. Although the genocide had ended, a new humanitarian crisis immediately blossomed: over a million Hutu refugees were crossing into Zaire, putting a severe strain on humanitarian aid. A United Nations spokesman called the flow of refugees an "absolute nightmare," given the impossibility of providing basics such as sufficient water and sanitation.[30]

THE AFTERMATH

In the aftermath of the genocide, some leading political figures expressed their remorse at not acting and called for a stronger response from the international community in the future. President Bill Clinton declared that "If the world community has the power to stop it, we ought to stop genocide and ethnic cleansing."[31] Seven years later, speaking at the Kigali airport he added,

> The international community, together with nations in Africa, must bear its share of responsibility for this tragedy, as well. We did not act quickly enough after the killing began. We should not have allowed the refugee camps to become safe haven for the killers. We did not immediately call these crimes by their rightful name: genocide.[32]

The UN Security Council quickly moved to set up the International Criminal Tribunal for Rwanda in November 1994 to prosecute those responsible for the genocide. That year, the Secretary-General also appointed an independent inquiry to examine the UN's actions in Rwanda at the time of the genocide.

As noted in Chapter 3, the genocide also triggered a new round of debate about when, and under what conditions, the international community should intervene in countries to protect humans, which produced a wave of support for the Responsibility to Protect norm and for the importance of prioritizing atrocity prevention.

The genocide in Rwanda had many negative repercussions as well. It contributed, directly and indirectly, to ongoing conflict in Central Africa, including a civil war in Burundi and two major wars in the Democratic Republic of Congo (DR Congo), both of which have claimed many more millions of lives. More than six million people died in DR Congo alone, from fighting and disease. As Human Rights Watch put it, the genocide "cast its shadow over all these conflicts, spinning actors in directions they would not otherwise have taken and coloring the analysis of events by the international community."[33]

WHAT WENT WRONG?

There is no shortage of arguments about how the United Nations and its member states failed to stop the Rwandan genocide. Some critics place the brunt of the blame on the United States; some on the United Nations Secretariat and bureaucracy; and some on the entire United Nations system, including its member states, Secretariat, and leadership. Many critics of the world's apathy believe that timely intervention may have averted the genocide. There is also an argument that it would have been difficult for any outside actor to stop the genocide once it began, due to the speed of the killing and the time it took before major actors truly realized what was going on.

Role of the United States

Samantha Power placed the brunt of the blame on the United States, which she argued not only failed to send troops, but in fact, led efforts to remove the UN peacekeepers. The United States worked hard to avoid any obligation to act, she writes, because "staying out of Rwanda was an explicit US policy objective."[34] She pointed to the weak leadership of the Clinton administration, which was dealing with other competing interests, and had a very narrow understanding what its possibilities for action were.[35] The Clinton administration worried that a mission to Rwanda might turn out poorly, such as those in Bosnia, Somalia, and Haiti, and it was fed up with what it considered to be endless UN demands for peacekeeping missions.[36] As National Security Advisor Anthony Lake later recalled, "I was obsessed with Haiti and Bosnia during that period, so Rwanda was, in journalist William Shawcross's words, a 'sideshow,' but not even a sideshow—a no-show."[37] Her emphasis on the United States as playing a key role in shaping UN actions toward Rwanda implicitly reflects a realist perspective. Action was not in the interests of the great power.

However, while most realists ignore the domestic sources of a state's interests, Power also paid attention to domestic politics, and argued that insufficient pressure from domestic sources of influence—such as the US congress, editorial boards, NGOs, and the public—was interpreted by US leaders "as an indicator of public indifference."[38] Even when it was quite clear that thousands of people were being massacred, the United States studiously avoided describing what was happening as "genocide," because US officials believed this would obligate the country to act, being a signatory of the 1948 Genocide Convention.[39] (That said, the convention does not specify *how* states should act.)

BOX 4.1 CONVENTION ON THE PREVENTION AND PUNISHMENT OF THE CRIME OF GENOCIDE (ARTICLES 1–3)

Adopted by Resolution 260 (III) A of the United Nations General Assembly on 9 December 1948.

Article 1

The Contracting Parties confirm that genocide, whether committed in time of peace or in time of war, is a crime under international law, which they undertake to prevent and to punish.

Article 2

In the present Convention, genocide means any of the following acts committed with intent to destroy, in whole or in part, a national, ethnical, racial, or religious group, as such:

- (a) Killing members of the group;
- (b) Causing serious bodily or mental harm to members of the group;
- (c) Deliberately inflicting on the group conditions of life calculated to bring about its physical destruction in whole or in part;
- (d) Imposing measures intended to prevent births within the group;
- (e) Forcibly transferring children of the group to another group.

Article 3

The following acts shall be punishable:

- (a) Genocide;
- (b) Conspiracy to commit genocide;
- (c) Direct and public incitement to commit genocide;
- (d) Attempt to commit genocide;
- (e) Complicity in genocide.

Source: http://www.hrweb.org/legal/genocide.html

When the State Department spokeswoman confirmed in June that "acts of genocide" occurred in Rwanda, a journalist asked, "What's the difference between 'acts of genocide' and 'genocide'? The awkward exchange that followed highlights the spokesperson's discomfort and need to avoid a direct answer.

> **Christine Shelly (State Department spokeswoman)**: Well, I think the—as you know, there's a legal definition of this . . . clearly not all of the killings that have taken place in Rwanda are killings to which you might apply that label . . . But as to the distinctions between the words, we're trying to call what we have seen so far as best as we can; and based, again, on the evidence, we have every reason to believe that acts of genocide have occurred.

> **Alan Elsner (Reuters)**: How many acts of genocide does it take to make a genocide?

> **Shelly**: Alan, that's just not a question I'm in a position to answer.[40]

Dallaire began using the "g-word" two weeks after the killing had begun, once he realized that the definition of genocide consisted of one group attempting to eliminate another.[41] In May, UN Secretary-General Boutros Boutros-Ghali stopped referring to the violence in Rwanda as "civil war" and publicly used the term genocide.[42] (To be fair, the United States wasn't the only member of the P-5 trying to avoid using the term. As late as June 1994, the word genocide was replaced with "acts of genocide" in a Security Council resolution, after China objected to the "g-word"[43].)

Scholar Alan Kuperman's argument contrasts directly with Power's.[44] He argued that even if major states had moved to act quickly, in particular by deploying 5,000 troops, it is unlikely the genocide could have been averted.[45] The problem, according to Kuperman, is more complex than a lack of political will from the United States or the West. Instead, he argued, the speed of the genocide was so quick, and the timing was such that a good deal of the killing was over before the West fully understood that what was going on was truly genocide, rather than civil war, and that much of the genocide was occurring in the countryside, outside the capital of Kigali.

According to Kuperman, writing in 2000, President Clinton could not have known that genocide was taking place until April 20, given how little US intelligence there was on the country and how the media also failed to capture the depth of what was going on. Even the existence of the "genocide fax" of January 11 was not sufficient proof that the UN knew what was going on relatively early. Kuperman argued that action shouldn't be authorized without confirming the accusation. He pointed out the fax also included a passage where Dallaire expressed some doubt about the credibility of the informant, and said "Possibility of a trap not fully excluded, as this may be a set-up."[46]

A lack of knowledge at the top levels of the US government coupled with the amount of time it takes to assemble troops, airlift them to Rwanda, reinforce them with armor or helicopters, and so on, would mean that there was little the West could do once the killing had begun. Even a rapid military intervention (and he focused on US intervention) could have saved up to 125,000 lives, but not have stopped the genocide in its tracks.

However, Kuperman did not conclude that the West should sit by idly and watch genocide unfold. Instead, he argued that the strongest lesson of the genocide was "intervention is no substitute for prevention." This means good old-fashioned diplomacy and negotiation must be strengthened in fragile situations. It also means that peacekeepers should be deployed "preventively" to forestall incipient violence, which also means that such forces should be large enough and sufficiently equipped to do their job.[47]

Indifference of the UN Bureaucracy

Others analyzing why the West did nothing to halt the genocide cast a wider net that goes beyond the United States' role. Scholar Barnett recognized that the United States worked hard to muzzle intervention, but went further to point out the moral responsibility of the UN—the Council and the Secretariat and the Secretary-General—had for the genocide.[48] The entire Security Council became silent when asked to contribute troops for intervening, which ultimately means that that the UN's indifference to genocide in Rwanda "is the sum of the individual indifferences of member states."[49]

But the bureaucracy of the UN was also indifferent. The Secretariat never informed the Security Council of the "genocide fax," while at the same time ordered peacekeepers to be "impartial." Boutros-Ghali's leadership, meanwhile, "leaves much to be desired," according to Barnett, since the Secretary-General "did not educate himself in even the most rudimentary way" about what was going on in Rwanda, did not cut short a trip to Europe in order to preside over the crisis, and generally appeared to be detached from a dangerous situation where peacekeepers had been killed and UNAMIR remained at risk.[50]

Yet, Barnett didn't conclude that the UN simply lacked spirit; rather he argued that the UN's inaction along with the view by the Security Council and the Secretariat that "withdrawal was ethical and proper" not "heartless or callous."[51] The rules of peacekeeping that the UN relied upon called for the UN to act in stable conditions. It is supposed to act after the fighting is finished, and not to create threat for peacekeepers. What was happening in Rwanda was in effect beyond the limits of UN peacekeeping rules and resources. As noted above, the "shadow of Somalia" contributed to the UN's lack of interest in getting involved with Rwanda. The UN initially defined the conflict in Rwanda as civil war, which also reduced its obligation to act. Indeed, Barnett suggests that the UN could perceive its inaction as both pragmatic and principled.[52]

Enough Blame to Share

An Independent Commission into the UN's actions during the Rwandan genocide, set up by then Secretary-General Kofi Annan, cast blame most widely, to include "each part" of the UN system: "in particular the Secretary-General, the Secretariat, the Security Council, and the Member States of the organizations." It argued that the absence of any political will by member states to act influenced the UN's ability to respond. The report calls for each part of the overall UN system to "assume and acknowledge their respective parts of the responsibility for the failure of the international community in Rwanda."[53] The bottom line was the lack of assertiveness by member states to act, along with a lack of resources, influenced the secretariat, the decisionmaking of the Security Council, and ultimately played itself out in UNAMIR's inability to get necessary troops, resources, and mandates to respond to the genocide. There is a rich literature on the genocide in Rwanda. These examples highlight some of the main arguments it offers, and show how different actors, including the UN, are identified as being a direct source of inaction.

CONCLUSION

Underlying all of the debates about what went wrong is an agreed fact: the perpetrators of genocide bear responsibility and blame for their actions. The individual studies presented above also show that arguments and debates about the sources of inaction from the international community point the finger in different directions (or in all directions). And these arguments resonate with some of the different theories of IO behavior presented in Chapter 2 in terms of arguing that the lack of political will by major countries (or all member states) is the root source of difficulties at the UN, or putting blame on the bureaucracy itself. It is interesting that the United States has been roundly criticized more than other UN members for its role, given that more evidence surfaced in the years following the genocide showing that the Belgians and French had a better sense of what was going on during the genocide than the United States. In any case, whether or not the United States knew what was happening early enough, it was obviously uninterested in getting involved.

The issues arising out of the international community's lack of involvement in the Rwandan genocide are alive and well. Powerful member states of the United Nations still struggle to gather the political will to prevent or mount a quick response to enormous tragedy arising out of conflict, as we have seen in the case of Darfur and also in the war in the DR Congo and Great Lakes region of Africa. Behind a UN member state's decision to act or not are factors that may include domestic political opinion, a state's strategic self-interests, and other factors that make government officials wary of intervening, especially in the midst of conflict. Many countries will not deploy ground troops in the midst of a civil war. The fact is that many states remain wedded to the norms of respecting state sovereignty, which clashes directly with the possibility of international intervention in a context where a government is one of the parties to the conflict. And, as Barnett has so eloquently argued, the UN's bureaucracy must also pay attention to its own survival. It is important to recognize the international community has had sufficient will to intervene in a number of conflicts with broad international support, such as East Timor (1999) and Kosovo (1999). But even when intervention occurs, effective intervention is still not as common as it should be.

As Chapter 3 noted, the ideas behind the R2P norm are noble, but so far have not taken root. In some ways, it is far easier for the international community to be helpful in offering old-fashioned humanitarian assistance, for example, in response to catastrophes that are not directly produced by conflict, such as tsunamis, earthquakes, or even food crises. But humanitarian aid can also be obstructed by international and domestic politics. Each crisis, whether traditional or not, tests the ability of the international community to cooperate in order to avert widespread catastrophe.

BIBLIOGRAPHY

Barker, Greg. "Ghosts of Rwanda." In *Frontline*, 2004.

Barnett, Michael N. *Eyewitness to a Genocide: The United Nations and Rwanda*. Ithaca, NY: Cornell University Press, 2002.

Bonner, Raymond. "Panic Kills 30—Refugee Total at 1 Million." *The New York Times*, July 18, 1994, A1, A7.

Central Intelligence Agency. "Rwanda." CIA, https://www.cia.gov/library/publications/the-world-factbook/geos/rw.html#People

Clinton, Bill. "Remarks by the President to Genocide Survivors, Assistance Workers, and U.S. and Rwanda Government Officials." Office of the Press Secretary, 1998.

Dallaire, Romeo. Fax to BARIL/DPKO/UNATIONS, New York, January 11, 1994.

Dallaire, Romeo. *Shake Hands with the Devil: The Failure of Humanity in Rwanda*. With Brent Beardsley. New York: Carroll & Graf, 2004.

de Waal, Alex. "Why Darfur Intervention is a Mistake." http://news.bbc.co.uk/2/hi/africa/7411087.stm.

Dobbs, Michael. "Warnings of Catastrophe" In *National Security Archive Electronic Briefing Book*. Washington, DC: National Security Archive, 2014.

Human Rights Watch. "Leave None to Tell the Story." New York: Human Rights Watch, 1999.

———. "Ten Years Later." New York: Human Rights Watch, 2004.

Kuperman, Alan J. "Rwanda in Retrospect." *Foreign Affairs* (January/February 2000): 94–118.

———. *The Limits of Humanitarian Intervention: Genocide in Rwanda*. Washington, DC: Brookings Institution Press, 2001.

Lewis, Paul. "Security Council Votes to Cut Rwanda Peacekeeping Force." *The New York Times*, April 22, 1994, 1.

Power, Samantha. *A Problem from Hell: America and the Age of Genocide*. New York: Basic Books, 2002.

———. "Bystanders to Genocide." *The Atlantic Monthly* (September 2001).

United Nations. "Report of the Independent Inquiry into the Actions of the United Nations During the 1994 Genocide in Rwanda." New York: United Nations, 1999.

5 The World Bank

The World Bank is the preeminent development finance organization in the world, for decades a powerful, influential source of loans, policy advice, and technical assistance for poor countries. Headquartered in Washington, DC, two blocks from the White House, the World Bank has an international staff of more than 11,000 people and its members range from 173 to 188 countries.[1] While its traditional work has been to provide loans to developing countries to finance individual projects, it has also grown over the years to provide loans for sectors and for broader economic policy reform and it also offers interest free loans and grants to the world's poorest countries. Like the other IOs covered in this book, its mission has expanded over time to dizzying heights. While its main mission is to reduce poverty and encourage economic development, in doing so it is actively involved in just about every sector and development issue imaginable, from agriculture to zinc mines. The bank provides financial support to build airports, roads, and power plants; improve access to primary schools; fight the spread of HIV/AIDS; improve irrigation and water distribution; rebuild bridges destroyed by war; modernize judicial systems; develop private sectors; and so on. The bank's emphasis on reducing human suffering through reducing poverty also puts it in a position to address directly or indirectly other problems that stem from poverty, such as disease, failed states, and even terrorism. In many ways, the bank's evolution reflects changes in its external environment—war, global financial crises, and the collapse of the Soviet Union, among others—as well as shifting conceptions of what *development* means in the scholarly and policy worlds. At each step of the way, the bank has implemented new ideas and approaches, and then has struggled with their negative effects or unintended consequences.

The bank has been seen by some as an institution that has learned from its mistakes, but it is also one constantly criticized for its performance.[2] Indeed, it has long been a favorite whipping boy of a range of critics, including anti-globalization protesters, politicians of various stripes in developed and developing countries, and people adversely impacted by bank projects. In a development that is either a strange twist of history or proof of learning, the current bank president, Jim Yong Kim, had previously criticized the bank for policy reduction strategies that "often exacerbate or leave unchanged the poverty in exactly those countries where it is worst."[3] If one looks at all the criticisms of the bank, it is clear that they range from arguments that the bank does too much (and should be shrunk) to too little in particular areas (and should take on more issues), and/or its performance is mixed to poor. On the extreme end are critics who think the institution is the source of enormous poverty and inequality, that it has blithely implemented policies benefiting corrupt officials, and should be abolished.[4] As to the source of its problems, critics point fingers at the bank's most powerful member state(s), its top management, its overall bureaucracy, its organizational incentive systems, and even civil society "watchdogs" who push the bank to do more and more. How to reform the bank is one of those longstanding debates that inspire various rounds of reform that may, in turn, be evaluated. Journalist Sebastian Mallaby summed up this conundrum nicely, speaking about the bank but also other IOs:

> [T]he World Bank shares the fragility common to most multilateral institutions. We veer between contempt for international bodies . . . and unrealistic pronouncements on what they ought to do: forge peace, banish financial instability, lift every person out of poverty. It has become commonplace to say that our global institutions are not up to the challenge of our unprecedented global interdependence. But the reason for this mismatch lies partly in our schizophrenia. Sometimes we pour scorn on the bank and other international bodies, and starve them of resources. Sometimes we talk as though they must have superhuman strengths, and we lumber them with impossible objectives.[5]

In recent years, the bank has also faced new challenges to its role. China's ExIm Bank in some years has lent more money to the developing world than the World Bank, and without the kinds of conditions on environmental, gender, or anti-corruption that are found in World Bank loans. The BRIC countries (Brazil, Russia, India, China, and South Africa) announced in 2014 the creation of their own, New Development Bank BRICS (NDB BRICS). China also launched, in October 2014, the Asian Infrastructure Investment Bank (AIIB), which allows for broader membership beyond Asia. While the United States and Japan opposed the new AIIB, other major countries signed up as founding members, including Great Britain, Germany, France, and South Korea. In broader geopolitical terms, many are wondering if these initiatives are indicative of the decline of American global influence. Indeed, the NDB BRICS' website explicitly states that it was set up "as an alternative to the existing US-dominated World Bank and International Monetary Fund."[6] More specifically, whether or not these new banks are a major threat to the World Bank will depend on the extent to which their lending policies, safeguards, and overall capacity create more opportunities for potential borrowers to engage in forum shopping. For example, if AIIB or NDB BRICS loans have fewer environmental and social safeguards and more attractive interest rates, borrowers will have more incentive to choose them over other options. The BRICS bank will have starting capital of $50 billion, increased to $100 billion over time, and the AIIB opens its doors with $100 billion in capital. This compares with $223 billion of subscribed capital for the World Bank.

This chapter discusses the birth and evolution of the bank, describing and highlighting the criticisms of the important ways in which it has sought to help promote economic development.

BIRTH OF THE BANK

The World Bank had a number of antecedents as financiers, government officials, and others had long thought about how to create more stable international trade, monetary, and financial relationships between states. In 1920, an International Financial Conference was held in Brussels, and its international participants put forward several proposals for an international financial institution that would make loans to governments to help rebuild Europe after World War I.[7] Dutch central banker Gerard Vissering, for example, called for the creation of an international credit bank to offer credits to countries that suffered from World War I, with resources provided by lending countries.[8] Some of these ideas were further explored, and others proposed, at a 1922 International Economic Conference held in Genoa.

The "father" of the bank and the IMF is undoubtedly US Treasury official Harry Dexter White, whose 1942 "Proposal for a United Nations Stabilization Fund and a Bank for Reconstruction and Development of the United and Associated States" built on past ideas and shaped the subsequent process of consultation with the British and others, which would ultimately produce both the bank and the fund. White was an economist with a PhD from Harvard who headed the US Treasury's monetary research division before becoming a close advisor to US Treasury secretary, Henry Morgenthau, Jr. White had a reputation for being clever and creative, but at times acerbic and truculent.[9] It turns out he was also a highly placed spy for the Soviet Union between 1941 and 1948, a fact that came to light much later (see Box 5.1).

A few years earlier, with World War II in full swing and many prominent people already thinking about the postwar order, US Treasury Secretary Henry Morgenthau asked White to draft a memorandum on a postwar fund that could help to stabilize currency fluctuation and promote trade. White had previously worked with experts from State, Treasury, the Federal Reserve System, and elsewhere to draft a proposal for an "Inter-American Bank" that never came into existence, but some of the ideas on the former were also reflected in the proposal for what came to be the World Bank.[10] White's ambitious suggestions called for a fund to help stabilize currency and a bank that would lend member states money for reconstruction and development, have its own currency (one "unitas" equal to $10), and help to promote democratic institutions within its member states. Morgenthau, in turn, passed White's proposal on to President Roosevelt, who endorsed them.[11] This was an important step in the process of an evolving idea that culminated with the birth of the bank.

BOX 5.1

In an interesting footnote to the birth of the World Bank, Harry Dexter White was, in fact, one of the Soviet Union's most highly placed agents in the American administration. His role for the KGB was alleged for years, but twenty recently released KGB documents spell out his assistance to Soviet intelligence in the mid-1930s and between 1943 and 1945. He was described as more of an independent "Soviet sympathizer" rather than a "disciplined" communist party member, with a reputation of someone who didn't take orders but did provide oral briefings and hand written documents to the Soviets. Essentially, he gave the Soviets information about US foreign policy and also offered advice on Moscow's negotiations on the United Nations. White was later appointed by President Truman in 1946 to be the first US executive director at the IMF. He resigned in March 1947, critical of US policy and suffering from health problems. In 1948, he responded to accusations that he assisted with Soviet intelligence by proclaiming his innocence. Three days after his testimony before the House Committee on Un-American Activities, he died of a heart attack.

Source: Benn Steil, The Battle of Bretton Woods: John Maynard Keynes, Harry Dexter White, and the Making of a New World Order (Princeton, NJ: Princeton University Press, 2013).

The British also played a particularly important role in the discussions. Over the next three years, a variety of British and American officials and other actors would work on the White proposal, and another proposal by distinguished British economist, John Maynard Keynes, who was the lead British negotiator. The details of both institutions were ironed out in 1943 and 1944, with plenty of heated discussions and debates. James Mead, a British official who authored a proposal for an international commercial union, recorded an October 5, 1943, meeting between White and Keynes in his diary:

> What an absolute Bedlam these discussion are! Keynes and White sit next [to] each other, each flanked by a long row of his own supporters. Without any agenda or any prepared idea of what is going to be discussed they go for each other in a strident duet of discord which after a crescendo of abuse on either side leads up to a chaotic adjournment of the meeting . . . [12]

The formal agreements that created the IMF and World Bank were hammered out at the United Nations Monetary and Financial Conference, which ran from July 1–22, 1944, at a mountain resort in Bretton Woods, New Hampshire. (This is why people refer to the World Bank and the IMF as the "Bretton Woods organizations.") President Roosevelt invited delegates representing 44 nations to the conference, and over 700 delegates participated.[13] The main purpose of the conference was to create an international monetary fund to promote currency stabilization (see Chapter 7). A Bank for Reconstruction and Development to provide resources to help rebuild the postwar world was seen as of lesser importance. The draft that acted as a basis for discussion of what ultimately became the bank's Articles of Agreement was a combination of the ideas presented by White and Keynes.[14]

It wasn't initially clear that the new institution would even be a bank. The British representative proposed calling it "the International Corporation for Reconstruction and Development." The French suggested "International Financial Institution for Reconstruction and Development."[15] In the end, it was called the "International Bank for Reconstruction and Development" (IBRD), but the debate over its name highlighted the fact that it was an organization born with a dual personality; it was partly a bank, partly something different, and over the years more akin to a development agency. Commission II, the group at Bretton Woods given the task of writing the bank's charter and chaired by Lord Keynes, noted in its report that the World Bank "was accidentally born with the name bank . . . mainly because no satisfactory name could be found in the dictionary for this unprecedented institution."[16]

The new institution agreed upon at Bretton Woods was similar to a private bank in the sense that it would make or guarantee loans primarily for postwar reconstruction (meaning countries devastated by World War II) and, second (after the first job was addressed), to development (meaning less developed countries). Like a private bank, its loans would have interest rates and would have to be repaid, and the institution would be able to issue bonds. Yet, the IBRD would differ from a private bank in many fundamental respects. Its shareholders would only be governments, it could only lend to governments or to public or private actors with a government guarantee of repayment; it would not receive deposits; it was set up on a nonprofit basis; and its loans typically would contain more conditionality than a

AP Photo/Abe Fox

United Nations Monetary and Financial Conference at Bretton Woods

private sector bank's. The fact that IBRD loans require a sovereign guarantee also impacts a government's incentives on whether to agree to a loan. Government budgets can limit the amount of guarantees authorized each year, which mean that IBRD loans are used for priority projects. IBRD loans also offer longer maturities and grace periods, and lower interest rates, than commercial loans.

The new bank's total capital would be $10 billion. The bank could make or guarantee a loan to a borrowing member-state government (or its representative) if the bank agreed the money was not available from other sources, if the bank felt the proposal merited a loan, and if the borrower was creditworthy. The loans and guarantees would be funded by the shareholders' capital subscriptions, plus principal and interest on the bank's loans, and later (and most importantly), funds the bank would raise itself from international capital markets. In reality, in the bank's early days, it could only actually lend around $727 million. This was the amount of the $1.6 billion in capital that was paid in, which was in gold or US dollars, resources that client states needed.[17] The amount available to lend was expanded by the bank's first public bond offering in July 1947 of $250 million, made through what was, at the time, the largest ever consortium of securities dealers in the US bond market.[18] It was a big deal, too, because the relationship between the bank and Wall Street did not start off well, and it took a great deal of lobbying by the bank to sell itself to the market. Richard Demuth, a senior bank official observed, when the bank's first president, Eugene Meyer (who had been a successful investment banker), first visited New York to meet investment bankers,

> They were however, thoroughly unenthusiastic about giving any financial support to the bank. . . . There were reasons for the complete disinterest of the bankers in buying our bonds. . . . In general, [the bank] was thought of as a do-good institution, as a wild idea, without any respectable support.[19]

Lending for Projects

The IBRD's loans were to go toward "specific projects . . . except in special circumstances." A project tends to involve building or developing something tangible, like roads or power plants. Projects are identified in a variety of ways, but ultimately involve appraisal by bank staff, approval by the bank board, and signature, disbursement, and payment of the loan. Often, large chunks of a bank loan to a developing country end up back in the coffers of rich country companies, who are hired to actually build the highway or power plant or water plant.

In the bank's early years, projects were geared to building a country's infrastructure. Projects are *not* loans for economic policy change. While today projects are the bread and butter of the bank's work, in its early days, countries were less interested in projects and more interested in loans to help stabilize their economies or reconstruct their monetary systems in the aftermath of a devastating world war, and therefore wanted loans to finance activities that fell outside the traditional project definition. The bank's first board of directors allowed for the latter types of loans early on, as fitting the "special circumstances" phrase, and when the bank opened its doors in June 1946, the latter type of "program" loan went to France, Netherlands, Denmark, and Luxembourg.

Governance Structure

The governance structure of the World Bank and fund were similar, and in fact the Articles of Agreement of the two organizations share virtually the same language in parts.[20] Indeed, the Articles state that bank membership is open to countries already members of the fund. Some countries' executive directors serve both institutions. Membership between the two international financial institutions was linked for two reasons: first, the founders believed that stable monetary conditions, which the fund directly addressed, were necessary for bank lending to be successful and second, fund membership required countries to take on certain obligations (such as rules on exchange rates), which were not required for membership in the bank.[21]

Both institutions have a three-tiered governance structure that consists of a board of governors, a board of directors, and the institution's management. At the top is the Board of Governors, which consists of a governor (and alternate) from each member country. The majority of the governors are finance ministers. The Board of Governors is the highest decision-making body at the two organizations, and it addresses the big strategic issues of its respective organization. The two boards meet each fall at the IMF/World Bank Annual Meeting.

BOX 5.2 WORLD BANK LOANS 1947 VS. 2014

World Bank Loans, 1947

France, loan to Credit National to help reconstruct and develop French economy. $250 million.

Netherlands, loan to government to reconstruct "productive facilities." $195 million.

Examples of World Bank (IBRD and IDA) Loans and Credits, 2014

Benin, IDA **Multisectoral Food, Health, and Nutrition Investment Project Financing Credit**, $28 million, to increase use of community-based interventions focusing on child growth and nutrition.

Ethiopia, IDA **General Education Quality Improvement Investment Project Financing Credit**, $130 million, to strengthen primary and secondary school learning conditions and administration.

China, IBRD **Integrated Modern Agriculture Development Investment Project Financing Loan**, $200 million, to develop sustainable, climate-resilient agriculture production systems in specific provinces, municipalities, and autonomous regions.

Indonesia, IBRD **Coral Reef Rehabilitation and Management Program-Coral Triangle Initiative Investment Project Financing Loan**, $47.4 million, to develop strong framework for sustainable management of coral reef resources.

Myanmar, IDA **Electric Power Investment Project Financing Credit**, $140 million, to improve capacity and efficiency of gas-fired power generation and helps strengthen the country's electric power-related institutions.

Philippines, IBRD **Second Inclusive Growth for Post-Typhoon Recovery Development Policy Loan**, $500 million, to help bridge financing gap due to Typhoon Haiyan, in order to help government response to human and economic impacts of typhoon.

Belarus, IBRD **Biomass District Heating Investment Project Financing Loan**, $90 million, to improve use of renewable biomass for heat and electricity generation in selected towns.

Ukraine, IBRD, **First Development Policy Loan**, $750 million, to promote good public sector governance, reforms utility subsidy system to make it more efficient and equitable.

Haiti, IDA **Cultural Heritage Preservation and Tourism Sector Support Investment Project Financing Grant**, $45 million, to make cultural heritage tourist sites more attractive, build government capacity to respond to emergencies, and address living environment for areas in the north of the countries.

Nicaragua, IDA **Sustainable Rural Water Supply and Sanitation Sector Investment Project Financing Credit/Grant**, $14.3 million credit, $15.7 million grant, to help selected areas have better access to sustainable services and assist government's ability to respond to emergencies.

Sources: World Bank Annual Report 1947, World Bank Annual Report 2014.

The Governors, in turn, delegate authority to the Board of Directors (also called executive directors or EDs), which is the body directly responsible for the organization's general operations. At the World Bank, for example, the EDs are responsible for considering and approving its loans and policies.[22] In effect, the executive directors are the main channel by which member states are involved in the bank's activities. They represent member states "principals," and often come from a country's finance ministry (the US Treasury, in the case of the

United States). That said, the principal-agent relationship between board members as agents to the countries they represent was a subject of debate and negotiation, not a given. The British, in fact, wanted the bank and IMF boards to be removed from domestic politics of their countries, but the American view, which prevailed, was that governments should have close control over their board members.[23] In the early years of the bank, there was often a tug of war between powerful members of the board and the bank's president, as the both sides sought to assert their power.

At both the World Bank and IMF, voting is weighted and is determined by the size of each country's capital subscription to the organization. At the bank's birth, only five of the largest shareholders had their own executive director. In the terms agreed to at Bretton Woods, these were supposed to be the United States, United Kingdom, China, France, and the Soviet Union, the same as veto-wielding members of the United Nations' Security Council. However, the Soviets did not ratify the Articles of Agreement, so India ended up being the fifth. The remaining countries were divided into groups represented by seven directors, for a total of 12 EDs.

At the bank's birth the United States provided around one-third of the money and received around one-third of the vote. It was therefore given the single largest stake at both Bretton Woods organizations. For example, in the bank's second year, when its annual report detailed voting share, the United States had 37.2 percent of the total vote. The next closest country was the United Kingdom, with 15.4 percent, followed by China at a distant 7.27 percent.[24]

While the United States' share has declined over time (currently at 15.99 percent at the World Bank and 16.75 percent at the IMF), the United States remains the single largest and most influential shareholder at both institutions. Its influence has always extended well beyond formal voting share, and in fact, since the board of directors at both institutions prefers to operate by consensus, formal voting is rare. Both organizations are based in Washington, DC, just blocks from the White House. The practice has also been since the beginning that the president of the bank is an American citizen, appointed by the US president, while the head of the IMF is a European. This practice has come under fire in recent years as being unfair. During the last search for a new World Bank president, for example, two non-American candidates were in the competition, but in the end only the American, Jim Yong Kim, had enough votes to win the race.

Today the IBRD has 25 EDs, representing 188 countries. The United States, France, Germany, Great Britain, and Japan have their own directors, as do Saudi Arabia, China, and Russia. The other countries are divided into groups—some of which contain over twenty members—that share an executive director and an alternate director.

Relations with the United Nations

Relations between the World Bank and the United Nations were never written in stone, but rather evolved over the years from a formal one, where the World Bank kept the UN at arm's length, to one that was more engaged and constructive. Both the United Nations Charter and the World Bank's Articles of Agreement contain language that there should be a relationship between the two institutions, but the bank's language was more vague. The bank's articles call for the institution to "cooperate with other international organizations," while the UN Charter states in a number of places that the UN should "coordinate" the activities of specialized agencies created by intergovernmental agreement. UN officials assumed that the bank was one of

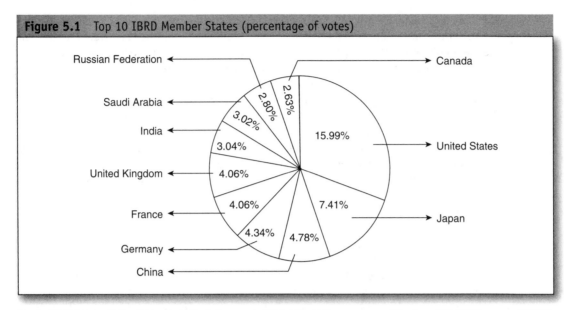

Figure 5.1   Top 10 IBRD Member States (percentage of votes)

Russian Federation — 2.80%
Canada — 2.63%
Saudi Arabia — 3.02%
India — 3.04%
United States — 15.99%
United Kingdom — 4.06%
France — 4.06%
Japan — 7.41%
Germany — 4.34%
China — 4.78%

Source: IBRD Country Voting Table, World Bank, January 4, 2016. http://siteresources.worldbank.org/BODINT/Resources/278027-1215524804501/IBRDCountryVotingTable.pdf

Note: Voting reform agreed to in 2008 and 2010 gave emerging market economies 4.59 percent more vote and moved China up the ladder to become the third largest voting member.[25]

these agencies.[26] The bank, in turn, wanted to remain as independent as possible, mainly because it didn't want to be dragged into political issues that might threaten its already fragile relationship with Wall Street. The IMF had similar views. Agreements between the UN and the Bretton Woods institutions were reached and passed by the General Assembly in 1947 stating the IMF and World Bank were "specialized" agencies of the UN, but each international financial institution "is, and is required to function as, an independent international organization."[27] In practice, this has meant that neither institution is beholden to the UN for financial support or any kind of approval. At the same time, both institutions participate in various UN meetings and report annually to ECOSOC. The World Bank set up cooperative arrangements with a number of UN agencies, such as the UN Development Programme (UNDP) and the Food and Agricultural Organization (FAO).[28] Operational relations remained strained between the UN and World Bank for the next few decades, until bank president George Woods began reaching out to the UN in a more constructive fashion.[29]

EVOLUTION

The bank's lending activities, policies, organizational structure, and driving ideas have changed many times over the years, influenced by the global economic and political environment in which it worked; internal leaders; politics and interests among shareholders; external criticism; and more broadly, the evolution of thinking about what development is and how it should be achieved. In the seventy plus years of its existence, the bank has faced a number of global economic and financial crises (each more frightening than the last), the Cold War, the subsequent collapse of the Soviet Union, the oil crisis, the rise of unfriendly watchdog NGOs, and an ever-growing number of issues deemed to be important by the bank's stakeholders. It has also coped with a few internal scandals.

Among the main changes in the bank's mission, strategies, and structure are the following: 1) the shift from early lending to Western Europe to a primary focus on lending to developing countries; 2) the creation of the bank's subsidiaries, which emphasize lending to the poorest countries and to private sectors, respectively; 3) a shift beyond infrastructure to include rural development, agricultural development, and a rapid expansion in the scale of lending in the 1970s; 4) structural adjustment lending, or lending to correct macroeconomic problems unaddressed by project lending, in the early 1980s; 5) in response to external and internal criticism, the addition of lending and policies on issues like the environment and gender in the 1980s and 1990s; 6) the Comprehensive Development Framework of the 1990s; 7) the focus on the Millennium Development Goals in 2000 (now replaced by the Sustainable Development Goals). Currently, the bank continues to focus on its broad overarching mission of "a world free of poverty," which it has operationalized as having two specific goals. The first is "end extreme poverty," or reducing to 3 percent globally the number of people living on under $1.25 a day by 2030. The second is "promote shared prosperity," or stimulating "income growth of the bottom 40% of the population in every country."[30] Both are very ambitious. As the bank notes, today around 21% of the developing world population lives in extreme poverty. That is over 1 billion people.[31]

The Impact of the Marshall Plan

The bank's first few years were far from successful. First, President Truman had a tough time finding someone to be president of the bank. Several people turned down the job or faced opposition. The first president, Eugene Meyer, a 70-year old with a distinguished career in public service who previously had been publisher of *The Washington Post* newspaper, abruptly resigned in December 1946, a mere six months into the job. He explained that he intended to remain until the bank's basic organization was in place, but observers thought Meyer was tired of fighting with the bank's US executive director and bureaucrats on issues such as loan policy and the relationship between the president and the board. Harold Smith, the bank's vice president, died in January 1947, and the bank was without a leader for another month, until John J. McCloy took the job of president.

Second, a year after its birth, the bank's planned emphasis on postwar reconstruction loans to Western Europe ran into trouble from a surprising source: the United States launched its Marshall Plan for Western Europe in June 1947. The plan, named after Secretary of State George C. Marshall, was a powerful way for the United States to help European nations return to "normal economic health" through US assistance that ultimately amounted to $12.4 billion, mostly in grants. Naturally, European countries vastly preferred US government grants (with no strings attached) to World Bank loans (that had to be repaid), so the Marshall Plan effectively took the wind out of the new bank's sails.[32] The loss of business in Western Europe resulted in the bank turning its attention to lending to the developing world. And third, the bank did not make its first loan until 11 months after its doors opened.

The May 1947 loan, for $250 million, was made to France to help it with reconstruction efforts. The French government originally asked for $500 million in its application, which was "a simple letter attached to an outline of the government's reconstruction program, the Monnet Plan."[33] The French wanted the funds to buy coal; equipment, such as ships, trucks, and coal mining machinery; and raw materials, such as fertilizers, copper, and tin. As such, this was a program and not a project loan. While the bank did not approve the full amount, it was still committing a good chunk of its loanable funds. In terms of how the bank should assess this application, one of its officials later recalled, "Nobody knew where to begin. We were inexperienced. We didn't know what kinds of questions to ask, what kind of investigation to make. We hadn't developed the kind of project approach that we worked out later."[34]

In those days, there wasn't yet sophisticated data to help bankers assess a country's creditworthiness. The emphasis at the time was to assess a country's behavior, in terms of deciding whether a country would be serious about servicing its debt. In fact, the bank had to be sure it wasn't lending money to dodgy recipients in order for it to be taken seriously in the US capital markets.[35]

The bank began to grow under the presidency of McCloy (1947–1949), a period during which it began borrowing on international capital markets, consistently making loans, and developing its policies and procedures for identifying, appraising, and negotiating loans. Lending focused on infrastructure-related projects such as electric power development (Luxembourg, Finland, and Brazil, for example), railway development (India), and equipment purchases for steel industries (Belgium, Luxembourg), timber production (Finland, Yugoslavia), and agriculture (Chile, Colombia, India).[36] By the end of its fiscal year for 1949 to 1950, the bank had lent a total of $832 million.[37]

New Affiliates and New Directions in Lending

Throughout its history, the bank's direction has been influenced by views from inside and from the broader development community on how to trigger and deepen economic development. Theories and arguments on how to best accomplish this have changed many times over the years, often as new ideas arise to correct some of the problems not well addressed (or problems caused) by the older ones. These changes reflect the bank's need to function and adapt within a changing global economic environment, its attempts to implement lessons it has learned along the way, and changing trends in developing economics and other academic disciplines. In the 1950s and 1960s, one impact of changing views on development was the creation of three new affiliates to address gaps unaddressed by the IBRD's work. The first was the *International Finance Corporation* (IFC), which was created in 1956 to lend money to private sector actors, without government guarantees. Its birth reflected thinking that development required growth in the private sector, and the IBRD was not able to easily lend directly to private sector actors. The *International Development Association* (IDA) followed four years later to offer interest-free loans and grants for the world's poorest countries. What good was a World Bank if some countries were too poor to take out its loans? This was also a time when new countries were proclaiming their independence throughout the developing world, and in the height of the Cold War, the bank's major donors wanted to make sure the new countries would be discouraged from looking to the Soviet Bloc for help. In 1966, the bank created ICSID, the *International Centre for the Settlement of Investment Disputes*, a novel quasi-judicial body to arbitrate and resolve disputes between member countries and foreign investors. The idea was that the resolution of these disputes would further enhance international investment. (A final affiliate was created in 1988, the *Multilateral Investment Guarantee Agency*, or MIGA, which offers insurance and other services to investment projects to help reduce losses due to factors like war, expropriation, or contract breaches.) Today, the IBRD and IDA are known as the World Bank, while those two plus IFC, ICSID, and MIGA are known as the "World Bank Group."

Rapid Expansion in the McNamara years

In the bank's first years, economists emphasized growth in gross national product (GDP) as the main engine powering development. Over time, some economists began to focus on other issues, such as entrepreneurship, literacy, social structures, and rural development, as it became clear that growth alone did not always trickle down to the poor and reduce human misery. What good were roads and power plants if poor farmers had trouble growing crops and had little or nothing to sell?

The content and scope of bank lending shifted dramatically under the tenure of Robert McNamara, who was president between 1968 and 1981. McNamara came to the World Bank following his controversial years as US defense secretary during the Vietnam War. Previously, he was an executive at Ford Motor Company, where he served as president for just a month before his move to the Pentagon.[38] During his years at the bank, McNamara placed poverty reduction at the top of the bank's policy agenda and rapidly expanded the issues and sectors it worked in.[39] Bank staff more than tripled in size, from approximately 1,575 to 5,200, and lending jumped from $953 million to $12.4 billion.[40] New departments were created in rural development, urban development, population, health, and nutrition, among others.[41]

In a speech to the bank's Board of Governors in 1973, McNamara said that a decade of unprecedented growth in developing country gross national product did not reach the poor people in those countries. In his 1973 "Address to the Board of Governors," McNamara stated

> Nearly 800 million individuals—40% out of a total of two billion—survive on incomes estimated (in U.S. purchasing power) at 30 cents per day in conditions of malnutrition, illiteracy, and squalor. They are suffering poverty in the absolute sense.[42]

He concluded dramatically: "The extremes of privilege and deprivation are simply no longer acceptable. It is development's task to deal with them."[43] (Shortly after his address, members of the Organization of Petroleum Exporting States or OPEC announced an oil embargo against the West, which resulted in the first "oil shock"—a quadrupling of oil prices, inflation, recession, and a global energy crisis, which impacted rich and poor countries alike.)

McNamara's position reflected a view among a number of economists that while economic growth was still as important as a driving engine of development, more attention needed to be paid to the distributional impact of growth. McNamara's strategy was to increase the role of the bank in rural areas by involving it in activities such as helping small farms increase production, making more water available for irrigation, and developing new agricultural extension services. During McNamara's tenure, the bank began to fund projects in the health and education and other nontraditional sectors for the first time. One example was a $2 million loan to Jamaica to support family planning programs, which included the construction of

10 rural maternity centers and a new wing for a Kingston hospital.[44] The bank also created the Consultative Group for International Agricultural Research (CGIAR) in 1971 to support old and create new agricultural research organizations. While over half of the bank's portfolio remained rooted in infrastructure projects, the new type of poverty-related projects shot up from under 19 percent of annual lending commitments in 1968 to over 31 percent by 1981.[45] In 1970, McNamara also launched the bank's first efforts to address environmental issues in its projects when he argued that development institutions should help developing countries avoid or reduce the damage that economic development can have on a country's environment.[46] (See Chapter 6 for a case study of the bank's environmental behavior.)

Many of McNamara's ideas showed foresight and vision, but implementing them was another story. Several analyses of the McNamara years highlight the drawbacks of his management style and are quite critical of the problems the bank faced in putting these ideas into practice. Environmental activist Bruce Rich argued that the means of implementing McNamara's vision "were infused with a disquieting lack of accountability, a structure of top-down control, and a thrust toward domination."[47] The technocratic approach that McNamara favored, Rich argued, also relied on easily quantifiable targets and the means to achieve those targets, and vastly increased pressure on bank staff to increase lending at the expense of project quality. Many loans, instead of benefiting the poorest of the poor, ended up in the pockets of powerful elites, and instances of corruption began to appear.[48] As more evidence surfaced of rural development projects ending in failure, it became clear that the bank's rapid expansion had left it overextended.[49]

Problems related to project quantity outpacing quality reflected the fact that McNamara instituted lending targets that in many regions or countries were hard for bank staff to meet without sacrificing quality. McNamara himself was optimistic that both quality and quantity could be achieved. Warren Baum, a senior bank official at the time said "He had one word that was not part of his vocabulary, and that was the word 'trade-off.' He thought you could have more of everything."[50]

Structural Adjustment Lending

The bank faced many big challenges in the 1980s. Among them were the international debt crisis of the early 1980s and the first major campaign by civil society actors attacking the bank for gross negligence in its environmental and social activities in the late 1980s.

The decade opened with dramatically higher interest rates (stemming from US Federal Reserve Chairman Paul Volcker's strategy to raise US interest rates in order to reduce inflation), a second oil price shock (1979–1980), and a continuing global recession. Many developing countries responded by borrowing more and more, mainly in dollars, to cope with higher import costs, less demand for their exports, and the need to pay off existing debt. Since the old debt was linked to US interest rates, every time US rates increased by one percentage point, developing country borrowers faced an additional four to five billion dollars a year in interest payments. By the second half of 1981, as an example, Latin American countries together were borrowing over a billion dollars a week, with most of the funds going toward paying off existing debt.[51] Finally, in 1982, Mexico triggered an international debt crisis when it announced that could not pay its debt. Over the next 12 months, over 30 countries joined Mexico in seeking to renegotiate their debt.[52]

The debt crisis had a major impact on the bank's sister institution, the IMF, which became the lead agency in negotiating debt rescheduling with countries, working alongside the US Treasury and Federal Reserve, their counterparts from other industrialized countries, major private banks, and the World Bank. An IMF-approved program was necessary to reopen the spigot of financial flows for suffering borrower countries, and thus avert what some feared could be a collapse of the entire international financial system. But, while the World Bank didn't play a leading role in debt rescheduling, it was still a major actor, and deeply impacted, as it worked to devise new lending programs for countries once IMF programs were agreed.

In particular, the crisis strengthened the role that new Structural Adjustment Lending programs (SAL) had in the bank's portfolio. SALs were launched in 1980 as loans that supported macroeconomic adjustment or changes to the policy environment rather than funding specific projects. In other words, they were loans to help governments change key economic policies, which was very different from loans for building infrastructure. The recessionary global economic environment prompted many economists inside, and outside, the bank to argue that reforms in trade, prices, taxes, and institutions were critically important in helping struggling economies return to health.[53] Related to this was the idea that loans for projects would be more successful if governments were encouraged to end policies that distorted markets in ways that impeded growth. As Willi Wapenhans, author of an important critique of the bank, noted, "The best investment project cannot succeed in a bad policy or regulatory environment!"[54] Indeed, many poor countries had built uncompetitive industries to supply their own markets; many were also printing money to pay for their increased spending. The free market advice dispensed by the World Bank was aimed at getting countries to cut their trade barriers, free prices, and encourage more competition and less state ownership.[55] Another advantage of adjustment lending was that it could be disbursed quickly and used to help governments with balance of payment financing in the middle of a crisis, whereas traditional project loans were disbursed more slowly.[56]

The bank's use of SALs increased dramatically as a result of the debt crisis, as they became part of new World Bank lending packages negotiated with countries under the bigger auspices of debt rescheduling.[57] One of the unintended consequences of this is that SAL was very similar to what the IMF asked countries to do and increased overlap and turf-battling between the two organizations. After some political ballet with the United States and other shareholders, the bank and fund agreed to some rules of collaboration to avoid overlap. These apparently were ignored in 1988 after the World Bank negotiated a loan with Argentina before the IMF had concluded its own negotiations with the government, prompting more feuding between the two organizations and ultimately a renewed attempt by the bank president and fund director to produce new guidelines to strengthen collaboration.[58]

SALs also faced growing criticism over the years, because in practice, adjustment and stabilization tended to impose more hardships on people, especially the poor. Adjustment usually required countries to reduce spending, for example, which slowed economic growth, increased unemployment, and cut programs in areas like education and health. The bank and the fund agreed that these policies were necessary to get at the underlying problems behind a country's poor economic health. Economist John Williamson later dubbed these policies, the *Washington Consensus*, a term that stuck, because the IMF and World Bank views were shared by the US Treasury, Federal Reserve, and some Washington, DC-based think tanks.[59] Some studies even argued that SAL could not be shown to have any positive effect on economic policies or economic growth.[60] SAL itself changed over time. It began with a focus on macroeconomic stabilization and adjustment but quickly grew to include a variety of other issues, such as the role of the government and producing greater market efficiency.[61]

Jumping ahead and foreshadowing the next section, in 2004 the bank replaced adjustment lending with what it called *development policy lending*. The new form encompassed a broader variety of instruments, including SAL, as well as poverty reduction support credits and sectoral adjustment loans. It was part of the broader thinking that governments should take ownership over policy sector reform in a process that should include consultation with stakeholders (and it didn't hurt to deflect criticism of the old SAL). By this time, such lending accounted for around one-third of total bank annual lending.

Growing Criticism

Attacks on the bank's practices emerged in the 1980s, and grew stronger and louder in the 1990s. As Mallaby noted, curiously, the attacks facing the bank came from both the political Right and Left. During the Reagan-Thatcher era, which emphasized deregulation and the promotion of free markets, the bank was criticized by the Right as being bloated and inefficient. How hypocritical it was, they observed, to have a bloated, bureaucratic public institution preach free market reforms to the world. The Left, in turn, criticized the bank's promotion of free market policies and argued whether the bitter economic medicine it was forcing down the throats of poor countries was leaving these countries even worse off.[62] In some cases, government budget cuts, or related actions, such as the reduction of food subsidies, triggered violent protests and riots.[63]

This decade saw the growing activism of nongovernmental organizations (NGOs), especially those that acted as watchdogs over the bank. As Chapter 6 discusses in detail, the first major campaign against the bank was launched by US-based environmental NGOs in the mid-1980s, which attacked the bank for funding projects that caused widespread environmental degradation.

In the 1990s criticism of the bank increasingly spilled over from environmental issues into other issues, such as high levels of poor country debt, the bank's insufficient attention to gender issues, and its overall performance. The array of critics also widened to include more international voices, and even internal bank voices. Indeed, some very strong criticism came from inside the bank itself. A 1992 in-house report on the quality of the bank's portfolio was scathing. Headed by bank president Lewis Preston's special advisor and bank Vice President, Willi Wapenhans, it argued that the bank's portfolio had deteriorated over the years, with a corresponding increase in projects with "major problems." These projects increased from 11 percent to 20 percent of the bank's portfolio between fiscal years 1981 and 1991. The number of projects that were "unsatisfactory" upon completion surged from 15 percent of the sample reviewed in fiscal 1981 to 37.5 percent in fiscal 1991.[64] Compliance by borrowers with legal covenants written into loans was "startlingly low." Five years later, another in-house review by the bank produced another highly critical report. It blamed both borrowers and bank staff for poor project outcomes. Borrower factors included weak or no government commitment, inadequate participation by beneficiaries, and broader macroeconomic instability. Bank weaknesses included overoptimistic staff and overambitious projects. "Institutional amnesia is the corollary of institutional optimism," it said.[65]

The 50th anniversary of the bank and fund in 1994 was a focal point for a variety of activists who criticized both institutions. A coalition of more than 200 US NGOs launched a "50 Years is Enough" campaign, aimed at the "immediate suspension of the politics and practices" of both institutions for causing "widespread poverty, inequality, and suffering among the world's peoples and damage to the world's environment."[66] Among the various disruptions NGOs accomplished at the 1994 Annual Meeting of the bank and fund in Madrid was one that occurred during the keynote speech by bank President Lewis Preston. As he began his speech, fake dollar bills rained down on the audience: one said "World Bankenstein;" another said, "This note is redeemable for ozone destruction." The audience looked up to see "two athletic activists," who "had scaled the steel girders high up in the roof, and were looking down on the armed police officers below with mocking impunity."[67]

Responding to Criticism, Facing New Challenges

The bank responded to criticism in a number of ways. For example, in the 1990s, it developed new policies on information disclosure (to be more transparent) and continued to expand its staff and safeguard policies in environmental and social areas; it created an Inspection Panel to increase accountability by investigating complaints from people affected by the bank's projects. It took on a greater leadership role in global environmental governance, for example, as a key player in the Global Environmental Facility (GEF), set up in 1991 to help poor countries address global environmental problems, and in the ozone depletion and biodiversity regimes.

Along with the IMF, the bank launched a new process by which qualifying highly indebted poor countries would have more say in their future by developing and implementing their own poverty reduction policies as a condition for debt relief. It also created new oversight mechanisms to monitor projects and make sure they complied with bank safeguard policies.

Many of the bank's efforts to placate critics took place under James Wolfensohn, bank president between 1995 and 2005. Wolfensohn, a successful investment banker, who was also deeply involved in philanthropic causes (he chaired New York's Carnegie Hall and the Washington, DC-based Kennedy Center for the Performing Arts, for example), knew he was inheriting a troubled institution and openly admitted the bank had made plenty of mistakes in the past.[68]

He took over the bank a few years after the collapse of the Soviet Union and end of the Cold War. This was a time when the former Soviet-bloc states were embarking on a dramatic and fundamental transformation of their economies from centrally planned to market based, and many of them depended heavily on the bank for its know-how and resources. Other new post-Cold War tasks arose, too, such as the reconstruction in the Balkans after a devastating war that ended in the mid-1990s. In the middle of Wolfensohn's first five-year term, the 1997 Asian financial crisis hit, rocking the world's financial foundation and causing millions to fall back into poverty and suffering.

Wolfensohn, like McNamara, felt strongly about putting poverty reduction front and center on the bank's agenda, and indeed he was a key figure at the bank championing debt relief for poor countries. By the time Wolfensohn took office, many developing countries were again drowning in debt. Uganda, for example, spent $2.50 per citizen a year on health, and $30 per citizen toward repaying its debt.[69] Many inside the bank and fund were concerned that this situation would lead to more financial instability. It also sent the wrong message to the debtor countries that were working hard to repay their debt. It seemed unfair if their less rigorous neighbors received relief. This is akin to a frugal consumer watching others who overspent and got into trouble with debt, receive government help.

Wolfensohn believed that for the bank to do a better job in alleviating poverty, it had to listen more to what borrowers wanted and widen the bank's approach to development. He launched several initiatives related to these ideas. One was an extensive restructuring of the bank to make it more client-oriented and less bureaucratic. In the late 1990s, the bank launched a "matrix management system," with a goal to improve the use of resources by allowing vertical and horizontal relationships to allow staff to more easily share information, and thus, work more efficiently. Matrix management was the latest fashion in the corporate world, where it was seen as promoting more teamwork and less hierarchy.[70] More staff moved from Washington, DC, into "the field," so they could work more closely with client countries. Wolfensohn also courted his critics, meeting with members of NGOs and sometimes siding with them against bank staff.[71]

Another initiative was the 1999 Comprehensive Development Framework (CDF), touted as a "holistic long-term vision" for poverty reduction. It called for countries to be in the driver's seat in terms of their development agenda; strong partnerships to be built between donors, borrowers, civil-society, and private sector actors; and a transparent development agenda. Wolfensohn's concept also called for development to advance on all fronts, from building roads to inoculating children against disease.

All of these ideas sounded good, at least on paper or in principle. It seems hard to refute the idea that bank staff should work more closely with client countries and let those clients have more say in their development process. It seems hard to refute a call for partnerships and public participation.

Yet, almost all of Wolfensohn's initiatives came under fire. The CDF was criticized inside the bank as being banal or lacking focus, in the sense that people were quite aware that development is complex and a holistic initiative trying to fix everything might end up fixing nothing. Some argued that the CDF reflected the impact of too much pressure from NGOs, who represented a variety of issues and were pushing the bank to move in too many directions. And what seems to be obvious at first glance may not be so upon deeper reflection. For example, closer relations between bank staff and client country have resulted, in some cases, in what has been called "clientitis," where overly cozy relations make it harder for the bank to cut off loan disbursements where there is evidence that borrowers are violating major loan conditions or are involved in corruption.[72] Getting involved in public participation also puts the bank smack in the middle of domestic politics, where it technically is not supposed to operate, and can create uncomfortable tensions with borrower governments that, in fact, are the bank's members. Nevertheless, despite various attacks on the framework, it was still embraced by the world's major donors. The matrix management system was also problematic in practice, given how it shifted budgetary power and added more layers of reporting complexity.[73]

Wolfensohn himself was also attacked as hurting the morale of bank staff with a management style that created mistrust and resentment. He was charismatic and passionate, but also famous for his temper and for having a poor relationship with top staff. Staff turnover was high during his tenure. It became more fashionable to deride the bank as its supporters dwindled. A commission set up by the US Congress in 1998 even proposed that the bank be dramatically scaled back, change its name to World Development Agency, and give funding for issues such as tropical disease and the environment.[74] Rich argued that Wolfensohn squandered an opportunity to choose priorities for the bank by "trying to be all things to all people and not choosing among what may be fundamentally irreconcilable priorities."[75] Financial journalist Stephen Fidler nicely summarized the position the bank faced by the end of the 1990s:

> If the World Bank were a private corporation, the 1990s would have been a decade of record profits, and the institution a growth stock. With the decline of communism, governments around the world became disillusioned with the public sector as an engine of growth and embraced market capitalism. . . . The bank's potential for influencing the path of the global economy seemed to be on the verge of an unprecedented expansion. But that potential was never realized. Without a clear mandate or well-defined products, the World Bank instead finds itself in crisis. . . . Critics speak freely of closing the institution altogether, or at least of radically shrinking it.[76]

The MDGs

In 2000 the United Nations launched the Millennium Development Goals (MDGs), a set of ambitious poverty reduction goals for the entire world to pursue. Heads of state from most of the world's countries endorsed these eight goals at a Summit meeting at UN headquarters amid great pomp and ceremony. The goals, discussed in Chapter 3, were touted as "an unprecedented promise by world leaders to address, as a single package, peace, security, development, human rights, and fundamental freedoms."[77]

The bank embraced the MDGs and said it was weaving them into its operations in a number of ways, including them in the Comprehensive Development Framework dialogues and various country and sectoral strategies it developed with client states. As Chapter 3 notes, implementing the MDGs was tougher than expected for everyone and the outcomes were mixed across regions and countries. The goals were challenging for the bank in part because they were not a good fit with the bank's own strategy on poverty reduction. The UN-driven MDG process focused on a comprehensive vision for the world, where all developing countries addressed the same millennium targets. Success was measured at the global level. But global goals may not fit an individual country's own goals. The bank and IMF developed a poverty reduction strategy called the poverty reduction strategy paper (PRSP) process, launched in 1999. Under the PRSP process, qualifying highly indebted poor countries (known as HIPC in the world of bank-related acronyms) were required to organize and implement a PRSP as a condition for debt relief, with the idea that resources freed up by debt relief could be used toward poverty reduction. The philosophy behind the PRSP was similar to that behind Wolfensohn's Comprehensive Development Framework, with the country in the "driver's seat," determining its own poverty reduction strategy for a three-year period, and presenting it through the PRSP. The PRSP was tailored to a country's specific circumstances to fit its limited resources and capacity.

There was some talk of using PRSPs to operationalize MDGs so a government could organize its priorities and coordinate external aid. For most countries, however, a realistic PRSP was simply not enough to reach the MDGs. And many countries had PRSP goals that differed from MDG goals. As countries tried to respond to both MDG and PRSP requirements, many felt they were jumping through hoops generated by externally driven processes that had little to do with their priority economic goals. Some countries felt they may have been in the driver's seat, but the car was more than likely a taxi, with the World Bank (and IMF) telling the driver where to go, how to get there, and paying the fare.

THE LAST DECADE

Public opinion of the bank went from bad to worse when Wolfensohn stepped down in 2005 and was succeeded by Paul Wolfowitz. Wolfowitz, appointed by US President George W. Bush, was highly unpopular among many of the bank's donor countries as well as bank staff; in a previous position as US Deputy Secretary of Defense, he had been a leading architect of the controversial US invasion of Iraq in 2003. He was a leading conservative foreign policy thinker, a personable intellectual, who also had a reputation throughout his 30-plus year career in Washington as lacking strong managerial skills. One bank critic immediately grumbled that Wolfowitz's appointment confirmed the views of some that the bank was a "tool of US foreign policy."[78] Wolfowitz had a brief honeymoon, as many were pleased he quickly won pledges from more donor aid at the G-8 Summit in Gleneagles, Scotland, while attacking US farm subsidies as a trade barrier to poor countries. But the grumbling continued. For example, Wolfowitz launched an anti-corruption initiative for countries receiving bank loans. Many staff were critical of the anti-corruption unit, which they argued seemed to target countries in an arbitrary way. Wolfowitz's decision to suspend aid to programs in India, Congo, and Uzbekistan was criticized as appearing to be ad hoc, since aid continued to flow to other countries with governance problems, such as Pakistan. Wolfowitz's supporters, in turn, believed that much of the criticism against him could be traced to European leaders who were critical of his role in the Iraq war, and others who were simply resistant to the changes he sought.[79]

Tensions between Wolfowitz and his in-house and external critics exploded after news was leaked that he approved a generous compensation package when his romantic partner, a World Bank employee, was reassigned outside the bank (due to their relationship). His partner, Shaha Riza, was upset she would have to leave her job at the bank once he began his new role, so, according to *The Economist*, he bowed to "her demand for a substantial rise in pay, sharp annual increases, and a big promotion (or two) on her return."[80] Wolfowitz argued that he followed the advice he received from the bank's ethics committee and directors, while a report by a committee of the bank's directors concluded that he violated the institution's rules and the "ethical obligations" of his contract.[81] One interesting aspect of this scandal was that many of the bank's staff campaigned noisily against Wolfowitz. There has never been such a vocal revolt by the staff of an international organization to remove its top official. Staff booed the president and wore blue ribbons that symbolized their support for "good governance," which meant removing Wolfowitz. Wolfowitz announced his resignation in May, effective June 30, 2007, after the bank's board accepted his assertion that the he had acted in an ethical manner and that his mistakes were made in good faith. *The Wall Street Journal*, which supported Wolfowitz, in turn, published an editorial calling his removal "a bureaucrats' coup via a made-up scandal, the real purpose of which was to undermine an anti-corruption agenda that threatened the bank's zero-accountability, self-dealing culture."[82] European officials, always hoping to end the practice of a US-chosen bank chief, agreed in advance that a quick Wolfowitz departure would earn their support for the United States choosing the next chief.[83]

The Bush administration moved quickly to nominate Robert Zoellick as Wolfowitz's successor and Zoellick's confirmation by the bank's board went smoothly. Zoellick, a protégé of James Baker (Treasury Secretary 1985–88 and Secretary of State 1989–1992), was president of the bank between 2007 and 2012. When he joined the bank, he was known for his leadership in international trade, for example helping to launch the Doha Round at the WTO when he was US Trade Representative (2001–05). He also pushed for trade pacts with a variety of countries around the world and played a key role in negotiations with China and Taiwan for membership in the WTO. While at the helm of the bank, Zoellick sought to better encourage sustainable growth and better assist the private sector. "Before long," he wrote, the bank was "shifting from debating existential questions to asking new, practical ones. What could it do to promote food security and better nutrition in the face of rising food and fuel prices?"[84] Indeed, months before the global financial crisis hit, Zoellick was trying to raise awareness of the impact sharply higher food and energy prices were having on the developing world, calling for an increase in aid and other responses. The bank then announced a Global Food Crisis Response Program that contained over $1 billion of lending.[85] Zoellick's other priorities were to continue promoting good governance and to reduce corruption, to use the bank as leverage to bring in other sources of financing, and to "democratize development," in part by launching an Open Data Initiative to make thousands of data sets freely available.

The Wolfowitz Scandal

Zoellick presided over the bank during the global financial crisis. Bank lending increased sharply as the bank lent over $230 billion in the period between 2007 and 2012, reaching a peak of $44.2 billion in commitments in fiscal 2010.[86] Between 2008 and 2009 alone, IBRD commitments increased by 144 percent from $13.5 billion to $32.9 billion.

When the global financial crisis hit, the bank did not have the same center stage role as the IMF, discussed in Chapter 8. But it responded quickly, with the top borrowers including middle income countries like Mexico, Poland, India, Brazil, South Africa, China, and Indonesia. The loans were mainly in the form of development policy lending rather than project lending.

Jim Yong Kim, who took over in mid-2012, was the first bank president with a background as a physician and anthropologist. Also unlike past presidents, he was an expert in public health. As noted above, one of his major goals is to eliminate extreme poverty by 2030. The bank estimates that 1.2 billion people live in extreme poverty, defined as under $1.25 a day.

Lending declined during Kim's first two years in office, given that the worst of the global financial crisis was over. From the peak of $44.2 billion committed in fiscal year 2010, IBRD commitments declined to $15.2 billion in fiscal year 2013, before showing signs of improvement to $23.5 billion in fiscal year 2015. For the first time in the bank's history, IDA commitments to the world's poorest countries surpassed IBRD commitments in fiscal year 2013, at $16.3 billion.

Kim's tenure at the bank has been rocky. He launched a major reorganization of the bank in 2013 after deciding the bank's structure was one of its major problems. He announced $400 million in cost cuts over three years, and he fired three top managers. Early reviews of the major restructuring were not positive. The *Financial Times*, for example, said the bank had "descended into a kind of restructuring hell," leaving the bank in "turmoil."[87] The new

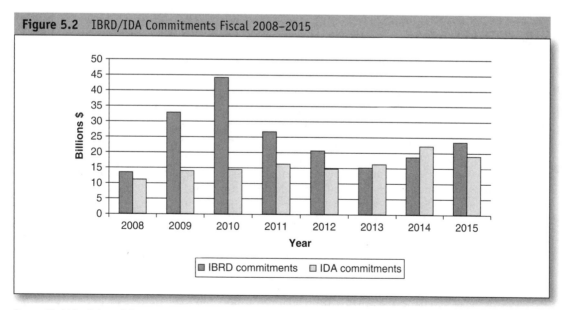

Figure 5.2   IBRD/IDA Commitments Fiscal 2008–2015

Source: World Bank Annual Report 2015.

structure moved power in the bank to 14 "global practices," which cover sectors such as agriculture, finance, water, and poverty. The previous matrix system had placed budgetary power in the regions and included specialist and country groupings, as well as "networks" that were meant to be "knowledge centers serving skill pools." For an outsider, understanding the complexity of the management structure could be very daunting. As the bank's Operation Evaluation Group described it:

> The matrix system—a dual matrix, bank-wide between the six Regions and four networks, and in each Region between Country Management Units and Sector Management Units—was to be facilitated by dual accountability for technical quality and an internal labor market for staff renewal and mobility.[88]

While the bank has seen several leadership changes in a relatively short period of time, and each leader puts his own imprint on the bank, the continuing expanding mission and clearly mixed performance have remained constant. In terms of mission, over the past decade the bank has focused more on issues of corruption, transnational crime, border porousness, and postconflict reconstruction. The bank remains a prominent actor in working with the global economic architecture and is today the largest source of funds for issues such as health-related programs in poor countries.[89] Yet, its expanding role has been accompanied by more evidence of mixed performance. The trend of declining lending, along with the existence of two new multilateral banks—the NDB BRICS and the AIIB—will mean more soul-searching about the bank's future and ability to respond to global development challenges. One open question is whether the current set of goals will be aided by the organizational restructuring. Stated differently, is the proposed solution a good fit with the identified problem?

PERSPECTIVES ON THE BANK

Scholars and practitioners have offered a number of arguments over the past decade to explain this, and some do not seem to become dated over time. As Jessica Einhorn, a former bank managing director wrote in 2001, the bank's mission "has become so complex that it strains credulity to portray the bank as a manageable organization."[90] She pointed the finger at the existence of too many constituencies pressuring the bank to address a growing number of issues. The problem she identified has not really changed in the subsequent years. Mallaby, who wrote a book about Wolfensohn, made a similar argument, but more dramatically, attributing the bank's performance problems to constant pressure from "an army of advocates" that "pounds upon the World Bank's doors, demanding that bank projects bend to particular concerns." He likened these advocates to a Lilliputian menace, bringing down the bank-as-Gulliver.[91] Naturally, leading advocates disagree. Rich has a different take on the bank's woes. He has argued that institutional incentives favor getting money out the door quickly—quantity over quality—is a leading problem, but more than that, the bank itself is a "microcosm of global society's geopolitical and environmental contradictions."[92]

Some scholars have applied a principal-agent model to explain the World Bank's performance problems, but in different ways. One argument is that bank performance has suffered in some issues when the bank-as-agent acted too independently and had to be reined in by its principals, the member state shareholders.[93] Another view argues that some of the bank's difficulties stem from the principals themselves, because it is they who have delegated conflicting or complex tasks that are simply too difficult for the bank to implement well.[94] An obvious example going all the way back to the bank's birth is that the institution was created to be both a financial institution and a development institution. It is a bank in the sense that its main function is to lend money; it is a development institution in the sense that it was created to promote a wide range of activities that go well beyond what a private bank does.[95] These two agendas don't always work smoothly together, such as cases where the bank is trying to urge borrowing governments to undertake policy reforms that are not directly related to the economy, such as social policies. Therefore, some of the tensions the bank struggles with are built into its character.

Another good example of the tension among bank tasks can be seen in attention to addressing good governance issues and the issue of corruption. These issues directly conflict with the provision in the bank's Articles that loans should be extended without regard to political considerations. Over time, the bank's shareholders have made it impossible for the bank *not* to address political issues in its work.

Bank analysts sometimes use the word *hypocrisy* when discussing the institution. Fidler, writing about the Wolfensohn years, argues that Wolfensohn wasn't simply a source of some of the bank's problems; rather, he was a "symptom of the hypocrisy of the leaders of rich countries." These are the people who "speak so eloquently on behalf of the world's poor yet do not care enough to prevent the decline of the world's top development institution."[96] Political scientist Catherine Weaver argued that "organized hypocrisy" inevitably arises at the bank, given the disparity between what it is expected to do and what it is able to do. Examples include its weak compliance with its own policies and tepid efforts to carry out new tasks.[97] This hypocrisy, she argued, plays a paradoxical role at the bank, because it can act as a tool or a liability. As a tool, in the form of paying lip service, it helps the bank shield itself from incompatible demands. But when the bank is caught in what she labeled "an act of hypocrisy," its legitimacy may be undermined, with further repercussions on its ability to do its work.[98]

Amid all the criticism, there are voices urging people to remember how difficult the bank's job truly is. The bank may be arrogant at times, argued Katherine Marshall, but it is also "tackling some of the world's hardest issues and should be expected to fail in many of its efforts."[99] Indeed, it should do a better job of openly acknowledging the difficulty of its work. Private sector investment in development countries, for example, often assumes a high degree of risk and expects a certain degree of failure. Devesh Kapur, John P. Lewis, and Richard C. Webb have pointed out that, in effect, the bank's project lending in developing countries has some similarities with venture capital investment, which, by definition, assumes a high degree of risk and expects a certain degree of failure. Some countries and sectors, by definition, are obviously more risky than others.[100]

CONCLUSION

It seems like almost every decade or so the bank is at a crossroads, deciding how best to face development challenges and external economic pressures, while reviewing its internal policies and structure. Critics perennially wonder about the bank's ability to translate its research into action, to learn from its mistakes, and to meet various external challenges and implementation challenges. There is almost constant concern that the bank is groping for relevance. While some of these issues reflect power politics among major shareholders, organizational politics, the politics and other conditions at the project and recipient country level, and issues related to bank leadership, it is also true that they reflect just how difficult it is to "do" development in practice. Economists, policymakers, civil society actors, and others have been thinking for decades about the best way to reduce poverty, for example, and we still don't have consensus. Whether one agrees with or criticizes the World Bank, it is likely to remain a central figure in the debates about the practice and goals of development.

BIBLIOGRAPHY

Beattie, Alan, and Edward Alden. "Shareholders' Dismay at Lack of Consultation." *Financial Times*, March 16, 2005.

Country Economics Department. "Adjustment Lending: An Evaluation of Ten Years of Experience." In *Policy and Research Series*. Washington, DC: World Bank, 1988.

Crider, John H. "Monetary Parley Called for July 1." *The New York Times*, May 27, 1944, 1.

Danaher, Kevin. *10 Reasons to Abolish the IMF & World Bank*. 2nd edition. New York: Seven Stories Press, 2004.

Drezner, Daniel W. "The System Worked: Global Economic Governance During the Great Recession." *World Politics* 66, no. 1 (2014): 123–64.

Easterly, William. "What Did Structural Adjustment Adjust? The Association of Policies and Growth with Repeated IMF and World Bank Adjustment Loans." *Journal of Development Economics* 76 (2005): 1–22.

Einhorn, Jessica. "The World Bank's Mission Creep." *Foreign Affairs* September/October (2001): 22–35.

Fidler, Stephen. "Who's Minding the Bank?" *Foreign Policy,* September/October (2001): 40–50.

Frieden, Jeffry A. *Global Capitalism: Its Fall and Rise in the Twentieth Century*. 1st ed. New York: W.W. Norton, 2006.

Garrett, Laurie, and Scott Rosenstein. "Missed Opportunities: Governance of Global Infectious Diseases." *Harvard International Review* 27, no. 1 (Spring, 2005): 64–69.

Gutner, Tamar. "The Political Economy of Food Subsidy Reform: The Case of Egypt." *Food Policy* 27 (2002): 455–76.

Gutner, Tamar L. *Banking on the Environment: Multilateral Development Banks and Their Environmental Performance in Central and Eastern Europe*. Cambridge: MIT Press, 2002.

———. "Explaining the Gaps between Mandate and Performance: Agency Theory and World Bank Environmental Reform." *Global Environmental Politics* 5, no. 2 (2005): 10–37.

Haas, Ernst B. *When Knowledge Is Power: Three Models of Change in International Organizations*. Berkeley: University of California Press, 1990.

Haines, Walter W. "Keynes, White, and History." *The Quarterly Journal of Economics* 58, no. 1 (1943): 120–33.

Harding, Robin. "Man on a Mission: World Bank." *Financial Times*, April 8, 2014, 9.

Huttlinger, James. "Robert S. McNamara at the World Bank Group: A Chronology of Significant Events." Washington, DC: World Bank, 2003.

Independent Evaluation Group. "The Matrix System at Work: An Evaluation of the World Bank's Organizational Effectiveness." Washington, DC: World Bank, 2012.

International Bank for Reconstruction and Development. "Fifth Annual Report to the Board of Governors 1949–1950." Washington, DC: World Bank, 1950.

——. "Second Annual Report." Washington, DC: International Bank for Reconstruction and Development, 1947.

Kapur, Devesh, John P. Lewis, and Richard C. Webb. "Introduction." In *The World Bank: Its First Half Century*, edited by Devesh Kapur, John P. Lewis, and Richard C. Webb. Washington, DC: Brookings Institution, 1997.

Kim, Jim Yong, Aaron Shakow, Jaime Bayona, Joe Rhatigan, and Emma L. Rubin de Celis. "Sickness Amidst Recovery: Public Debt and Private Suffering in Peru." In *Dying for Growth: Global Inequality and the Health of the Poor*, edited by Jim Yong Kim, Joyce V. Millen, Alec Irwin, and John Gersham, 127–53. Monroe, ME: Common Courage Press, 2000.

Kraske, Jochen. *Bankers with a Mission: The Presidents of the World Bank, 1946–91*. New York: Oxford University Press, 1996.

Mallaby, Sebastian. *The World's Banker: A Story of Failed States, Financial Crises, and the Wealth and Poverty of Nations*. New York: Penguin Press, 2004.

Marshall, Katherine. *The World Bank: From Reconstruction to Development to Equity*. New York: Routledge, 2008.

Mason, Edward S., and Robert E. Asher. *The World Bank since Bretton Woods*. Washington, DC: Brookings Institution, 1973.

McNamara, Robert S. "Address to the Board of Governors." Washington, DC: International Bank for Reconstruction and Development, 1973.

Meltzer, Allan (Chairman). "Report of the International Financial Institution Advisory Commission." Submitted to the US Congree and US Department of the Treasury. Washington, DC: March 8, 2000.

Moggridge, D. E. *Maynard Keynes: An Economist's Biography*. New York: Routledge, 1992.

Nielson, Daniel L., and Michael J. Tierney. "Delegation to International Organizations: Agency Theory and World Bank Environmental Reform." *International Organization* 57, no. 2 (2003): 241–76.

Phillips, David A. *Reforming the World Bank: Twenty Years of Trial—and Error*. New York: Cambridge University Press, 2009.

Pollack, Jacques. "The World Bank and the IMF: A Changing Relationship." In *The World Bank: Its First Half Century*, edited by Devesh Kapur, John P. Lewis, and Richard Webb, 473–521. Washington, DC: The Brookings Institution, 1997.

Portfolio Management Task Force. "Effective Implementation: Key to Development Impact." Washington, DC: World Bank, 1992

Quality Assurance Group. "Portfolio Improvement Program: Draft Reviews of Sector Portfolio and Lending Investments." Washington, DC: World Bank, 1997.

Rich, Bruce. *Foreclosing the Future: The World Bank and the Politics of Environmental Destruction*. Washington, DC: Island Press, 2013.

———. *Mortgaging the Earth: The World Bank, Environmental Impoverishment, and the Crisis of Development*. Boston, MA: Beacon Press, 1994.

———. "The World Bank under James Wolfensohn." In *Reinventing the World Bank*, edited by Jonathan R. Pincus and Jeffrey A. Winters, 26–53. Ithaca, NY: Cornell University Press, 2002.

Steil, Benn. *The Battle of Bretton Woods: John Maynard Keynes, Harry Dexter White, and the Making of a New World Order*. Princeton, NJ: Princeton University Press, 2013.

Stern, Nicholas, and Francisco Ferreira. "The World Bank as 'Intellectual Actor.'" In *The World Bank: Its First Half Century*, edited by Devesh Kapur, John P. Lewis, and Richard Webb, 523–609. Washington, DC: The Brookings Institution, 1997.

Theunis, Georges. "Report of Commission II (International Bank for Reconstruction and Development) to the Executive Plenary Session, July 21, 1944." In *Proceedings and Documents of the United Nations Monetary and Financial Conference*, 1100–05. Washington, DC: United States Government Printing Office, 1944.

United Nations General Assembly. "Agreement between the United Nations and the International Monetary Fund." New York: United Nations, 1947.

United Nations General Assembly. "Outcome Document of the Special Event to Follow up Efforts Made toward Achieving the Millennium Development Goals." New York: United Nations, 2013.

United Nations. "The Millennium Development Goals Report 2005." New York: United Nations, 2005.

Vice President and Corporate Secretary. "Second Report of the Ad Hoc Group." Washington, DC: World Bank, 2007.

Volcker, Paul A., Gustavo Gaviria, John Githongo, Jr., Ben W. Heineman, Walter Van Gerven, and John Vereker. "Independent Panel Review of the World Bank Group Department of Institutional Integrity." Washington, DC, 2007.

Wapenhans, Willi A. "Efficiency and Effectiveness: Is the World Bank Group Well Prepared for the Task Ahead?," edited by Bretton Woods Commission. Washington, DC: Bretton Woods Commssion, 1994.

Weaver, Catherine. *Hypocrisy Trap: The World Bank and the Poverty of Reform*. Princeton, NJ: Princeton University Press, 2008.

Weisman, Steven R. "Deal is Offered for Chief's Exit at World Bank." *The New York Times*, May 8, 2007, 1.

Winters, Matthew S. "The World Bank and the Global Financial Crisis: The Reemergence of Lending to Middle-Income Countries." *Whitehead Journal of Diplomacy and International Relations* 12, no. 2 (2011): 57–72.

Wolfowitz, Paul. "An Outsider's Fate." *The Economist*, May 19, 2007, 65.

Woods, Ngaire. *The Globalizers: The IMF, the World Bank, and Their Borrowers*. Ithaca, NY: Cornell University Press, 2006.

World Bank. "Annual Report 1989." Washington, DC: World Bank, 1989.

———. "Annual Report 2012." Washington, DC : World Bank, 2012.

———. "Annual Report 2013." Washington, DC: World Bank, 2013.

———. "Bretton Woods Conference." http://web.worldbank.org/WBSITE/EXTERNAL/EXTABOUTUS/EXTARCHIVES/0,,contentMDK:64054691 ~ menuPK:64319211 ~ pagePK:36726 ~ piPK:36092 ~ theSitePK:29506,00.html.

———. "Pages from World Bank History: Richard Demuth." January 24, 2003. http://web .worldbank.org/WBSITE/EXTERNAL/EXTABOUTUS/EXTARCHIVES/0,,contentMDK:20087 352 ~ pagePK:36726 ~ piPK:36092 ~ theSitePK:29506,00.html.

———"The World Bank's First Loan May 9, 1947." Washington, DC: World Bank. http://web .worldbank.org/WBSITE/EXTERNAL/EXTABOUTUS/EXTARCHIVES/0,,contentMDK:20035 704 ~ pagePK:36726 ~ piPK:36092 ~ menuPK:56273 ~ theSitePK:29506,00.html.

———"World Bank Group Strategy." Washington, DC: World Bank, 2013.

World Bank and International Monetary Fund. "2005 Review of the Poverty Reduction Strategy Approach: Balancing Accountabilities and Scaling up Results." Washington, DC: The World Bank, The International Monetary Fund, 2005.

Ziegler, Chuck. "The World Bank's First Loan May 9, 1947." Washington, DC: World Bank. http://web.worldbank.org/WBSITE/EXTERNAL/EXTABOUTUS/EXTARCHIVES/0,,content MDK:20035704 ~ pagePK:36726 ~ piPK:36092 ~ menuPK:56273 ~ theSitePK:29506,00 .html.

Zoellick, Robert B. "Why We Still Need the World Bank." *Foreign Affairs* 91, no. 2 (2012): 66–78.

"Zoellick's Clean-up Duty." *The Wall Street Journal*, May 31, 2007, A14.

6 World Bank Case Study
Environmental Behavior and Performance

The World Bank's activities in the area of environment offer insights into the challenges the institution has faced over the years in trying to juggle its various mandates, meet the needs of its member state shareholders, respond to civil society accusations and criticism, deal with public relations fiascos, and understand how to actively engage in changing definitions of *development*.

This is a tale of contradictions and possibly hypocrisy.[1] It is a tale of how the bank's work in the 1980s prompted the first major campaign by environmental nongovernmental organizations (NGOs) against it. The NGOs accused the bank of promoting enormous environmental destruction, which resulted in hurting, rather than helping, people in developing countries. That campaign provided a model for subsequent anti-globalization (and other) campaigns against the bank and other major international organizations and the more wide-ranging criticisms of its action (or inaction) in other areas, such as human rights and gender. The bank responded to criticism by environmentalists with a variety of institutional and policy reforms over the years, including its efforts to mainstream environment into all of its work, rather than treating it as a stand-alone area of activity. Its responses in the area of environment have also influenced its broader efforts to reform itself.

Since the late 1980s, the bank has become a global leader in many transboundary environmental issues. It is an implementing agency for the Global Environmental Facility (GEF), set up in 1991, and for the Montreal Protocol's Multilateral Fund, set up in 1990. It has played a leadership role in several international environmental programs related to seas (including the Baltic, Caspian, Red, and Mediterranean). In the late 1990s, it helped to set up the World Commission on Dams. The bank is a major international source for funding to support biodiversity. It is also a leader in efforts to combat climate change. The Group of Eight (G8) industrialized countries in 2005 called for the bank to develop a "clean energy investment framework," or a plan for promoting clean energy investments in developing countries.[2] Its 2013 strategy for reducing extreme poverty and improving prosperity also calls for "raising the profile of climate change as a leading development issue," with the argument that climate change risks impact development.[3] It makes billions of dollars in loans to mitigate against climate change and also for adaptation and oversees billions in climate investment funds. It finances solar energy projects, offers social safety nets to people impacted by drought, and studies flood risks in countries vulnerable to increases in sea level. It also publishes research reports on climate change, which make suggestions for how countries can respond. Finally, the bank has also declared that it is becoming carbon neutral and is reducing its own greenhouse gas emissions.

Despite these apparent accomplishments external and even internal criticism are still present. The bank is attacked for financing environmentally controversial projects and not heeding its own policies, or having policies or projects that are at cross-purposes. For example, in the area of climate change, some commentators have pointed out that while the bank is trying to address climate change it is also continuing to finance coal-fired power plants.[4] One environmental group argued that the bank has been the second largest source for publicly financed coal-fired power plants in the past 14 years.[5] The bank's internal independent evaluation group has piped in, stating that while the bank's environmental project performance has improved since the mid-1990s, there is still wide variation between successful and unsuccessful projects throughout the world, and it has continued to do a poor job in monitoring and evaluating the environmental impact of its projects and programs.[6] The bottom line is that the bank's environmental performance is more a zigzag than an example of slow and steady improvement. Forward steps have been accompanied by some backward steps, sometimes simultaneously.

This chapter begins by posing and answering two basic conceptual questions: what is the relationship between environment and development, and how do the bank's development activities impact the environment? It then describes the evolution of the environment initiative at the bank and shows the various factors along the way that prompted or pushed the bank into an ongoing series of reforms. It shows the uneven nature of the bank's efforts to address environmental issues in its work. The chapter then turns to some of the analytical perspectives on the issue, highlighting the views of scholars and other analysts on whether and how the bank's environmental performance has improved or deteriorated and why.

ENVIRONMENT AND DEVELOPMENT

The major activity of a multilateral development bank (MDB) such as the World Bank is to promote economic development. As Chapter 5 explained, what development means and how it should be nurtured is a moving (and expanding) target. Over the years, there has been growing awareness that economic development is inextricably linked to the environment. Development clearly puts pressure on the environment, because it involves changes such as clearing land, building power plants and highways, or damming rivers. Even poverty reduction can hurt the environment when it results in more cars, refrigerators, or other trappings of higher income. Economic growth obviously can exacerbate environmental problems. It can mean more factories producing more goods (that use natural resources or are wrapped in plastic) and more pollution. It can mean deforestation from logging, the overuse of water resources, soil degradation, and so on. The relationship between development and the environment is complex. For example, more roads may reduce traffic jams (and emissions), but they may also result in more people buying and driving cars (more emissions).

Global awareness of the relationship between environment and development started coalescing in the 1960s, and the ways that we think about this relationship has evolved considerably over the subsequent years. The 1972 United Nations Conference on Human Development, also called the Stockholm Conference, was the first global conference to focus on a single issue. It helped to legitimize the idea that environmental issues were something that all countries should care about, but it was also clear at the conference that many developing countries still believed that environmental concerns were rich country problems. One African delegate made the provocative statement that his country wouldn't mind more pollution, if that's what it took to industrialize.[7] It is worth pointing out a virtually forgotten fact that the World Bank was called upon to help define the issues that the conference would address, and an early document the bank produced was used as a foundation for the conference's final declaration.[8] The 100 plus states that attended (which did not include the Soviet bloc) signed the declaration that contained 26 very general principles on how the global environment should be managed. For example, Principle 4 states that

> Man has a special responsibility to safeguard and wisely manage the heritage of wildlife and its habitat, which are now gravely imperiled by a combination of adverse factors. Nature conservation, including wildlife, must therefore receive importance in planning for economic development.[9]

The conference also produced an "Action Plan," with 109 additional recommendations. Perhaps its most notable accomplishment was its role in recommending the creation of the United Nations Environment Programme (UNEP), which is a focal point of the UN's work on environmental issues.

In the 1980s a number of large environmental disasters played a role in growing global interest in environmental issues. These included the following disasters:

- The 1984 chemical accident in Bhopal, India, where tons of toxic gases were released at a Union Carbide pesticide plant, ultimately killing thousands of people.
- The 1986 major explosion of the Soviet nuclear reactor in Chernobyl, which released radioactive clouds across the western Soviet Union and throughout Europe (east and west).
- The 1986 spill of around 30 tons of herbicides and insecticides from a Sandoz chemical plant into the Rhine River, near Basel, Switzerland. This resulted from a fire at the plant.[10]
- The 1989 *Exxon Valdez* oil spill in Alaska, one of the world's largest oil spills (over 10 million US gallons of Prudhoe Bay crude oil), which killed enormous numbers of birds, sea mammals, and fish.

An important moment in the development of global norms on development and environment issues was the 1987 publication of *Our Common Future*, a report of the UN's Commission on Environment and Development. This report, also known as the Brundtland Report, named after its chair, former Norwegian prime minister Gro Harlem Brundtland, was an international best seller. It argued that environmental degradation was hardly a rich country problem; rather, economic development was inextricably linked to the environment. For example, it pointed out that

> agricultural policies may lie at the root of land, water, and forest degradation. Energy policies are associated with the global greenhouse effect, with acidification, and with

AP Photo/John Gaps III

Cleaning up the Exxon Valdez
oil spill at Prince William Sound,
April 13, 1989.

deforestation for fuelwood in many developing nations. These stresses all threaten
economic development. Thus economics and ecology must be completely integrated in
decision making and lawmaking processes not just to protect the environment, but also
to protect and promote development. Economy is not just about the production of
wealth, and ecology is not just about the protection of nature; they are both equally
relevant for improving the lot of humankind.[11]

The report defined and popularized the term *sustainable development*, which is now widely
used as a way to talk about integrating environment and development. Sustainable development is defined as economic activity that "meets the needs of the present without compromising the ability of future generations to meet their own needs."[12] Stated differently, it means
development that lasts (is sustainable) without making future generations worse off.
This obviously general definition inspired an entire literature trying to translate it into more
practical terms and/or criticizing it for being so vague.

The bank itself contributed to operationalizing and conceptualizing sustainable development with suggestions on how to turn the general ideas into workable government
policies. Its 1992 *World Development Report* examined specific ways that environment
and development are connected and brought in an economic perspective, such as how to
think about trade-offs, how to build costs into decision-making, and when and how
market-based incentives and regulation may be appropriate to help change people's
behavior.[13]

That same year, the 1992 United Nations Conference on Environment and Development
(called UNCED, or the Earth Summit) was held in Rio de Janeiro and at the time was the largest
international conference in history. More than 110 heads of state, over 9,000 official delegates

attended, with 2,400 NGO representatives and another 17,000 people involved in a parallel forum for NGOs.[14] The conference was held on the twentieth anniversary of the Stockholm Conference, with a goal of taking a big step forward to forge strategies to address environmental degradation while promoting development. In the two decades following Stockholm, problems such as climate change, ozone depletion, and deforestation, among others, grew worse, with more scientific evidence pouring in all the time. The UNCED conference had an ambitious agenda. It produced the Rio Declaration of Environment and Development (27 nonbinding principles on how states should promote sustainable development); a nonbinding statement on forest management to encourage sustainable management of different types of forests; and a 294-page nonbinding "Agenda 21" with chapters on a variety of sectors and topics that describe problems (such as poverty, desertification, and land degradation) and offered policy suggestions for addressing them. Two international treaties were also signed at the Earth Summit: the UN Framework Convention on Climate Change and Convention on Biological Diversity.

The Earth Summit raised global consciousness about the relations between environment and development. Nonetheless, it was not considered to be a big success. Developing countries were concerned about the costs of making additional commitments to the environment, and "aid fatigue" was also an issue in the years following the Summit. Indeed, the cost of implementing the recommendations made in Agenda 21 was estimated to be $625 billion, but nowhere remotely near that amount was pledged at the Earth Summit (or since).[15] NGOs remained critical that governments around the world would not pay enough attention to the environmental consequences of globalization.

The next big stop in the evolution of the environment/development connection was the 2000 Millennium Summit, where heads of state endorsed the Millennium Development Goals (MDGs). They, included Goal 7, "Ensure environmental sustainability," which was broken down into three indicators and eight specific targets (see Table 6.1). The existence of this specific goal as one of the eight affirms the fact that world leaders acknowledge the intersection of environmental sustainability with other goals linked to poverty reduction.

As noted in Chapter 3, the newest initiative is the Sustainable Development Goals (SDGs) that also contain a number of specific goals on sustainable development, including the areas of water and sanitation, energy, climate change, marine resources, and terrestrial ecosystems. Like the MDGs, they are also ambitious.

Today there is definitely more widespread recognition that the pursuit of environmental sustainability, poverty reduction, and economic growth are interconnected. The norm has spread, although action often lags far behind. There are undoubtedly pockets of successful activities that have produced positive outcomes for development and the environment at the local, regional, and global levels, but also constant evidence of unsustainable development and environmental degradation.

HOW MIGHT BANK ACTIVITIES IMPACT THE ENVIRONMENT?

Before turning to the history of the bank's relationship with the environment, we can identify some of the direct and indirect impacts it might have on the environment through its lending and nonlending (analytical) activities.

Table 6.1   Indicators and Targets for Goal 7

Target 7.A

Integrate the principals of sustainable development into country policies and programmes and reverse the loss of environmental resources

Indicators
7.1 Proportion of land area covered by forest
7.2 CO_2 emissions, total, per capita and per $1 GDP
7.3 Consumption of ozone-depleting substances
7.4 Proportion of fish stocks within safe biological limits
7.5 Proportion of total water resources used

Target 7.B

Reduce biodiversity loss, achieving, by 2010, a significant reduction in the rate of loss

Indicators
7.6 Proportion of terrestrial and marine areas protected
7.7 Proportion of species threatened with extinction

Target 7.C

Halve, by 2015, the proportion of the population without sustainable access to safe drinking water and basic sanitation

Indicators
7.8 Proportion of population using an improved drinking water source
7.9 Proportion of population using an improved sanitation facility

Target 7.D

Achieve, by 2020, a significant improvement in the lives of at least 100 million slum dwellers

Indicators
7.10 Proportion of urban population living in slums

Source: United Nations, *Official List of MDG Indicators*, http://mdgs.un.org/unsd/mdg/Host.aspx?Content=indicators/officiallist.htm

The bank's *direct impact* can be positive or negative. The most obvious *direct positive impact* is through a project designed specifically to address major environmental issues. An example would be projects to increase energy efficiency or conservation in a municipality, to provide sewage treatment, to improve land management, or to protect nature or promote conservation of biodiversity in a particular region. One example is a bank-funded "efficient lighting and appliances" project in Mexico that included replacing 23 million inefficient light bulbs with compact fluorescent lamps in medium-income homes.[16] Even projects or other activities that are not explicitly "environmental" can have a positive impact on the environment. For example, a loan by the bank's private sector financing arm, the International Finance Corporation (IFC), which allows for the purchase of modern manufacturing technology, may reduce pollution simply by replacing older technology.[17]

An example of *direct negative impact* would be a project that causes environmental degradation. Given that almost everything the bank does has some impact on the environment, the question is how to define *negative*. In practice, critics of the bank focus on projects that have caused enormous environmental degradation. They are less likely to criticize something like a mass transit project, which creates pollution, but in decreasing the number of cars on the road may simultaneously result in a net decrease of harmful emissions.

Examples of an *indirect positive* impact would be research or advice from the bank that contributed to a change in government policy toward the environment. An example would be bank leadership in agenda setting exercises that lead to a new consensus on a country's or region's environmental priorities. Another example would be the bank's safeguard procedures resulting in a project design altered to avert environmental damage.

An *indirect negative* impact might include something like lending for macroeconomic policy changes that reduce government spending for the environment, and this reduction in spending then contributes to an increase in environmental degradation. Another example would be cases where bank loans allow a government to free up resources to pursue actions that damage the environment.

Table 6.2   Examples of Environmental Impacts

	Positive	Negative
Direct Impact	A project that improves the environment	A project that causes environmental degradation
Indirect Impact	— Loans for policy and institutional reform (versus projects) that result in more energy efficiency or reduced pollution — Research and advice that contribute to changes in government policy or institutions that ultimately result in improved environment	— Loans for policy and institutional reform (versus projects) that reduce government spending, which then impacts environmental spending — Research and advice that contribute to changes in government policy that harms environment

EVOLUTION OF BANK'S ENVIRONMENTAL ACTIVITIES, POLITICS, BEHAVIOR

The bank's environmental history can be broken into three parts.[18] The first part, from around 1970 to 1987, began with the birth of environment as an issue to be directly addressed and the subsequent emergence of evidence that some bank projects were, in fact, causing enormous environmental harm. The second period, 1987 to the late 1990s, was a dynamic period of change in the bank's policies, staffing, environmental actions, and portfolio, which was also accompanied by some problematic projects and ongoing criticism by environmental groups. The third period, from the late 1990s to the present, is characterized by some uneven steps. Some organizational and policy changes reduced the importance of the environment as a sector, along with efforts to fold it into broader issues of poverty reduction via the MDGs. In fact, in the latest period there has largely been less attention to the "greenness" of individual projects. This may be changing under Jim Yong Kim's presidency, with its emphasis on climate change, and the fact that "environment and natural resources" is one of the bank's new 14 global practices.

Birth of an Environmental Initiative

Bank president Robert McNamara launched the bank's first attempts to address environmental issues in its work in 1970, when he announced that the bank had a role to play in helping countries avoid or mitigate the environmental damage caused by economic development. He created a new unit within the bank to address environmental issues, the Office of Environmental and Health Affairs, which later became the Office of Environmental Affairs (OEA). In fact, the bank's leadership in this area was acknowledged at the time, and McNamara was the keynote speaker at the 1972 Stockholm Conference. Bank staff officials also drafted an early document that resulted in the conference's "Declaration, Principles, and Recommendations."[19]

Unfortunately, the OEA had little power and staff. With only three specialists by 1983 (growing to five by 1985), it sought to try to reduce environmental damage of bank projects, but only saw project documents late in the project preparation cycle. This meant it was too late to make changes. The small team also had no ability to block projects from board approval. The bank's environmental actions were generally superficial. As Robert Wade noted, "what the bank did under the label of 'the environment' included residual things like the relocating of a power line so as not to spoil the view from a game lodge, matters that no one else wanted to deal with."[20]

By the early 1980s, the environmental movement had taken off and grown, and a group of Washington, DC-based environmentalists became increasingly aware that a number of World Bank projects were causing enormous environmental degradation. This group, which included the Natural Resources Defense Fund (NRDC), the Environmental Policy Institute (which later merged with Friends of the Earth), and the National Wildlife Federation, began investigating the bank's environmental claims and found more evidence of destruction, which prompted them to launch a campaign for environmental reform at the bank. Many other groups joined them, and soon the campaign became international. The environmentalists succeeded in getting the US House Subcommittee on International Development Institutions and Finance to hold hearings on the topic of multilateral banks and the environment. When the hearings opened June 29, 1983, according to Bruce Rich, who was a lawyer with NRDC and one of the leaders of the NGO campaign,

> The witnesses recounted case after case of environmental and social disasters financed by the bank and its sister institutions: huge dams that displaced indigenous peoples, botched irrigation schemes that contributed to the spread of waterborne diseases such as malaria and schistosomiasis, cattle ranching schemes that destroyed tropical forests, and massive resettlement projects . . .[21]

Two of the most egregious projects were the Polonoereste project in northwestern Brazil and the Transmigration program in Indonesia. For the former one, officially known as the Northwest Regional Development Program, the bank lent more than $450 million in the early 1980s to promote agricultural colonization and road building in the state of Rondônia. The idea behind the highways was to link the more populous parts of Brazil in the south to the northwest, through the pristine rainforests that were home to thousands of indigenous people. The agricultural component was to build settlement centers and attract settlers to grow export crops, such as coffee and cocoa. Ironically, the project documents explicitly note the goals of protecting the environment and the indigenous population.[22] The NGOs gathered evidence that the project had encouraged the unexpected, massive migration of colonists and that this migration, in turn, overwhelmed support efforts. The large number of colonists overwhelmed support efforts and resulted in slash and burn agriculture and then deforestation that ravaged huge swaths of land. Life-threatening diseases also spread through the area and hit the indigenous communities especially hard.[23] The project was clearly a disaster and was the topic of its own special hearing of the House Science and Technology Subcommittee on Natural Resources, Agricultural Research, and Environment.[24]

In Indonesia, the infamous Transmigration project was an attempt to resettle millions of poor Indonesians from the more populated inner islands to the sparsely populated outer islands, which were also the location of indigenous tribes and pristine rainforests. The $500 million project attracted millions more in bilateral and other aid and aimed to reduce poverty in the inner islands, while promoting the economic development of the outer islands.[25] The ideas sounded fine, but in practice, human rights and environmental critics pointed out that the project was political in nature, since it allowed Indonesia's corrupt military regime to move Javanese people from the inner islands to a more "politically unreliable" part of the country, where guerrilla warfare had been going on for twenty years.[26] The result of the project, as Rich noted, was "a legacy of environmental ruin," which included tens of thousands of kilometers of deforestation, an increase (rather than decrease) in poverty, and failure on a large scale. Settlers abandoned areas where agriculture was impossible due to poor soils, and violent conflicts and massacres occurred in several of the sites.[27]

In the end, more than twenty hearings on MDB performance were held by six Congressional subcommittees between 1983 and 1987. The US Congress responded by developing recommendations for environmental reform of the MDBs, which included an increase in environmental staff, greater consultation with NGOs and environmental and health ministries in project preparation, and more environmentally beneficial projects. The NGO campaign also succeeded in gaining support from other major bank shareholders and as important, the US Treasury, the World Bank's official US shareholder. The bank was under fire as never before.

1987 to the Late 1990s: Criticism Prompts Reform, and More Criticism

In July 1986, former Republican Congressman Barber Conable became the president of the bank. He was sympathetic to the NGOs' concerns and launched a major reform of the bank's organizational structure and environmental approach. Conable publicly admitted the bank's behavior was poor. Among the organizational changes were the creation of a new central environmental department to take the lead in developing policies and undertaking research; new environmental offices in the bank's regional technical departments to be the "watchdogs" over bank projects; and a growing number of new environmental positions, which over the next handful of years would total around 300 staff and long-terms consultants. Congress also pushed the bank, through the Treasury, to propose new environmental assessment (EA) procedures to ensure projects were better designed to avert or reduce potential environmental harm.

The bank seemed to turn itself around relatively quickly from being the source of so many environmental disasters to being an environmental leader. It continued to develop new policies and other due diligence procedures. It developed a portfolio of projects that had the environment as a primary goal. It developed several policies on the environment in between the late 1980s and late 1990s, including management of wildlands (1986), environmental policy for dam and reservoir projects (1989), water resources management (1993), indigenous people (1991), and a revised policy on environmental assessment (1991).[28] As noted in this chapter's introduction, the bank became the lead implementing agency of the Montreal Protocol's Multilateral Fund in 1990 and the GEF in 1991. It became the agenda setter, facilitator, and leader in a number of regional environmental initiatives in the late 1980s and early 1990s. It moved environmental staff into country departments so they could more actively involved in project design and implementation. In 1992, the year of the Rio conference, as noted above, the bank published the seminal report, *Development and the Environment*. In 1993, the bank set up an Inspection Panel, a three-member commission, to investigate complaints against the bank's work; and in 1994, it adopted an information disclosure policy. By 1995, the bank had an active portfolio of $10 billion in loans in 62 countries, where the primary objective of the loan was improving environmental management.[29] These are all examples of ways that the bank responded to criticism by NGOs and major shareholders, and the changes reflected the growing importance of issues such as accountability and transparency. The changes reflected growing understanding in parts of the bank about the intersection of environment and other major bank development goals, and much of this work reflected the activities of individuals inside the bank who were experts on different aspects of environmental in different sectors where the bank worked.

But while many of these changes were taking place, the bank continued to work on some very controversial projects and receive criticism from different quarters. The evidence of contradiction created fresh momentum for NGO criticism of the bank. One disastrous set of projects involved the Narmada River in India, where the Indian government planned to build a series of large and small dams over many years for hydropower, irrigation, and drinking water. Unfortunately, these plans also required submerging thousands of villages, destroying forests, and displacing tens of thousands of poor people. Opponents argue the projects would produce an enormous social and environmental tragedy.[30] The bank agreed to provide $450 million in loans and credits for the first stage of this scheme, the construction of the Sardar Sarovar dam and its related canals, as early as 1985. Somewhat ironic in light of the protest against the project that followed was the fact that bank staff were thinking about environmental issues in designing the first dam and canals to reduce waterlogging and salinity.[31]

The grassroots campaign by Indians resisting the projects eventually gained the support of an international group of NGOs, which included many of the people already putting pressure on the bank. By 1987, the transnational campaign against Narmada called on the bank to stop funding the dam because the bank had no clear resettlement plan and had not resolved the environmental issues related to the dam's construction. This was a passionate campaign that ultimately involved around 250 groups from 37 countries.[32]

The Sardar Sarovar dam controversy was the topic of one of the US congressional oversight hearings held in 1989, which, of course, was two years after the bank had announced its environmental reforms. For environmentalists like Rich, the controversy showed more than ever the bank's inability to reform itself.[33]

In late 1990, thousands of people protested in India by taking a "long march" through the three states most impacted by the dam. Their goal was a nonviolent occupation of the site. A standoff with police at one of the borders promoted some of the leaders to begin a hunger strike that ended 26 days later on the announcement that the bank would order an independent review.[34] The resulting Morse Commission's review (named for former US Congressman and former director of UNDP Bradford Morse, its lead writer) was a scathing criticism. It bluntly stated that both the bank and India shared responsibility for the fact that the projects were flawed and the bank was not enforcing its own environmental and resettlement policies. The involuntary resettlement caused by the projects, it said, "offends recognized norms of human rights."[35] It concluded, "There appears to be an institutional numbness at the bank and in India to environmental matters. . . . The tendency seems to have been to justify rather than to analyze; to react rather than anticipate."[36]

The World Bank's board first voted to continue, despite the fact that major shareholders such as the United States, Germany, Japan, Canada, and the Nordic countries favored suspension. A year later, in 1993, the balance finally tipped toward cancelling, so the Indian government decided not to ask for additional bank funding in order to avoid a formal vote. This was seen as a face saving effort for both parties.[37]

Sardar Sarovar was one of a handful of other controversial projects in the late 1980s through the mid-1990s. And along with protests and criticism came more bank reform. In the early 1990s, in response to the criticism, the bank commissioned an internal review of its portfolio. The review team, led by former bank President Lewis Preston's special advisor and bank vice president Willi Wapenhans, found evidence that the bank's portfolio had deteriorated over the years. Over a third of the bank's completed projects were seen as "unsatisfactory." Projects with "major problems" jumped from 11 percent in 1981 to 20 percent in 1991.[38]

Some of the controversial projects involving the bank were also dams, like Sardar Sarovar, which made the bank the focus of an international coalition of dam opponents. Its 1993 water policy sector guidelines acknowledged the poor performance of some of its projects. In 1997, the bank and the World Conservation Union (IUCN) hosted a Large Dams Workshop that brought together NGO critics, bank staff, and officials from companies that built dams. Although the atmosphere was not always collegial, the group agreed to set up a world commission on large dams with a goal of developing new criteria for standards for dams and guidelines to promote "best practices."[39] The resulting World Commission on Dams began meeting in May 1998 with twelve commissioners, including environmental and human rights NGOs, a multinational engineering firm, government officials from Australia, China, South Africa, and others. It produced its conclusions in November 2000. The report acknowledged many problems associated with large dams, such as their negative impact on aquatic ecosystems, significant impact on "poor, vulnerable, and future generations," and tendency toward cost overruns and below target-generation performance. It recommended a focus on more comprehensive assessment for water and energy that shifted away from dams and the importance of devising "core values" for accountability, equity, and efficiency in the decision-making process.[40] The response to the report was predictably mixed, with dam opponents generally more positive than dam proponents.[41] The bank's response was to announce it would "reengage" with this type of large and controversial project, but with a "more effective business model," that would "put development impact first."[42]

Late 1990s to the Present: Zigzag Performance

The two plus decades have been a period where the uneven nature of bank environmental actions continues. The big question is, "how does it all add up?" Most of the scholarly literature is critical of the bank for not finding a way to match its leadership aspirations with its environmental practices.

As noted in Chapter 5, bank president James Wolfensohn (1995–2005) initiated a number of activities to placate bank critics. Focusing specifically on the environment, some of the positive moves during his presidency included the establishment of a new quality assurance and compliance group to oversee staff compliance with bank safeguard policies; increased lending for biodiversity, energy efficiency, and renewable energy projects; a fuller range of advisory and analytical activities; and ongoing attempts to mainstream the environment into all of the bank's activities. The idea of mainstreaming is that environmental issues shouldn't be treated as a separate set of projects or policies within the bank, but rather as issues that should be integrated into everything the bank does, such as its sectoral work.

A 2001 bank-wide environmental strategy report affirmed that promoting sustainable environmental development was a part of the bank's overarching development and poverty reduction goals. The strategy proposed moving forward by emphasizing areas where the environment/poverty reduction links are strong: mainstreaming, particularly across sectors, and focusing on issues where global and local benefits intersect.[43] The challenge at the heart of the strategy is that it was full of ideas of activities the bank can undertake but also recognized that the commitment of its borrowers is central to the strategy's success.

The most recent strategy, for the period from 2012 to 2022, lays out a vision for what the bank calls "a green, clean, and resilient world for all."[44] It defines *green* as "a world in which natural resources, including oceans, land, and forests, are sustainably managed and conserved to improve livelihoods and ensure food security." *Clean* is low pollution. *Resilience* has to do with responding to shocks and better adapting the problem of climate change. While the 2001 strategy focused on the World Bank itself, the new strategy includes the IFC and MIGA (its Multilateral Investment Guarantee Agency). The strategy has a long list of actions that the World Bank will undertake, including developing better accounting measures to address the ecosystem, more partnerships with a variety of actors to work on cleaning up the oceans, helping countries to reduce pollution, and working on regional environmental issues and strategies.

Meanwhile, the bank deepened its collaboration with environmental NGOs in issues like conservation, forests, and biodiversity. Finally, as noted, the bank has taken on a leading role in climate change governance. A big move in this direction took place under Robert Zoellick's presidency, where the bank argued that climate change is a clear threat to development and not just a matter for rich countries. A 2008 Strategic Framework for Development and Climate Change document adopted by the bank sought to mainstream climate change issues at the country and project levels. It also contained a number of ambitious goals, including a pledge to sharply increase its financing for energy efficiency and new renewable energy and hydropower.[45] Energy efficiency financing increased following this initiative, with the bank lending $7.5 billion for such projects between fiscal years 2008 and 2013.

The bank has also played a leading role in managing new carbon funds, as the major industrialized countries tasked the bank in 2008 with oversight over $7 billion in climate investment funds (CIFs), which offered developing countries low-interest loans and grants to finance projects and programs to confront climate change.[46] The bank is also active in the global carbon market that started up in the 2000s. Under the Kyoto Protocol's Clean Development Mechanism (CDM) and Joint Implementation (JI), industrialized countries can meet some of their greenhouse gas reductions by investing in projects that reduce emissions in other countries (developing countries under CDM, and essentially developed under JI).[47] The idea is that it does not matter where in the world emissions are reduced, as long as they are reduced somewhere. The bank managed the first carbon fund to finance projects that would count under the CDM and JI. The fund, set up in 2000, was a partnership with six countries and 17 countries and has capital of $180 million. Today, the bank is the trustee of 15 such carbon initiatives, funded by wealthy countries and companies, which are capitalized at more than $3 billion and have funded 145 projects in 75 countries.

In spring 2013, World Bank President Kim and UN Secretary-General Ban Ki-moon co-chaired the first "Sustainable Energy for All" advisory board. This is a UN initiative aimed at promoting energy efficiency, universal access to electricity, and renewable energy. Under the Kim presidency, climate change was confirmed as a "leading development issue" and the bank has committed billions more in lending with "mitigation co-benefits" and "adaptation benefits."[48] Recent projects include a $20 million IDA grant, with other sources contributing an additional $124 million for a wind farm in Yemen, and a $110 million IDA project aimed at improving climate resilience in Sri Lanka.

While these steps by the bank are positive and important, there are also several trends that may be seen as backward steps. First, environmental lending has not seen a clear upward trend. In fact, environmental lending, as measured by the bank, declined sharply between 1994 and 2002, from 18 percent of the bank's total commitments in 1994 to just 5 percent in 2002, which was also linked to a decline in specific projects that focused on pollution management and environmental health.[49] While there have been signs of recovery over the past decade, in fact 45 percent of all bank environmentally related commitments went to only four countries: Brazil, China, India, and Mexico. Africa has received the smallest percentage of resources for the environment relative to its share of total bank commitments.[50] Looking at the bigger picture, the Independent Evaluation Group (IEG) concluded in 2014 that the performance of the bank's investment portfolio overall declined between fiscal years 2010 and 2012 to 69 percent of projects being "moderately satisfactory or better" in terms of their outcomes, which was down from 75 percent in fiscal years 2008 to 2010. The IEG blamed overambitious project design and poor supervision as being among the causes, although it recognized the borrowers' own performances have been impacted by the global financial crisis.[51]

Second, as noted above, environmental watchdog organizations are still pointing out inconsistencies between rhetoric and action. The Bank Information Center (BIC) pointed out that in 2008 alone, the World Bank and IFC investment in fossil fuels more than doubled, compared with an 11 percent increase in funding for solar, wind, biomass, and other renewable energy projects. Obviously, fluctuations in lending mean that data for one year may not mean much, but the BIC report identified a trend in increased lending for fossil fuels over several years.[52]

Rich agrees there is "an operational disconnect" between the bank's work on climate change mitigation and adaptation and the fact that it is a major source of publicly financed coal-fired power plants. He pointed out that the bank ignored the recommendations of the 2004 Extractive energy Review (EIR) study the bank itself sponsored, which argued that the bank should focus not on new coal-fired power plants, but on investments in energy efficiency and conservation, emission-reducing projects, energy resource development, and similar issues.[53] During Zoellick's tenure, between 2007 and 2012, program lending grew as project lending shrunk, and the bank's environmental and other social safeguard policies did not apply to the former. There are also more recent efforts inside the bank to weaken its safeguard policies.

A theme of Rich's criticism is the bank's hypocrisy. For example, he noted that part of the Climate Investment Funds can be used to support coal-fired power plants, albeit the more efficient kind. "Even as the bank was promulgating its new climate strategy, it went on a coal-plant financing binge," he concluded. Between 2008 and 2010, "Massive loans . . . totaling some $6.75 billion were dished out for coal plants and associated infrastructure in the Philippines, Chile, Botswana, India, and South Africa," making a mockery of the broader strategy.[54] Hypocrisy was not just confined to issues of climate. For example, he cited an IEG report that pointed out 75 percent of 20 major bank projects in or near tiger habitats between 1994 and 2004 actually posed a direct threat to the habitats. Two-thirds also posed indirect threats. An example would be where a project encouraged tiger poaching. Given that tigers are an endangered species the bank has pledged to help protect, these data are disappointing.[55]

SOME QUASI-INTERNAL CRITIQUES

As this chapter has shown, the bank itself has often been a good source of studies that evaluate its behavior. Internal reports, as well as assessments from its IEG, have been critical as the previous examples have shown, although in general, and unsurprisingly, they often emphasize perceived successes more than most external analyses.

The 2001 environmental strategy report suggested that three broad factors can explain why the bank has only been "partially successful" in supporting environmental sustainability in borrower countries. First, it admitted the bank has been overoptimistic in its attempts to do everything from set environmental objectives to designing complex interventions. This does not allow for all of the "complexity and practicalities of implementation." Second, it pointed out that mainstreaming hadn't yet become a reality. It noted, "Although bank professionals in general are aware of the importance of environmental issues, they often see them as a self-standing agenda and not as an element of their core task of supporting development and poverty reduction." And third, it said client countries themselves are still evolving in their awareness of environmental issues.[56] That was a diplomatic way to say that many client countries did not place environment high on their list of development priorities and need more political will and commitment for the bank's efforts to help and to succeed.

A 2002 report by the bank's internal performance auditor (named the Operations Evaluations Department at the time, but later renamed the Independent Evaluation Group) was even more blunt. Examining the bank's environmental performance in the 1990s, it said, "Environmental sustainability was not integrated into the bank's core objectives and country strategies, and linkages between macroeconomic policy, poverty alleviation and environmental sustainability were not explicitly forged."[57] It concluded, "The modest extent of mainstreaming the environment into the bank's overall program is disturbing."[58]

A 2008 IEG report looked at the effectiveness of the entire World Bank Group in supporting the environment between 1990 and 2007. The report paints a picture of unevenness, with a central argument that while the bank was a global leader in "calling attention to the global importance of environmental sustainability," it has not been successful in moving from what it calls its "upstream" analytical work to its "downstream" activities in its efforts to "integrate these efforts centrally into country programs, incorporate them as requirements for sustainable growth and poverty reduction, and provide lending to help countries address environmental priorities."[59] Even serious environmental problems have been "treated unevenly in bank analytical and/or lending activity."[60] A big problem, the report admitted, was "lukewarm interest" from borrowing countries. But the report didn't just blame borrowing countries. The bank's monitoring and evaluation systems are weak, which prevents the bank from properly assessing, at an aggregate level, the environmental impacts and results of its projects.[61] The IFC in turn, was criticized as insufficiently supervising projects undertaken by intermediaries. MIGA, finally, was critiqued as having insufficient monitoring of the environmental requirements and standards set for some of its projects.[62]

A 2009 IEG "Annual Review of Development Effectiveness" report reviews the implementation of the 2001 Environment Strategy and concludes that the results are "quite mixed." Bank lending levels and general project performance have improved, but the bank's efforts to mainstream environmental initiatives in sectors such as transport and water sanitation have fallen short, and the bank's environmental stewardship is also uneven.[63]

And finally, a 2013 IEG report evaluating the bank's response to addressing climate change concludes that while there have been some good projects, overall its top findings were that "Guidance is lacking on when and how to incorporate climate risks into project design and appraisal"; "Current procedures are ad hoc. Climate risks are sometimes neglected. At the other extreme, climate projects based on complex global models have not been useful for many project-level applications."[64]

EXTERNAL VIEWS AND DEBATES

Most of the external literature on the World Bank is critical of bank performance in general, as previously noted in Chapter 5. The sub-literature on the bank's activities in the environmental sector is predominantly critical, too, but there is still a range of argument and debate.

In the scholarly literature on the bank's environmental performance, Daniel Nielson and Michael Tierney's work made the rare argument that, in fact, after 1994 the bank's environmental performance dramatically improved in terms of its environmental lending portfolio and behavior, mainly due to pressure from bank shareholders and principals that succeeded in reining in the bank (as agent). They argued that there was a statistically significant increase of 15 percent in stand-alone environmental projects between 1994 and 2000.[65]

This author disagreed with those conclusions, arguing in turn that Nielson and Tierney conflated *behavior* with *intention* and used a faulty coding of bank projects that cannot accurately measure environmental behavior or environmental lending.[66] The authors, for example, looked at data on loan commitments, but not implementation, so they had no way to know if a project that was meant to be "pro-environment" in fact resulted in environmental damage.

Several of the bank's most environmentally destructive projects were meant to be *green* in some shape or form.

Susan Park offered an alternative explanation for the environmental changes within the World Bank Group by privileging the role of transnational environmental advocacy networks in determining that and influencing how the World Bank and its affiliates should change their environmental behavior. In her view, nonstate actors have an impact on how IOs internalize norms and ideas, and they do so through socialization.[67]

On the opposite end of the spectrum from Nielson and Tierney is Michael Goldman, who argued the bank's response to criticism of its environmental behavior spurred the expansion of what Goldman calls the bank's "green hegemony." The bank's response was to reinvent itself by adding environmental issues to its neoliberal economic agenda. This, in turn, has given the bank a way to expand the tentacles of its knowledge and power throughout the world. While the bank's influence on knowledge may be less well documented than its role in disastrous projects, it is still extremely important, according to Goldman.[68]

Wade attributed the bank's mixed environmental behavior to what he called the "slipping clutch" of its incentive system. He pointed out gaps between more procedural measures of individual performance, and more outcome-oriented budgetary and rewards systems. It is this incentive gap that has done much to hinder the bank's efforts to mainstream.[69]

And finally, Rich pointed to a variety of reasons behind the bank's poor environmental behavior. The pressure for bank staff to get the money out the door quickly ("pressure to lend") will inevitably hurt project quality; the powerful bureaucracy, driven by a culture of expansion also adversely impacts project choices and design; a culture of secrecy and lack of accountability; some examples of poor leadership at the top of the bank; and more decision-making power for borrowing countries such as China and India, who do not appreciate limits on the types of projects they can borrow money for.[70]

This chapter has framed the bank's environmental performance as mixed, with examples of positive and negative steps. The principal-agent model is useful in explaining some of the gaps in performance, especially where it recognizes the problem of *antinomic delegation*, or the fact that member-state principals give the bank conflicting or complicated tasks that are quite difficult to implement. Examples of this include the macro-level problem of mission creep at the bank and the everyday challenge the bank faces in acting as part financial institution and part development institution.[71] Not everything is automatically the fault of bank staff with member states sitting innocently on the sidelines.

CONCLUSION

While just about everyone, including bank staff, agrees that the bank has a lot of work to do in better addressing environmental issues in its work, there is a wide range of explanations as to what is wrong and how to fix it. It is also true that most of the research to date focuses more on the forest—the big picture—rather than the trees, the individual areas in which the bank works. A more nuanced picture of the bank, focusing mainly on specific issues like biodiversity, climate change, or energy, would offer a clearer account of specific bank actions. But the issue of how to add up the individual sectors is still important.

One of the challenges facing insiders and outsiders who seek to evaluate the bank's environmental performance is that it is not that easy to measure. The World Bank and other multilateral banks have traditionally defined environmental performance via funding objectives and/or showing the degree of compliance with due diligence and safeguard procedures. Emphasizing funding objectives can be done by projects that explicitly have primary environmental goals (i.e., pollution abatement) or projects that have significant environmental components (i.e., energy efficiency measures in a power project). Highlighting due diligence procedures, in turn, is a way of showing how the bank has sought to mitigate or avert environmental degradation in its project, for example, through environmental assessment. In telling the public how it is addressing environmental issues, the bank points out what it is doing in the area of research, agenda setting efforts, and advising borrowers on how to develop priorities and policies.

However, these measures are also imperfect and it is difficult to measure their impact. Funding objectives listed in a project document may not translate into project design or implementation. Indeed, the bank has been accused in the past of funding forestry projects that actually cause deforestation. Pooling together loan amounts to offer an aggregate amount of "environmental lending" doesn't capture the fact that smaller projects may have a greater environmental impact than larger projects. And quantifying activities, such as research and outreach and their impact on domestic policies or specific environmental improvement, is difficult to do.[72] The bank's efforts to mainstream its environmental actions, in turn, also have the negative effect of reducing its attention to individual projects with environmental goals.

The World Bank's 2012 environmental strategy is ambitious. It says everything a good strategy should say. It talks about building on past lessons, finding new solutions, working in partnerships, strengthening knowledge, and prioritizing issues such as climate change and low-emission clean energy development. It lays out green, clean, and resilience agendas for each region of the world. It correctly recognizes that such ideas depend on other ingredients to be successful. (It calls these potential pitfalls "implementation risks.")[73] These include financing from donor countries and capacity in recipient countries. We can add to those a few more conditions for success: political will at both the donor and recipient government level; support from other parts of the bank that may conflict with the strategy (i.e., reduce the number of coal-fired power plants); and attention to project implementation. While it is highly likely we will see uneven implementation, we can hope that the latest set of ideas continues to seep through the bank and its various stakeholders.

BIBLIOGRAPHY

Chomitz, Kenneth, Dinara Akhmetova, and Stephen Hutton. "Adapting to Climate Change: Assessing the World Bank Group Experience." Washington, DC: Independent Evaluation Group, 2013.

Clapp, Jennifer, and Peter Dauvergne. *Paths to a Green World: The Political Economy of the Global Environment*. Cambridge: MIT Press, 2005.

Clark, Dana, Jonathan Fox, and Kay Treakle. *Demanding Accountability: Civil Society Claims and the World Bank Inspection Panel*. Lanham, MD: Rowman & Littlefield Publishing, 2003.

Conca, Ken. *Governing Water: Contentious Transnational Politics and Global Institution Building*. Cambridge: MIT Press, 2006.

Goldman, Michael. *Imperial Nature: The World Bank and Struggles for Social Justice in the Age of Globalization*. New Haven, CT: Yale University Press, 2005.

Gutner, Tamar. "World Bank Environmental Reform: Revisiting Lessons from Agency Theory." *International Organization* 59 (Summer 2005): 773–83.

Gutner, Tamar L. *Banking on the Environment: Multilateral Development Banks and Their Environmental Performance in Central and Eastern Europe*. Cambridge: MIT Press, 2002.

———. "Explaining the Gaps between Mandate and Performance: Agency Theory and World Bank Environmental Reform." *Global Environmental Politics* 5, no. 2 (2005): 10–37.

Independent Evaluation Group. "Annual Review of Development Effectiveness: Achieving Sustainable Development." Washington, DC: World Bank, 2009.

———. "Environmental Sustainability: An Evaluation of World Bank Group Support." Washington, DC: World Bank, 2008.

———. "Results and Performance of the World Bank Group 2013." Washington, DC: World Bank, 2014.

Khagram, Sanjeev. *Dams and Development: Transnational Struggles for Water and Power*. Ithaca, NY: Cornell University Press, 2004.

Mainhardt-Gibbs, Heike. "World Bank Energy Sector Lending: Encouraging the World's Addiction to Fossil Fuels." Washington, DC: Bank Information Center, 2009.

Morse, Bradford, and Thomas Berger. "Sardar Sarovar: Report of the Independent Review." Ottawa, Canada: Resources for the Future, Inc., 1992.

Nielson, Daniel L., and Michael J. Tierney. "Delegation to International Organizations: Agency Theory and World Bank Environmental Reform." *International Organization* 57, no. 2 (2003): 241–76.

———. "Theory, Data, and Hypothesis Testing: World Bank Environmental Reform Redux." *International Organization* 59 (2005): 785–800.

Park, Susan. *World Bank Group Interactions with Environmentalists: Changing International Organisation Identities*. Manchester, UK: Manchester University Press, 2010.

Rich, Bruce. "Foreclosing the Future: Coal, Climate and Public International Finance." Washington, DC: Environmental Defense Fund, 2009.

———. *Foreclosing the Future: The World Bank and the Politics of Environmental Destruction*. Washington, DC: Island Press, 2013.

———. *Mortgaging the Earth: The World Bank, Environmental Impoverishment, and the Crisis of Development*. Boston, MA: Beacon Press, 1994.

United Nations, *Official List of MDG Indicators*, http://mdgs.un.org/unsd/mdg/Host.aspx?Content = indicators/officiallist.htm.

United Nations Environment Programme. "Declaration of the United Nations Conference on the Human Environment." 1972.

van Gils, J. A. G. "Modelling of Accidental Spills as a Tool for River Management." Paper presented at the Chemical Spills and Emergency Management at Sea, Amsterdam, Netherlands, 1988.

Wade, Robert. "Greening the Bank: The Struggle over the Environment, 1970–1995." In *The World Bank: Its First Half Century*, edited by Devesh Kapur, John P. Lewis, and Richard Webb, 611–734. Washington, DC: Brookings Institution Press, 1997.

Weaver, Catherine. *Hypocrisy Trap: The World Bank and the Poverty of Reform*. Princeton, NJ: Princeton University Press, 2008.

World Bank. "Annual Report 2013." Washington, DC: World Bank, 2013.

——. "Climate Change Projects and Programs." World Bank, http://www.worldbank.org/en/

——. "Development and Climate Change: A Strategic Framework for the World Bank Group." Washington: DC, 2008.

——. "Effective Implementation: Key to Development Impact." Washington DC: World Bank, 1991.

——. "Mainstreaming the Environment: The World Bank Group and the Environment since the Rio Earth Summit." Washington, DC: World Bank, 1995.

——. "Making Sustainable Commitments: An Environmental Strategy for the World Bank." Washington, DC: World Bank, 2001.

——. "Promoting Environmental Sustainability in Development: An Evaluation of the World Bank's Performance." Washington, DC: World Bank, 2002.

——. "Restructuring Paper on a Proposed Restructuring of the Efficient Lighting and Appliances Project to the United Mexican States Approved on November 23, 2010." Washington, DC: World Bank, 2012.

——. "Toward a Green, Clean, and Resilient World for All: A World Bank Group Environmental Strategy 2012–2022." Washington, DC: World Bank, 2012.

——. "World Development Report 1992: Development and the Environment." Washington, DC: World Bank, 1992.

——. "Loan Agreement, Northwest Region Development Program—First Phase, between Federative Republic of Brazil and International Bank for Reconstruction and Development." Loan Number 2061. Washington, DC: World Bank, 1981.

"World Bank Climate Funds: 'A Huge Leap Backwards.'" *Bretton Woods Project* Update no. 60 (2008). http://www.brettonwoodsproject.org/art-560997.

World Commission on Environment and Development. *Our Common Future.* New York: Oxford University Press, 1987.

7 The International Monetary Fund

If the IMF had a dollar for every criticism of its purpose and role by the Right, the Left, and the Center, it would perhaps never again have to approach its shareholders for more money to sustain its operations.[1]

The IMF is the scapegoat of first resort.[2]

Recall from Chapter 5 that the IMF was born at the Bretton Woods conference to help manage the international monetary system, to make it more stable and less prone to crises. Over the years, the IMF has become the most powerful source of lending to countries facing economic crisis. Governments that are low on the foreign currency they would use to pay for imports or debts turn to the IMF for short-term loans in hard currency to tide them over. The IMF, in turn, will negotiate a program with the country that requires economic policy changes designed to help the country regain economic health. The "doctor-patient" metaphor is often used to describe the IMF's work—its job is to treat an ailing country with sometimes bitter medicine. Since the early 1980s, the IMF's imprimatur has been necessary for countries in economic trouble to receive fresh loans from the World Bank or private sector banks. The IMF has also been described as a sort of *financial cooperative* whose members are countries. They contribute certain amounts of their own currency and gold to the IMF, called *quotas*, based on their global economic strength. Countries that need help can then draw money from the IMF in globally strong currencies such as the dollar or euro.

Making sense of the IMF has been trickier for the public than making sense of the World Bank, because unlike the bank, the IMF does *not* make loans for *projects*, which are more visible and tangible. In fact, the typical IMF loan is called a lending "arrangement." The IMF works in the area of economic stabilization, and more specifically, through mostly macroeconomic policy tools. When we examine World Bank projects, we can often point to very visual things like the construction of a highway or power plant. Where bank projects have caused harm, we can also literally see it, for example, where a project results in deforestation or the destruction of habitat. It is not as obvious how one can see or explain the harm or good caused by the IMF's recommendations on macroeconomic policy reform. Put differently, it's easier for the average person to understand how a traditional World Bank project may impact poverty or the environment than to understand the effects of monetary or fiscal policy changes on a country. (Let's not forget, however, that the World Bank also makes loans for economic policy reform that are similar to what the IMF does.)

In order to understand what the IMF does and how it works, one must know some basics from international economics, including answers to the following questions: Why do exchange rates matter? What is a trade deficit? How do interest rates affect an economy? What are the causes of economic crisis in an individual country, and how and why does it spread to other countries? What economic policy prescriptions work best when a country is experiencing an economic crisis?

This chapter will answer these questions as it describes and explains the changing role of the IMF in the international economy. It begins by explaining what the IMF was set up to do and how it is governed, before turning to a discussion of the major turning points in the IMF's history. The chapter then examines the views from some major scholars and critics of the IMF and some of the ways the IMF has responded.

The year 2009 was a banner year for the International Monetary Fund (IMF), as the global financial crisis instantly lifted the institution up from a steady decline in lending and legitimacy and put it back into the frontline of actors working to help countries hit hard by external and budgetary crises. The IMF's lending (arrangements approved) had dropped precipitously from over SDR 41 billion[3] in its fiscal year 2002 to SDR 600 million in 2007, as an improved global economy gave many developing countries alternative lending options, and the IMF suffered under the glare of a variety of critics. In 2008 it began cutting its staff, amid a shrinking loan portfolio. This all changed after the crisis hit. For the first time since the late 1970s, even developed countries were seeking help, including Iceland, whose economy faced a sharp meltdown as its banking system collapsed. In 2013, the biggest borrowers were not developing countries, but rather Greece, Portugal, and Ireland.[4] The IMF's role in the global financial crisis is the topic of Chapter 8.

Protestors dressed like zombies at a rally against the visit of IMF Managing Director Christine Lagarde, Manila, November 2012.

Like the World Bank, the IMF has been criticized for causing more harm than good and has drawn the ire of anti-globalization protestors and others who say the IMF increases poverty and suffering in its borrower countries. The IMF's conditionality, the policy strings attached to its loans, has been under attack for years, and for numerous reasons, including: it is too intrusive, it helps to cause financial crises (that the IMF then has to help to fix), and it is too homogenous and not tailored enough to countries with different domestic situations. Like the World Bank, the IMF is trying to redefine its identity to meet, and sometimes resist, changing and growing demands.

THE IMF'S MANDATE AT BIRTH

The IMF was created at Bretton Woods to tackle the types of monetary imbalances and other economic problems that plagued the international economy during the interwar years and contributed to the onset of World War II. The IMF would be at the center of an international monetary system aimed at keeping exchange rates stable. If a country was in economic trouble and needed money (more specifically, because it has a temporary balance of payments deficit), the IMF could offer it a loan. Before proceeding with the IMF's history, it is important to take a step back and understand why the IMF was given these roles, and what they meant in practice.

What Are Exchange Rates, and Why Is Stability a Good Thing?

An exchange rate is the value, or price, of one currency expressed in the other. It is how many dollars you can buy per euro, or how many yen you can buy for a Swiss franc. As J. Lawrence Broz and Jeffry Frieden note, "The exchange rate is the most important price in any economy, for it affects all other prices."[5] It is easy to imagine that the more stable and predictable these rates are, the more confidence investors have to put their money in other countries, and the more confidence importers and exporters have to buy and sell goods from or to other countries. It is less risky for anyone to put money in another country when there is reassurance the other country's currency won't lose its value. This impacts the average individual, too. If your country's currency is weak, it is more expensive for you to travel abroad and to buy certain imported goods.

During the Bretton Woods negotiations, negotiators were keen to set up a system of currency stability to avoid the terrible impact and legacy of the Great Depression, where world trade shrunk dramatically, commodity prices collapsed, and unemployment rose to unprecedented levels. Many countries responded by devaluing their currencies in order to gain some competitive edge vis-à-vis their trading partners. These competitive devaluations were an example of what was called a *beggar-thy-neighbor policy*.[6] If one country, Country A, lowered the value of its currency relative to other currencies, that would make its products relatively cheaper. The result would be Country A would increase its exports and thus the amount of money it was receiving. But if its trade partner, Country B, responded by lowering *its* currency, a vicious cycle began.

The competitive devaluations of the 1930s followed the collapse of what was called the *gold standard*, a system where most of the major industrialized countries at the time promised to exchange its currency for gold, at a set price. This system was formally adopted by Britain in 1819 and took root in most of the other major economies by the 1870s, as countries realized that this type of stability—a currency always convertible to a specific amount of gold—was great for international trade, investment, and even migration, because it created predictability. As Frieden noted, "The gold standard rates of exchange . . . were so fixed for so long that, it is said, schoolchildren learned them by rote because they seemed as stable as the multiplication tables."[7] The system collapsed during World War I, and a form of it was revived between 1925 and 1931. By the time of the Bretton Woods negotiations, many policymakers, businesspeople, and even union officials were wary of returning to the rigidity of the gold standard. They wanted something more flexible, so that governments could use policy tools to help manage the economy in ways that were impossible under the old system.[8]

The fund was designed to manage a new monetary system that was more flexible than the old gold standard, but also more stable than a system of freely floating currencies. The new system was a "modified fixed rate" system, or a "par value" system, where currencies were fixed to the dollar, and the dollar was fixed to the price of gold, at $35 per 1 ounce. The United States government stood behind the agreement and would exchange gold for dollars at this rate. The flexibility built into the system allowed countries to adjust their exchanges rates when necessary (if one felt its exchange rate was too high or too low, for example), but a change of over 1 percent required the IMF's consent. This system allowed for relatively stable and predictable exchange rates, which, in turn, helped to encourage global trade and deepened people's confidence in international investment.

What Is a Balance of Payments "Problem," and What Can the IMF Do About It?

Roles
___
Maintain
 exchange
 rate
Lend $

The fund's other central role was to lend money to countries running low on hard currency. A typical example is a country that is overspending in its trade with other countries. It is buying more (importing) from the world than it is selling to the world (exporting). Since it pays for goods from other countries in dollars, Euros, or other major currencies, having a trade deficit can literally mean that the country's central bank is running out of hard currency. Looking at trade alone, we would say the country is running a *trade deficit*. Looking at the country's larger balance of payments—its complete set of payments and receipts vis-à-vis the rest of the world—we would say it has a *current account deficit*, or a "balance of payments problem."[9] The current account is broader than the trade balance. It includes trade and other measures, such as aid flows. As Paul Blustein aptly put it, discussing the imaginary country Shangri-la, an example used in some of the IMF's teaching materials:

> [I]f Shangri-la runs too large a tab, it may suddenly find itself in the same situation as the individual who has maxed out on his credit cards. Maybe there's an unexpected shock—a sudden surge in the price of imported oil, for example, or a dip in the price of a key export, such as coffee or computer chips. . . . Sources of hard currency from abroad dry up, because foreign lenders conclude that for the foreseeable future, Shangri-la has little prospect of generating enough proceeds from its exports to pay all its obligations to foreigners. At this point, Shangri-la's finance minister and central bank governor are likely to be found stepping out of a limousine in that curved driveway in front of IMF

headquarters. The IMF is the only place an overextended country like Shangri-la can obtain the hard currency it needs to obtain vital imports and keep its economy functioning.[10]

The IMF was set up to be able to give countries short-term loans that would offset the balance of payments imbalances, which, in turn, helped the country avoid readjusting its exchange rates. Since making loans gave the IMF something of a bank-like personality, it naturally sought to make sure that countries would be able to repay these loans, and it wanted to be sure that borrowers were fixing their economic problems, so it began attaching *conditionality* to its loans. Conditionality can be thought of as the policy changes the IMF deems necessary for the country to regain its economic health. As the IMF explains it,

> Conditionality is a way for the IMF to monitor that its loan is being used effectively in resolving the borrower's economic difficulties, so that the country will be able to repay promptly, and make the funds available to other members in need.[11]

What happens is the IMF agrees to lend a specific amount of money to a country, and in return the country complies with the IMF's conditions.[12] The IMF's main form of nonconcessionary assistance is the Stand-By Arrangement, which typically lasts one to two years, with repayment due between three and one-quarter and five years of disbursement. The disbursement of the funds is conditional on the country reaching its economic targets.

In the IMF's early years, conditionality was implicit in some of its lending decisions. Conditionality became codified in the 1950s, and since then it has become extremely controversial, as loan recipients and other critics argued that it was too intrusive and often made things worse rather than better. For example, if the IMF determines that a country has been spending too much, then IMF conditionality may call for spending cutbacks, such as reducing the

A critical view of IMF conditionality.

government's budget. Over time, the IMF's preferred choice of conditionality was clearly what is called in the language of economics as "macroeconomic stabilization based on controlling aggregate demand through fiscal and monetary policy."[13] This meant that a country's balance of payments problems were seen as caused by too much demand (relative to output). The traditional solution, then, was to reduce this demand through fiscal (government revenue collection/spending) or monetary (interest rate, exchange rate) policies. These policy measures tend to create austerity in countries, which can manifest itself as increased unemployment, poverty, malnutrition, and other social and economic ills. Even governments that readily agree to IMF loans with this type of conditionality attached often find it useful to treat the IMF as a scapegoat, blaming it for the country's ills. The IMF's response has been that it is treating the problem, albeit with bitter medicine, but was not the cause of the country's problem.

IMF conditionality was relatively narrow for many years, but increased in number and scope in the 1980s and 1990s, in response to the fund's growing involvement in developing countries as well as the 1982 debt crisis and the 1997 Asian financial crisis, which are discussed below. Instead of having a dozen or so requirements attached to a loan, the IMF imposed 50 plus requirements. As Devesh Kapur noted, "the Asian countries have had to sign agreements that look more like Christmas trees than contracts, with anywhere between 50 to 80 detailed conditions covering everything from the deregulation of garlic monopolies to taxes on cattle feed and new environmental laws."[14] Facing great criticism, the IMF began cutting back on conditionality and produced revised guidelines on conditionality in 2002. Nonetheless, the IMF's Independent Evaluation Office found in a 2007 report that the number of structural conditions had not declined, which resulted in fresh calls by the IMF's board to better implement its new conditionality guidelines. As discussed in Chapter 8, in response to the 2009 crisis, the IMF reviewed its lending framework and announced a number of ways that it would increase flexibility, including streamlining conditionality.

IMF MEMBERSHIP AND GOVERNANCE

Chapter 5 discusses the governance system of both Bretton Woods sisters. Today, the IMF has 188 members, which includes virtually every country in the world. The handful of members of the United Nations that are not members of the IMF include small city states such as Andorra and Monaco, as well as the Communist nations of North Korea and Cuba.

A country is assigned its quota when it joins the IMF, and then it can draw on the currencies it needs when it faces economic difficulty. It pays at least 75 percent of its subscription in its own currency, and the remainder in widely accepted currencies or using the IMF's unit of accounting, the SDR.[15] The size of the quota determines how much money a member can get from the IMF. A member can borrow up to 300 percent of its quota each year; although under special circumstances it can receive more.[16] In fact, the Flexible Credit Line introduced in 2009, allows qualified countries to access much higher percentages of their quota (even up to and beyond 1000 percent) for longer periods of time to protect them from "volatility and spillovers" that may result from global crises.[17] As noted in Chapter 5, the country's voting power reflects the size of its quota.[18]

From time to time the quotas are readjusted to account for a country's changing position in the global economy. The most recent effort to adjust quotas, which was designed to give more voting weight and "voice" to the BRIC countries (Brazil, Russia, India, and China) and other developing countries, is discussed in Chapter 8. Yet, it is also important to recall, as James Vreeland aptly notes, that while the IMF's voting structure is based on a complicated account-ing system, the fact is the board rarely votes. It mainly operates on consensus. Official votes are uncommon, although one of the top officials of the IMF may "keep track of straw polls" so that there is still a sense of what the majority view is.[19] This means that a focus on "chairs and shares" as a way of understanding how the IMF is governed can be misleading. At the same time, though, the board is important since it meets three times a week and makes decisions about IMF programs, policy, and strategy. Board

MAJOR TURNING POINTS IN THE IMF'S HISTORY

The IMF has evolved in many ways over the years, but less dramatically so than the World Bank. The IMF launched new financing facilities, took on new countries, and broadened and deepened its economic advice and lending. Some of these changes have been in response to broader trends and/or crises in the international economy; others have been in response to criticism, of which there has been no shortage. Among the most important times of change for the IMF are the closing of the gold window in 1973; the 1982 debt crisis; the 1997 to 1998 Asian crisis; and the 2008 global financial crisis. This chapter examines the first three important times of change, and the subsequent chapter looks in-depth at the fourth.

1973: Closing of the Gold Window

The IMF had a few growing pains in its early years, but then functioned fairly well as a referee of the international monetary system, until the system became shaky in the late 1960s. Like the World Bank, it was not able to be a truly global institution at its birth, because the Soviets decided not to join either, and instead, set up their own institution for economic coop-eration for East bloc countries, the Council for Mutual Economic Assistance, or COMECON. After the fund opened its doors in 1947, its first years were spent with its board and staff developing policies and lending instruments, and welcoming new members. The first loans were made to France, the Netherlands, and Mexico. There were also some early tensions between France and the rest of the IMF's board, when France was declared ineligible to use fund resources in 1948 when it proposed differential exchange rates for the franc. These were not allowed under fund rules, and the board feared the French plan would destabilize other European currencies.[20]

By the late 1960s, the par-value system was under enormous strain. The fatal flaw of the system was that all currencies were valued vis-à-vis the dollar, and the dollar's own value was off. The United States was spending an enormous amount of money in the 1960s. One reason was its support of the Viet Nam war, which meant rising US military spending. Domestically, President Lyndon Johnson had launched a domestic reform agenda called the "Great Society," that also involved increased government spending. Whereas the United States had trade surpluses in the mid-1960s, by 1971 the trade balance was in the red.[21]

Another way to state the problem is that the supply of dollars floating around the world was much greater than the demand for those dollars. Normally, when the supply of something exceeds demand, all things being equal, the price of that item will decline. If currencies had been floating freely, the value of the dollar vis-à-vis other currencies would have declined. Two choices were possible under the Bretton Woods par value system: either the dollar should be devalued or all the other currencies should be revalued. Neither option was seen as politically viable. As confidence in the dollar eroded, more and more people began exchanging their dollars for gold. This resulted in a massive outflow of gold from the United States and increased worries that the US economy could collapse. In a dramatic speech in 1971, US President Richard Nixon announced the closing of the gold window, which meant ending the convertibility of the dollar into gold.[22] The dollar promptly dropped around 10 percent over the next few months, and by 1973 the Bretton Woods system formally linking currencies to the dollar, and the dollar to gold, officially ended.[23] After that, IMF member states had a lot of flexibility on foreign exchange arrangements. Many let their currencies float; some pegged their currency to another one (like the dollar or French franc) or to a basket of currencies, and some joined a currency "bloc."

At IMF headquarters, staff circulated a tongue-in-cheek obituary, "We regretfully announce the not unexpected passing away after a long illness of Bretton Woods, at 9 p.m. last Sunday. Bretton was born in New Hampshire in 1944 and died a few days after his 27th birthday."[24] However, despite the demise of the dollar-gold convertibility system, the IMF did not declare failure and shut its doors. Instead, it began a new chapter of its existence.

The first oil crisis of 1973, when OPEC members quadrupled the price of oil and embargoed oil sales to the United States, triggered an energy crisis, worldwide recession, and ultimately high levels of inflation. All of this meant the IMF was quite busy making loans to countries facing economic trouble, and it also set up new facilities to help countries meet the increased cost of oil imports and to allow members to borrow higher percentages of their quotas in

BOX 7.1 FLOATING EXCHANGE RATE BASICS

When currencies *float*, it means that they rise and fall with respect to other currencies based on factors such as supply, demand, market psychology and liquidity, and the economic health of a given country or region. Central banks at times intervene, buying and selling currencies to try to nudge the value of their currency (or another currency) one way or another. Many smaller countries tend to link their currency to a major currency, or allow it to float with careful government intervention. Currencies are traded, internationally, in what is called the "foreign exchange market," where daily turnover is now in the trillions of dollars. The 24-hour foreign exchange market consists of major dealer institutions (banks and other financial institutions) located around the world, who buy and sell on behalf of their corporate and other clients. Some of these dealers are what are called *market makers*, which means they buy and sell at the prices quoted, making a profit on the *spread*, or difference between the two prices.

exceptional cases. The fund established a new Trust Fund in 1976 to help developing countries receive loans with very light conditionality and a concessional interest rate of 0.5 percent a year.[25] By 1977, Great Britain and Italy were also in the queue of countries seeking IMF assistance, joined by the United States in 1978. Drawings by advanced industrialized countries stopped in the late 1970s and did not resume until Iceland knocked on the IMF's door for assistance in the 2009 financial crisis. Meanwhile, in the late 1970s, there was a second sharp increase in oil prices, while US interest rates rose sharply in an effort by Federal Reserve Chairman Paul A. Volcker to curb US inflation. This had a double whammy effect on oil-importing developing countries, whose growing debts were largely denominated in dollars (and hence, based on US interest rates). The simmering problems that resulted came to a boil in 1982.

The 1982 Debt Crisis

The 1982 Latin American debt crisis marked a major new phase in the IMF's evolution. The IMF stepped onto the center stage as the lead crisis manager, organizing the creditor banks and negotiating with debtor countries. The crisis was sparked when Mexico, staggering under a heavy burden of debt, told US and IMF officials on August 12, 1982, that it was facing default on its loans, since it could not make the next payment to US commercial banks and other ·

Figure 7.1   IMF Lending, 1950–89

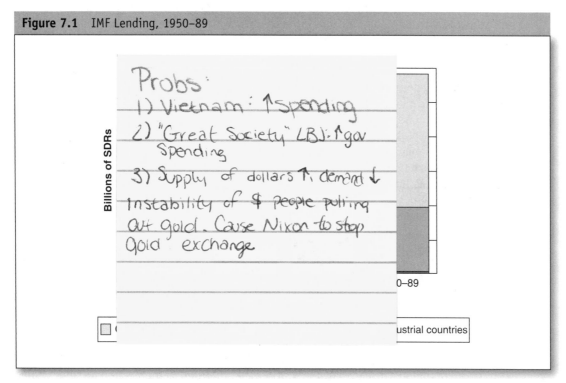

Source: Boughton, James M. *Silent Revolution: The International Monetary Fund, 1979–1989*. Washington, D.C.: International Monetary Fund, 2001, 18.

major banks. The next day, Friday, August 13, 1982, Mexican finance officials arrived in Washington, DC, to work with US and IMF officials to organize emergency help. The negotiations produced $3 billion from the United States, some of which could be used by Mexico to meet the payments to banks due on Monday.[26] But more money was needed, and quickly. On Friday, August 20, Mexico informed its bankers that it wouldn't be able to make its next payment on the loan principal due on Monday. The negotiations that followed resulted in the IMF gaining a powerful position in working with debtor countries and their creditors throughout the crisis.

The prospect of a Mexican default shook the financial world, as people feared other countries facing enormous debt would follow suit. Several Eastern European countries had already faced possible default in the early 1980s, but Mexico exacerbated the problem because its external debt was so large, at $80 billion; a default could trigger the collapse of major international banks and therefore create a full-blown global financial calamity. Many developing countries were suffering from the effects of high debt, high global interest rates, weak economies, and skittish bankers. There has been a lot of finger pointing about the causes of the crisis.[27] Some observers and participants blamed the developing countries for pursuing heavy external borrowing to support their domestic spending. Others blamed the big international banks for happily lending without paying close enough attention to what was going on in some of the borrowing countries. Staff members at the IMF itself had expressed concern over Mexico's growing levels of external debt, but according to IMF historian James Boughton, these warnings were "muted" and resulted in complacency by the IMF board.[28] Sixteen of the 27 nations seeking to reschedule their debt by October 1983 were Latin American. The four largest—Mexico, Brazil, Venezuela, and Argentina—together owed $176 billion dollars, almost three-quarters of total outstanding developing country debt.[29] US banks, meanwhile, were the source of most of the Latin American loans.

The fund stepped in by offering Mexico significant financial support, if Mexico would in turn negotiate an adjustment program with the fund. The Mexican team, led by Mexico's Secretary of Finance, Jesús Silva Herzog, worked closely with the IMF and US officials in a process that was not without its bumps and high drama. At the end of the day, an IMF program was seen as important to show Mexico was making appropriate economic reforms and to act as a green light to Mexico's creditors to justify and offer new loans. But banks were not exactly standing in line to offer Mexico more money. The fund's managing director, Jacques de Larosière, put unprecedented pressure on the commercial banks to come up with new money for Mexico to fill a gap between what was already available and what Mexico needed to stay afloat.[30] The fund was well placed to take on this leadership role. The hundreds of banks (large and small) with outstanding loans to Mexico and other developing countries needed some outside actor to help them coordinate themselves; the fund was obviously more of an independent actor than an individual creditor country, plus it had long experience in helping to coordinate its member states. As Boughton concluded,

While there was no specific mandate that made it more natural for the IMF to play that role [of coordination] than, say, the World Bank, the fund demonstrated an ability to step in quickly and forcefully when the indebted countries requested its assistance.[31]

Ngaire Woods called the IMF conditionality the "first rendition of what would later be called the Washington Consensus."[32] The IMF's conditionality for Mexico and other countries affected by the crisis emphasized a reduction in government spending, including government subsidies on basic consumer goods, higher taxes, and policies to reduce inflation.

Following Mexico, a number of other countries lined up to negotiate a deal that included new loans and tough IMF conditionality. These included Brazil, Argentina, Chile, Ecuador, Peru, and Uruguay. Outside Latin America, the Philippines and Côte d'Ivoire were also affected in 1983 and 1984.[33] Fears of a global crisis began to recede by 1984, even though developing country debt continued to grow and economic growth remained stagnant.

Major creditor countries started talking about the possibility of debt relief for countries, ways for banks to write off principal, reduce the interest rates on loans, or other measures that effectively reduce the amount of money countries' owed. Two plans launched by the United States, the 1985 Baker Plan (named after US Treasury Secretary James Baker III) and the 1989 Brady Plan (named after US Treasury Secretary Nicholas Brady) offered ways to respond to the fact that debtors were still drowning in debt and banks were not eager to increase net lending. Baker's program called for debtor countries, specifically 15 heavily indebted countries, to renew their efforts at reforming and liberalizing their economies, with increased lending from the World Bank and Inter-American Development Bank, as well as significant increased net lending from commercial banks. The Brady Plan went further, calling for banks to voluntarily come up with debt-reduction schemes, and possibly new lending, for debtor countries engaged in economic liberalization. Debt reduction is anathema to private banks and many inside the IMF, and there was strong opposition to this plan. Countries also doing their best to meet their debts also don't like to see their neighbors getting a free lunch. Nonetheless, the Plan went forward, with the fund deeply involved in negotiating the details with banks and the countries seeking relief.[34] The fund also launched new policies to allow countries to buy back some of their own debt with fund resources. By the middle of 1994, 18 countries received deals under the Brady Plan, resulting in debt forgiveness of $60 billion, and new loans from banks, as well as the World Bank and IMF.[35] By the early 1990s, the debt crisis was over. Looking back on it, economists argued that this was a crisis of liquidity, rather than insolvency. That meant it was a temporary crisis caused by the inability of countries to come up with enough foreign exchange to make required payments on their debt. It wasn't a permanent problem that countries simply could not earn foreign exchange.

1997–1998 Asian Crisis

The 1990s, unfortunately, were no easier on the IMF than the 1980s. The decade began with the fall of Communism and the heady challenges the formerly socialist countries faced in dramatically reorienting their economies to a market-based system. Criticism of the fund began to pick up speed, with some arguing it was providing an inadequate amount of support to the region, or offering counterproductive advice, or even that its policies helped to contribute to the onset of the crisis. The "Fifty Years Is Enough Campaign" was launched in 1994, on the 50th anniversary of the bank and fund. It argued that the Bretton Woods institutions promoted unsustainable development, which was environmentally destructive and resulted in increased poverty.

Mexico faced another crisis in 1994, dubbed the "peso crisis." The IMF responded by approving its largest ever financial package to date. But this paled next to the more frightening, far-reaching crisis that occurred in East Asia in 1997 and 1998. To put things in perspective, in 1982, the IMF provided Mexico with $3.7 billion dollars. During the peso crisis, it provided $17 billion, out of a $40 billion dollar total package. The amounts given to East Asia were even higher, totaling over $100 billion. The IMF ended up lending a total of $35 billion dollars, and rounding up an additional $77 billion from other sources. These large IMF "bailouts" were quick, emergency lending arrangements to countries made in hopes of averting the spread of crisis to an ever growing number of countries. The IMF's role in the Asian crisis was highly controversial, and prompted a fresh round of criticism that the institution was seriously misguided or incompetent, or both.

What Was the Asian Financial Crisis?

The crisis was a series of sharp declines in a number of Asian countries' currencies and stock markets. It spread to Russia (1998) and then to Brazil (1999) and stood poised to threaten the rest of the world, too. It began in Thailand and quickly spread to Indonesia, Malaysia, the Philippines, and South Korea before heading up to Russia and across the globe to Brazil. The crisis was defined by enormous economic disruptions, contracting economies, bank closures, political instability and the resulting painful human costs—increases in unemployment and poverty—and the corresponding declines in living standards.

Many observers were quite surprised that a major economic crisis would have East Asia as its epicenter, because for many years these Asian countries were admired for their rapid economic growth and increases in living standards. Indeed, East Asian countries were seen as a role model for other developing countries.

What Happened?

The crisis was triggered by a collapse in Thailand's currency, the baht, on July 2, 1997, when it lost around a quarter of its value overnight.[36] The initial problem was mainly about exchange rate speculation, but it quickly blew into something much bigger. A number of external and domestic factors created the conditions for this to occur. One contributing factor on the external side was the rapid growth in private capital flows. Private capital flows are money flowing from one country to another between private sector actors. Some examples are purchases by investors in one country of stocks or bonds in another, foreign direct investment (where companies or investors from one country invest in business opportunities in another country), lending by banks in one country to banks or companies in another country, and so on. Net private capital flows to Thailand and other Asian countries had grown dramatically between 1990 and 1996, surging from around $21 billion to 107 billion dollars.[37] But this money was heading into countries with mixed, and often weak, levels of regulatory supervision over banks, problems compounded in some cases by corruption. The weak domestic context created a situation that undermined domestic banking systems. Looking back, commentators observed that no one was keeping a close eye on whether Asian companies and banks were taking on too much risk, or borrowing too much. Some observers also criticized the IMF for urging the East Asian countries to liberalize their capital markets, exactly the type of actions that allowed so much capital to flow in, and later, out. In other words, this capital market liberalization played a role in the subsequent regional and global instability. One of the most visible signs of crisis was the fact that when Western investors, banks, companies, and hedge funds get nervous (or want to speculate, especially in the case of hedge funds) they can rather quickly take their money and run. The money rolled out as quickly as it rolled in, which greatly exacerbated an already precarious situation.

The match igniting this explosive mix arose from the relationship between the baht, the dollar, and the yen. The baht was relatively fixed in terms of the dollar, at roughly 25 bahts per dollar, and was kept stable by daily purchases or sales of dollars by the central bank.[38] In the summer of 1997, the Japanese yen declined about 35 percent vis-à-vis the dollar. Japan is one of Thailand's major trading partners, so suddenly the baht was much stronger in relation to the yen. That meant that Thailand's exports became more expensive to Japanese consumers, and therefore Thai exports declined.[39]

Investors grew nervous. Thailand, and other countries in the region, also had inflated stock market values and property prices. Confidence in the Thai economy and in neighboring economies started declining. These circumstances put pressure on the baht to decline, but it couldn't—it was tied to the dollar. Foreign investors began selling their holdings in Thailand (for dollars and other currencies). Some market participants, like hedge funds, sold the Thai *short*.[40] This is a technique used in financial markets where you can actually sell something before you buy it. In this case, hedge funds sold baht, betting that they would buy it back at a much cheaper rate at a later date. The Thai central bank was in a real fix—it couldn't keep producing foreign exchange, and it couldn't keep propping up the baht. Finally, in July, the baht began its decline and by January 1998 it had lost half of its value. Billions of dollars in capital began to hemorrhage out of Thailand and then its neighbors, too, including Indonesia, Taiwan, South Korea, and Hong Kong. Some of this occurred because investors and speculators were betting which country would be the next to see its stock market in freefall. The central banks of these countries, in turn, were seeing the foreign exchange reserves drained, which would mean they couldn't provide dollars and other currencies to their big corporations, or others, that needed the money to run their business and make payments to their foreign creditors. Journalist Thomas Friedman popularized the term "Electronic Herd" to describe the big international players, which included commercial banks, pension funds, mutual funds, and insurance companies, and other actors trading stock and currencies.[41]

The IMF played a central role in trying to defuse this crisis, by organizing the massive bailout packages to help governments avoid defaulting on their foreign debts and to try and restore investor confidence in these markets. The IMF's basic approach was to try to reestablish financial market confidence in these countries by making sure the vulnerable countries had enough money to dissuade speculators and others from attacking their currencies, money that could be used by domestic firms to repay their dollar-based loans. (Of course, one of the side effects of this provision of hard currency is that rich people inside the country could get dollars at an attractive exchange rate, and then send those dollars out of the country.)[42] The packages to Thailand, Indonesia, and South Korea, for example, included loans that central banks and governments could use to repay debts and macroeconomic plans that included high interest rates (to attract investors). But the IMF staff felt they shouldn't just put short-term Band-Aids on the problem, but instead, should try to get at the deeper problems facing these economies. The IMF packages included major restructuring of the financial sectors, which included closing banks. They also called for other far-reaching measures, often very specific, detailed reforms.[43] For example, the Indonesia agreement included the elimination of the company that monopolized sugar and flour, the elimination of a Clove Marketing Board, and the end of barriers to investment in palm oil plantations.[44]

Journalist Paul Blustein, in his book *The Chastening*, does an excellent job of bringing to life how dramatic and tense the negotiations were and explaining the perspective and role of individual participants from the involved countries, banks, and international institutions. Thailand, for example, refused to negotiate a rescue loan with the IMF even as the baht was declining rapidly, because its key officials (the central bank governor and his deputy, among them) were ambivalent about IMF support and policy conditionality. In Indonesia, the fund called for the closure of sixteen shaky banks, but did not simultaneously work to strengthen the banking system. The result was that people became nervous that other banks might also be weak, which prompted a run on Indonesia's privately owned banks and fears that the nation's entire banking system might collapse.[45]

The South Korea case was probably the most dramatic. By early 1997 South Korea seemed like it was in relatively good shape, with strong exports and even government surplus. The weak link was that a few of the country's major conglomerates, called *chaebol,* had gone bankrupt, and this weakened the banking system. The threat of default by South Korean banks would make a bad situation even worse. As the crisis unfolded, Blustein details how it was US officials behind the scenes that were influencing the IMF and calling for deep structural change in Korea's economy that went well beyond what the IMF traditionally called for. After several days of nonstop negotiations the resulting deal included a record $21 billion from the IMF and more than $55 billion from the World Bank, Asian Development Bank, and the United States and other countries. South Korea agreed to major structural reforms that would result in a more open economy, more competition in its financial sector, the ability of foreign investors to greatly increase their involvement in public companies, updated and more transparent corporate accounting practices, and more.[46] Five days later, on December 8, the Korean won came under attack, falling by its 10 percent limit against the dollar each day for five days.[47] The financial markets detected some back-paddling from the Korean side and became aware of how low Korea's foreign exchange reserves really were. Simplifying the resulting negotiations to their barebones minimum, Blustein explains that in the end, the crisis in Korea abated when international banks agreed to reschedule their short-term loans. The banks, concludes Blustein, "got away with murder. They foolishly injected billions of dollars of short-term loans into a country with a shaky financial system, yet they were suffering no losses."[48]

Assessing the IMF Role in the Asian Crisis

While there had been criticism of the IMF before the Asian crisis, the discussion was especially relevant by the late 1990s because, for many, the crisis showed that the IMF had truly failed in its mission to promote global stability; it did not avert the crisis, and its lending policies during the crisis were seen by many as wrong-headed. Some high-profile economists, such as Paul Krugman, Jeffrey Sachs, Joseph Stiglitz, and Jagdish Bhagwati, argued that the IMF's actions exacerbated East Asia's economic problems. Some of the criticism became remarkably personal. Stiglitz, the former chief economist of the World Bank, for example, mused that

> the older men who staff the fund—and they are overwhelmingly older men—act as if they are shouldering Rudyard Kipling's white man's burden. IMF experts believe they are brighter, more educated, and less politically motivated than the economists in the countries they visit. In fact, the economic leaders from those countries are pretty good—in many cases brighter or better-educated than the IMF staff, which frequently consists of third-rank students from first-rate universities.[49]

When asked in an interview to respond to Stiglitz's critique, IMF chief Michel Camdessus replied that he would not, because,

> Here in France you are in a country where people like soccer, and of course, in soccer you should never score against your own team—the Bretton Woods team, in this case. Stiglitz' lack of intellectual integrity in all of these comments does not leave him very well placed to criticize our performance. Such unjustified and misguided criticisms don't deserve to be answered.[50]

Beyond the personal criticisms, the Asian crisis forced the international community to consider what went wrong and how global financial institutions, policies, and structures might be reformed to strengthen what was commonly called "the global financial architecture." It is true that criticism of the IMF came from across the political spectrum, so it would be misleading to think there was any international consensus about what the IMF did wrong. One major line of criticism attacked the IMF's conditionality—it was too intrusive, or detailed, or simply the wrong policy choices for the problem at hand. A second line was that IMF involvement in such massive bailouts increases the problem of *moral hazard*.

Problems with IMF Conditionality

Many commentators and economists argued that the deep structural reforms the IMF urged countries to undertake had nothing to do with the short-term problem behind the crisis—speculation on the financial markets. Asking a country to make deep structural reforms may unnecessarily intrude on a country's sovereignty. For example, the IMF asked Indonesia to end government corruption.[51] One can argue that this is certainly not a bad thing to do, and it would result in a more efficient and healthy economy. But the fact is that these deep changes may be moving away from the immediate issues behind the crisis.

Moreover, critics argued that the IMF's policies in East Asia were the same traditional ones it used in other parts of the world, like Latin America in the 1980s, and that these were not appropriate to use in Asia.[52] The traditional policies, as noted above, are aimed at reducing government spending and tightening credit, and they are useful for countries experiencing balance of payments deficits caused by excessive demand. But in Asia, excessive demand was not the source of the problem for most countries. A particular problem was that higher interest rates effectively strangled already weak economies. When interest rates are higher, people and businesses take out fewer loans to use to buy things (such as homes or equipment or new workers). One side effect of these various problems is that they may result in more intense crises if countries, fearful of the IMF's far-reaching conditionality, try to avoid going to the IMF when they are in trouble. Martin Feldstein added to the medical metaphors surrounding the IMF by comparing it to the "painful dentist," whose patients avoid going in until it is absolutely necessary.[53]

Moral Hazard

Many commentators argued that the Asian crisis raised the problem of *moral hazard*. Moral hazard refers to situations where insurance against bad outcomes encourages more risky behavior. In other words, if you have an old car that is fully insured, you may not be careful about locking it up or getting into a fender-bender because you know you'll receive insurance money if it is stolen or dented. Something that is supposed to *protect* (in this case, insurance) can ultimately *undermine* safe behavior.

This term was first used to discuss the unintended consequence of setting up central banks to act as a lender of last resort in case a domestic banking system is threatened with collapse. The problem is that if banks know they have a regulatory safety net, they may take more, rather than fewer, risks because they know they will be bailed out if something goes wrong. Unsurprisingly, we have seen this term used many times in the current financial crisis.

In the case of the IMF, there has been concern that if investors, banks, and governments know the IMF will arrive with large bailout packages in times of trouble, this may result in more reckless behavior by all of the above. Investors may make more risky investments and governments may encourage looser regulation. Scholar Kapur added a twist to the term, arguing it can apply to the IMF itself. In other words, the IMF may have an incentive to take risks in its own policy advice to countries, because it has its own form of insurance: No IMF staff ever gets fired for poor policy advice. In addition, the IMF is usually first in line of creditors to be repaid.[54]

Other Critiques

As one of the opening quotes of this chapter inferred, there are plenty of other critiques. The Meltzer Commission, a special US Congressional commission (2000) that made recommendations on how to reform international financial institutions, considered 12 principal criticisms in its report. They ranged from "The IMF is too powerful" to "the IMF's interventions have not been associated, on average, with any clear economic gains to recipient countries."[55]

The Meltzer Commission concluded that the IMF, as well as the World Bank and regional development banks, would improve their performance if they were more accountable and "had a clearer focus on an important, but limited set of objectives."[56] For the IMF, this would mean making short-term loans for countries that need short-term liquidity. Some of the Commission's recommendations were seen in subsequent efforts by the IMF to revise and make more flexible its lending policies.

Blustein argued that the IMF was simply too ill-equipped to stand up against the enormous flows of private capital that can enter and exit countries with such great speed. The size of markets and disruptions overpowers the fund's capacity. In the end, he concluded, "the fund's efforts to contain the crises were analogous to a team of well-trained orthopedic surgeons trying to cure a ward of patients experiencing emotional breakdowns."[57] The problem wasn't just the IMF's alone, because the institution was working with high-ranking officials at the US Treasury, Federal Reserve, and related agencies from the other Group of 7 (G7) advanced economies—none of whom proved any better at safeguarding the global economy.[58]

IMF Response

Unsurprisingly, the IMF made various attempts to defend its actions. Kenneth Rogoff, the IMF's chief economist, argued in an article entitled "The IMF Strikes Back" that it isn't true the IMF encourages moral hazard, because very often private investors don't escape as easily as some believe. He cited data that private investors lost more than $325 billion as a result of the Asian crisis and the Russian debt default of 1998.

In terms of the common criticism that the IMF austerity program increases a country's suffering, he reminded us that "developing countries don't seek IMF financial assistance when the sun is shining; they come when they have already run into deep financial difficulties, generally through some combination of bad management and bad luck."[59] Governments also find it politically helpful to blame the IMF when they have to take difficult policy actions, like cutting government spending. Rogoff also raised the counterfactual—what would happen to countries in crisis if the IMF didn't step in? Things could be worse if countries defaulted on their loans or found their currency in free fall. "Blaming the IMF for the reality that every country must confront its budget constraints is like blaming the fund for gravity," he concluded.[60]

PERSPECTIVES ON THE IMF

Many scholars, including economists and political scientists, have conducted research that seeks to explain in more detail what factors shape how the IMF performs and behaves.

One area of research examines how effective fund programs have been at helping countries get back onto their economic feet. Political scientist J. R. Vreeland surveyed the literature on this topic and concluded that it produces contradictory results on indicators that include inflation, balance of payments, and economic growth.

He explains that a major reason for this is because evaluating the IMF's activity is complicated. Countries seeking help face different circumstances. There is consensus that the IMF has had a positive, significant impact on balance of payments problems, but not on whether the IMF has helped to lower inflation.[61] In the area of promoting economic growth, the IMF has been weak, with some studies even showing the IMF has a negative impact on economic growth.[62] The mixed results may or may not mean the IMF is doing something wrong. The recipient countries play a role, too. They may not be complying with the IMF's policies. Vreeland also cites studies that show compliance in some areas is higher than others.[63]

Scholars also admit measuring compliance is tricky, and even when we know that countries are not complying, it is not always easy or possible for the IMF or its major shareholders to punish noncompliance.

Political scientists Michael Barnett and Martha Finnemore present a constructivist argument on what is wrong with the IMF and why it matters. They argue that IMF staff have gained a great deal of authority and autonomy as a result of their specialized expertise in economics. They developed and disseminated the economic models that shape how the IMF has responded to countries. In particular, this explains the IMF's emphasis on balance of payments problems and the policy prescriptions that follow. When policies failed, the IMF's response has been to expand conditionality, rather than to retrench. The result of this logic of expansion, they argue, has been an unmanageable proliferation in IMF goals, which can result in organizational dysfunction. This dysfunction can occur as the organization struggles to do too much with limited resources, or as the goals themselves may clash. An excellent example of the latter is how the goal of capital market openness conflicts with the goal of economic stability, as we have seen with the Asian financial crisis.[64]

Economist William Easterly has argued that a central problem with the IMF, as well as other major international organizations who give money to developing countries, is that they advocate a "top-down" approach in foreign aid, an approach that applies global blueprints without following through on implementation and results. He calls the big aid organizations "Planners," and he contrasts them with "Searchers," people and organizations who work "at the bottom" in developing countries to find out what is really needed. "In foreign aid," Easterly argues

> Planners announce good intentions but don't motivate anyone to carry them out; searchers find things that work and get some reward. Planners raise expectations but take no responsibility for meeting them; Searchers accept responsibility for their actions. Planners determine what to supply; Searchers find out what is in demand.[65]

His argument was inspired, in part, by his observation that Western nations have spent over $2 trillion dollars on foreign aid in the last fifty years and still cannot get inexpensive medication to prevent poor children from dying of malaria. Yet, somehow, other people on the same planet can manage to deliver millions of copies of Harry Potter books to bookstores by the launch date. This illustrates the differences between Planners and Searchers.

He also argues that the multilateral organizations are too centralized, an observation repeated elsewhere. Of the major multilateral organizations, the IMF is one of the more centralized. For example, while the World Bank has moved a lot of its staff to developing countries in the past decade, the IMF typically has only one "resident representative" in each country, and that person has limited powers. Most of the work is done in Washington, DC, and IMF staff then fly to countries for brief visits, spending their time in finance ministries, central banks, and nice hotels. As Stiglitz passionately noted,

> Modern high-tech warfare is designed to remove physical contact: dropping bombs from 50,000 feet ensures that one does not "feel" what one does. Modern economic management is similar: from one's luxury hotel, one can callously impose policies about which one would think twice if one knew the people whose lives one was destroying.[66]

These are examples of a variety of perspectives on what is wrong with the IMF, and there is no consensus on how to reform the institution. Critics who passionately argue that the IMF should be shrunk or abolished have counterparts who argue that it should be expanded with greater powers. We should now expect more evaluation of the IMF's performance in the euro crisis, as the latest chapter in thinking and debate about how the institution can continue to evolve to handle future challenges.

CONCLUSION

This chapter has charted some major points in the IMF's history, and we can see that, like the World Bank, it has sought to evolve and adjust to global economic and financial issues and pressures. This chapter has shown some of the ways that it has been less institutionally flexible than the World Bank and offered examples of its modest adjustments. The bank, for example, over time has hired staff with PhDs in a variety of areas beyond economics, including environmental engineering, sociology, political science, and anthropology. The IMF still relies primarily on economists. The bank has played a leadership role, albeit contested, in issues such as poverty reduction and the environment. It more actively engages with civil society than the IMF. The IMF points out that its work is essential in issues such as reducing poverty, but clearly that is not the central focus of its work in fostering international monetary cooperation and seeking to ensure global stability. At the same time, the bank is struggling more with the sheer number of goals and mandates than the IMF, which has been more successful at avoiding mission creep. Perhaps one of the best tests of the IMF's legitimacy and performance will be to see how all of the changes that have taken place impact its ability to prevent or react to the next global financial crisis. After all, some scholars remind us that such crises are a permanent fixture of life, and the question is not "whether," but "when."[67]

BIBLIOGRAPHY

Barnett, Michael N., and Martha Finnemore. *Rules for the World: International Organizations in Global Politics*. Ithaca, NY: Cornell University Press, 2004.

Bird, Graham R. *The IMF and the Future: Issues and Options Facing the Fund*. New York: Routledge, 2003.

Blustein, Paul. *The Chastening: Inside the Crisis That Rocked the Global Financial System and Humbled the IMF*. New York: Public Affairs, 2001.

Boughton, James M. *Silent Revolution: The International Monetary Fund, 1979–1989*. Washington, DC: International Monetary Fund, 2001.

Broz, J. Lawrence, and Jeffry A. Frieden. "The Political Economy of Exchange Rates." In *The Oxford Handbook of Political Economy*, edited by Barry R. Weingast and Donald A. Wittman, 587–97. New York: Oxford University Press, 2006.

Cline, William R. *International Debt: Systemic Risk and Policy Response*. Cambridge: MIT Press, 1984.

Curry, Timothy. *History of the Eighties—Lessons for the Future*. Vol. 1, Washington, DC: FDIC, 1997.

Easterly, William Russell. *The White Man's Burden: Why the West's Efforts to Aid the Rest Have Done So Much Ill and So Little Good*. New York: Penguin Press, 2006.

Eckes, Alfred E. *A Search for Solvency: Bretton Woods and the International Monetary System, 1941–1971*. Austin: University of Texas Press, 1975.

Feldstein, Martin. "Refocusing the IMF." *Foreign Affairs* 77, no. 2 (March-April 1998): 20–33.

Folkerts-Landau, David, Donald J. Mathieson, and Garry J. Schinasi, eds. *International Capital Markets: Developments, Prospects, and Key Policy Issues*. Washington, DC: International Monetary Fund, 1997.

Frieden, Jeffry A. *Global Capitalism: Its Fall and Rise in the Twentieth Century*. 1st ed. New York: W.W. Norton, 2006.

Friedman, Thomas L. *The Lexus and the Olive Tree*. Thorndike, ME: Thorndike Press, 1999.

Gould, Erica R. *Money Talks: The International Monetary Fund, Conditionality, and Supplementary Financiers*. Stanford, CA: Stanford University Press, 2006.

Horsefield, J. Keith. *The International Monetary Fund, 1945–1965: Twenty Years of International Monetary Cooperation*. Vol. I, Washington, DC: International Monetary Fund, 1969.

Humphreys, Norman K. *Historical Dictionary of the International Monetary Fund*. 2nd ed. Lanham, MD: Scarecrow Press, 1999.

IMF. "Fund Facilities." http://www.imf.org/external/np/exr/faq/facilitiesfaqs.htm.

———. "IMF Conditionality." http://www.imf.org/external/np/exr/facts/conditio.htm.

———. "Special Drawing Rights (SDRS)." http://www.imf.org/external/np/exr/facts/sdr.htm.

———. "The IMF at a Glance." International Monetary Fund, http://www.imf.org/external/np/exr/facts/glance.htm.

Kapur, Devesh. "The IMF: A Cure or a Curse?" *Foreign Policy,* 111 (Summer 1998): 114–29.

Meltzer, Alan (Chairman). "Report of the International Financial Institutional Advisory Commission." Washington, DC, 2000.

Naim, Moises. "The FP Interview: A Talk with Michael Camdessus About God, Globalization, and His Years Running the IMF." *Foreign Policy* 120 (September-October, 2000): 32–45.

Radelet, Steven, and Jeffrey Sachs. "The East Asian Financial Crisis: Diagnosis, Remedies, Prospects." In Harvard Institute for International Development, 1998.

Reinhart, Carmen M., and Kenneth S. Rogoff. *This Time Is Different: Eight Centuries of Financial Folly*. Princeton, NJ: Princeton University Press, 2009.

Rogoff, Kenneth. "The IMF Strikes Back." *Foreign Policy* 134 (January-February 2003): 39–46.

Stiglitz, Joseph E. *Globalization and Its Discontents*. 1st ed. New York: W. W. Norton, 2002.

———. "The Insider." *The New Republic*, April 17, 2000.

Stone, Randall W. "IMF Governance and Financial Crises with Systemic Importance." In *Studies of IMF Governance: A Compendium*, edited by Ruben Lamdany and Leonardo Martinez-Diaz, 369–74. Washington, DC: International Monetary Fund, 2009.

Vasquez, Ian. "The Brady Plan and Market-Based Solutions to Debt Crises." *Cato Journal* 16, no. 2 (1996): 233–43.

Vreeland, James Raymond. *The International Monetary Fund: Politics of Conditional Lending*. New York: Routledge, 2006.

Woods, Ngaire. *The Globalizers: The IMF, the World Bank, and Their Borrowers*. Ithaca, NY: Cornell University Press, 2006.

8 International Monetary Fund Case Study

The IMF and the Global Financial Crisis

The global financial crisis erupted in September 2008, triggered by the collapse of Lehman Brothers, which caused credit markets to seize up and left economic and unemployment crises in its wake. The roots of the global crisis were in a subprime housing loan crisis in the United States. The resulting "Great Recession" was the worst the world had experienced since the Great Depression of the 1930s and put enormous stress on existing efforts to further global economic governance. Capital flows dried up, trade contracted dramatically, and unemployment rose in the subsequent months. Global economic growth of 1.9 percent in 2008 turned into a contraction of 2.1 percent the following year, which marked the first such decline in over sixty years.[1] US Federal Reserve economists estimated that if the United States economy continued along its pre-crisis trajectory, it would have produced a staggering $1 trillion more in goods and services each year.[2] Major banks were hard hit, but the human impact was much greater. Rising food and oil prices were already taking a toll on low-income countries. The crisis pushed millions more people into extreme poverty.[3]

It also made all governments painfully aware that more cooperation was needed to address financial regulations and practices in ways to prevent a catastrophe from repeating itself or turning into something even worse. The crisis was a major test of the IMF's importance and role in the global economy and in global economic governance. Before the crisis, many argued the IMF was losing credibility and relevance. Its lending was declining and its staff was shrinking. The crisis dramatically changed the IMF, infusing it with fresh life and importance as the centerpiece of global economic governance. The G20 leaders turned to the IMF to be a financial firefighter, and the IMF moved quickly to respond. The G20 leaders announced in April 2009 a dramatic tripling of IMF's lending resources to $750 billion. By 2013, these resources were nearly $1 trillion. IMF lending skyrocketed between 2007 and 2011, from an astonishingly low SDR 600 million (less than $1 billion, or around $912 million) to a peak of more than SDR 142 billion (around $220 billion).[4] Once the euro crisis exploded in the spring of 2010, the IMF became part of the "Troika" of creditors, along with the European Commission and European Central Bank, that has played a central role in Europe's response. While the initial financial panic was contained by the response of major central banks, which injected billions of dollars of liquidity into global financial markets, the IMF still played a key role in the response in a variety of ways.

There are many angles from which one can evaluate the IMF's role in the crisis. Given the IMF's central role in safeguarding international monetary stability, the obvious major categories for evaluating the IMF's performance are: how well it predicted the crisis; how quickly it responded with its lending and other assistance; and how well it sought to strengthen its ability to be better prepared for the next crisis. This chapter will show how the IMF was poorly prepared in the run-up to the crisis and how it also responded quickly in its role as financial crisis firefighter, given a mandate to do so by its shareholders. Its performance in the third category is mixed. It made a number of positive institutional changes but has not yet implemented a major set of governance reforms.

The chapter begins by describing and explaining the crisis itself and what sparked it, before turning to IMF's role in the run-up to the crisis, in the midst of the crisis, and in the aftermath of the crisis. In the run-up to the crisis, the obvious questions are: did the IMF have an inkling a crisis might erupt? Was it working with countries to prevent such crises, especially through its surveillance activities? Surveillance is the fund's system of monitoring the global economy and member states' economic and financial policies. It advises countries on risks and the policies they might adopt to promote economic stability and reduce their vulnerability to crises. In the midst of crisis, the chapter examines how the IMF was given a major role by G20 countries to act quickly to offer support to countries in dire need of funding. The large increase in IMF resources was a significant change for the institution, which was still struggling at the time with criticism of its role in the Asian crisis of the late 1990s.

The chapter then discusses and evaluates the major changes in IMF policies and activities that emerged as a result of the crisis. Member states also created a number of important new initiatives to better manage the global financial and economic system. If we fast forward to today, we can say that global recovery has continued. But even major countries are still coping with some of the fallout from the crisis, including weak economies in Europe. Unemployment remains high in Europe and the United States. Some emerging markets have continued to struggle, and slower growth in China has rattled world stock markets. And there is still a lot of anger—toward the powerful banks and wealthy bankers, toward governments with weak regulatory systems, and so on. If history is a guide, there will be more such crises in the future. Do the G20 leaders and the IMF have sufficient political will to produce a stronger response? No one can say "yes" with confidence. And while there is plenty of criticism about the IMF's role in global economic governance, it is also true that for now, the global economy has survived.

WHAT SPARKED THE CRISIS?

Many factors came together to create the conditions for the crisis. The epicenter was in the US housing market sector, which had seen hefty increases in housing prices and the availability of easy-to-obtain mortgages, even for people with poor credit histories who were high-risk borrowers. Meanwhile, big banks created fancy financial products that pooled (increasingly bad) mortgages and sold them in an environment where investors incorrectly assumed there was little risk. Heavy borrowing was prevalent throughout the US financial system and economy. Low, apparently stable, short-term interest rates made investors more comfortable about taking higher risks in borrowing to invest in higher-yielding, more risky securities. Adding to these shaky underpinnings, regulatory oversight was fragmented and weak and contributed to destabilizing financial innovations.

More broadly, in the midst of high world economic growth, there was a major imbalance between the large United States current account deficit and the large current account surpluses in Asia and in oil exporting countries. This imbalance was of concern to some economists (even at the IMF) because if something made investors nervous, they might reverse the large capital inflows going into the United States, which would make matters worse. The global imbalances, in the words of IMF economists, "played a role in the build up of systemic risk. They contributed to low interest rates and to large capital inflows into US and European banks. . . . these two factors then contributed to a search for yield, higher leverage, and the creation of riskier assets."[5]

US housing prices basically moved in one direction for most of the period since WWII—up. The pace increased in the late 1990s and early 2000s, with real house prices up nearly 30 percent between 1997 and 2002. Mortgage rates were inching lower and lower. By 2004, US home ownership was at a record high of 69.2 percent.[6] Loans called "subprime" were easy to get. A subprime loan is one that may be given to someone who does not qualify for a regular (prime rate) loan. Subprime loans have higher rates than prime rate loans, but interest rates were so low in the years leading up to the crisis, that they were quite attractive.

Meanwhile, in the world of finance, the mortgages were being *securitized*, or turned into securities that could be sold to investors. One type of *mortgage backed security* pooled mortgages into different sets of bonds with different interest rates and maturities. Another type was set up so that the interest and principal paid by the homeowner would be distributed to the investor through some type of intermediary. These were ultimately risky instruments dressed up to look less risky. If home prices are rising and interest rates are low, there are fewer defaults and investors at the end of the line do well. But if interest rates start to rise and people start to default on their mortgages, then the investors at the end of the line are not doing well. And that is precisely what happened. Banks selling such securities were also loose and fast in meeting proper standards and guidelines. By late 2013, the US Securities and Exchange Commission had charged a long list of banks, brokerages, and other financial institutions with misconduct and fraud, such as concealing risks from investors and improperly pricing their collateralized debt obligations. Banks had to pay hundreds of millions to settle these charges.[7]

By late 2005, the housing party was over. Rapid growth of housing sales slowed. Mortgage rates rose by around 1 percent, which impacted many first-time home owners. Soon, prices stalled and started to drop throughout 2006. By 2007, the decrease in sales accelerated. The bubble had popped. Foreclosures were rising, and the US subprime mortgage crisis began to impact broader credit markets. The largest US subprime lender, New Century Financial, filed for bankruptcy protection in April 2007, with liabilities of more than $100 million.[8] Another large mortgage company, American Home Mortgage, did the same in August, followed by a British mortgage lender, Northern Rock. The latter prompted the first major run on a UK bank in 140 years, which only stopped when British regulators agreed to guarantee all existing deposits.[9] The bank was later nationalized.[10]

In early August 2007, BNP Paribas became the first major bank to react to the risk of its subprime mortgage-related assets exposure by freezing three of its funds.[11] By the end of 2007, large financial institutions were reporting huge losses, which were mainly due to their holdings of securities linked to subprime mortgages. For example, Citigroup announced in October that its third-quarter profit was down 57 percent, reflecting its mortgage-backed securities woes.[12] Merrill Lynch announced a $2.24 billion third-quarter loss, and Morgan Stanley posted a loss of $3.59 billion, reflecting similar problems. Swiss bank USB followed with an announcement of a whopping $10 billion in write-downs.

As *The Economist* summed it up,

> When America's housing market turned, a chain reaction exposed fragilities in the financial system. Polling and other clever financial engineering did not provide investors with the promised protection. Mortgage-backed securities slumped in value, if they could be valued at all. Supposedly safe CDOs (collateralized debt obligations) turned out to be worthless, despite the rating agencies' seal of approval. It became difficult to sell suspected assets at almost any price. . . . Trust, the ultimate glue of all financial systems began to dissolve in 2007 . . . as banks started questioning the viability of their counterparties.[13]

Flimsy regulation also played a role in the meltdown. In the United States, there was no real attempt to address the housing bubble. European central bankers did not actively address a surge in borrowing. International capital ratios for banks, which were meant to ensure that banks hold a sufficient amount of capital relative to their assets, were also weak. Banks could get away with holding minimal capital aside, and they were also adept at moving debt off of the balance sheet or doing other creative accounting to allow them to take on more debt than was wise.[14]

More financial institutions began to totter and fall in 2008. In March, JPMorgan Chase bought Bear Stearns, one of Wall Street's largest securities firms (close to $400 billion in total assets), for the shockingly low price of $2 a share (about $236 million). This was less than one-tenth of the firm's market price on the last trading day before the weekend deal. Another unusual aspect of the deal is that the Federal Reserve provided financing for the deal and the Fed and Treasury were involved in the negotiations to save the firm.[15] The New York Fed also offered a $12.9 billion weekend bridge loan to Bear Stearns to make sure it could meet its obligations the Friday before the weekend deal making.[16] The New York Fed then created a limited liability company to absorb part of Bear Stearn's mortgage trading portfolio that JPMorgan Chase thought was too risky to take on, to get those dodgy assets off of Bear Stearns' books. The New York Fed extended another $29 billion in credit for this part of the deal.[17]

In June 2008, US Senator Charles E. Schumer (D-NY), the chairman of the congressional Joint Economic Committee, asked several US regulators to check the financial health of IndyMac Bancorp, a large mortgage lender with $32 billion in assets as of March 2008. Schumer was concerned about "serious problems" with the bank's financial health, due to its mortgage portfolio. The result was a run on the bank, with IndyMac customers withdrawing an average of $100 million a day. The bank promptly collapsed and was seized by federal regulators. It was the biggest US bank failure in 24 years.

SEPTEMBER 2008: THE CRISIS ERUPTS

In September 2008, the global financial system seized up as the crisis blossomed and spread. It was a harrowing month. "Day after day during the crisis," wrote then US Treasury Secretary

Henry (Hank) Paulson, "another corner of the markets seemed to unravel, each one worse than the one before. The week that Lehman went down was absolutely brutal—easily the worse week of my life."[18] The first drama was when the US government stepped in to take over Fannie Mae and Freddy Mac on September 7. The move was called the US government's "most dramatic market intervention in years," by *The Wall Street Journal*, which reported the government promised up to $200 billion to help the companies cope with the losses stemming from worthless mortgages.[19] Fanny Mae and Freddy Mac, two casual-sounding names for the Federal National Mortgage Association (Fannie) and the Federal Home Mortgage Corporation (Freddy), were the two largest mortgage finance lenders in the United States, which owned or guaranteed almost 50 percent of US residential mortgages.[20] They were unusual creatures. Fannie Mae was born in the Great Depression, created by the federal government to purchase loans from banks and create a secondary market to encourage home purchases and mortgages. It became privately owned in the late 1960s, with the requirement that it devote "a reasonable portion" of its mortgage purchases to "low- and moderate-income housing."[21] Freddie Mac was created by Congress in 1970 to buy long-term mortgages from "thrifts" (federally chartered savings and loan institutions, which offered basic banking services to individuals and small business, with an emphasis on mortgage lending) to help these institutions better manage their own interest rate risks. Freddie joined Fannie as a privately owned institution in the late 1980s.

Between 2004 and 2007 both Fannie Mae and Freddie Mac were aggressive actors in the mortgage market, purchasing large quantities of risky mortgages and mortgage-backed securities and ignoring warnings from internal officers. They held over $5 trillion dollars in debt and mortgage-backed securities.[22] They "basically loaded their balance sheets with more dry brush than California in August," quipped *Time* magazine.[23] The two institutions rapidly lost billions of dollars when the housing market headed south beginning in 2007. There was also evidence of shady behavior, such as instances where Freddie Mac reported its earnings as $5 billion higher than they should have been between 2000 and 2003, and where Fannie Mae added an extra $10.6 billion to its earnings report between 1998 and 2004. Both were later accused by their regulator of inappropriately tinkering with their accounting rules.[24]

Exactly a week after the seizure of the mortgage giants, "the American financial system was shaken to its core," as Lehman Brothers collapsed on Monday September 15, hours after Bank of America decided to buy Merrill Lynch & Co.[25] Lehman was the oldest and one of the largest investment banks in the United States, with $600 billion in assets and 25,000 employees. Its collapse shocked global markets and created financial panic as credit markets dried up. It was the largest bankruptcy in history. A dramatic weekend of secret negotiations failed. Bank of America, a possible suitor, decided it could not manage a deal without federal aid, and so turned around and instead bought Merrill Lynch & Co., another troubled investment bank. This time, the US government decided not to help out the potential buyers. Lehman was later broken up with various parts sold to different buyers. The decision by the Fed and the Treasury to let Lehman die remains controversial, since it did not stop a financial meltdown and since it happened shortly after the Fed supported the sale of Bear Stearns to JP Morgan.

Lehman had been hit hard by the subprime mortgage crisis, and its stock had plunged in value throughout the year. It had bought too much US property on borrowed money. Investor confidence disappeared. The US Treasury had worked for a number of months with Lehman, trying to get it to raise more capital and trying to get Bank of America (BofA) to buy it. Looking back on that fateful weekend, Paulson said that things might have ended up worse if BofA bought Lehman instead of the much larger and more globally connected Merrill. "Had BofA bought Lehman," he wrote, "I believe Merrill would have failed—with even worse consequences for the market than the Lehman collapse."[26] The stock market took a huge beating that day, closing down over 500 points in the largest single decline since the 9/11 attacks. As investors panicked, credit markets dried up.

All of this was just Monday. On Tuesday, giant insurance firm AIG was crumbling under the weight of enormous losses that stemmed from its London branch getting deeply involved in risky credit default swaps. The Fed stepped in to rescue it with an $85 billion loan and the equivalent of a 79.9 percent stake.[27] Unlike in the case of Lehman, AIG was seen as too big to fail, since its collapse would impact small investors invested in supposedly safe money-market funds that in turn invested in AIG's debt.[28] Fed Chairman Benjamin Bernanke, New York Fed President Timothy Geithner, and Treasury Secretary Paulson all agreed that such federal intervention was necessary to avert catastrophe in financial markets. Morgan Stanley and Goldman Sachs were the next focus of bearish investors pulling funds out in a trading frenzy. A day after AIG was rescued, shares of Morgan Stanley sunk by 24 percent and Goldman's were down 14 percent.[29] Financial institutions would not lend to one another. Major US firms could not raise money.[30] In Russia, the government suspended the stock market after it went into free-fall despite the government helping the country's three largest banks with $44 billion.[31] On September 21, in response to their precarious position, Goldman and JPMorgan Chase changed their status from investment banks to bank holding companies. International investors, such as the Chinese, were rapidly pulling money out of US markets.

The drama continued for weeks with the US government rolling out a package bit by bit. In early October 2008, Congress passed and President Bush signed into law the Emergency Economic Stabilization Act of 2008, which created a $700 billion Troubled Asset Relief Program (TARP) set up to buy troubled assets from banks. Global stock markets responded with steep declines.[32] As part of the program, the US Treasury made $250 billion available to shore up financial institutions and nine large ones tapped into this for $125 billion. In return, the Treasury temporarily ended up with stocks in these institutions. The United States also dramatically increased the size of bank deposits it was willing to insure and then guaranteed all money market funds. A number of other steps were also taken to strengthen banks and inject new life into mortgage markets.

Meanwhile, governments around the world were taking actions to keep their banking systems afloat as the financial crisis morphed into a deeper economic crisis. Central banks injected heavy doses of liquidity into financial markets. It also turns out that countries that had relatively lower current account deficits at the time of the crisis ended up weathering the storm better than others. Latin America's current account deficits were moderate, and East Asian governments had accumulated reserves and run current account surpluses as part of their response to the crisis of the late 1990s. The magnitude of crisis contagion in these regions ended up being less than many had feared.[33]

ENTER THE IMF

The IMF didn't become a major player in the crisis right when the market imploded. As this chapter has shown, the initial story was really one about major United States and European financial institutions and their regulators and governments. Unlike the other crises in recent decades, this one originated in the United States and first spread to other rich countries. It was not immediately about emerging markets or other developing countries, the IMF's main clients. But given the IMF's role in surveillance and advising countries on economic policy, one can fairly ask whether the IMF anticipated the crisis or whether its policy advice to countries may have an impact on what transpired.

The two types of surveillance are *multilateral* (focusing on the stability of the global economy) and *bilateral* (addressing individual members). Since 1981, the IMF has published *World Economic Outlook*, which is the main document reflecting its multilateral surveillance operations. A second important annual surveillance document is the *Global Financial Stability Report*, which was first published in 2002. In terms of bilateral surveillance, IMF staff typically meet annually with each member country for what are called "Article IV consultations," which are a required part of a country's membership in the IMF. IMF staff missions assess the country's economic and financial conditions and policies, meeting with government and central bank officials. IMF staff often also meet with other domestic actors, including members of parliament and representatives of business, labor, and civil society more broadly. The IMF Executive Board then reviews the staff report to assess the member state's actions and policies and ensure that it is complying with the IMF Articles of Agreement. In 2007, the Board clarified that a country's external economic stability is the driving goal behind the Article IV consultations.[34]

The IMF did not anticipate the crisis. Commentators pointed out that the IMF did notice that housing prices were unsustainable in many advanced economies, but right up until the crisis itself, it was forecasting stable conditions because it did not understand what would happen to banks and other financial institutions if housing prices took a sharp downward turn.[35] The fund did not connect the dots between the risk across different sectors, especially the financial sector, and it underestimated how financial sector spillover could produce such dramatic macroeconomic consequences.[36] Its *World Economic Outlook* report in April 2007, for example, concluded risks to the global economy were very low.

Perhaps the biggest criticism of the IMF in the run-up to the crisis came from the IMF's Independent Evaluation Office (IEO), which examined the IMF's actions before the crisis and produced a scathing report that concluded the IMF was "woefully unprepared."

According to the IEO,

> the IMF provided few clear warnings about the risks and vulnerabilities associated with the impending crisis before its outbreak. . . . The IMF's ability to correctly identify the mounting risks was hindered by a high degree of group-think, intellectual capture, a general mind-set that a major financial crisis in large advanced economies was unlikely, and inadequate analytical approaches. Weak internal governance, lack of incentives to work across units and raise contrarian views, and a review process that did not "connect the dots" or ensure follow-up also played an important role, while political constraints may have also had some impact.[37]

IMF Managing Director Dominique Strauss-Kahn did not argue with the conclusions when the report was published in 2011, but noted that the IMF had itself acknowledged that it did not sound an alarm "in a sufficiently early, pointed, and effective way."[38] To put the situation in perspective, it is worth recalling that there was also an absence of alarm bells from leading economists and government bodies, as few people predicted the crisis. Most economists and policymakers either assumed financial firms could self-regulate, or they did not pay enough attention to other relevant indicators of trouble. Many thought that the United States could not fall prey to crisis, given its large capital markets and innovative financial system.[39] As economist Paul Krugman noted,

> almost nobody predicted the immense economic crisis that overtook the United States and Europe in 2008. . . . On the eve of crisis in 2007 the officials, analysts, and pundits who shape economic policy were deeply, wrongly complacent. They didn't see 2008 coming; but what is more important is the fact they even didn't believe in the possibility of such a catastrophe.[40]

Rapid Response

The IMF moved quickly once the crisis hit to get money out the door and help coordinate global and regional initiatives. Once the global economy began to contract, countries lined up for IMF assistance. By late October 2008, Strauss-Kahn announced at the annual meetings with the World Bank that the IMF's Emergency Financing Mechanism was up and running, ready to give out loans in a speedy process. Under the new mechanism the IMF board would rapidly approve loans, within 48 to 72 hours after the IMF and the national government had reached their own agreement. In October and November 2008, the IMF agreed to over $43 billion in loans—$16.5 billion to Ukraine, $15.7 billion to Hungary, $7.6 billion to Pakistan, $750 million to Georgia, and $2.1 billion to Iceland. The latter was especially dramatic, since it followed the collapse of Iceland's banking system and was the first time a Western European country had borrowed from the IMF in over 30 years. The vast majority of these loans were supported by other commitments, which mean that total financing could be much higher than the IMF loan itself. For example, the total resources that went to Hungary totaled almost $26 billion, as the IMF loan was accompanied by resources from the European Union and the World Bank.[41] Additional resources to Iceland gave the country a total of $11.3 billion.[42]

The IMF also announced plans to set up a $100 billion new short-term lending facility (loans of three months) to middle-income countries that included Mexico, South Korea, and Brazil. This would be especially novel in that the loans did not include policy conditionality, which would certainly help get the money disbursed quickly.

An extraordinary first meeting of the G20 heads of state and finance ministers took place November 14 to 15, 2008, in Washington, DC. The leaders of 19 large, industrialized economies, plus the EU assembled on relatively short notice at US President George W. Bush's invitation to craft a response to the global financial crisis, which included a 47-point action plan.[43] The idea was to show that the most senior authorities, accounting for around 85 percent of global GDP, were serious about cooperating to respond to the crisis and indicated a prominent role for this group in global economic governance.

The leaders agreed that they would implement reforms aimed at strengthening financial markets and regulation. They stressed the IMF's important role in the crisis and also agreed to

G20 Summit
on Financial
Markets and the
World Economy,
November 2008

Official White House Photo by Joyce N. Boghosian

"ensure that the IMF, World Bank and other MDBs (multilateral development banks) have sufficient resources to continue playing their role in overcoming the crisis." They also announced their commitment to reforming voting power in the IMF and World Bank so that emerging and developing countries would have a greater voice. G20 members account for 63.4 percent of votes at the IMF. Right before the global summit, Japan announced it would offer up to $100 billion to the IMF to help emerging economies facing emergency.[44] This was the single largest supplemental contribution ever by an IMF member.[45]

A number of observers thought the new G20 was an exciting innovation in global governance. It brought in more countries than the old G8, which was seen as too small and insufficiently representative to essentially act as the world's "economic steering committee."[46] Bringing a wider array of countries comprising 90 percent of the world's economy and two-thirds of its population could be seen as raising legitimacy.[47] At the same time it is still a self-appointed group that has not fully delivered on its promises for financial reform and more open markets.

The crisis rolled on for the next few months, with some debates between the major powers about issues like how tough financial regulations should be and whether the IMF could improve its surveillance and early warning tools. Between late 2008 and spring 2009, *The Economist* argued

> the global economy has fallen off a cliff. Consumers have cut back their spending. Companies have slashed production, postponed investment and laid off workers in their millions. The financial system remains dysfunctional. Trade flows are shrinking at the fastest rates since the Second World War. . . . Private capital flows are collapsing, devastating those emerging economies, especially Eastern Europe, that rely on foreign borrowing.[48]

The IMF was painfully aware that to address the precrisis drop in lending and to be seen as stepping up to make a difference to countries tackling the crisis, it needed to adapt itself to the new environment. One response was to overhaul its lending framework in ways that would increase flexibility and make it easier for countries to access fund resources. It announced in March 2009 a new Flexible Credit Line, which would even allow countries that had strong policies to receive large infusions of IMF funding without any conditionality at all. It also announced it would work on simplifying the conditionality and adding flexibility to its regular stand-by arrangements, its "workhorse lending instrument." It also announced it would speed up the ability of low income countries access to its Exogenous Shocks Facilities.[49]

In April 2009, the G20 leaders met again, this time in London. The leaders announced a dramatic tripling of the IMF's lending resources to $750 billion. This included $250 billion to be made available immediately by the EU and Japan. They also agreed to, at minimum, double the IMF's concessional resources for low-income countries and to increase the IMF's allocation of SDRs by the equivalent of $250 billion, which would help to inject liquidity into the global economy. Finally, they agreed to sell $6 billion worth of IMF gold, to provide more concessional finance for poorest countries. "Together with the measures we have each taken nationally," the leaders stated in their communiqué, "this constitutes a global plan for recovery on an unprecedented scale." The leaders announced they were deeply engaged in "unprecedented" fiscal stimulus policies, and that they would work to build stronger regulatory and supervisory frameworks for their financial sectors.[50] This seemed to marry the United States' emphasis on the importance of fiscal stimulus and the interest of major European countries, such as France and Germany, to focus on an overhaul of financial sector rules. As a step to strengthening the global financial system, the leaders agreed to create a new Financial Stability Board (FSB) to succeed the Financial Stability Forum (FSF). It would include the FSF's members along with the rest of the G20 members, Spain, and the European Community.[51] The FSB's job is to help coordinate financial stability efforts and promote effective implementation of related policies.

The G20 also pledged to reform the IMF's and other international financial institutions' "mandates, scope and governance." This pledge included their commitment to implementing IMF reforms on quotas and voting that were previously agreed to in April 2008. As noted in Chapter 7, the 2008 reforms were intended to increase the role and voice of low-income countries on the IMF's board. Further, they agreed that the leadership of the top international financial institutions should be appointed in "an open, transparent, and merit-based process," in response to criticism of the old-boy network way of doing things in past, where the leader of the World Bank was always an American, and the leader of the IMF was always a European.[52]

But the G20's interest in strengthening the IMF was also ambiguous in parts. For example, at the next G20 summit in September 2009, it called for modernizing IMF governance but also gave the IMF a subsidiary role when the G20 created a Mutual Assessment Process, or MAP, by which countries would work directly with each other to correct global imbalances, in a sort of "peer review mechanism."[53] Later on, at the G20 Seoul meeting in 2010, the IMF was asked to play a larger role in the MAP, possibly because the MAP had not made much impact in correcting macroeconomic imbalances.

By the end of the IMF's fiscal 2009 year (April 2008-June 2009) it had approved a record 66.7 billion SDR (around $100 billion) in lending to 15 countries.[54] Figure 8.1 shows IMF lending pre- and post-crisis. By 2012, lending was focused on the euro crisis, with 90% of new

Figure 8.1 IMF Arrangements Approved during Financial Years Ended April 30, 2006–2015 (in billions of SDRs)

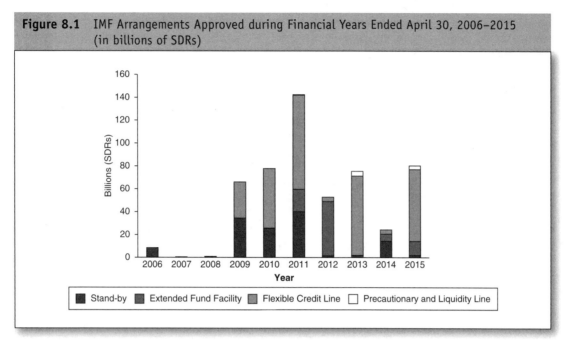

Source: IS IMF Annual Report, 2015.

gross commitments going to Greece and Portugal. To put things in perspective, it is also important to note that the US Federal Reserve was the real lender of last resort at the height of the crisis, injecting over $600 billion in liquidity, which it generated through central bank swap arrangements with a number of European central banks; the European Central Bank itself; and the central banks of Japan, Canada, Australia, and New Zealand. It also set up $30 billion swap lines to the central banks of Brazil, South Korea, Mexico, and Singapore in October 2008, ending in April 2009. ASEAN members, plus China, Japan, and South Korea, had previously agreed in May 2008 to raise the availability of currency swaps to $80 billion.[55] Central bank swaps basically allow central banks quick access to dollars or other currencies they may need in responding to the crisis. Central bank swaps were important and made a difference in the crisis, but they are also selective and ad hoc in nature.[56]

For the remainder of the year and into the first half of 2010, the global economy started sputtering back to life, albeit unevenly. Major countries led the way in cutting their interest rates as low as possible, and many increased government spending to jump start their economies. But eurozone countries were sinking into their own euro crisis, discussed in Chapter 12, and millions of people were still unemployed.

The IMF faced a surprising new challenge to its legitimacy in 2011, when its managing director, Strauss-Kahn, resigned in May in the midst of the first of a series of sex scandals. The 2011 one revolved around a hotel housekeeper accusing him of sexual assault. The charges were later dropped, but others surfaced, including one that he was involved in a French prostitution ring, for which he was later acquitted. After his resignation, the IMF appointed the first woman director of any IFI, former French Finance Minister Christine Lagarde. Many had hoped that for the first time a developing country candidate could win the top job. But in the end, as former IMF chief economist Kenneth Rogoff noted, the result had "all the suspense of a Soviet-era election."[57]

Institutional Responses

Under Strauss-Kahn and Lagarde, the IMF launched a number of new policies and initiatives and other institutional reforms to be more responsive in its lending and better equipped to prepare countries for future crises. There is little analysis of how effective these have been, in part because many of them are fairly new. But the changes do show willingness by the fund to respond to the problems identified by staff and external observers.

In terms of surveillance, the fund worked to better integrate its multilateral and bilateral surveillance. It created in 2011 a new Spillover Report to examine the impact on the "systemic five" largest economies (China, euro area, Japan, United States, United Kingdom) on other economies. The following year it launched a new External Sector Report as another way to examine the impact of the large economies on the rest of the world. The fund has worked to better tailor its policy advice to individual countries, and it has moved to strengthen its financial surveillance. It also created a new global risk assessment matrix. The fund has also sharply increased the money it provides under its nonconcessional financing facilities.

It also created new additions to its lending toolkit. Colombia, Mexico, and Poland were the first to access the new Flexible Credit Line, mentioned above. The Precautionary and Liquidity Line is for countries that would not be eligible for the Flexible Credit Line. For low-income countries there are new concessional facilities with higher access limits and more concessional financing terms.

IMF research has turned more to issues like policies for better managing global capital flows, the adequacy of international reserves, and how to respond to gaps in data that were noticeable in the crisis. The fund is also collaborating with the Financial Stability Board (FSB) on Early Warning Exercises to assess a range of risks to the global economy and suggests ways of mitigating them. The fund issued an updated communication strategy that emphasized the importance of being more responsive to individual country needs and helping to build trust. Internal reviews, such as the 2014 Triennial Surveillance Review, call for the fund to do more to strengthen policy dialogue by doing better at "delivering difficult messages," being more candid in its surveillance, and following up on past policy advice beyond implementation.[58]

These advances have been overshadowed by US blockage of a set of IMF quota and governance reforms agreed to in 2010. The reforms agreed to in 2008 went live in 2011, giving 54 member states quota increases, which would translate into stronger voting power for these countries. In late 2010, finance ministers decided to go further, with a larger reform package. This package called for giving emerging market economies and other developing countries an additional 6% of quota shares. The proposed move would lift the BRIC countries (Brazil, Russia, India, and China) into the top 10 fund shareholders, meaning their economic power would be better reflected in their voting power. China, for example, would jump to being the third largest IMF member, behind the United States and Japan, the same as with the World Bank. The big European countries on the Board agreed to reduce their combined presence from eight of the 24 executive directors to six. The reforms also called for all board members to be elected (instead of appointed).[59]

This second set of reforms were stalled due to opposition by conservative Republicans in the US House of Representatives. Under IMF rules, three-fifths of its members representing 85 percent of total voting power must approve. In effect, support by the United States, with 16.74 percent of total voting power, is critical, giving it the ability to veto major IMF decisions. The short story is that even though the United States has been a leader in calling for IMF reform, the reforms were tied to the US budget approval process. One obstacle to approval occurred with the Republican-dominated House Appropriations Committee sought to link IMF reform funding with White House compromises in health care and the Internal Revenue Service.[60] After a five year delay, the US Congress finally approved the reforms in late December 2015. They were part of the overall spending bill that President Barack Obama immediately signed into law.

The delay in passing these reforms is one of the reasons behind China and the other BRIC countries' decision to set up their own new NDB BRICS and China's decision to set up the new AIIB. While new multilateral development banks compete directly with the World Bank, not the IMF, the moves do reflect frustration that the existing IFIs are stuck in the past and do not adequately represent these important contributors to global economic growth, especially China.

EVALUATION OF RESPONSES AND ACTIVITIES

Many scholars and analysts view the crisis and responses to it as indicative of the failures of global economic governance, which implies the IMF was somehow lacking in leadership, ideas, or coordination—before, during, and/or after—given its historic role in global economic governance. Most analysis does not single out any one particular actor. This makes sense since the most powerful states are the major actors in global economic governance, and this crisis originated in the United States and first spread to other rich countries. Jeffry Frieden, Michael Pettis, Dani Rodrik, and Ernesto Zedillo argued that "the structure of international cooperation on economic issues seems seriously deficient" and in most global economic issue areas other than monetary cooperation, "international cooperation is stalled, flawed, or non-existent." The reasons, they stated, include the fact that governments face domestic political obstacles with increased cooperation, and that the major international economic players have different goals and interests on some of the major issues.[61] Naazneen Barma, Ely Ratner, and Steven Weber agreed that member states interests differ, which makes a coordinated response elusive.[62] Bremer and Roubini argued that instead of living in a "G20 world," we are in a "G-Zero world," because "no single country or bloc of countries has the political and economic leverage—or the will—to drive a truly international agenda." They expect the future holds more conflict over international macroeconomic coordination and financial regulatory reform. The strong consensus seen at the November 2008 and April 2009 G20 meetings were more the result of common fear than agreement, but once the fear abated, so did the forward movement.[63]

But is the picture really this bleak? One can argue that, in fact, global trade and capital flows did show significant recovery in many parts of the world. That can be seen as a sign of success. The IMF's rapid response with emergency financing during the crisis also counts, as does agreement to increase its funding. As Chapter 12 notes, the IMF members eventually boosted IMF resources by more than $430 *billion* to help address the worsening euro sovereign debt crisis. The result would give the IMF access to more than $1 *trillion* dollars to lend. Some scholars, such as Barry Eichengreen, called for expanding the role of the IMF in the wake of the crisis, for example, by giving it more responsibility in coordinating international financial market and banking reform. It could also act as a market maker for an expanded role of the SDR in international transactions (i.e., if the SDR were treated more like an international currency). He acknowledged, though, that we rarely see dramatic changes in the international financial architecture, where the norm has been incremental change.[64] But many individual pieces of incremental change can add up. The IMF's independent evaluation arm argued that, in the end, the IMF has strengthened the global financial safety net because it quadrupled its credit capacity and vastly increased its nonconcessional lending while making its revised lending toolkit more flexible.[65] Joseph Joyce's review of the IMF concluded that while the IMF underestimated the global financial system's state of health and stability before the crisis, during the crisis, it did react quickly to provide assistance and with more flexible terms. This, he explained, made a difference to the recovery and vastly improved the IMF's reputation.[66]

Others have argued that if you dig more deeply, you will find that economic governance overall worked better than we thought. Daniel W. Drezner, for example, argued "global economic governance responded quickly and robustly" to the Great Recession and with a remarkable degree of "institutional resiliency and flexibility."[67] He defined global economic governance as "a set of formal and informal rules that regulate the global economy and the collection of authority relationships that promulgate, coordinate, monitor, or enforce said rules." He measured performance in terms of economic outcomes, policy outputs, and institutional resilience and found in all cases we are no worse off, and at times better off, than at the height of a crisis. Global economic growth, trade flows, and foreign direct investment have all rebounded. His evidence included the rapid response by central banks, finance ministries, the G20, and the IMF in 2008 and 2009. Eric Helleiner had a different take on how all the actions by the IMF, states, and other actors add up. He predicted that in the wake of the crisis we will see increasing fragmentation on global financial governance, which will result in more decentralization of regulation. But he concluded that this may actually be a good thing because it will fit better with the different varieties of capitalism that exist in the world. He implied that this will result in a reduced role for the IMF, for example, as developing countries try to reduce their dependence on the IMF by accumulating large reserves of foreign exchange to help buffer the impact of a future crisis.[68]

CONCLUSION

The global financial crisis of 2008 triggered a rapid response by powerful states and their central banks and resulted in moving the IMF back onto the center state of global economic and financial governance. The IMF was the recipient of a large infusion of resources and quickly moved billions of dollars out the door to countries in need. After dropping the ball in terms of foreseeing a crisis, it acted nimbly after the crisis hit and became a major crisis manager, although central banks were probably the lead managers in the end. The IMF created new instruments, streamlined old ones, reformed its governance structure, and even adjusted some of its long standing views on appropriate economic policies. It even weathered a steamy scandal surrounding Strauss-Kahn. This was a dramatic moment in the IMF's history. Somehow, it overcame the widespread perception that its days might be numbered, even though its surveillance ahead of the crisis was lacking. It secured its place in global economic and financial governance after a period of declining demand for its lending and interest in its advice. The global financial panic was ultimately contained. But the IMF really had no time to bask in any sort of glory. By 2010, it was immersed in the burgeoning euro crisis. Again, it was outside its comfort zone, its usual area of expertise that focused on working with developing countries. It had to turn its attention to Greece, Ireland, and Portugal and maneuver in a politically challenging environment working with European governments, the European Commission, and the European Central Bank. One obvious lesson of these crises is that no region's finances can be understood in isolation. Another is that while the IMF acted quickly once the crisis hit, it must do more to assist member states in preventing crises.

BIBLIOGRAPHY

Barma, Naazneen, Ely Ratner, and Steven Weber. "The Mythical Liberal Order." *The National Interest* 124 (March-April 2013): 56–67.

"Be Bold." *The Economist*, April 2, 2009. http://www.economist.com/node/13405306.

Board of Governors of the Federal Reserve System. "Bear Stearns, JPMorgan Chase, and Maiden Lane Llc." US Federal Reserve, http://www.federalreserve.gov/newsevents/reform_bear-stearns.htm.

Bradford, Colin I., Johannes F. Linn, and Paul Martin. "Global Governance Breakthrough: The G20 Summit and the Future Agenda." In *Policy Brief #168*. Washington, DC: The Brookings Institution, 2008.

Bremmer, Ian, and Nouriel Roubini. "A G-Zero World." *Foreign Affairs* 90. no. 2 (March–April 2011).

Callis, Robert R., and Melissa Kresin. "US Census Bureau News: Residential Vacancies and Homeownership in the Third Quarter 2013." Washington, DC: US Department of Commerce, 2013.

"Crash Course." *The Economist*, September 7, 2013.

Dash, Eric. "Citigroup Profit Fell 57% in Third Quarter." *The New York Times*, October 15, 2007.

Drezner, Daniel W. "The System Worked: Global Economic Governance During the Great Recession." *World Politics* 66, no. 1 (2014): 123–64.

"East Asian Ministers Working to Expand Currency Deals." *The New York Times*, May 4, 2008.

Eichengreen, Barry. "Out of the Box Thoughts About the International Financial Architecture." In *IMF Working Paper*. Washington, DC: International Monetary Fund, 2009.

Federal Housing Finance Agency Office of Inspector General. "A Brief History of the Housing Government-Sponsored Enterprises." Washington, DC: Federal Housing Finance Agency Office of Inspector General, 2013.

Frieden, Jeffry, Michael Pettis, Dani Rodrik, and Ernesto Zedillo. "After the Fall: The Future of Global Cooperation." In *Geneva Reports on the World Economy*. Geneva, Switzerland: International Center for Monetary and Banking Studies, 2012.

Hagerty, James R., Ruth Simon, and Damian Paletta. "U.S. Seizes Mortgage Giants." *The Wall Street Journal*, September 8, 2008.

Haggard, Stephan. "Politics in Hard Times Revisited: The 2008–09 Financial Crisis in Emerging Markets." In *Politics in the New Hard Times: The Great Recession in Comparative*

Perspective, edited by Miles Kahler and David A. Lake, 52–74. Ithaca, NY: Cornell University Press, 2013.

Helleiner, Eric. "Reregulation and Fragmentation in International Financial Governance." *Global Governance* 15, no. 1 (2009): 16–22

Independent Evaluation Office. "IMF Performance in the Run-up to the Financial and Economic Crisis: IMF Surveillance in 2004–07." Washington, DC: International Monetary Fund, 2011.

International Monetary Fund. "Annual Report 2009." Washington, DC: International Monetary Fund, 2009.

———. "Annual Report 2011." Washington, DC: International Monetary Fund, 2011.

———. "Global Financial Stability Report." Washington, DC: International Monetary Fund, 2008.

———. "IMF Executive Board Approves 12.3 Billion Euro Stand-by Arrangement for Hungary." Washington, DC: International Monetary Fund, http://www.imf.org/external/np/sec/pr/2008/pr08275.htm.

———. "IMF Management and Staff Respond to the Report by the Independent Evaluation Office on IMF Performance on the Run-up to the Financial and Economic Crisis." Washington, DC: International Monetary Fund, 2011.

———. "Lending by the IMF." Washington, DC: International Monetary Fund. http://www.imf.org/external/about/lending.htm.

———. "London Summit-Leader's Statement." Washington, DC: International Monetary Fund, 2009.

Joyce, Joseph P. *The IMF and Global Financial Crises: Phoenix Rising?* New York: Cambridge University Press, 2013.

Karnitschnig, Matthew, Deborah Solomon, Liam Pleven, and Jon. E. Hilsenrath. "U.S. to Take over AIG in $85 Billion Bailout; Credit Dries Up." *The Wall Street Journal*, September 16, 2008.

Kingsley, Patrick. "Financial Crisis: Timeline." *The Guardian*, August 7, 2012. http://www.theguardian.com/business/2012/aug/07/credit-crunch-boom-bust-timeline.

Krugman, Paul. "Why Weren't Alarm Bells Ringing?." *The New York Review of Books*, October 23, 2014.

Lamdany, Ruben, and Sanjay Dhar. "IMF Response to the Financial and Economic Crisis." Washington, DC: Independent Evaluation Office, 2014.

"Lessons of the Fall." *The Economist*, October 18, 2007.

Mollenkamp, Carrick, Susanne Craig, Serena Ng, and Aaron Lucchetti. "Lehman Files for Bankruptcy, Merrill Sold, AIG Seeks Cash." *The Wall Street Journal*, September 16, 2008.

Nishikawa, Yoko. "Japan to Offer IMF up to $100 Billion from Fx Reserves." *Reuters*, November 13, 2008.

Paulson, Henry M. *On the Brink: Inside the Race to Stop the Collapse of the Global Financial System*. 1st ed. New York: Business Plus, 2010.

Rogoff, Kenneth S. "After the Scandal, More of the Same at the I.M.F." *The New York Times*, June 15, 2011.

Samans, Richard, Klaus Schwab, and Mark Malloch-Brown. "Running the World, After the Crash." *Foreign Policy*, January 3, 2011.

Saporito, Bill. "Freddie Mac and Fannie Mae Shareholders." *Time*, November 3, 2008.

Sorkin, Andrew Ross. "JP Morgan Pays $2 a Share for Bear Stearns." *The New York Times*, March 17, 2008.

Strauss-Kahn, Dominique. "The IMF and Its Future." Washington, DC: International Monetary Fund. http://www.imf.org/external/np/speeches/2008/121508.htm.

Taylor, John B. "Obama and the IMF Are Unhappy with Congress? Good; the International Monetary Fund Needs to Get Its House in Order before Washington Green-Lights More Money." *The Wall Street Journal*, February 13, 2014.

"The World This Week." *The Economist*, September 20, 2008, 10.

US Securities and Exchange Commission. "SEC Enforcement Actions: Addressing Misconduct That Led to or Arose from the Financial Crisis." Washington, DC: US Securities and Exchange Commission, http://www.sec.gov/spotlight/enf-actions-fc.shtml.

Weiss, Martin A. "International Monetary Fund: Background and Issues for Congress." Washington, DC: Congressional Research Service, 2013.

Wessel, David. "Top Economists Rethink Post-Crisis Policy; Old Remedies Not Helpful for Spurring Growth, Preventing Calamity." *The Wall Street Journal*, November 13, 2013.

World Bank. "Annual Report 2009."Washington, DC: World Bank, 2009.

———. "Annual Report 2010." Washington, DC: World Bank, 2010.

9 The World Trade Organization

If you are someone who doesn't know much about international trade, an interesting exercise is to look at the label on the shirt you are wearing. Chances are it was not made in the same country that you are living in at the moment. *International trade*, or the buying and selling of goods and services across national borders, is such a ubiquitous part of our lives we are hardly aware of it. We eat foods grown or processed in other countries; we drink water bottled in other countries and shipped overseas to us. No doubt a high percentage of your personal belongings were made in many different countries. Some goods, like cars, are built with parts produced in numerous countries. Raw materials from one country are regularly shipped to another to be made into a final product. One study showed that 97 percent of the factory gate price of an iPhone4 "made" in China actually consisted of materials, components, and intellectual property that came from South Korea, the United States, Germany, Japan, and elsewhere.[1] In fact, international trade is a major issue for environmentalists, because all of that shipping back and forth emits greenhouse gases and other pollutants that contribute to climate change, acid rain, and other environmental problems. Lori Wallach, a prominent critic of the trading system, once pointed out that US timber companies have harvested timber to make into chopsticks that are sent to Japan, while a Japanese company harvested timber in Malaysia to make into toothpicks that are shipped to the United States. She cynically concluded, "Somehow, with all that transportation, all of that extra processing and labeling and translating, that trade is more worthwhile than trees in the United States going into our toothpicks, and the trees in Asia going into the Japanese market."[2]

The great classical economist Adam Smith remarked in the 18th century that trade is deeply embedded in human nature, since humans have a propensity to "truck, barter and exchange one thing for another," a trait he observed can be found in no other species.[3] "Nobody ever saw a dog make a fair and deliberate exchange of one bone for another with another dog," he wrote.[4] In today's world, we depend on international trade for basic goods and even natural resources.

Trade flows are huge and have been choppy in recent years. In 2009, the year after the Great Recession set in, the volume of global trade contracted 12 percent from the year before—the largest contraction since World War II—even though global trade in goods and services still stood at an astonishing $15 trillion.[5] Other global challenges have impacted trade as well, but trade remains the lifeblood of the global economy. According to the WTO, world trade in goods zoomed from $2 trillion in 1980 to almost $19 trillion in 2013. Trade in services grew at an ever-quicker pace, from $367 billion in 1980 to $4.6 trillion in 2013.[6] Figure 9.1 shows world trade as a percentage of GDP, increasing from 38.7 percent in 1980 to 59.4 percent in 2013. The lion's share of this trade is taking place in North America, Europe, and Asia. The US

Figure 9.1   Volume of World Trade, Percentage of GDP, 1980–2013

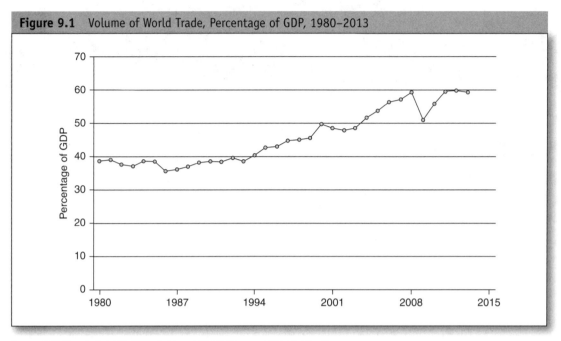

Source: WTO Secretariat, "World Trade Report 2013" (Geneva: WTO, 2013), 19.

monthly trade deficit is well into the tens of billions of dollars, although there is also a surplus in services trade.

International trade is a powerful topic in international and domestic politics for many reasons. It not only underpins economic growth, but also creates a variety of winners and losers. When working properly, trade stimulates both economic growth and efficiency. It allows companies to find new customers by expanding in overseas markets, it increases competition between companies and countries, and it allows consumers to have more choices in the goods and service they buy and to buy these goods and services more cheaply. When not working properly, trade can fan tensions between countries, harm the environment, increase poverty, hurt health, and fuel conflict, among other negative outcomes. An example of trade impacting health is the case of the EU banning imports of hormone-treated US beef starting in the late 1980s as part of a ban on the use of growth-promoting hormones in raising beef, a wide-spread practice in the United States that concerned European consumers. The United States, in turn, banned imports of beef from the EU amid concerns about mad cow disease, or Bovine Spongiform Encephalopathy after an outbreak in the late 1990s. An example of trade impacting social welfare is the use by some developing countries of child labor to produce goods—especially those for export, which fetch much needed foreign currency. The use of child labor to produce goods like carpets and rugs in countries such as India has been documented by reports that children as young as eight have been sold into bonded labor to weave rugs up to 16 hours a day.[7] The International Labour Organization in Geneva has prohibited this practice and many countries have adopted legislation to combat it, but it is difficult to police.

Trade is a major issue for emerging and developing countries. In terms of the former, China, Mexico, and India, for example, rank as numbers 1, 15, and 19, respectively, in the world's leading exporters of merchandise trade in 2013, and as numbers 2, 14, and 12 in the world's leading importers of merchandise trade.[8] For poor countries, it is especially important that they can sell their goods and services to other countries so they can receive foreign currency to use for purchasing goods and services from other countries. When they are denied access to rich country markets, their own economies may shrink, hurting the ability of trade to help alleviate poverty. International trade can cause a variety of other negative consequences as well. For example, developing countries that depend on exports of primary commodities also have a great deal of income inequality, since the key beneficiaries of commodity exports are usually landowners or mining companies.[9] Fluctuations in commodity prices can cause problems for their broader economies as well.

It will come as no surprise, then, that international trade is a contentious political issue. Workers may suffer when their industries are threatened by cheap foreign imports. Consumers, by contrast, benefit from cheap foreign goods. International trade can put some companies out of business and help others expand rapidly. It can benefit some countries and economies and hurt others. Governments regularly set up barriers to keep foreign competition out and then negotiate to reduce trade barriers.

The reduction of trade and tariff barriers coupled with an increase in volumes of international trade flows in past decades has given rise to the appearance and widespread use of the term *globalization* and debates about its impact on global politics and governance. The expansion of trade and elimination of some regulations and the upsurge of borderless commerce has been accompanied by increased travel, waves of migration, and capital flows between countries and trading blocs. Globalization is defined in numerous ways, but most definitions have, at their heart, the idea of economic integration at the global level.[10] The world today is more integrated than at any other time in the past century. That being said, some people have the impression that national economies are far more integrated than they actually are. For example, the United States produces over 80 percent of what is consumed in the United States.[11] Between-country trade is nowhere close to being as important as within-country trade. Nonetheless, there are lively and widespread debates about globalization that have to do with the extent to which it helps or hurts people (labor, the poor), the environment, human rights, culture, sovereignty, and a host of other issues. "Globalization," said former World Trade Organization (WTO) Director-General Mike Moore, is "the defining feature of our time." While it is part of an opportunity to "build better living standards and a safer and more secure world," at the same time, "such enormous upheaval is unsettling, especially when it seems unpredictable and uncontrollable."[12]

Today, the WTO is at the center of the international trading regime, although its position has been challenged by critics and the fact that the latest trade round—called the Doha Development Agenda—failed. The WTO is an international organization that is the successor to a trade treaty, the General Agreement on Tariffs and Trade (GATT), that governed international trade negotiations for over forty years. The GATT was enormously successful in achieving growing liberalization of world trade, especially in the lowering of tariff barriers. The WTO, in turn, has widened and deepened the scope of trade agreements, but has done so amid growing trade politics and macroeconomic realities that have stalled the latest round of negotiation. It also has a novel mechanism for resolving trade disputes between member states, which essentially acts like a court with rulings that are compulsory and binding to member states. This mechanism is seen as a major advance in the judicial powers of international organizations. Like the other organizations examined in this book, the WTO is also a source of controversy. While the WTO has been praised for contributing to economic growth, it is also plagued by criticism of its accountability, legitimacy, and the sometimes negative impact of free trade on issues like labor and the environment. Its 1999 meetings in Seattle were met by a major anti-globalization protest, with over 30,000 demonstrators protesting against the WTO. As former WTO Secretary-General Renato Ruggiero noted,

> As the WTO becomes more important to the world economy, it also becomes a growing focal point for public hopes and concerns: How should the world protect endangered species and promote sustainable development? Should trade be linked to labor standards and human rights? Can we preserve cultural identities in an age of borderless communications? Can we have an open world economy without a stable financial system? And what about eradicating poverty, reducing inequalities, and promoting the rights of women? These and many other issues are a world away from "traditional" trade concerns such as tariffs or quotas. And yet all find themselves part, directly or indirectly, of the new trade agenda.[13]

All of these changes mean that the WTO is inextricably linked to geopolitics. Its rules impact state policies, economies, and even security interests. There is also political and economic tension at its core: Countries turn to the WTO because they want to see the benefits from trade, but they also want to maintain their ability to restrict trade in some areas, as no country on earth allows completely free trade with nary a trade-constraining rule.

This chapter begins by briefly discussing the pros and cons of the promotion of free trade, which is the primary goal underpinning the GATT and WTO. The fact that international trade has both benefits and costs and both winners and losers fuels the debates surrounding the international trade regime and organizations. The chapter then turns to the birth of the GATT, its goals, evolution, accomplishments, and shortfalls, before presenting the WTO and its own growth and challenges. The international trade regime has been very successful in some respects; namely, reducing tariff barriers to trade and in expanding what sorts of items fall under the negotiating umbrella. It has been less successful in addressing agriculture, the role of developing countries, environmental and social issues, and some other grey areas of trade like protectionism. The failure of the current Doha round has also hurt the WTO's leadership role in global trade.

OPEN MARKETS, PROTECTED MARKETS

The debates about trade, over the centuries, have been between those who support more open and free trade, or trade unencumbered by government meddling,[14] and those who support regulating trade for other reasons, which may be related to power, sovereignty, development, labor, security, health, social welfare, and the environment. The debate about the goodness of economic openness goes back hundreds of years. Free trade ideas represent what is called the *liberal perspective* in economics. This is somewhat different than traditional liberal political theory, which emphasizes equality and liberty, although the two perspectives may overlap depending on the thinker or time.[15]

One of the most famous free trade proponents, Smith, argued in the 18th century that the "wealth of nations" increases if market barriers are removed and people are left to pursue their trucking, bartering, and trading. Certainly it is common sense that if a country is good at producing something, it will benefit by selling that item abroad. Less intuitive is the idea that even if country A produces everything *less* efficiently than country B, it *still* benefits through trade. This is the concept of *comparative advantage* that was laid out by David Ricardo in the early 19th century. Ricardo used the example of Portugal being able to produce both wine and cloth more efficiently (with less labor) than England.[16] At first glance, one might conclude that it wouldn't make sense for Portugal to trade in one or both of these items with England. However, if Portugal itself is better at producing wine than cloth, comparative advantage means that it still makes sense for Portugal to focus more on producing wine and less on cloth, and therefore to sell wine to Britain and buy cloth from Britain. Another simple example might be a corporate executive and her assistant. It may be that the executive is better with administrative tasks than her assistant, but it still makes sense for the executive to devote her time and energy to those things her assistant cannot do and delegate to the assistant the administrative duties. The upshot of Ricardo's theory is that specialization can be beneficial to both trading partners, even if one produces everything more efficiently than the other. Since Ricardo's time, many economists have produced new models (or extended old models) to show why trade between countries is beneficial.

Although the benefits of free trade are widely touted in the discipline of economics, no country in the world has ever completely opened its borders to allow free trade across all economic sectors. More commonly throughout history, governments have sought to create trade barriers in a variety of sectors for a variety of reasons, all of which serve to benefit the country vis-à-vis others. Mercantilism, for example, was a "system of economic control" used by Europe's colonial powers in the 1700s to exploit their colonies' markets in order to enrich "the crown" and strengthen the colonial power's military force.[17] Mercantilists believed trade and economic growth should be harnessed to strengthen the state. For mercantilists, the economy was subordinate to the state and national security and exports were more beneficial than imports. A related idea is that industrial self-sufficiency is preferable for national security reasons than being dependent on other countries for specific goods. Indeed, Adam Smith's own work was promoted by his reaction against mercantilist thinking.

A more modern variation of mercantilism argues that self-sufficiency is necessary to help promote development in poor countries. This was the idea behind *import-substitution-industrialization*, a policy favored by many Latin American and African countries in the twentieth century as a means to reduce dependence on industrialized economies by encouraging domestic production of manufactured products, even if they could be purchased cheaper from other countries. Unsurprisingly, low-skill, labor-intensive industries in developed countries that face "high and rising import penetration" will also be highly protectionist. Alternatively, industries and multinational corporations that are mainly export-oriented are less protectionist.[18] Throughout the world, labor working for industries that face competition from imports often favors government protection. (However, it is also the case that when some jobs are destroyed by trade, others may be created. This is the concept of *creative destruction*.[19]

One well-cited example is how the loss of textile manufacturing—and jobs—in North Carolina, gave rise to the Research Triangle Park, with high paying, better jobs in the high-tech and biotech industries.) More recently, interest groups that were not used to cooperating in the past have found common interest in protectionism. Labor unionists and environmentalists marched side by side at the 1999 Seattle protests against the WTO.

Today we see that efforts toward more liberalized trade and efforts toward protection often occur simultaneously. Countries like the United States that negotiate for more liberalized world trade at the GATT/WTO also negotiate bilaterally to receive preferential treatment on specific products or sectors. There are also many regional trade agreements that give a region preferential treatment over the rest of the world. The largest and most economically important one has been the European Economic Community (EEC, now the European Union). The six founding members of the EEC agreed to gradually eliminate barriers to trade among member states and create a common external tariff for the rest of the world. Another is the North American Free Trade Agreement (NAFTA). The GATT/WTO rules do allow member states to enter into bilateral and regional agreements, as long as they do not increase trade barriers to nonmembers. While the many bilateral and regional trade agreements lower trade barriers among their members, they may also be eroding the WTO's central role in the international trade regime. One thing is clear: the broad debate about the pros and cons of free trade is a perennial one with plenty of data supporting either side. More precise answers come from policymakers and scholars who drill down into the specifics of individual countries, regions, time periods, policies, domestic politics, and economic circumstances, which better illuminates who wins and loses.

THE GATT

The creation of an international trade organization was also on the minds of the US and British officials involved in creating the Bretton Woods organizations as World War II was ending, and took place parallel to discussions on money and finance that resulted in the birth of the World Bank and IMF. While the Bretton Woods conference recognized the importance of a trade institution, its participants represented finance ministries rather than trade ministries, so the issue was not fully pursued.[20] The discussion of trade was also politically more difficult, and ultimately, the proposed International Trade Organization (ITO) never came into being when it was clear that it would not receive enough support in the US Congress to pass. One problem was, as Jeffry Frieden explained, "trade policy pitted powerful firms whose profits depended on protection against other powerful firms whose profits depended on the removal of trade barriers."[21] Congress also feared the impact of the ITO on sovereignty since its draft charter was an ambitious document that sought to address issues beyond trade, such as employment rules and restrictive business practices. US politicians saw this as too intrusive.[22]

Part of the group of states negotiating the ITO also began in 1945 to discuss how to reinvigorate trade liberalization by reducing tariffs. Tariffs, which are taxes on imports, were governments' main instrument of trade policy. Taxing an import makes it relatively more expensive vis-à-vis a domestic product. That, in turn, is expected to reduce the demand for the import relative to the domestic product. So, if similar US and Chinese appliances cost $100, but the Chinese appliance faces a $20 tariff, and now costs $120, consumers will hopefully gravitate toward the cheaper appliance and benefit the US company relative to the Chinese company. Of course, things get interesting and complicated if the Chinese decide to sell below cost, which is called *dumping*, or if consumers continue to prefer the Chinese product for reasons other than cost. Rising tariffs were particularly problematic in the 1930s, when the United States Smoot-Hawley Tariff Act of 1930 caused US tariffs to increase dramatically, which triggered retaliatory actions from US trading partners. These same *beggar-thy-neighbor* policies were behind the Bretton Woods negotiators' interest in creating an IMF to promote currency stability.

As was the case with the IMF and World Bank discussions, the United States played the lead role in influencing the birth of GATT, with the strong involvement of Great Britain, and the support of other allies as well. In 1947, 23 states signed the General Agreement on Tariffs and Trade, which was supposed to be an interim agreement that would eventually operate under the forthcoming ITO. The ITO was never born, but the GATT continued on its own and remained a "provisional" agreement for its 47 years of existence.[23] The GATT was therefore a strange creature, technically neither a formal organization nor a treaty (since it never came into force). While the states negotiating the ITO then agreed to a Charter just weeks after the GATT was signed, the fact that some states would not ratify it, including the powerful United States, meant that by 1951 the ITO was essentially finished.[24]

What Was the GATT?

The GATT was an agreement that sought to liberalize world trade by promoting open, non-discriminatory trade, mainly through rounds of negotiations that pursued reductions in tariffs. The contracting parties actually weren't committing themselves to *free* trade with zero tariffs; rather, they were agreeing to treat all signatories the same in applying tariffs on imports. That meant that any tariff concessions agreed at the negotiating rounds extended to all other contracting parties.[25] It is therefore more accurate to understand the GATT, and its successor the WTO, as a system of rules to promote more open and fair competition, rather than undiluted free trade. The GATT set rules on the types of policies countries can use to improve their own trade position vis-à-vis the rest of the world. The GATT's legal structure ended up being, in trade scholar John Jackson's words, "a complex mixture of almost 200 treaty texts (protocols, amendments, rectifications, etc.)" forever clouded by its awkward provisional status.[26]

At its heart are two principles: *most-favored nation treatment* and *national treatment*, both of which were meant to encourage countries to reduce or avoid discrimination in their trade policies and relations. Most-favored nation (MFN) is actually a slightly confusing term, because it means the opposite of one nation favoring another; it means that if one member grants a tariff concession or other trade advantages to another member, it has to grant the same benefit to all other GATT members. It means that one country will *not* favor another in granting a trade privilege. The concept of national treatment is similar, but it has to do with trade that has already entered a country's border. It means that Country A has to treat other countries' products the same way as it treats its own products. Country A, then, cannot create obstacles to Country B's products by introducing special domestic taxes, spurious licensing requirements or ancillary charges that discriminate against Country B's products or services. Such obstacles are essentially offering protection to Country A's products. National treatment, therefore means, that a country must treat its domestic producers and foreign producers equally.

In addition to the principle of nondiscrimination, the GATT signatories committed themselves to the principles of transparency in their trading practices; consultation and dispute settlement where conflict arose; and *reciprocity*, or the idea of maintaining balance in trade relations with mutually agreeable rules.[27]

The negotiators of the GATT did realize that some exceptions to these principles of free trade might make sense from time to time. Article XX of the GATT agreement, for example, also says countries can use protectionist measures to protect human, animal, or plant life or health; public morals; national treasures; and a few other issues, as long as such steps are not a disguised form of protectionism. Naturally, this list created a contentious gray area of disputes, in which one country's concern about a health issue inspires its trading partner's cries of protectionism. Article XXI allows exceptions relating to national security issues. And Article XXIV allows for the fact that countries might band together in smaller groups, like a region, to create a "preferential trading arrangement." Under regional or preferential trade agreements, the group of countries creates freer trade among each other, but still may raise barriers against the rest of the world. This does seem to be a contradiction to the idea behind MFN. Jagdish Bhagwati explains this by noting when the GATT was negotiated, most people thought this exception would rarely be used because it meant that members of a preferential agreement would have to make substantial concessions in lowering almost all tariffs, and therefore, it would be less attractive than the GATT version.[28]

The GATT operated through eight negotiating trade rounds, each of which involved more countries and took on new issues. The trade rounds brought together trade ministers to negotiate tariff-reducing measures, as well as agree on rules for trade policies. The focus of GATT for its first five rounds was in the negotiation of tariff reductions. As mentioned above, 23 contracting parties were involved in the first round; by the eighth round (the Uruguay Round, 1986–94), 123

Table 9.1 GATT Trade Rounds

Year	Place/name	Subjects covered	Countries
1947	Geneva	Tariffs	23
1949	Annecy	Tariffs	13
1951	Torquay	Tariffs	38
1956	Geneva	Tariffs	26
1960–1961	Geneva Dillon Round	Tariffs	26
1964–1967	Geneva Kennedy Round	Tariffs and antidumping measures	62
1973–1979	Geneva Tokyo Round	Tariffs, nontariff measures, "framework" agreements	102
1986–1994	Geneva Uruguay Round	Tariffs, nontariff measures, rules, services, intellectual property, dispute settlement, textiles, agriculture, and creation of WTO	123

Source: http://www.wto.org/english/thewto_e/whatis_e/tif_e/fact4_e.htm.

contracting parties were present. The value of trade covered by the negotiating rounds went from $10 billion in the first round (Geneva Round) to over $4 trillion by the end of the Uruguay Round.

The GATT was more of an institution in the broad sense—a set of rules that governed state behavior—than in the narrow sense of being a formal organization. It was also a "member-driven" institution in the sense that it had a very small secretariat. Trade rounds were events where trade ministers came together to negotiate on behalf of their governments. This meant the GATT's bureaucracy was marginal. Even the WTO's bureaucracy today is extremely small relative to other major international organizations, with fewer than 650 staff. (However, there is a growing literature that argues even such a small secretariat is an active actor that can have influence on shaping member state interests.)[29] The GATT and its successor the WTO are institutions that reflect a realist perspective of IOs more than anything else. Their actions primarily reflect bargaining and negotiation that takes place among their member states.

How Did the GATT Evolve?

The GATT negotiations were quite successful in convincing countries to reduce their tariff barriers. Even the first round, held in Geneva, succeeded in producing an agreement on concessions on 45,000 tariffs that impacted $10 billion (or around one-fifth) of global trade.[30] Each subsequent round continued bringing tariffs down. The Kennedy Round, concluded in 1967, included an across-the-board tariff cut of 35 percent on 60,000 different products. By the GATT's end, average tariffs were a fraction of their rates before the GATT existed. For example, by the mid-1990s, tariff rates on industrial goods produced by industrial countries were below 4 percent.[31] World trade in goods grew steadily at an average annual rate of 8 percent for the first twenty years (1950–1974), before showing signs of slowing down.[32]

By the mid-1960s, it became apparent that countries were reducing tariffs at the same time they were creating new barriers to trade. These new barriers were called *nontariff barriers* (NTBs), or *nontariff measures*, which include government subsidies (such as export subsidies), antidumping duties, government procurement rules, and also packaging or labeling rules that, in effect, discriminate against a foreign producer. They may also include what are called "technical barriers to trade" and sanitary and phytosanitary measures. Some of these barriers are developed to protect consumers or the environment, but they are often developed to protect domestic producers. Sometimes a measure kills two birds with one stone. For example, in the 1980s, a Danish government regulation called for beer, soft drinks, and mineral waters to be marketed only in a limited number of government-approved container types that allowed for a large proportion to be returned, recycled, and reused. The idea was innovative from an environmental perspective, especially in calling for reuse of containers. But foreign manufacturers complained that this rule discriminated against them, since they would have to pay high costs to redesign their containers and to find ways of refilling them. Foreign companies were also suspicious that the Danish rules didn't apply to wine and milk, drinks where there was little foreign competition in Denmark.[33] The issue for the GATT was when these NTBs distort trade.

GATT negotiations started tackling NTBs in the mid-1960s at the Kennedy Round, and more extensively at the Tokyo Round in the 1970s.[34] By the time of the Uruguay Round, it was clear that the GATT had been successful in reducing tariffs on products and expanding the range of trade addressed, but it also had several weak areas. On the plus side, the decline in tariffs contributed to a large gain in trade between industrial countries and to growing economic interdependence among countries. On the minus side, plenty of restrictions still existed in other areas of trade, especially in agriculture. The GATT was also relatively less successful in addressing the thousands of NTBs. The GATT also had a weak dispute settlement mechanism. The panel of experts organized under the GATT system could listen to one country's complaint against another and even rule on it, but the accused country could not be forced to comply with the ruling. The dispute resolution system operated on the basis of diplomacy rather than rules to solve trade disputes. As the WTO itself has noted, "By the early 1980s, the General Agreement was no longer as relevant to the realities of world trade as it had been in the 1940s."[35] It pointed out that global economic recession and rising rates of unemployment in the 1970s and early 1980s spurred governments to renew their efforts to protect sectors facing foreign competition. Meanwhile trade in new areas, like services, was growing, and countries were becoming adept at exploiting loopholes in the GATT. The GATT needed to be strengthened or reformed to avoid losing even more credibility.

The Uruguay Round, launched in 1986, was the most ambitious round in the GATT's history. Its goal was not only to continue to lower tariff and nontariff barriers to trade, but to produce agreements for trade in new issue areas of trade in services, intellectual property, and agriculture. Services included banking, insurance, and tourism. Intellectual property included patents, copyrights, and trademarks. And agriculture was a long-term, politically-hot issue where European and American farmers lobbied strongly to continue being protected.

The Uruguay round was negotiated for seven years, ending in 1994, lasting almost twice as long as its original schedule. Ministers from 109 countries signed the agreement, in Marrakesh, Morocco, pledging to reduce tariffs by an average of 40 percent and producing agreements on services, intellectual property rights, textiles, and financial services. The agreement was 22,000 pages long and weighed 385 pounds.[36] To give one an idea of the level of detail involved, Paul Blustein offered an example:

> The variety of duties that U.S. customs officers would assess on poultry, which took up an entire page, included a tariff on live chickens of 0.9 cents per bird; a levy on fresh, chilled, or frozen chicken meat that was not cut in pieces of 8.8 cents per kilogram; a charge on "cuts and offal, fresh or chilled," of 17.6 cents per kilogram; a duty of 15 cents per kilogram on turkeys that were "not cut in pieces, fresh or chilled," and so on.[37]

It was the largest trade negotiation in history and covered a wide range of trade, including toothbrushes, power boats, HIV treatment, and genes of wild rice.[38] During the negotiations, which included dramatic moments of deadlocks and breakthroughs, many were pessimistic that negotiators would reach a successful outcome. Trade issues had become more complex, as issues beyond trade in goods became more prominent, and frustration grew in many quarters about the lack of action on major issues like agriculture. In addition to the new side agreements mentioned above, the Uruguay Round also produced an agreement by rich countries to phase out the 1974 Multi-Fiber Arrangements, which protected their textile industries from cheaper developing country imports.[39] The ministers also put forth an agenda and timetable for future negotiations on issues that ranged from maritime services to telecoms. Perhaps most importantly, the round established the new WTO, which was a vast improvement over the GATT, creating a formal international organization that was created to be on par with the IMF and World Bank to oversee the global economy. Business left unaddressed by the Uruguay Round, including environmental, social, and labor issues, would be tackled by the new organization.

WTO BIRTH, GOVERNANCE, DISPUTE SETTLEMENT

The new WTO came into being on January 1, 1995, housed in the same Geneva building as the GATT, on the shores of Lake Geneva. Peter Sutherland, the GATT's Director-General, changed hats and became the WTO's first Director-General.[40] Jackson, a trade expert, proposed creating a new organization to replace the GATT in the early 1990s. The Canadian trade minister, John Crosbie, helped to propel the idea forward with a formal proposal that the creation of a new trade organization be part of the Uruguay Round Agreement.[41] A stronger organization was seen as necessary to solve some of the weaknesses of the GATT.

Technically, the new WTO was created to administer the GATT and its new related agreements. The new WTO contained all the rules from the GATT including the agreements negotiated at the Uruguay Round, the General Agreement in trade and services, and the Agreement on Trade-Related Intellectual Property Rights (TRIPS). The WTO agreements included special treatment for developing countries and required that its members regularly inform the WTO about their trade laws and measures in an effort to make trade policies more transparent. Other annexes of the agreement deal with specific sectors and issues, including agriculture, rules of origin, textiles and clothing, and health regulations for farm products, for example. By 2015, WTO membership stood at 161 members, up from 128 by the end of the Uruguay Round. Members can be states or "customs territories" that have autonomy in conducting trade policy. This means that the European Union is a member, in addition to EU member states. Taiwan, while not officially recognized by all countries as a sovereign state, is also a member, since 2002.

How Does the WTO Work?

The WTO is more of a member-driven organization than the IMF and World Bank, since it has a much smaller bureaucracy of around 635 staff and its emphasis is on trade negotiations between governments. Its budget is also rather small at under 200 million Swiss francs (2014), with member contributions based on their state's (or economy's, in the case of members like Taiwan) share of world trade.[42] The WTO's highest authority is the Ministerial Conference, where trade ministers meet at least once every two years to negotiate trade agreements. For the most part, decisions are made by consensus, not voting, although voting is possible where consensus is not. At the WTO, consensus has meant that no participating member states actively opposes. In many cases, the process has been that small groups of key countries meet to hammer out an agreement, and then beyond this group, consensus occurs if there is no opposition.[43] Formally, the WTO operates on a "one country, one vote" basis, akin to the UN General Assembly, but in practice this does not mean small countries have the same weight as the United States or the European Union. Indeed, the two largest trading members have the most important trading markets in the world, so the leverage and power of the US and EU is far greater than that of other WTO members. This can be a problem given that there is more competition between the EU and the US, which may not work well in an organization relying on consensus in making decisions.[44] Scholars have argued that the US and EU also strengthen their leverage in WTO negotiations through techniques such as *forum-shifting*, where they negotiate with different countries in different fora simultaneously, which gives the powerful countries more opportunities to use incentives to get what they want.[45] Negotiations can be lengthy and difficult. As former Director-General Moore once wrote, "It is consensus by exhaustion."[46]

Figure 9.2 WTO Organogram

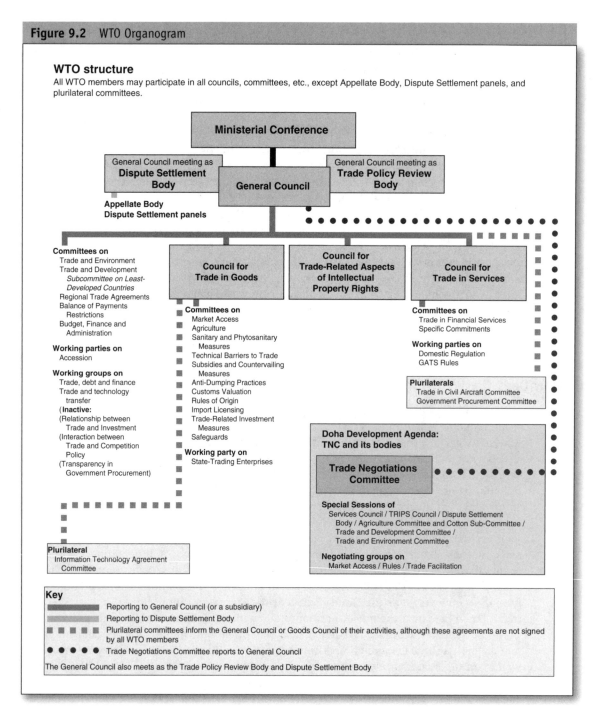

Source: http://www.wto.org/english/thewto_e/whatis_e/tif_e/organigram_e.pdf

Under the Ministerial Conference is the General Council, which handles the WTO's daily work, and consists of the senior member state officials from all the WTO member states. These are typically ambassadors. In fact, many developing countries will have one official represent their country at the WTO and at other Geneva-based UN organizations. The General Council wears different hats. For example, it can meet as the WTO's Dispute Settlement body (discussed below) or its Trade Policy Review Body. Three additional councils operate under the General Council: one on trade in goods (Goods Council), one on trade in services (Services Council), and one on trade-related aspects of intellectual property rights (TRIPS Council). There are various other committees and subsidiary bodies that handle smaller subsets of issues.[47] The role of the small secretariat is supposed to be purely administrative: to organize meetings, provide technical support, and help support member governments on the various WTO activities. As the WTO website states, the Secretariat "has no decision-making powers."[48] However, in the scholarly field of international organizations, there is a growing literature that looks at ways even the most administrative bureaucracies can help to influence member state interests or actions. For example, Frank Biermann et al. argued that cognitive influence (changing knowledge and belief systems), normative influence (impacting norm-building on specific issues), and executive influence (assisting country efforts in ways that impact interests) are ways in which international bureaucracies influence their member states and other political actors.[49] Sikina Jinnah, in turn, has argued these mechanisms have operated in the WTO's Secretariat, along with additional mechanisms of litigation facilitation (legal support in dispute settlement) and strategic framing of information and ideas to influence public opinion. This has meant that in the area where trade and environmental issues overlap, at times these mechanisms have increased the secretariat's authority and ability to influence member states.[50]

The WTO's Dispute Settlement Body (DSB) is one of the most important innovations of the WTO. The DSB acts as a quasi-court and can make judgments that force countries to change their domestic laws. It provides an example of how an IO can actually intrude upon state sovereignty. Its powers, say some observers, are "unprecedented," because its decisions are compulsory and binding.[51] Its Appellate Body has been called "an autonomous judiciary," which can produce decisions that are not in line with powerful state interests. Further, it can authorize the winners of cases to punish the losers for noncompliance.[52] It was the United States, which so often throughout its history has feared intrusions into its sovereignty, that championed a strong dispute resolution mechanism. The United States proposed both that panel reports be automatically adopted and that a new Appellate Body be created, giving parties a right to appeal.[53]

Under the old GATT, as noted above, dispute settlement was accomplished (or not) more by diplomacy than rules. The countries on either side of the dispute had to agree to set up a panel and to accept the panel's ruling. It was easy for one of the parties to block the process or drag it on for years. There was no enforcement mechanism. Under the dispute settlement mechanism, there are clear rules, processes, and timetables, and no party can block the process.[54] The rule of law is what largely influences dispute settlement under the new mechanism, compared with the softer approach of the old one. The new system is certainly being used. During the forty plus years of GATT, member states filed 535 complaints.[55] By contrast, during the dispute settlement mechanism's first twenty years, there have been over 450 cases.[56] The cases have addressed a wide variety of issues, from antidumping measures on frozen shrimp to protection of intellectual property rights. The current dispute settlement procedures have clearly strengthened the WTO's authority in international trade.

WTO disputes arise when one member accuses another of violating the WTO agreements. The ideal first step is for the countries to settle the dispute themselves through consultation. If that fails, a panel of three to five respected trade experts is chosen by the Dispute Settlement Body (which consists of all member states, wearing a different hat) and the panel examines the evidence and makes a decision about which side is right. The panel process consists of both parties submitting written legal arguments that present their interpretation of the issues and the laws. The panel meets to hear each side's presentation and to ask questions. Third parties can also be involved. The Panel's rulings tend to be long, detailed legal documents.[57] Officially, the panel is presenting its decision to the Dispute Settlement Body, but in practice it is tough for member states to reject the panel's conclusion, because it can only be done by consensus.[58] Interestingly, more than half of all WTO cases are resolved between the time the complaint is filed and before the panel issues a ruling.[59]

One novel part of the WTO's dispute settlement process is that either party (or both together) can appeal the panel's decision. This is where the Appellate Body comes in. The Appellate Body is a seven-member group of well-respected international trade or law specialists appointed by the Dispute Settlement Body for four-year terms. Three members will hear the appeal, and the Body can uphold, modify, or reverse the initial panel ruling. Again, the DSB can only reject the conclusions by consensus. This "rule of negative consensus," by which reports by a panel or Appellate Body are adopted unless there is a consensus to block them, is seen as making the dispute settlement process work more smoothly and effectively.[60] Finally, after all the various procedures (and there are many) are followed and the country accused of violating a trade provision does not change its policy, then the harmed party can ask the DSB to allow it to impose what are essentially retaliatory trade sanctions against the other country. Enforcement is up to the states. This means that the success of enforcement depends on the interest and ability of member states to keep an eye on their trade partners' trade barriers.[61]

One very political example of how this process works is when the EU won a case in 2003 against the United States involving steel subsidies. In March 2002, President George W. Bush imposed temporary tariffs of more than 20 percent against steel imports. The US steel industry had been hurt by cheaper imports, and the steel unions, most US steelmakers, and powerful members of the Congressional steel caucus argued that these import prices were unfair. The tariffs were to last until 2005 to give the industry a chance to recover, invest in new technology, and negotiate better terms with labor. The EU and seven countries responded by filing formal complaints with the WTO. The WTO ruled in July 2003 that these tariffs violated international trade rules, prompting the US to appeal. The EU made it clear that if it were allowed to retaliate it would slap $2.2 billion in tariffs on a wide range of US products, which included apples, citrus fruit, toilet paper, rowboats, men's suits, fruit juices, drums, and ink-jet printers. What did these products have in common? They were products that sold well in Europe, and were produced in states like Florida that were important in the looming 2004 US presidential elections.[62] The EU would hit the Bush administration where it hurt. Japan, China, and Norway were among other countries also poised to impose retaliatory tariffs on the United States. The Bush administration had to make a tough decision, because if it backed down, there might also be ramifications in steel-producing states like Michigan, Ohio, and Pennsylvania. Domestic politics came to the fore.

To no one's surprise, the WTO's Appellate Body ruled in November 2003 that the US steel tariffs violated trade rules. As *The Wall Street Journal* wryly noted, "The U.S. appeal to the July WTO ruling against the tariffs never had a snowball's chance in a steel furnace of success."[63] While the United

States tried to work out some sort of compromise with Europe, China announced it would take punitive action against the United States, raising tariffs on some US products, if the United States did not abide by the WTO ruling. China's announcement came shortly after the Bush administration announced it would try to slow the growth of Chinese exports to the United States of goods that included bras and bathrobes.[64] This steel tariff dispute finally ended in early December when President Bush decided to withdraw the tariffs. The conclusion of this particular trade dispute was seen as a boost for the legitimacy and credibility of the WTO and its ability to get even a powerful country such as the United States to abide by its rules.

Even though the WTO's dispute settlement mechanism can be seen as a challenge to state sovereignty, in fact the most powerful WTO members use this mechanism the most. As Shaffer has noted, the United States participation rate as a party or third party in "fully litigated WTO cases" stands at around 97 percent, and the EU's rate is 82 percent.[65] The big players and their powerful multinational corporations also have the legal expertise and financial resources to devote to complex, time-consuming litigation at the WTO.[66] Stated differently, many poor countries simply can't afford to use the DSM.

EVOLUTION

Battle in Seattle

The Ministerial Conference planned for Seattle in late 1999 was intended to launch a new round of multilateral trade negotiations. Instead, negotiations were overwhelmed by a torrent of tens of thousands of antiglobalization protestors who called the WTO undemocratic and unaccountable and criticized its weak or nonexistent efforts to address labor, environmental, human, and consumer rights issues, among others. Some people were there to protest other issues like third world debt or the influence of multinational corporations. The protests brought together a somewhat curious combination of groups, including labor unionists, students, farmers, and environmentalists (some of whom were dressed up as sea turtles).[67] Organizations such as the Oklahoma Wheat Commission, OXFAM, the North Carolina Peanut Growers Association, and the World Rainforest Movement were represented.[68] Most of the protestors were nonviolent, and spent time singing, dancing, chanting, and also meeting before and after the protests for teach-ins and parties. Some protestors carried giant puppets through the streets. The big protest on November 30 blocked city streets and ended in a huge rally. Some demonstrators chained themselves to pipes or blocks. Small groups of anarchists and other demonstrators smashed store windows. The police fired tear gas and pepper spray in some areas. The protests succeeded in paralyzing the city and making it impossible for some of the delegates to attend the opening ceremony. That evening the mayor declared a state of emergency, and the National Guard arrived the next morning as some sporadic protests continued. Trade officials did manage to meet from December first to third, but there was little progress, and the meetings did not produce any declaration.

In the aftermath of the "Battle in Seattle," there was a lot of finger pointing to determine what went wrong and why. Scholars and commentators blamed factors such as a flawed negotiation processes that made consensus building difficult; the fact that the Director-General of the WTO and some of the leading negotiators were new on the job; the impact of the demonstrations on the meeting; the lack of consensus between the members of the Quad (referring to the United

States, European Union, Japan, and Canada); the Clinton administration's poor job in handling the politics and organization of the meeting; and the gulf between developed and developing country views on how to address issues that might be included in the new trade round.[69]

Doha Round

The Doha Round was launched in late 2001 in the capital of Qatar (far away from most protestors) and is widely acknowledged to be stalled or dead. Its failure may have repercussions on the authority and role of the WTO itself. As Manfred Elsig wrote, in the Doha trade round, the WTO has "stumbled from one missed deadline to the next."[70] The current round was more formally known as the "Doha Development Agenda," since its objective was to address trading issues that would benefit developing countries. The Ministerial declaration, adopted on November 14, 2001, noted that trade can "play a major role in the promotion of economic development and the alleviation of poverty," and laid out a work program that would focus on agriculture, trade in services, trade-related aspects of intellectual property rights (the TRIPS agreement), trade and environment, and a number of other relevant issues.[71] The Doha round was also launched in the aftermath of the 9/11 attacks, and some people hoped that offering concessions to the developing world would help to reduce rising animosity toward the developed world.

The round did not have an auspicious start. In a climate of shrinking world trade flows there were gaps between the priorities of major developed and developing countries. The United States, for example, hoped to focus on lowering agriculture trade barriers. Japan and many developed countries wanted to tackle the problem of antidumping rules. Brazil and India, speaking for a host of developing countries, wanted exceptions to international patent rules for drugs to treat malaria and HIV in order to save money and cope with health crises.[72]

The negotiations collapsed at the September 2003 ministerial meeting in Cancun, Mexico, where the growing gap between developed and developing country goals was starkly evident. Delegates from a number of developing countries walked out of the meetings arguing that the rich countries were not willing to compromise enough on the big issues, like agriculture. Developing countries noted the hypocrisy of the rich countries, which give the equivalent of over $300 billion in subsidies each year to their farmers, while at the same time, try to get poor countries to open up their agricultural markets. Disagreements flared anew at subsequent meetings in 2005, 2006, and 2008. At the July 2008 meeting, the ministerial board imploded after a long, nine-day gathering.[73] Today, many trade officials see little hope in Doha ever being completed, and as a result there are separate, stand-alone negotiations on the Trade in Services Agreement. The idea would be to take the services component of Doha and create a separate pact.

Why Did Doha Fail to Produce an Agreement?
What Are Some Implications?

Scholar Kent Jones surveyed the literature on Doha and produced a laundry list of ten factors that may have contributed to Doha's failure. These include the fact that the WTO's large membership of 157 countries makes it difficult to achieve consensus; the WTO operates on the basis of a *single undertaking*, which means "there is no agreement until everything is agreed." This contributes to the difficulty of coming up with a single concluding package; faster-growing developing countries such as China, India, and Brazil are exercising more voice and influence in negotiations; other global crises (terrorism, the 2008 financial crisis) have distracted trade negotiators; and multinational corporations are more interested in bilateral treaties and preferential trade agreements (PTAs) that have provisions for investment policy.[74] Beyond the structural problems, there are the usual politics. In areas such as agriculture, for example, there is little agreement on how the sector should be liberalized.

Some scholars and policymakers have expressed concern about what the failure of Doha means to the international trade regime. As trade specialists Gary Clyde Hufbauer, Jeffrey J. Schott, and Woan Foong Wong warned, "continued drift in the Doha Round negotiations will foster broad-scale neglect of the multilateral trading system, causing irreparable harm to the WTO's credibility as a negotiating forum, which would, over time, also undermine its valuable dispute settlement mechanism."[75]

One result of stalled multilateral negotiations is a rise in protectionism. Protectionism has been increasing since the 2008 financial crisis, even though global trade has rebounded since that difficult year. And while G20 members specifically pledged multiple times to promote free trade in the wake of the crisis, according to one trade scholar, G20 member states were actually responsible for almost 80 percent of protectionist actions in 2012.[76] Often these were "emergency" measures countries implemented in an attempt to limit the damage caused by the crisis. Global trade has been hampered by Europe's crisis but also by slower domestic demand in China and global concerns about the US budget deficit and fiscal issues.[77] Many of the protectionist measures popping up in recent years (so-called "behind the border" barriers) are also harder for authorities to identify and police—they include things like regulatory or licensing policies that effectively restrict trade.[78]

Another result of the failed Doha Round is a rapid growth in the number of PTAs between countries. PTA is a generic term referring to trade agreements between two or more countries. They include bilateral agreements, regional agreements, and plurilateral agreements. The latter refer to agreements that impact subgroups of WTO members. PTAs have risen from under 80 in 1990 to over 300 today. Just about every WTO member participates in at least one PTA, with some members participating in over a dozen. The only WTO members not involved in any PTA are Mongolia, Djibouti, Democratic Republic of the Congo, and Madagascar.[79] The United States, for example, is involved in more than 10 PTAs, starting with NAFTA. In early 2013 it began negotiating a PTA with the EU, the Transatlantic Trade and Investment Partnership. It is also negotiating a Trans-Pacific Partnership (TPP) with countries in Asia and Latin America. In addition to the United States, TPP members include Canada, Japan, Mexico, Australia, Brunei, Chile, Malaysia, New Zealand, Peru, Singapore, and Vietnam. This would be a powerful trading bloc that covers 40 percent of global GDP. The open question is: what about China? At this stage it is unclear whether China would be a potential member, whether it would be threatened by the TPP nations, or whether it would have to respond to the TPP policies.[80] China would not be able to enter until it undergoes significant domestic economic reform, and several TPP countries want to conclude a high standard agreement before letting China enter. If left out of TPP, China stands to lose billions of dollars in regional trade to its Asian neighbors.

Meanwhile, China has proposed a 16-nation Regional Comprehensive Economic Partnership (RCEP). Trade experts are divided as to whether the RCEP will compete with the TPP or whether the two may work in parallel, as well as with other free trade areas in the region. The RCEP's standards will likely be weaker, since it will not include labor and environmental protection issues.

The literature often uses the terms *PTA*, *regional trade agreement*, and *free trade agreement* as synonyms, although some agreements called regional trade agreements (RTA) aren't even regional, such as the US-Australia agreement or the EU's trade agreements with countries like Chile and South Africa. The important point is the fact that so many countries are involved in so many of these agreements creates, according to an OECD study, "webs of overlapping trade agreements each with its own set of market access rules and regulatory frameworks."[81] PTAs tend to call for tariffs and other trade barriers to be eliminated over a period of time (often a decade) within the member countries. Naturally, there are debates about whether PTAs aid or harm world trade. After all, they allow for freer trade between members, but not with nonmembers. That means they promote both free trade and protectionism. Quite clearly they undermine the most-favored nation principle at the heart of the GATT/WTO where members impose the same non-discriminatory tariff on all other members.

In fact, the GATT/WTO rules do allow for preferential trading groups under Article 24, which exempts free trade areas and customs unions from MFN treatment. This apparent contradiction can be traced to the negotiations surrounding the International Trade Organization. The United States was behind the idea because it wanted to accommodate a secret free trade agreement with Canada, a treaty that was never signed.[82] While Article 24 was meant to be restrictive, in practice these restrictions were ignored over time.[83]

Critics of PTAs are concerned that such agreements divert trade to members and away from nonmembers. This diversion is especially bad if members produce goods at higher costs than nonmembers, because that means that an individual member is paying more for imports than it might otherwise pay. Critics also worry that countries' emphasis on preferential initiatives may hurt their interest in multilateral ones. Some are also concerned that regional trading arrangements may create tensions between groups of countries.[84] Bhagwati, a prominent critic, has called PTAs "termites in the trading system" and "a pandemic and a pox on the world trading system" that systematically undermine trade.[85] In addition to the reasons above, he is also concerned about what he calls a "mish-mash" of barriers. By this he means that if a country is a member of multiple such agreements, any single commodity will have different tariff rates and tariff reduction schedules. Rules of origin also get confusing if they vary between members, nonmembers, agreements, and products.[86] The mish-mash of barriers also impacts suppliers, who must tailor their products to meet the various rules of origin. Customs officials, in turn, must assess different tariffs on the same project, depending on its origin, which makes the trade agreement murky.[87]

Proponents of PTAs counter that such arrangements may, in fact, exist in harmony with, or even promote, multilateral arrangements—the two are not a zero sum game. For example, economist C. Fred Bergsten has argued that regional arrangements can "lock in domestic reforms" and push trade liberalization ideas that can later fit into multilateral negotiations. He and others have also argued that regional arrangements allow "learning by doing," by helping governments get used to liberalizing trade, and this can also help at the multilateral level. Finally, proponents argue that in most free trade arrangements, trade creation exceeds trade diversion.[88] Scholars have also argued that domestic institutions and interest groups (especially exporters seeking better access to international markets) also favor the creation of PTAs for their own strategic interests, including a response to discrimination abroad.[89]

Some studies paint more nuanced pictures. For example, an OECD study looked at whether or not tariffs are actually reduced by PTAs. It examined more than 50 regional trade agreements covering 158 tariffs and found over 90 percent of tariffs on average were eliminated by the end of the implementation period. It also found higher degrees of tariff elimination between South-South agreements (over 92%) than North-South agreements (87%).[90] At the same time, it found great variation in terms of which tariffs were reduced, and across countries and sectors. Other studies show more mixed results, often depending on the approach and the sector analyzed.

The bottom line, ultimately, is that whether or not such preferential agreements are helpful or harmful depends on other factors—how they are managed, whether or not they divert trade, the extent to which they result in domestic regulations that apply beyond specific trade partners, and whether they leave developing countries marginalized. The specific details of the PTA/RTA matter.

LOOKING AHEAD

Looking ahead, the WTO faces a number of challenges in the coming years. First, the rise in regionalism will continue. The question is how this will impact WTO legitimacy. If the WTO can play a role in coordinating regional pacts, that would increase its relevance.

Second, issues of trade and development will remain very important, especially given the link to poverty reduction. As noted above, the Doha Round was supposed to create more opportunities for developing countries to share in the gains from trade. More developing country involvement in trade, in turn, was supposed to help lift millions of people out of crushing poverty. Developing countries continue to face numerous hurdles when it comes to engaging in international trade. Not only do developed countries still place obstacles against developing country imports, but the vast majority of tariff barriers developing countries face (70%) are imposed by other developing countries.[91] And while PTAs can help developing countries gain access to international markets and promote competitiveness, very often PTAs challenge government capacity. As economists Jean-Pierre Chauffour and Jean-Christophe Maur have noted, developing countries interested in PTAs may face "the added burden of covering an increasingly large and complex set of issues with limited administrative resources for negotiation and implementation, and frequently no preexisting experience."[92] Another uncomfortable fact is that sub-Saharan Africa still has a very small share of nonoil world trade, and since at least 25 percent of its exports are in agricultural trade, it is more affected by commodity price volatility than more diversified economies.[93] Finally, we know that some countries that have opened up have still only achieved poor performance or were hurt by global economic downturns, such as many countries in Latin America.[94] Facing a quite different scenario than sub-Saharan Africa are the leading emerging markets. These are likely to be major drivers of global economic growth in near-term, which will have an impact on world trade patterns. One analyst predicts India, Vietnam, and China will post the strongest export growth by 2020, with annual growth in the double digits.[95] Trade policy and liberalization are clearly necessary but hardly sufficient to efforts at reducing poverty.

Third is the issue of agriculture, which has a great impact on developing countries. The agricultural sector accounts for over 50 percent of the labor force in those countries. It is a major area of world trade that has seen little progress in liberalization, especially in the United States and Europe. Although world trade experienced tremendous growth in the post-World War II decades, the agricultural sector did not. Agriculture's share of world trade fell from 34 percent to 14 percent between 1950 and 1976.[96] By the end of the Uruguay Round, global trade in agriculture was far from being open. OECD governments give the agricultural sector huge subsidies, especially in the areas of wheat, rice, and maize, where there are powerful farm lobbies. But the issue is complicated, because it is not necessarily the case that removing subsidies to rich country farmers will help poor countries. Economist Jeffrey Sachs, for example, has noted that cutbacks in European subsidies for wheat and maize may actually hurt the least developed countries in Africa, since they are net food importers, and higher prices for such staples would hurt consumers, even though it would help farmers.[97] Rich countries also continue to maintain high tariffs on many developing country agricultural products. The history of WTO disputes is full of "food fights." Indeed, the longest running dispute (twenty years) in the GATT/WTO was over bananas, triggered by Europe restricting banana imports from outside Africa, the Caribbean, and Pacific. Negotiators in the Uruguay Round created an Agreement on Agriculture that included a reduction in tariffs on agricultural products, a reduction in domestic subsidies, and liberalization in market access. But in practice, there was little change.[98] Agriculture was to be a central issue in the Doha Round.

These are three key issues facing the WTO in coming years, but there are also many others. Debates continue about the role of trade impacting global and regional environmental problems, and of the impact of trade on health and labor, for example. Individual countries also have specific challenges on their trade agendas. For the United States, as an example, many issues surround its trade with China. China is the largest source of US imports and the third largest destination for US exports. However, on the US side, policymakers are concerned about China's undervalued currency, its poor record in upholding intellectual property rights, and other unfair trade practices. Evidence of Chinese corporate espionage, including stealing or compromising corporate trade secrets, prompted the United States to push successfully for a deal with China where the two countries would work together to stop corporate espionage.

PERSPECTIVES ON THE WTO

There are numerous strands of literature on the WTO system and the various trade rounds. Scholars specializing in international political economy, economics, and law, in particular, study a range of issues that include the politics of the negotiations; the legal analysis of the trade agreements, institutions, and dispute settlement bodies; the economics of trade; the history and evolution of trade, capitalism, and crisis; the impact of trade on domestic politics, policies, and sectors; trade and development; trade and security; and so on.

One traditional political science strand of research has focused on the WTO's role in trade liberalization.[99] A more recent strand has examined how the GATT and WTO have resolved trade conflicts, especially through the dispute resolution mechanism, and the role domestic politics plays in why governments choose this adjudication process.[100] A third strand examines the response of countries excluded from trade pacts.[101] A fourth strand is interested in the role that the WTO's small secretariat plays in influencing trade governance.[102] As noted earlier in this chapter, scholars also evaluate the effectiveness of the trade regime under the WTO.[103]

Some scholars analyze aspects of the trade regime, such as intellectual property rights.[104] Trade economics has focused on ways of promoting efficiency from fewer barriers to trade. Trade law specialists have argued over time for more legalization in the trade regime, and their work also highlights issues related to dispute resolution and compliance. Political scientists and legal scholars have also focused on the issues related to the WTO's "democratic deficit," its lack of transparency, and its lack of accountability and legitimacy.[105] This is linked to policy-related literature by advocates of a more democratic, green, and fair WTO.

Given increasing pressures on the WTO to address traditionally nontrade issues areas, such as labor, health safety, environment, and human rights, one important question facing scholars is what factors will determine whether the WTO makes progress in areas linked to trade, and why it has already made more progress in some areas than others. Some have argued that states will pursue deeper linkages when it improves the WTO's legitimacy and states' sense of fairness. Others argue that the most powerful states will determine how successful the WTO is and whether it has strong or weak links to nontrade issues areas.[106] A third is that the standards adopted reflect the ability of domestic interest groups to have an impact on the policy debates.[107]

CONCLUSION

Today, the WTO presents a mixed picture of strengths and weaknesses. It has succeeded in creating a deeper framework of trade rules, and it has a strong system of dispute resolution. Certainly, the world it faces is dramatically different than the world that existed when the GATT was born in 1948, and therefore, it is no surprise that it has taken on so many new issues (like all the other institutions covered in this book). But if we are judging its ability to produce new trade agreements that successfully address some of the toughest issues in trade, then it has failed. Blustein called the WTO "the most essential element in the glue that holds the global-ized economy together," and is concerned that its eroding authority will result in member states ignoring their commitments.[108] Political scientist Rorden Wilkinson, by contrast, has argued that all the past collapses of ministerial meetings were ultimately followed by forward movement in the trade agenda. Collapse, then, is not fatal, but perhaps even procedural, according to Wilkinson.[109] Over the next decade, how the WTO deals with the issues of legitimacy, negotiation, PTAs, and the linkage between trade and other global issues will make more clear whether it remains relevant or not. Of particular importance is the political will and preferences of the world's largest economic powers. If they are not interested in making the global trade system less fragmented, the WTO will become sidelined.

BIBLIOGRAPHY

"After Seattle: A Global Disaster." *The Economist*, December 11, 1999, 19–20.

Baldwin, Richard. "Multilateralizing Regionalism: Spaghetti Bowls as Building Blocs on the Path to Global Free Trade." *World Economy* 29, no. 11 (2006): 1451–518.

Barton, John H., Judith L. Goldstein, Timothy E. Josling, and Richard H. Steinberg. *The Evolution of the Trade Regime: Politics, Law, and Economics of the GATT and the WTO.* Princeton, NJ: Princeton University Press, 2006.

Beattie, Alan. "Economic Gloom Puts Free Trade at Risk: News Analysis." *Financial Times*, June 14, 2012, 5.

Bergsten, C. Fred. "Open Regionalism." In *Working Paper 97-3*. Washington, DC: Peterson Institute for International Economics, 1997.

Bhagwati, Jagdish N. *Termites in the Trading System: How Preferential Agreements Undermine Free Trade*. New York: Oxford University Press, 2008.

Biermann, Frank, Bernd Siebenhüner, Steffen Bauer, Per-Olof Busch, Sabine Campe, Klaus Dingwerth, Torsten Grothmann, Robert Marschinski, and Mireia Tarradell. "Studying the Influence of International Bureaucracies: A Conceptual Framework." In *Managers of Global Change: The Influence of International Environmental Bureaucracies*, edited by Frank Biermann and Bernd Siebenhüner, 37-74. Cambridge: MIT Press, 2009.

Blustein, Paul. *Misadventures of the Most Favored Nations: Clashing Egos, Inflated Ambitions, and the Great Shambles of the World Trade System*. 1st ed. New York: PublicAffairs, 2009.

"Bush's Steel Opening." *The Wall Street Journal*, November 5, 2003, A2

Chase, Kerry A. "Multilateralism Compromised: The Mysterious Origins of GATT Article XXIV." *World Trade Review* (2006): 1-30.

Chauffour, Jean-Pierre, and Jean-Christophe Maur. "Beyond Market Access." In *Preferential Trade Agreement Policies for Development* edited by Jean-Pierre Chauffour and Jean-Christophe Maur, 17-36. Washington, DC: The World Bank, 2011.

Clapp, Jennifer. "WTO Agriculture Negotiations: Implications for the Global South." *Third World Quarterly* 27, no. 4 (2006): 563-77.

Collier, Paul. *The Bottom Billion: Why the Poorest Countries Are Failing and What Can Be Done About It*. New York: Oxford University Press, 2007.

Davis, Christina L. *Why Adjudicate? Enforcing Trade Rules in the WTO*. Princeton NJ: Princeton University Press, 2012.

Dollar, David. "Globalization, Poverty, and Inequality." In *Globalization: What's New?*, edited by Michael M. Weinstein, 96-128. New York: Columbia University Press, 2005.

Dür, Andreas. "EU Trade Policy as Protection for Exporters: The Agreements with Mexico and Chile." *Journal Common Market Studies* 45, no. 4 (2007): 833-55.

Elsig, Manfred. "The World Trade Organization at Work: Performance in a Member-Driven Milieu." *Review of International Organizations* 5, no. 3 (2010): 345-63.

Esserman, Susan, and Robert Howse. "The WTO on Trial." *Foreign Affairs* 82, no. 1 (2003): 130-40.

Flora, Liz. "Complete Transcript: Thomas Donilon at Asia Society New York." New York: Asia Society New York, March 11, 2013.

Frieden, Jeffry A. *Global Capitalism: Its Fall and Rise in the Twentieth Century*. 1st ed. New York: W.W. Norton, 2006.

Fulponi, L., M. Shearer, and J. Almeida. "Regional Trade Agreements: Treatment of Agriculture." *OECD Food, Agriculture and Fisheries Working Papers* (2011).

Gargan, Edward A. "Bound to Looms by Poverty and Fear, Boys in India Make a Few Men Rich." *The New York Times*, July 9, 1992, A8.

Gilpin, Robert, and Jean M. Gilpin. *The Political Economy of International Relations*. Princeton, NJ: Princeton University Press, 1987.

Gowa, Joanne, and Soo Yeon Kom. "An Exclusive Country Club: The Effects of GATT 1950-94." *World Politics* 57 (2005): 453-78.

Gruber, Lloyd. *Ruling the World: Power Politics and the Rise of Supranational Institutions*. Princeton, NJ: Princeton University Press, 2000.

Hoekman, Bernard. "North-South Preferential Trade Agreements." In *Preferential Trade Agreement Policies for Development* edited by Jean-Pierre Chauffour and Jean-Christophe Maur, 95–109. Washington, DC: The World Bank, 2011.

Hufbauer, Gary Clyde, Jeffrey J. Schott, and Woan Foong Wong. *Figuring out the Doha Round*. Washington, DC: Peterson Institute for International Economics, 2010.

Irwin, Douglas A. "Trade and Globalization." In *Globalization: What's New?*, edited by Michael M. Weinstein, 19–35. New York: Columbia University Press, 2005.

Jackson, John Howard. *The World Trade Organization: Constitution and Jurisprudence*. London: Royal Institute of International Affairs, 1998.

Jinnah, Sikina. "Overlap Management in the World Trade Organization: Secretariat Influence on Trade-Environment Politics." *Global Environmental Politics* 10, no. 2 (2010): 54–79.

Jones, Claire. "Emerging Markets Exports to Drive Growth." *Financial Times*, February 27, 2013.

Jones, Kent. *The Doha Blues: Institutional Crisis and Reform in the WTO*. New York: Oxford University Press, 2010.

Kahler, Miles, and David A. Lake. "Globalization and Governance." In *Governance in a Global Economy*, edited by Miles Kahler and David A. Lake, 1–30. Princeton, NJ: Princeton University Press, 2003.

Kahn, Joseph. "Amid Trade Agenda Talks, Sharpened Focus on Rich-Poor Disputes." *The New York Times*, November 1, 2001, C1.

Kenen, Peter B. *The International Economy*. Englewood Cliffs, NJ: Prentice Hall, 1985.

Krueger, Anne O. "Introduction." In *The WTO as an International Organization*, edited by Anne O. Krueger, 1–27. Chicago, IL: Chicago University Press, 1998.

Lake, David A. "Rightful Rules: Authority, Order, and the Foundations of Global Governance." *International Studies Quarterly* 54, no. 3 (2010): 587–613.

Lamy, Pascal. "Multilateral and Bilateral Trade Agreements: Friends or Foes?" New York: Annual Memorial Silver Lecture, Columbia University, 2006.

Macrory, Patrick F. J., Arthur E. Appleton, and Michael G. Plummer, eds. *The World Trade Organization: Legal, Economic, and Political Analysis*. New York: Springer, 2005.

Milner, Helen V. "International Trade." In *Handbook of International Relations*, edited by Walter Carlsnaes, Thomas Risse, and Beth A. Simmons, 448–61. London: Sage, 2003.

"Ministerial Declaration." In *WT/MIN (01)/Dec/1*. Geneva, Switzerland: Doha WTO Ministerial, 2001.

Moore, Mike. "In Praise of the Future." Geneva, Switzerland: WTO, 2000.

Naim, Moises. "Lori's War." *Foreign Policy*, no. 118 (April 1, 2000): 28–55.

OECD. "Global Value Chains: Preliminary Evidence and Policy Issues." Paris: OECD, 2011.

Pollack, Mark A., and Gregory C. Shaffer. *When Cooperation Fails: The International Law and Politics of Genetically Modified Foods*. 1st ed. New York: Oxford University Press, 2009.

Reddy, Sudeep, and Alex Frangos. "Trade Slows around World—Declining Growth in Exports Dims Prospects for U.S. Economy; Europe Cuts Imports." *The Wall Street Journal*, October 1, 2012.

Rhodes, Carolyn. *Reciprocity, U.S. Trade Policy, and the GATT Regime*. Ithaca, NY: Cornell University Press, 1993.

Riding, Alan. "109 Nations Sign Trade Agreement." *The New York Times*, April 16, 1994, 35.

Rodrik, Dani. "Globalization for Whom?" *Harvard Magazine* (July-August 2002).

Rosendorff, Peter, and Helen Milner. "The Optimal Design of International Trade Institutions: Uncertainty and Escape." *International Organization* 55, no. 4 (2001): 829–57.

Sachs, Jeffrey D. *The End of Poverty*. New York: The Penguin Press, 2005.

Sampson, Gary P. "Overview." In *The Role of the World Trade Organization in Global Governance*, edited by Gary P. Sampson, 1–27. Tokyo: United Nations University Press, 2001.

Schneider, Howard. "On Asia Trip, Obama Presses Economic Counter to China." *The Washington Post*, November 19, 2012.

Schott, Jeffrey J., ed. *The WTO After Seattle*. Washington, DC: Institute for International Economics, 2000.

Schumpeter, Joseph A. *Capitalism, Socialism and Democracy*. New York: Harper & Row, 1942.

Sell, Susan K. *Private Power, Public Law: The Globalization of Intellectual Property Rights*. New York: Cambridge University Press, 2003.

Shaffer, Gregory. "Power, Governance, and the WTO: A Comparative Institutional Approach." In *Power in Global Governance*, edited by Michael Barnett and Raymond Duvall, 130–60. New York: Cambridge Universitiy Press, 2005.

Smith, Adam. *An Inquiry into the Nature and Causes of the Wealth of Nations*. London: Printed for W. Strahan and T. Cadell, 1776.

"The Price of Tariffs." *The Wall Street Journal*, July 15, 200.

US Office of Technology Assessment. "Trade and the Environment: Conflicts and Opportunities." Washington, DC: Government Printing Office, 1992.

Wilkinson, Rorden. *The WTO: Crisis and the Governance of Global Trade*. New York: Routledge, 2006.

Wonacott, Peter, and Scott Miller. "China Weights Tariffs on U.S. Goods." *The Wall Street Journal*, November 21, 2003.

World Trade Organization. "Understanding the WTO." Geneva, Switzerland: World Trade Organization, 2010.

———. "World Trade Report 2013." Geneva, Switzerland: World Trade Organization, 2013.

———. "World Trade Report 2014." Geneva, Switzerland: World Trade Organization, 2014.

———. "Chronological List of Disputes Cases." Geneva, Switzerland: World Trade Organization. http://www.wto.org/english/tratop_e/dispu_e/dispu_status_e.htm.

———. "The General Agreement on Tariffs and Trade (GATT 1947)." Geneva, Switzerland: World Trade Organization. https://www.wto.org/english/docs_e/legal_e/gatt47_e.pdf.

———. "International Trade Statistics ". Geneva, Switzerland: World Trade Organization, 2010.

———. "Overview of the WTO Secretariat." Geneva, Switzerland: World Trade Organization. http://www.wto.org/english/thewto_e/secre_e/intro_e.htm.

———. "The Uruguay Round." Geneva, Switzerland: World Trade Organization. http://www.wto.org/english/thewto_e/whatis_e/tif_e/fact5_e.htm.

WTO History Project. "NGO Attendees-2." Seattle: University of Washington. http://depts.washington.edu/wtohist/orgs.htm.

10 World Trade Organization Case Study
Intellectual Property, Trade, and Access to Medicine

The issue of poor country access to medication has prompted an ongoing contentious debate pitting powerful, rich-country drug companies against developing country governments. As trade scholar Susan Sell succinctly put it, proponents of access to medicine want to *expand* access, while large pharmaceutical companies have sought to *ration* access.[1] The tension is often presented more dramatically as one of profits versus human life. Diseases like malaria, HIV/AIDS, and tuberculosis (TB) kill millions of people a year, primarily in developing countries.[2] Mortality rates have declined sharply in recent years, given more emphasis on prevention, care, education, and more available drugs, but these diseases are still killers. HIV is still the leading cause of death from a single infectious agent, followed by TB, each of which still kills over a million people a year.[3] In fact, at least one-third of those who have HIV also have TB. More than 70 percent of people with HIV, or 25 million people, live in sub-Saharan Africa, which also saw the majority of AIDS deaths. The United Nations reports that more than half of the 35 million people who have HIV don't even know it.[4]

On the positive side, there have been great advances in getting medication to developing countries, scientific innovations, and global efforts to fight these diseases. Prices for expensive medicines, such as for HIV, have fallen dramatically. Access to essential medicines was part of the Millennium Development Goals (MDGs). Goal 6 was "Combat HIV/AIDS, Malaria and other diseases." The new Sustainable Development Goals also include a health component. Goal 3 is "Ensure healthy lives and promote well-being for all ages," with targets including ending AIDS, TB, and malaria epidemics by 2030. Yet, it is too early to be wholly enthusiastic about success. The poorest countries still have very weak health infrastructures, which became sadly clear during the Ebola outbreak that began in late 2013, where overstretched West African nations were woefully unequipped to respond quickly to the growing epidemic. Tensions still exist between pharmaceutical companies, governments, activists, and patients. It is also the case that poorer countries still struggle with access to affordable treatment for noncommunicable diseases, such as cancer, and expensive medical devices.

Intellectual property issues are inherent in these challenges. For example, access to medication involves pharmaceutical companies that have patents on their products. They argue that the average cost of developing a new drug can be around $500 million and it can take years before a new drug is on the market. Of course, there are always medicines or other medical products that do not get approved after millions of dollars have been invested in research and development. Companies that make copies of brand-name drugs (called *generic drugs*) typically sell the copies at steeply discounted prices and take business away from the brand-name manufacturer. Pharmaceutical companies also point out that generic producers aren't actually making new drugs, although many diseases evolve. This supports pharmaceutical companies' arguments for patent protection as a means to encourage innovation.[5] If they cannot protect their patents, which give them a period of time where no one else can make, use, or sell the product or process, they may not have incentives to invest millions of dollars on research. And if they do not have an incentive to invest in "diseases of the poor," they may also choose to concentrate more on health problems that impact richer countries (e.g., cholesterol and high blood pressure) versus those that impact developing countries (such as malaria and TB).[6] World Health Organization (WHO) Director-General Margaret Chan stated the conundrum succinctly when noting that

> The essence of the ethical argument is straightforward. People should not be denied access to life-saving or health promoting medicines for unfair reasons, including those with economic cause. Yet the pharmaceutical industry operates in response to economic factors and market forces. This is a profit-driven industry, and not a philanthropist, not a humanitarian enterprise. What incentives does this industry have to fix prices according to their affordability among the poor? . . . Of all the issues discussed at WHO governing bodies, access to medicines consistently sparks the most heated, sometimes divisive, and potentially explosive debates. This is all the more so since these discussions almost inevitably turn to questions of prices, patents, intellectual property protection, and competition.[7]

The international global health regime or regime complex (since there are overlapping clusters of players depending on the issue) includes government initiatives, international organizations, large pharmaceutical companies, generic drug firms, and many types of corporations and business groups, activist groups and other NGOs, and philanthropic and private foundations like the Bill & Melinda Gates Foundation. There are also a number of public-private partnerships in global health, such as the Global Fund to Fight AIDS, Tuberculosis and Malaria (Global Fund), which has given tens of billions of dollars toward programs to fight those diseases. The WHO is an important actor at the center of the global health regime and was historically a leader in global health issues. In recent years, though, it has not been particularly strong and effective. Loss of staff, budget cuts, and a number of other organizations working on global health issues have impacted the WHO's current ability to set and implement a strong agenda for global health issues. It has also been slammed for its inability to respond rapidly and effectively to international health emergencies, such as the Ebola crisis.[8]

Where does the WTO fit in? As international law scholar David P. Fidler has noted, global health governance cuts across issues of "health, trade, labor, humanitarian, human rights, and environmental law."[9] The WTO has been centrally involved where trade and trade rules intersect with public health objectives and challenges. Indeed, the interaction between trade and global health issues has a long history, going back at least to government efforts to curb the spread of cholera and yellow fever in the 1830s, given that these diseases were spread, in part, by trade. Trade is what allows medications to cross borders from the company that produced them to the people who need them. Trade encourages competition and impacts pricing and the availability or predictability of supply. More broadly, trade intersects in complex ways with poverty reduction, which can impact health. Debates about trade, health, and access to medicine also played a role in increased attention on health from the global human rights community and the appearance of a growing "right to health" norm.[10]

This chapter emphasizes the particular nexus of where the WTO has (and has not) played a role in global health governance by focusing on access to medicine. This particular focus highlights the challenges of weighing developed country and corporate interests with saving lives. Intellectual property, overall, is still an area where the rich have more power than the poor. What has the WTO done and what can it do to contribute to balance the different interests in a way that saves more lives?

In fact, there has been great progress toward increasing poor countries' access to important medications, although we certainly have not reached the "universal access" that is a goal for many public health officials. The WTO has played a role in moving the issue along, many times working in conjunction with organizations such as the WHO. It has especially been a key forum for states to negotiate intellectual property issues that impact access to medicine. The tensions

Figure 10.1   Intersections of Trade, Public Health, and Intellectual Property

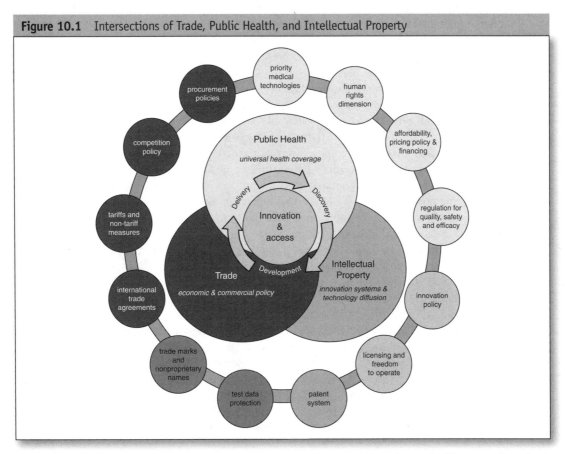

Source: © World Trade Organization (WTO) 2015, "Promoting Access to Medical Technologies and Innovation" (Geneva: WTO, 2012), 15.

between developing countries seeking cheaper medications and pharmaceutical companies are not going to disappear anytime soon. And it is still the case, as Chan noted, that "the gaps in health outcomes are greater today than at any time in recent history. A person in a wealthy country can expect to live more than twice as long as someone from a poor country."[11]

TRADE AND PHARMACEUTICALS

The Uruguay Round agreement that created the WTO in 1995 included the creation of the TRIPS (the Agreement on Trade Related Aspects of Intellectual Property Rights), which was an annex to the agreement creating the WTO. TRIPS was a watershed moment in how international property rights are governed. As scholars Ethan Kapstein and Joshua Busby noted, "From its inception, TRIPS became the focal point of debate over whether the rights of companies should trump public health."[12] TRIPS, according to legal scholar Laurence Helfer, "has teeth. It contains detailed, comprehensive substantive rules and is linked to the WTO's comparatively hard-edged dispute settlement system."[13]

TRIPS, based on four existing intellectual property rights agreements, set high minimum standards for the protection of intellectual property rights. TRIPS required signatory nations to adopt patent terms of 20 years. It also allowed longer compliance deadlines for developing countries (four extra years for developing countries, and 10 years with possible extensions for the poorest countries), as well as a provision permitting compulsory licensing. The TRIPS agreement addressed issues like copyright protection, trademarks and industrial designs, and patents. The balance, in this case, weighed heavily on the side of pharmaceuticals. The agreement reflected concerns of rich country multinational corporations, including pharmaceutical companies, about protection from "piracy" of their goods and counterfeit products. India, for example, had a 1970 patent law that did not offer patent protection for pharmaceutical products. This allowed the country to develop a robust generic drug industry that made and sold copies of drugs that were still under patent in developed countries.[14] Brazil was also a large producer of generic drugs, given that it did not grant patents on medicines before TRIPS. Under TRIPS, all member countries would eventually have to offer protection for post-1995 patents, which meant that the main beneficiaries were developed countries and large pharmaceutical companies.[15] As scholars John Odell and Susan Sell have noted, "Big Pharma" companies, including Merck and Pfizer, had a voice and role in shaping the agreement.[16] Developing countries accepted the deal because they were also promised concessions on the export of their agricultural and textile products to the developed world.[17]

According to trade scholar John Barton, Article 27 was especially important to drug companies because it required that "patents shall be available for any inventions, whether products or processes, in all fields of technology." According to him, "the clear intent was to prohibit exclusions of drug products such as those contained in Indian law."[18] Some aspects of the TRIPS rules were either ambiguous or open to interpretation. An important one is Article 31, which allows for *compulsory licensing* of patented products. Governments can issue compulsory licenses to domestic production firms without the patent holder's consent under certain conditions to "authorize use or production of a patented item by a domestic party other than the patent holder."[19] The idea is for a government to allow the local production of medicines if justified in the public interest in order to help people have access to essential medications. The patent holder, in turn, is supposed to receive "adequate remuneration" depending on the case. TRIPS limits the use of compulsory licensing in several ways, including cases where there is a "national emergency or other circumstances of extreme urgency."[20] Such emergencies could include public health crises, but who would decide when and how to define such crises? The licenses were also to be used "predominantly for the supply of the domestic market" to make clear this production was not for export. But this provision also left open the question of what a country should do if it did not have a domestic manufacturing company able to receive such a license.

Developing countries, NGOs, and others criticized TRIPS. Economist Jagdish Bhagwati went as far as to argue intellectual property protection was not an appropriate issue for the WTO to handle. Instead of having to do with mutually beneficial trade, for most poor countries, it is "a simple tax on their use of such knowledge." The TRIPS agreement, he argued, turned the WTO "into a royalty-collection agency."[21] The UNDP argued that TRIPS was "highly questionable for large parts of the developing world" precisely because it "has the potential to restrict access to medicines, technology and knowledge, with disturbing implications for indigenous knowledge and food security."[22] Even some protestors in the Battle in Seattle accused the WTO of blocking generic medication from poor nations. Campaigns by activists framed the issue as one of drug company policies killing people by being more concerned with profits than lives.[23]

Because HIV/AIDS was spreading quickly throughout places like sub-Saharan Africa in the 1990s, many different actors were paying close attention to how access to medicines would actually work under TRIPS. In the late 1990s, US trade officials pressured Thailand to drop its plans to issue a compulsory license to manufacture a generic version of an AIDS drug produced by a US firm. In 1997, South Africa passed a law that allowed the health minister to override patent laws in a health emergency. The country had the highest number HIV positive people of any country in the world. At the time antiretroviral (ARV) drugs cost around $1,000 a month. In a country where the average annual income was $2,600, this was a crisis. The law allowed the Ministry of Health to permit compulsory licensing of drugs, as well as parallel importation. The compulsory licensing meant local companies could produce generic versions of needed drugs, and parallel importation meant importers could buy patented name brand drugs from the cheapest possible sources. Unsurprisingly, large pharmaceutical companies like Merck, which produced an ARV medication, and the United States, immediately demanded the appeal of this Act. The United States went as far as denying some trade benefits and threatening trade sanctions. A group of South African and multinational drug companies brought a suit against the South African government. But there was also a public response against this suit, including efforts by AIDS activists and NGOs, like South Africa's Treatment Action Campaign, Doctors Without Borders, and Oxfam, and demonstrations in Washington, DC. As scholar Adrian Flint noted, the court case was, for the pharmaceutical companies, "an unmitigated public relations disaster that appeared to confirm the primary stereotype associated with Big Pharma; the prioritization of profits over human life."[24]

The global AIDS crisis prompted growing concern that something had to be done to make life-saving medications affordable to the world's poor. Activists were lobbying for changes. In 2000 alone, the G8 leaders agreed they would "implement an ambitious plan on infectious diseases, notably HIV/AIDS, malaria and tuberculosis" and committed themselves to

South African protesters demand free access to ARV medications in 2000.

reductions in HIV-infected young people, TB deaths, and the "burden of disease associated with malaria" in coming years.[25] The UN General Assembly adopted a "Declaration of Commitment on HIV/AIDS" with a list of actions to be taken, ranging from efforts to prevent the spread of the disease, to calls for strengthening care, support, and treatment for those with the disease. Notably, the declaration called for the need for cheaper drugs "in close collaboration with the private sector and pharmaceutical companies." As noted earlier, the new United Nations Millennium Development Goals included a goal on combating HIV/AIDS, malaria, and other diseases.[26] On the civil society organization front, Oxfam partnered with other groups on a Cut the Cost Campaign in 2001 to call for affordable prices in poor countries for life-saving medicines.

Yusuf Hamied, owner of the Indian generic drug company, Cipla, caused a great stir when announcing in September 2000 that his company would sell the ARV drugs for $800 per person per year, compared with the going rate of around $12,000 per patient per year charged by the large pharmaceutical companies. He went even further in December 2000, offering to sell such drugs to NGOs for $350 dollars a year, or around $1 a day.[27] Suddenly, it became possible to treat large numbers of people and for donor countries to seriously consider supporting such programs. Aware that public sympathy had turned against them, some drug companies also moved to reduce the price of their AIDS drugs in Africa through a UN initiative.[28] The companies finally dropped their South Africa case in 2001, given public outrage.[29] By late 2001, the price of the ARVs was substantially lower than a mere year earlier. Brand name drugs dropped to $712 dollars a year, and generics were as low as $295. By 2007, people could receive generic combinations of the medicines for under $100 per person per year. In 2009, one large pharmaceutical company, GlaxoSmithKline, announced it would reduce the price of all of the medicines it sold to the 52 poorest countries, and invest 20 percent of its profits from sales to least-developed countries into their own health care infrastructures. The company also agreed to create a patent pool to donate small molecules and processes to spur research on neglected diseases.[30]

NOVEMBER 2001 DOHA DECLARATION AND 2003 CANCUN AGREEMENT

The TRIPS agreement was a major issue on the agenda of the 2001 Doha ministerial. Many countries, excluding the United States, felt that the language had to be clearer and that the agreement had to better address the problems facing developing countries. NGOs were also advocating for greater access to medication, as were other international organizations such as UNAIDS and the UN Sub-Commission for the Protection and Promotion of Human Rights. The South African case also encouraged developing countries to seek some revision to TRIPS in terms of more clarity on the issue of access versus patent rights. The resulting "Declaration on the TRIPS Agreement and Public Health" reaffirmed that countries have some wiggle-room in their actions to protect public health. It gave the least developed countries an extension until 2016 for implementing the parts of TRIPS related to adopting pharmaceutical patents, marketing rights, and data protection. Stated more plainly, these countries do not have to protect patents on pharmaceutical products until then. The Declaration also specified that member countries had the right to determine what exactly constituted a national health crisis and included "HIV/AIDS, malaria, and tuberculosis and other epidemics" in that determination. In fact, some international drug companies and pharmaceutical associations hoped to narrow Doha to only include reference to AIDS, but their efforts failed. In addition, it reiterated that members could grant compulsory licenses and laid out the various terms and conditions for doing so.

One lingering problem was that the agreement implied that only countries that could manufacture a drug could have the right of compulsory licensing. This would certainly not help poor countries without such manufacturing capacity, mostly in sub-Saharan Africa. The Doha Declaration called the WTO Council on TRIPS to come up with a solution to this issue. WTO members came up with a new agreement on this issue in August 2003. This became an amendment and annex to the 1994 TRIPS agreement. The agreement waived Article 31 (f) of the original TRIPS agreement (which limited compulsory licenses primarily for use in the domestic market) for countries with limited manufacturing capacity and for exports to the least developed countries.[31] This meant a country without manufacturing capacity could use a compulsory license to import needed medicine from a generic producer in a different country. The WTO Director-General, Supachai Panichpakdi, announced that this step was "a historical agreement for the WTO . . . (that) proves once and for all that the organization can handle humanitarian as well as trade concerns."[32]

EVALUATING THE DOHA DECLARATION

The Doha Declaration was praised by many public health officials as being an important advance in raising public health issues over intellectual property rights in certain situations. Yet, access to medication involves other hurdles that go beyond the compulsory license issue. These can include the absence of trained medical personnel to administer the drugs and the absence of smoothly functioning (or even existing) systems to distribute medications. These are components of the bigger issue—a reliable health system. Pascal Lamy, then the EU's trade negotiator, noted that the new agreement essentially solved "about 10 percent of the problem of access to medicines by developing countries."[33] In addition, most developing countries were not actually using the compulsory license options.

Powerful countries, such as the United States, sought ways to strengthen intellectual property rights standards beyond TRIPS and Doha. These "TRIPS-plus" policies are found in bilateral and regional trade agreements. For the issues of trade and drugs, for example, TRIPS-plus agreements may contain provisions such as longer patent terms and a longer period of exclusivity on pharmaceutical safety and efficacy test data.[34] Such agreements negotiated by the United States since 2001 include patent protection for pharmaceuticals that go beyond the 20 years term of TRIPS. The TRIPS-plus standards are seen as undermining some of the flexibility embedded in TRIPS and, in some cases, raising drug costs. The regional and bilateral agreements also have other possible impacts on health, for example where they impact a farmer's ability to share seeds or a company's ability to avoid stating a plant's origins.[35]

These agreements may also restrict a developing country's ability to issue compulsory licenses and add new restrictions that reduce generic producers' ability to sell their medicines. As scholar Flint has noted, "As the WTO has worked towards making TRIPS acceptable to poorer countries, so the US, at the instigation of Big Pharma, has worked towards circumventing concessions."[36] Countries that agree to expand intellectual property protection may receive, as the carrot, lower tariffs on some of the goods they seek to sell to the United States.

To date, very few countries have imported needed medicines through compulsory licensing. Over 30 countries (mostly developed) have announced that they will not even use the compulsory license system to import drugs or that they will only do so in case of emergency. On the positive side, many pharmaceutical companies have lowered the prices of their ARV medications and medication for other diseases.[37]

IMPORTANT INITIATIVES OUTSIDE OF THE WTO

While intellectual property issues are essential to international access to medicine issues, many very important advances in helping to get medications to developing countries took place outside the WTO and resulted, for example, in sharply lower prices for ARV medicines and countless lives saved. Looking specifically at HIV/AIDS, one of the largest programs is the President's Emergency Plan for AIDS Relief (PEPFAR), set up by former US President George W. Bush in 2003, which was the largest effort by one country to fight one disease. PEPFAR was set up to buy drugs for 2 million people infected with the disease in poor countries that were originally not allowed to buy generic drugs, as well as to offer care for patients and children orphaned by the disease. To date it has provided $52 billion toward addressing HIV/AIDS. Its first phase focused on emergency response. The next phase turned to promoting sustainable country programs through a shared partnership with the US that emphasized the country should take leadership and "own" their programs. Its goals included supporting prevention, care, training of new health care workers, and strengthening domestic health systems.[38]

Another advance for poor country access to medications for HIV/AIDS, malaria, and tuberculosis took place in 2006, the governments of five countries (Brazil, Chile, France, Norway, and the United Kingdom) established UNITAID, an international drug purchasing facility that is based in Geneva and hosted by the WHO. Its source of financing is innovative: around half of its resources come from a tax on airplane tickets in several countries. It also brings in funding from governments, NGOs, and the Bill & Melinda Gates Foundation. It works by using its resources and leverage to negotiate price reductions and get drugs to people more quickly. In 2010, it created a "Medicines Patent Pool" specifically to lower the price of HIV medications.

The MPP works by inviting holders of patents of priority HIV medications to negotiate to "license to the MPP," which means that the patent holders agree that other producers may produce and market low-cost versions of the medicines under specific terms, and the original patent holders then receive small royalties. UNITAID has also worked with the Clinton Foundation HIV/AIDS Initiative to negotiate deals with pharmaceutical companies to bring further reductions in the prices of generic ARV drugs, especially second-line drugs.[39]

The World Bank has also been a significant player in responding to HIV/AIDs since the late 1990s, when it began working with countries on national strategies and structures for coping with the disease. It launched a Multi-Country HIV-AIDS Program for Africa in 2000, to focus on prevention, care, and treatment. It funds a range of projects that work on areas such as capacity building for government and civil society actors, government's ability to respond to the disease, and "mainstreaming" AIDS interventions. It has spent over $4.5 billion to date.[40]

Expanding beyond AIDS to include tuberculosis and malaria, one of the largest international initiatives is the Global Fund to Fight AIDS, Tuberculosis, and Malaria, set up in 2002. Former UN Secretary-General Kofi Annan hoped to create some type of mechanism to fight these three diseases. The idea received support from the G8 Summit in Okinawa in 2000 and was later endorsed at the 2001 summit in Genoa. The fund, based in Geneva, Switzerland, has disbursed over $24 billion dollars to date. In the latest period, 2014 to 2016, it has $12 billion to disburse. The money funds antiretroviral and TB treatment for millions of people, the distribution of hundreds of millions of nets treated with insecticide (to prevent malaria), and support for strengthening health care systems. Its board includes representatives of donor and recipient countries, NGOs, private sector actors, and local communities. The World Bank is the fund's trustee.

All of these and other efforts have contributed to considerable progress toward combatting HIV/AIDS, as well as TB and malaria. For the former, more people than ever are receiving necessary treatment. AIDS drug costs have plummeted over 100 times since 2000. Today such drugs cost less than $100 per year, per person.[41] Pharmaceutical companies now offer different levels of pricing for their HIV drugs, tailored to reflect average per capita income. This means prices are lowest in the poorest countries. TB is still second to AIDS as the "greatest killer worldwide due to a single infectious agent," according to the WHO, which also notes that the death rate from TB shrunk by a dramatic 45 percent between 1990 and 2012.[42] TB is an infection caused by a bacterium and is curable, although there are strains that are resistant to multiple drugs. The WHO is a global leader in disseminating policies and strategies, technical support, and shaping a broader research agenda for this disease.[43] The story for malaria is similar, in the sense that mortality has declined by a dramatic 42 percent over the past decade or so, but it is still a killer. WHO data show over 200 million malaria cases and over 600,000 deaths caused by malaria in 2012 alone.[44] Malaria is caused by a parasite carried by mosquitoes.

OTHER CURRENT ISSUES OF WTO, HEALTH, AND TRADE

The WTO and WHO have cooperated over time on health and trade. In 2000, the organizations co-published a study on WTO agreements and public health, although outside observers argued that the study was "cautiously worded and largely descriptive," reflecting the need for compromise.[45] The WHO's World Health Assembly also produced a 2008 Global Strategy and Plan of Action on Public Health, Innovation and Intellectual Property that resulted in more interaction and cooperation between the WHO, WTO, and WIPO (World Intellectual Property Organization) on these issues. That year, the head of the WTO invited the heads of WHO and WIPO to deepen their dialogue on how the three institutions could better work together on the issue of poor country access to medicines. The institutions now meet regularly to hold workshops or symposia or to exchange information on their respective activities.[46] One output is a joint study the three organizations produced in 2013, "Promoting Access to Medical Technologies and Innovation: Intersections between Public Health Intellectual Property and Trade."

Medical technologies is a term that includes medicines, but also includes vaccines and medical devices. The report notes that in the area where health policy, intellectual property, and trade intersect, there has been growing interest in recent years on issues such as medical devices and medicines for noncommunicable diseases (such as cancer and heart disease). Indeed, noncommunicable diseases and chronic diseases cause the majority of deaths worldwide today, but receive a tiny percentage of donor funding for health issues, because they primarily impact countries that do not need aid. Scholar Jeremy Youde calculates that donors spend less than 3 percent of their health spending on these health issues, although these diseases cause over 60 percent of deaths worldwide.[47] The WHO, WTO, and WIPO report predicted continuing and large declines in deaths related to the main communicable diseases, but warned that we will also see steep increases in deaths due to noncommunicable diseases in the next 25 years. The report expected that such diseases would account for around 75 percent of all deaths by 2030.[48] It does make sense that as communicable diseases decline more people will die from noncommunicable disease.

There has also been more attention to equitable access to vaccinations, spurred in part by outbreaks of influenzas that have crossed species, like the avian influenza (A) H5N1 in 1997 and the 2009 outbreak of influenza (A) H1N1 (or "Swine Flu"). As authors Friede et al. noted, developing countries "would be last in the queue to benefit from a pandemic vaccine." In 2009, global production capacity for seasonal flu vaccines stood at 900 million doses, far below the 13.4 billion doses estimated as required to vaccinate the world population to a pandemic if two doses are necessary.[49] The WHO launched an initiative in 2006 aimed at encouraging more vaccine manufacturing in developing countries, the overall supply of vaccines, and more research and development related to influence vaccines. The intellectual property issues related to producing vaccines have to do with access to technology and knowledge, rather than patents. A helpful development was that the WHO was able to receive a royalty-free license on technology from Merck (then called Nobilon) that would allow manufacturers in developing countries to produce and sell seasonal and pandemic nasal spray vaccine for influenza.[50]

A final issue of importance is that of trade in counterfeit medications, which has been an issue since the mid-1980s. These are medications that may correctly mirror a legal version, but they may also include the wrong dosage, completely lack an active ingredient, or they may even include toxic ingredients.[51] Counterfeit drugs obviously hurt the profits of legitimate manufacturers, but they also have a real human impact if they make a condition worse, lead to resistance, or result in death. The TRIPS agreement did speak to the issue of pirated and counterfeited goods, but it did little to slow trade in such goods. Japan and the United States put the issue on the agenda of the 2006 G8 Summit in St. Petersburg, where leaders agreed to instruct their experts to look into how to strengthen the international legal framework to enforce intellectual property rights. In 2011, eight countries (Japan, United States, Australia, Canada, South Korea, Morocco, New Zealand, and Singapore) signed the Anti-Counterfeiting Trade Agreement (ACTA) in Tokyo. It was a TRIPS-plus agreement since it based on the idea that TRIP sets a floor for protecting intellectual property rights. It is a plurilateral agreement in the sense that it is an intellectual property agreement negotiated by a group of countries. This particular agreement was negotiated in secrecy. The idea behind it is to give custom officials in signatory countries more power to seize counterfeit goods, including medications, and also allows for relevant judicial authorities to order the infringer to pay damages to the right holder. It raised a firestorm of criticism from internet activists, especially in the EU, who argued it would restrict internet freedom and privacy amid concerns that it would allow border guards to search laptops, smart phones, and other potential sources of illegal content (think of all the programs and music that are illegally downloaded). ACTA was rejected by the European Parliament in 2012, and to date it is still not in effect.[52] Scholar Sell argued that the ACTA negotiations are an example of vertical forum-shifting, since powerful states could have gone through WIPO but chose a different way of trying to achieve higher intellectual property standards.[53]

PERSPECTIVES ON WTO, INTELLECTUAL PROPERTY, AND GLOBAL HEALTH GOVERNANCE

Scholars addressing the specific intersection of the WTO, intellectual property, and global health governance approach the issues from a number of different perspectives and disciplines. The examples below offer a sense of some of the important areas of research.

One strand of research that has produced a robust literature in recent years examines global health governance more broadly and address, in part, how the consellations of actors, including the WTO, WHO, WIPO, national governments, NGOs and other civil society actors, and others, succeed or fail to work together. As Youde noted, global health was seen as a relatively unimportant issue during the Cold War, given the prominence of international security issues and concerns. The HIV/AIDS pandemic and the growing problem of infectious diseases such as malaria and TB helped to give the topic more prominence. Countries are much more aware today of how global health can have a significant impact on security, economic development, and other issues. The sluggish international response to the Ebola epidemic has turned more attention to understanding and improving global health governance. One thing we do know is that effective global health governance is an area that requires close cooperation between national and international actors. Infectious diseases do not respect borders (and sometimes even species). But we also know that cooperation on most issues does not come easily. The global health regime faces a number of problems, including those related to specific diseases, the poor capacity of many domestic health systems, poor coordination among donors, and insufficient resources for a number of issues.[54] As international law professor Fidler noted,

Taken together, the challenges presented by health threats, social determinants of health, and the normative imperatives of human dignity and social justice make the current scale and content of global health governance breathtaking. At the same time, this expansive scope complicates effective cooperation. The collective action mechanisms available to states, intergovernmental organizations, and nonstate actors are not well suited to producing health-centric, coordinated governance across all necessary policy areas. As a result, holes, fissures, and shifting sands appear in contemporary global health governance.[55]

Related to the broader issue of global health governance is the narrower issue of how actors make use of different institutional fora or regimes to pursue their interests. Helfer has argued that the TRIPS agreement had "unanticipated effects on international intellectual property lawmaking" because it helped to diffuse interest in intellectual property issues across a variety of international organizations and other actors. In his view, this reflects the fact that developing countries and NGOs have been unhappy with many of the TRIPS provisions, and so their strategy has been to try and "recalibrate, revise, or supplement the treaty" by moving the discussion about intellectual property rights issues to other organizations where they feel their interests are better met. As noted in Chapter 2, Helfer argued this is an example of *regime shifting*.[56] Indeed, he observed that such regime shifting had already occurred on this issue, when the United States and European Community worked to move intellectual property rights issue to the GATT/WTO from WIPO in advance of the TRIPS agreement. Political scientist Sell sees something similar happening, but from the perspective of powerful countries, which she argued have greatly benefited from shifting TRIPS-related intellectual property issues to other bodies. This has created a "more congested and complex" arena for intellectual property policymaking that has primarily benefited the "stronger parties who seek to ration access to intellectual property."[57] Interest in regime or forum shifting, in this case, may be seen across a wide variety of actors.

Sell and her political scientist colleague Odell have examined the politics leading up the 2001 Doha Declaration. A coalition of developing countries, which typically lacks influence in such international fora, were able to achieve some of their main objectives in the negotiation process, in part because of the coalition's ability to reframe the issue as one of public health (rather than one of trade). Kapstein and Busby studied how a group of advocates (social activists and policy entrepreneurs in both the public and private sectors) pushed to dramatically lower the price of ARVs and make treatment available for everyone with AIDS. They argued that the WTO was a major focal point of the advocates' activities because the TRIPS agreement contained ambiguities on issues like public health. This made it well suited as a target of attack by those seeking to lower ARV prices, also allowing advocates to offer advice and information to developing country governments.[58]

CONCLUSION

Former WTO Director-General Pascal Lamy once summarized the complexity of access to medicine, showing how entangled it is with trade, intellectual property rules, and other factors. He said "access to medicines requires the right mix of health policies, intellectual property rules and trade policy settings, and involves the judicious and informed use of a range of measures including competition policy, procurement strategies, attention to tariffs and other trade related drivers of cost, and choices within the IP system."[59] In a world where these issues are highly political, involve powerful public and private sector actors, billions of dollars of profit, and impact human health, we are unlikely to see a "right mix" that satisfies everyone. Because the trade component of access to medicine issues will remain a central issue, the WTO/TRIPS will remain an important actor at the intersection of intellectual property and public health. At the same time, its broader legitimacy will be influenced by how well it continues to address access-to-medicine issues.

BIBLIOGRAPHY

Barton, John H. "TRIPS and the Global Pharmaceutical Market." *Health Affairs* 23, no. 2 (2004): 146–54.

Bhagwati, Jagdish N. "Patent Protection Does Not Belong with WTO." *Financial Times*, February 20, 2001.

Block, Robert. "South Africa May Reject Use of AIDS Drugs—Having Beaten Back Lawsuit, Pretoria Now Is Hedging on Antiretroviral Agents." *The Wall Street Journal*, April 20, 2001.

Chan, Margaret. "Opening Remarks: Creating Synergies between Intellectual Property Rights and Public Health." World Trade Organization, http://www.wto.org/english/tratop_e/trips_e/techsymp_july10_e/techsymp_july10_e.htm#chan.

Chase, Marilyn. "Clinton Foundation, Unitaid Strike Deals on Price Cuts for AIDS Drugs." *The Wall Street Journal*, April 29, 2008.

Cooper, Helen, Rachel Zimmerman, and Laurie McGinley. "Patents Pending: AIDS Epidemic Traps Drugs Firms in a Vise: Treatment Vs. Profits—Suit in South Africa Seeks to Block Generic Copies." *The Wall Street Journal*, March 2, 2001.

Fergusson, Ian F. "The WTO, Intellectual Property Rights, and the Access to Medicines Controversy." In *CRS Report for Congress*. Washington, DC: Congressional Research Service, 2006.

Fidler, David P. "The Challenges of Global Health Governance." In *International Institutions and Global Governance Program*. New York: Council on Foreign Relations, 2010.

Flint, Adrian. *HIV/AIDS in Sub-Saharan Africa: Politics, Aid and Globalization*. New York: Palgrave Macmillan, 2011.

Friede, Martin, Laszlo Palkonyay, Claudia Alfonso, Yuri Pervikov, Guido Torelli, David Wood, and Marie Paule Kieny. "WHO Initiative to Increase Global and Equitable Access to Influenza Vaccine in the Event of a Pandemic: Supporting Developing Country Production Capacity through Technology Transfer." *Vaccine* 20S (2011).

G8 Information Centre. "G8 Communique Okinawa 2000." http://www.g8.utoronto.ca/summit/2000okinawa/finalcom.htm.

Gurry, Francis. "Opening Remarks: Creating Synergies between Intellectual Property Rights and Public Health." Paper presented at the WHO-WIPO-WTO Joint Technical Symposium, Geneva, Switzerland, July 16, 2010.

Helfer, Laurence R. "Regime Shifting: The TRIPS Agreement and New Dynamics of International Intellectual Property Lawmaking." *Yale Journal of International Law* 29, no. 1 (2004): 2–83.

Kapstein, Ethan B., and Joshua W. Busby. *AIDS Drugs for All: Social Movements and Market Transformations*. New York: Cambridge University Press, 2013.

Lamy, Pascal. "Coherence between Health, Intellectual Property and Trade Key to Access to Medicines." Geneva, Switzerland: World Trade Organization, 2013.

Lee, Kelley, Devi Sridhar, and Mayur Patel. "Bridging the Divide: Global Governance of Trade and Health." *Lancet* 373, no. 9661 (2009): 416–22.

Marlink, Richard G., and Alison G. Kotin. *Global AIDS Crisis: A Reference Handbook*. Santa Barbara, CA: ABC-CLIO, 2004.

Odell, John, and Susan K. Sell. "Reframing the Issue: The WTO Coalition on Intellectual Property and Public Health 2001." In *Negotiating Trade: Developing Countries in the WTO and NAFTA*, edited by John Odell. New York: Cambridge University Press, 2006.

Oxfam International. "GSK Breaks with Industry Ranks to Improve Access to Medicines." http://www.oxfam.org/en/pressroom/pressreleases/2009-02-17/gsk-breaks-industry-ranks-improve-access-medicines.

PEPFAR. "Executive Summary of PEPFAR's Strategy." United States President's Emergency Plan for AIDS Relief, http://www.pepfar.gov/about/strategy/document/133244.htm.

Saini, K., N. Saini, and A. Baldi. "Impact of Anti-Counterfeiting Trade Agreement on Pharma Sector: A Global Perspective." *Journal of Current Pharmaceutical Research* 6, no. 1 (2011): 4–10.

Sell, Susan K. "TRIPS Was Never Enough: Vertical Forum Shifting, FTAS, ACTA, and TPP." *Journal of Intellectual Property Law* 18 (2011): 447–78.

———. "TRIPS-Plus Free Trade Agreement and Access to Medicines." *Liverpool Law Review*, no. 28 (2007): 41–75.

Solon, Olivia. "Acta La Vista, Baby! European Parliament Rejects Controversial Trade Agreement." *Wired*, July 4, 2012.

UNAIDS. "UNAIDS Report Shows That 19 Million of the 35 Million People Living with HIV Today Do Not Know That They Have the Virus." http://www.unaids.org/en/resources/presscentre/pressreleaseandstatementarchive/2014/july/20140716prgapreport/.

United Nations. "Millennium Development Goals and Beyond 2015." New York: United Nations, 2014.

United Nations Development Programme. "Making Global Trade Work for People." New York: Earthscan, 2003.

World Bank. "World Bank and HIV/AIDS: The Facts." http://www.worldbank.org/en/topic/hivandaids/brief/world-bank-and-hivaids-the-facts.

World Health Organization. "Tuberculosis." Geneva, Switzerland: World Health Organization. http://www.who.int/mediacentre/factsheets/fs104/en/.

———. "Tuberculosis: WHO Global Tuberculosis Report 2014." Geneva, Switzerland: World Health Organization, 2014. http://www.who.int/tb/publications/factsheet_global.pdf

———. "World Malaria Report 2013." Geneva, Switzerland: World Health Organization, 2013.

WTO. "Decision Removes Final Patent Obstacles to Cheap Drug Imports." Geneva, Switzerland: WTO, 2003.

WTO, WIPO, WHO. "Promoting Access to Medical Technologies and Innovation: Intersections between Public Health, Intellectual Property and Trade." Geneva, Switzerland: WTO, WIPO, WHO, 2013.

Youde, Jeremy R. *Global Health Governance*. Malden, MA: Polity Press, 2012.

Latin America has a number of regional economic organizations (Latin American Integration Association, Mercosur, NAFTA, Central American Common Market (CACM)), as well as a regional development bank and regional courts (Andean Tribunal of Justice, Central American Court of Justice). It has some of the oldest ROs, such as the OAS, with its broad range of mandates, from democratization to poverty reduction. Africa is home to the African Union (AU) (which replaced the old Organisation of African Unity in 2002 and is the subject of the next chapter), the East African Community, Common Market for Eastern and Southern Africa, the Economic Community of Central African States, the Economic Community of West African States (ECOWAS), and the Arab Magreb Union, the Community of Sahel-Saharan States, the Inter-governmental Authority on Development, and the Southern African Development Community, for example. In the Middle East, regional organizations include Organization of Petroleum Exporting Countries, the Gulf Cooperation Council, and the Arab League.[15] Table 11.1 offers some examples of regional organizations in a handful of major sectors.

DEBATES ABOUT REGIONALS

The literature on regional organizations is rich and deep. It includes work on integration, inter-regionalism, and the role of regional organizations in individual sectors and issue areas. It evaluates the performance of regional organizations, explains their rise and decline, and looks at how they interact with one another and with states and other national and civil society actors. Perhaps one of the main debates that cuts across institutions and sectors is whether ROs complement or conflict with IOs.

On one hand, there is a literature that argues that regional organizations are helpful to global ones. As noted above, ROs may provide a stepping-stone between national and global governance. Ramesh Thakur and Luk Van Langenhove, for example, argued that states and international organizations are not enough for effectively solving many global problems. Regionalism, they argued, is "an integral part of contemporary multilayered and multi-actor governance."[16]

In many ways global organizations encourage the existence of regional ones, directly or indirectly. Article 51 in Chapter VII of the UN Charter reaffirms that collective self-defense is allowable in the face of an armed attack, before the Security Council can take necessary measures to maintain peace and international security. Article 51 also allowed for the creation of a number of regional security alliances, such as NATO, the Southeast Asia Treaty Organization (1954), and the Warsaw Pact (1951).[17] The UN Charter's Chapter VIII, "Regional Arrangements," is explicit that there is a role for regional arrangements in maintaining international peace and security and such arrangements are consistent with the UN's purposes and principles. The idea behind this is that regional organizations are closer to many of the issues that most impact member states. The Security Council would still get involved, if necessary, but ROs can be a first, and possibly final, stop. Likewise, parts of the UN family focus on regions, such as the UN's regional commissions. A number of regional organizations, including the African Union, Caribbean Community, and League of Arab States, have permanent observer status at the General Assembly.

Former UN Secretary-General, Boutros Boutros-Ghali, argued in the 1992 *Agenda for Peace* that ROs could play a role lightening the Security Council's burden and contributing "to a deeper sense of participation, consensus and democratization in international affairs."[18] His successor Kofi Annan agreed that a greater depth of UN cooperation with ROs was important to producing more effective outcomes.[19] For example, ROs have an interest in how to manage conflict (though different countries in the region may want different outcomes) and they have local knowledge. Their local role can give them legitimacy.

Some scholars and policymakers have argued that ROs can counter the problematic practices or limitations of IOs. NATO, for example, can more quickly deploy forces than the Security Council and its troops tend to be better equipped and trained. In the area of development, regional development banks may be seen as focusing on the specific development challenges of a region while cooperating with the World Bank.

A number of scholars argue that ROs have many weaknesses. ROs may be biased as they pursue their own regional interests. They may be corrupt or lack experience or capacity. They may not be helpful or good. They may be just as bureaucratic as large IOs. Usually, they lack the legitimacy of a global organization. The old Organization of African Unity had a history of stunning failure in addressing regional conflicts and civil wars, including the Rwandan genocide. A number of regional integration institutions in Africa, including ECOWAS and the East African Community, have been ineffective in promoting integration or increased trade. In Latin America, the OAS performed poorly at averting or halting civil wars in Central America during the 1980s and 1990s. In Asia, ASEAN has often been hampered in acting effectively to address conflict given the different interests of its members.

Another overarching critique of ROs is that they may draw legitimacy away from global institutions. As noted in the WTO chapter, the rise of bilateral and regional free trade agreements and economic regionalism are seen by many as eroding the central role of the WTO. There are concerns that the new Asian Infrastructure and Investment Bank and New Development Bank BRICS will hurt the IMF and World Bank. Regionals may not always complement or help IOs.

THE EUROPEAN UNION

The institutionalization of Europe is a profound process that has directly impacted hundreds of millions of lives. It began as a process of economic integration, but over time the issues it addresses have expanded and today include issues such as social policy, immigration, and security policy. The process has moved forward in fits and starts, with some periods of rapid institutional building (from 1950 through the mid-1960s) followed by what has been called "euro-stagnation" in the 1970s due to the oil crisis and global recession. Starting in the 1980s there was another burst of institution-building and an increasing scope and deepening of what integration meant.[20] Today, EU decisions impact domestic policymaking actions and European law impacts a broad range of issues that includes parental leave, gender equality, agricultural prices, minimum standards for drinking water, and even the cost of cell phone roaming charges. EU citizens can take prescriptions for medication written in one EU country and fill them in another EU country. There are common European standards on everything from how cosmetics are manufactured to how construction products are manufactured. A citizen of any EU member state can live, study, work, shop, and retire in any other member states. The EU today embodies a huge body of law that impacts member states, individuals, and even, indirectly, other countries.

euro and is now challenged by the euro crisis. While economic integration has been on the European agenda for decades, EMU was a major step forward in calling for a common monetary policy and currency, with coordination in fiscal policy.

EMU has been tested in many ways. For example, even the most powerful EU economies—France and Germany—found themselves by 2003 in breach of agreed fiscal requirements set by the Maastricht Treaty, which led to the requirements being relaxed. EU scholars have long pointed out the inherent structural challenge where monetary policy is a "one-size fits all" conducted outside of member states that still control their individual fiscal policies, a situation that can create conflict policy preferences and outcomes.[35] The euro crisis has focused more attention on this issue.

The euro crisis erupted in the spring of 2010 and was a surprising additional act in the drama that began on the other side of the Atlantic Ocean. European banks were deeply invested in the US mortgage market, and many also required governments to bail them out. The banking crisis in Europe morphed into a sovereign debt crisis as investors began to focus on weak government finances in Europe. In some cases European governments did not have the healthy finances needed to rescue their banks. Some European countries were not meeting the fiscal principles they agreed to, which made it difficult to maintain a common currency. Economists also noted that the EU's thin level of integration in labor and product markets did not help.[36] The bottom line is that it was really tough for so many countries to share a currency given the economic context. "Europe," noted a financial journalist,

> created a single currency before its member nations were ready for it. Their economies had not converged sufficiently for one currency to fit all. As a result, the common currency tended perversely to push the nations further apart, with the nations of the periphery, such as Spain and Ireland, booming unsustainably.[37]

All of these factors together created a perfect storm in Europe resulting in economic contraction, rising unemployment, stagnant growth, and in some areas—political unrest. By July 2012 there were real concerns that the euro might collapse, and ECB president Mario Draghi famously pledged that July to "do whatever it takes" to save it. The crisis ended up bringing down a number of European governments and also revealed some of the major flaws and tensions in the structure of the eurozone.

Greece was at the center of the crisis. It announced in fall 2009 it had a large budget deficit, which was much higher than expectations (over 12% of GDP, well above EU guidelines of 3%), as the new government revealed past dodgy accounting practices were used to mask the accurate levels.[38] It also had a current account deficit and a crippling level of public debt. Investors became jittery about Greece's ability to pay its debts and manage its deficits, and the euro started to weaken as investors sold it and European stocks. For Greece to cut its deficits, it would need to cut spending sharply, tackle endemic tax evasion and raise taxes, and take other actions pushed by the EU. Public concerns about these actions prompted strikes and demonstrations. By the end of the year thousands of workers went on strike, concerned about the spending cuts the EU was pushing as a way for Greece to reduce its deficit and improve its creditworthiness.[39] The dramatic austerity package announced in March 2010, welcomed by the Commission, ECB, and IMF (dubbed "the Troika"), further fueled riots on the streets. Greek Finance Minister,

George Papaconstantinou, said the country had to make a choice between "collapse or salvation."[40]

To ensure the Greek government did not default on finance repayments to its international creditors, including other European banks and the IMF, eurozone finance ministers agreed on a massive €110 billion bailout package for Greece in May 2010, a package designed by the Troika. This three-year package of emergency loans included €80 billion in bilateral loans from euro area countries and a €30 billion IMF standby arrangement. It was the largest ever fund program, relative to quota, at 3,212 percent of quota, and it was the first fund program with a member of the euro area. [41] It was also widely unpopular in Germany. Greece, in turn, had to agree to more dramatic spending cuts, which would be monitored by the Troika. Soon after, eurozone leaders announced a stunning €750 billion deal to help stabilize the euro more broadly, which included €500 in financing that could be supplemented with another €250 billion from the IMF.[42]

Worries about Greece's finances soon spread to two other countries facing problems with high levels of sovereign debt, as investors grew concerned that the debt might have to be restructured, or that countries might default. Portugal and Ireland sought bailouts within the year, later followed by Cyprus.[43] There were also concerns about Italy and Spain, which avoided similar bailouts but were helped by other actions, such as the ECB buying back their bonds. While there was variation in the economic problems each country faced, they all shared the euro and could not devalue their currency to help them out of crisis.

At the height of the crisis, it did not seem realistic for Greece to consider leaving the euro. There was concern that such a move would hurt European banks that had lent money to Greece and that investors would start betting on which country might be next to exit. Exiting the euro was also seen as humiliating in Greece, and it would be a move that would cause the country further economic pain, as its own currency would undoubtedly sink dramatically.[44] As the crisis unfolded, the EU responded with a number of actions. The ECB lowered interest rates to record lows and undertook numerous other actions to help calm the markets. By 2012, it was clear that the 2010 rescue was not enough to solve Greece's problems. In fact, the IMF later admitted that its hopes that dramatic Greek reforms would solve the country's economic problems were overly optimistic. Greece succeeded in reducing its fiscal deficit, but was also in the midst of a deep recession, its banks were undercapitalized, unemployment was still rising, and it still had too much public debt. In March 2012, the eurozone nations agreed to a second bailout for Greece, totaling €130 billion, with a €28 billion contribution by the IMF. Again, loan disbursements were tied to specific actions by the Greek government in revamping its economy. All of these "shows of strength" were meant to calm the markets and reduce speculation that the eurozone might break up.

At the same time, the crisis highlighted the difficulty the EU faces in responding nimbly, given that policy cooperation has involved 17 to 19 countries and the main EU institutions. As Randall Henning noted, while European policymakers were deliberating about how to respond to Greece's woes in winter and early spring 2010, "the amount of money that would later be required to calm the markets probably tripled."[45] Financial markets often viewed the actions taken by the EU and the IMF as "too little and too late."[46]

By 2015, it was unclear whether or not the crisis was over. On the positive side, Ireland and Portugal successfully completed their bailout programs by mid-2014. But the Greek crisis remained. In early 2015, Greek voters, fed up with austerity and unemployment, elected a new leader who sought to challenge the austerity policies that the country pursued since the start of the crisis. The drama of the crisis reached a new boiling point in the summer of 2015 when Prime Minister Alexis Tsipras held a referendum to ask Greek voters whether they would accept the latest offer by the county's creditors, and voters overwhelmingly rejected the deal. However, subsequent talks between the Greek government and its creditors did revolve around new and painful austerity measures.

While Greece and its creditors subsequently moved away from the brink, there are still concerns that the slump caused by slow growth and high unemployment in Greece will not be that easy to solve even with yet another bailout program.

PERSPECTIVES ON THE EU

Scholars who specialize in the EU examine a wide range of issues, including work on European integration as a process, the EU as a political system, the effectiveness and impact of specific EU policies or policies in specific sectors, issue areas, EU institutions, and member states. They are interested in how the EU works, how it has evolved, whether and how EU institutions matter, and what explains success and failure in EU actions in different issue areas and over time. They also study patterns of European governance, policymaking, international presence, and more. Major debates in the EU scholarly world include the impact of integration on member state sovereignty, and whether the EU is becoming more or less democratic. Some of the schools of thought reflect broader theoretical debates in international relations and international organizations, including the realist, institutionalist (mentioned above), and constructivist perspectives. Policy network theory is also a prominent strand of theorizing in the EU literature, with a focus on the "clusters" of actors who shape outcomes in individual policy sectors.[47] A number of universities have special research centers on the EU. There are also academic journals entirely devoted to the study of the European Union, including the *European Union Politics*, the *Journal of Common Market Studies*, the *Journal of European Public Policy*, and the *Journal of European Integration*, among others.

The euro crisis has also renewed disillusionment with EU institutions and policies. In Britain there is talk of a voluntary exit, or "brexit" in the press. Greece may be pushed out of the euro. As Matthijs and Kelemen noted, "Many citizens, especially the young, no longer associate the EU with greater freedom and opportunity; instead they blame it for financial pain, prolonged joblessness, and a lack of democratic choice."[48] Scholars have also argued that the euro crisis also reflects a failure of governance, including the fact that members of the Troika did not always share preferences or goals reflecting some of the negative side effects of institutional overlap.[49] Even the IMF recognized that the Troika did not work especially well, given that it lacked a clear division of labor, the European institutions tended to analyze the situation differently (looking at how it impacted Europe) from the IMF (which takes a country focus), and the members sometimes had very different projections on growth. The fund even acknowledged that it underestimated how dramatic Greek's economic contraction would be after the first bailout.[50]

CONCLUSION

This chapter has highlighted the important roles that ROs play in international relations and global and regional governance and has shown examples of the variation in their efforts, influence, performance, and legitimacy. They vary in their structure; their interaction with member states, their global counterparts, and one another; the scope of their activities; and their performance. ROs can offer options to states that are forum shopping, but ROs may also contribute to some of the downsides of institutional overlap. ROs also provide another point of engagement for other actors in global governance, including civil society actors, private sector actors, and so on. The chapter highlighted the EU as a special example of the most complex and highly-developed regional organization—so much so that there is discussion on how exactly to define what it has become but also widespread acknowledgment of the powerful role it and its institutions are having in member states and in global governance.

BIBLIOGRAPHY

Authers, John. *Europe's Financial Crisis: Short Guide to How the Euro Fell into Crisis, and the Consequences for the World.* 1st ed. Upper Saddle River, NJ: FT Press, 2013.

Bomberg, Elizabeth E., John Peterson, and Richard Corbett. *The European Union: How Does It Work?* The New European Union Series. 3rd ed. Oxford, UK: Oxford University Press, 2012.

Boutros-Ghali, Boutros. "An Agenda for Peace: Preventive Diplomacy, Peacemaking and Peace-Keeping." New York: United Nations, 1992.

Caporaso, James A. "The European Union and Forms of State: Westphalian, Regulatory or Post-Modern?" *Journal of Common Market Studies*, 34, no. 1 (2008): 29–52.

Cowles, Maria Green, and Stephanie Curtis. "Developments in European Integration Theory: The EU as 'Other.'" In *Developments in the European Union 2*, edited by Maria Green Cowles and Desmond Dinan. New York: Palgrave MacMillan, 2004.

Delegation of the European Union to the United States. "What is the European Union?" Washington, DC: Delegation of the European Union to the United States. http://www.euintheus.org/who-we-are/what-is-the-european-union/.

Egan, Michelle, and Maria Helena Guimaraes. "Compliance in the Single Market." *Business and Politics* 14, no. 4 (2012): 1–28.

European Commission, "About the European Commission," http://ec.europa.eu/about/index_en.htm.

European Investment Bank, "Financial Report 2013," 3. http://www.eib.europa.eu/attachments/general/reports/fr2013en.pdf.

European Parliament at your Service, "European Citizen's Initiative," http://www.europarl.europa.eu/aboutparliament/en/001eb38200/European-citizens%27-initiative.html

European Union. "Living in the EU." http://europa.eu/about-eu/facts-figures/living/index_en.htm.

"Eurozone Approves Massive Greece Bail-Out." *BBC News*, May 2, 2010.

Goldgeier, James M. "The Future of NATO." New York: Council on Foreign Relations, 2010.

Hardt, Heidi. *Time to React: The Efficiency of International Organizations in Crisis Response.* New York: Oxford University Press, 2014.

Kahler, Miles. "Economic Crisis and Global Governance: The Stability of a Globalized World." In *Politics in the New Hard Times: The Great Recession in Comparative Perspective*, edited by Miles Kahler and David A. Lake, 27–51. Ithaca, NY: Cornell University Press, 2013.

——. *International Institutions and the Political Economy of Integration*. Washington, DC: The Brookings Institution, 1995.

——. "Regional Institutions in an Era of Globalization and Crisis." In *Integrating Regions: Asia in Comparative Context*, edited by Miles Kahler and Andrew MacIntyre, 3–27. Stanford, CA: Stanford University Press, 2013.

Kahler, Miles, and David A. Lake. "Introduction." In *Politics in the New Hard Times: The Great Recession in Comparative Perspective*, edited by Miles Kahler and David A. Lake, 1–24. Ithaca, NY: Cornell University Press, 2013.

Katzenstein, Peter J. *A World of Regions*. Ithaca, NY: Cornell University Press, 2005.

Mansfield, Edward D., and Helen V. Milner. "The New Wave of Regionalism." *International Organization* 53, no. 3 (Summer 1999): 589–627.

Matthijs, Matthias, and R. Daniel Kelemen. "Europe Reborn: How to Save the European Union from Irrelevance." *Foreign Affairs* (January/February 2015).

Obama, Barack. "Remarks by President Obama and NATO Secretary-General Rasmussen before Meeting." Washington, DC: White House Office of the Press Secretary http://www.whitehouse.gov/the-press-office/2014/03/26/remarks-president-obama-and-nato-secretary-general-rasmussen-meeting.

Peterson, John. "Policy Networks." In *European Integration Theory*, edited by Antje Wiener and Thomas Diez, 105–24. New York: Oxford University Press, 2009.

Pevehouse, Jon C. "With a Little Help from My Friends? Regional Organizations and the Consolidation of Democracy." *American Journal of Political Science* 46, no. 3 (July 2002): 611–626.

Pisani-Ferry, Jean. *The Euro Crisis and Its Aftermath*. New York: Oxford University Press, 2011.

Pollack, Mark A. *The Engines of European Integration: Delegation, Agency, and Agenda Setting in the EU*. New York: Oxford University Press, 2003.

Russett, Bruce M. "International Regions and the International System." In *Regional Politics and World Order*, edited by Richard A. Falk and Saul H. Mendlovitz, 181–87. San Francisco, CA: W. H. Freeman & Co. Ltd., 1973.

Sbragia, Alberta. "Thinking about the European Future: The Uses of Comparison," in *Euro-Politics: Institutions and Policymaking in the 'New' European Community,* Alberta M. Sbragia, ed. Washington, DC: The Brookings Institution, 1992.

Schmidt, Vivien A. "The European Union: Democratic Legitimacy in a Regional State?" *Journal of Common Market Studies*, 42, no. 5 (2004): 975–997.

Schuman, Robert. "The Schuman Declaration." May 9, 1950.

Smith, Helena. "Strikes Hit Greece as Debt Crisis Grows." *The Guardian US,* December 17, 2009. http://www.theguardian.com/business/2009/dec/17/greece-protests-strikes-debt-crisis.

Thakur, Ramesh, and Luk Van Langenhove. "Enhancing Global Governance through Regional Integration." *Global Governance* 12, no. 3 (July-September 2006): 233–40.

Union of International Associations, ed. *Yearbook of International Organizations 2014–2015*. Brussels, Belgium: Brill, 2014. Figure 2.1. http://ybio.brillonline.com.proxyau.wrlc.org/sites/brill.uia.org/files/pdf/v5/2014/2_1.pdf.

12 Regional Organizations Case Study

African Union Peace Operations

The Organization of African Unity (OAU) was born in 1963 amid great fanfare with the goals of liberating Africa from the vestiges of European colonization, safeguarding member-state sovereignty, building solidarity among African states, and creating a unified continent. It began with 32 members and over time most African states joined. It also developed a very poor reputation, given that it did very little to curb conflicts in the region, including Ethiopia, Angola, Chad, Somalia, Liberia, the Democratic Republic of Congo, Sierra Leone, and elsewhere, where its members were often implicated. It did not stop leaders like Idi Amin in Uganda or General Sani Abacha in Nigeria, who butchered thousands of people. It did not avert genocide in Rwanda. The OAU was also criticized for doing little to address other major issues in the region, including promoting economic growth and combatting corruption. In 2002, the African Union (AU) replaced the OAU, with a mission to be a more effective institution that would promote African economies, address major development issues, and act more forcefully to prevent, manage, and resolve conflict in the region. Today the AU comprises 54 member states, and its secretariat is based in Addis Ababa, Ethiopia.[1]

One of the central ideas behind creating the AU was to move away from OAU's emphasis on supporting liberation movements and ending apartheid (which did end in 1994), and toward promoting economic development and integration and a commitment to democratic principles. For some there were hopes of reviving earlier visions of an institution that would produce even deeper Pan-African ties. A 2007 summit of AU leaders, for example, focused on creating a "United States of Africa."[2] But other leaders were critical of this initiative and argued it was impractical. In fact, the new AU's structure was patterned on the European Union, with bodies that include a Commission, a Court (the African Court of Human and People's Rights), and a Pan-African Parliament; although in practice these institutions work in different ways than the EU's bodies, with dramatically smaller budgets. Box 12.1 lists the objectives of the AU.

Perhaps the most novel aspect of the new AU is its move away from the OAU's support of the principle of *non-interference* in member states, an idea related to the sacrosanct principle of sovereignty. The AU was created with the right to intervene in member states in situations of "grave circumstances, namely: war crimes, genocide and crimes against humanity."[3] This change in focus was influenced in some ways by the emerging Responsibility to Protect norm discussed in Chapter 3. The OAU, by contrast, privileged sovereignty and territorial integrity of member states. This meant it stood aside in the face of conflict and even genocide.

BOX 12.1 AFRICAN UNION OBJECTIVES

To achieve greater unity and solidarity between the African countries and the peoples of Africa;

To defend the sovereignty, territorial integrity, and independence of its Member States;

To accelerate the political and socio-economic integration of the continent;

To promote and defend African common positions on issues of interest to the continent and its peoples;

To encourage international cooperation, taking due account of the Charter of the United Nations and the Universal Declaration of Human Rights;

To promote peace, security, and stability on the continent;

To promote democratic principles and institutions, popular participation and good governance;

To promote and protect human and peoples' rights in accordance with the African Charter on Human and Peoples' Rights and other relevant human rights instruments;

To establish the necessary conditions which enable the continent to play its rightful role in the global economy and in international negotiations;

To promote sustainable development at the economic, social, and cultural levels as well as the integration of African economies;

To promote cooperation in all fields of human activity to raise the living standards of African peoples;

To coordinate and harmonize the policies between the existing and future Regional Economic Communities for the gradual attainment of the objectives of the Union;

To advance the development of the continent by promoting research in all fields, in particular in science and technology;

To work with relevant international partners in the eradication of preventable diseases and the promotion of good health on the continent.

Source: "AU in a Nutshell," http://www.au.int/en/about/nutshell

The AU's Constitutive Act also called for the "condemnation and rejection of unconstitutional changes of governments," which was a significant departure from its predecessor's rejection of any interference in member states internal affairs. To help implement what was called a principle of "non-indifference," the AU's member states created in 2003 a Peace and Security Council (PSC) as "a standing decision-making organ for the prevention, management and resolution of conflicts" in the region. The PSC, which began its work in 2004, was entrusted with promoting "peace, security, and stability" in the region, with a range of activities that include peace-making, peace-building, and post-conflict reconstruction activities. The new PSC has been fairly active in its short life. It has helped to manage conflicts in a number of member states. It has sent peacekeeping missions (which it calls peace support operations) to places that include Burundi, Sudan, Somalia, and the Comoros. It has also imposed sanctions to express condemnation against unconstitutional government changes in Central African Republic, Togo, Mauritania, Niger, Mali, and Madagascar, among others.[4]

This chapter examines the creation of the PSC and some of its major peace operations to highlight the challenges facing an important regional organization that seeks to create a more peaceful Africa. The PSC's peace operations are an important indicator of whether the AU is able to reconcile the old OAU's tradition of nonintervention with the AU's modern commitment to democracy and the rule of law. To date the PSC's impact on managing conflict in the region has been mixed. On one hand, it has not played a leading role in many of the region's conflicts. UN troops and/or French troops were the key actors involved in responding to conflicts in Central African Republic, Mali, Niger, and Côte d'Ivoire. NATO and the UN took the lead in Libya. Where the PSC has been directly involved, it has not always been successful, such as its 2004 to 2007 mission in Darfur. The AU's planned standby forces do not yet exist, despite millions of donor dollars in training. The peace operations also heavily depend on outside funding, which has never been sufficient. On the other hand, the AU's peacekeeping forces succeeded in pushing al-Shabab forces outside of Somalia's capital. AU peacekeeping troops contributed to stability in Burundi, at least for a while. The AU's response rate to crises is more rapid than the UN's response and that of other regional organizations. The ability to be nimble in responding to crises can literally save lives and contribute to more effective outcomes.[5] Scholars argue that despite the mixed performance of the PSC, it has, and will continue to have, an impact on the region's security dynamics and therefore deserves closer attention and analysis.

FROM THE OLD OAU TO THE NEW AU

As noted above, the OAU had a terrible reputation in the international community as it put preserving state sovereignty above goals such as stopping human rights abuses by some of its leaders. In fact, Ugandan dictator Idi Amin was actually the chairman of the OAU in the middle of his reign of terror. As scholars Samuel Makinda and F. Wafula Okumu noted, the OAU "often behaved like a mutual preservation club." It was also widely known as merely "talking shop," because lofty words were not translated into action.[6] Ugandan president Yoweri Museveni called the OAU a "trade union of criminals."[7] Its relationship with the United Nations was also testy at times. When the UN Security Council imposed sanctions against Libya over the 1988 bombing of a Pan Am transatlantic flight over Lockerbie, Scotland, the OAU agreed to defy the sanctions. The OAU was also a weak institution that operated without clear rules or procedures.[8]

By the 1990s, many African leaders realized it was time for states to try something new and therefore the OAU agreed to establish the new AU with a different focus. Many observers greeted the metamorphosis with scepticism. After all, the controversial long-time Libyan dictator Muammar el-Qaddafi was competing for leadership of the new organization (which he did not succeed in getting). He was critical of African leaders working with the West, and his dictatorship did not fit other leaders' views that the new organization should be strengthening democracy and accountability in Africa.[9]

The constitutive act of the new AU was signed on July 11, 2000, and the new organization became operational in July 2002. The new AU was loosely modeled on the European Union. Its Assembly of Heads of State and Government is the "supreme organ" and meets once a year. The Executive Council consists of the ministers from the member states, makes decisions on policies, and is responsible to the Assembly. Its Commission is the main administrative body and includes eight Commissioners, each of whom is responsible for a portfolio.

The Commission's Peace and Security Directorate contains the Peace Support and Security Operations Division, which mandates the AU's peace support operations. There is a Pan-African Parliament and also a Court, the African Court on Human and Peoples' Rights, which delivered its first judgment in 2009. (This is different from the envisioned Court of Justice in the AU's constitutive agreement.)

THE PEACE AND SECURITY COUNCIL

As noted above, the PSC was set up in 2004, based on a 2001 decision. African leaders released white doves on the announcement of the new PSC and hailed the move to *non-indifference* from the old, sacrosanct principle of *non-interference*.[10] The PSC consists of 15 members, the same number as the UN Security Council. Members are elected by the AU Executive Council with Central Africa, East Africa, and Southern Africa each having three representatives, North Africa having two, and West Africa having four. Unlike the Security Council, the PSC has no permanent members and there is no veto. Five members have three-year terms, and the remaining 10 have two-year terms. Members have equal voting rights. The PSC's chair rotates each month, in alphabetical order of member state names, in English.[11] The PSC's permanent representatives meet at least twice a month at the Addis Ababa AU headquarters.

In addition to its goal of promoting peace, security, and stability in the region, the PSC's other central goals are to "anticipate and prevent conflicts"; "promote and implement peace-building and post-conflict reconstruction activities"; "coordinate and harmonize continental efforts in the prevention and combating of international terrorism"; "develop a common defense policy for the Union"; and "promote and encourage democratic practices, good governance and the rule of law, protect human rights and fundamental freedoms, respect for the sanctity of human life and international humanitarian law," all of which are seen as important in helping to prevent conflict. One seemingly contradictory aspect of the PSC's Articles is that the principles of non-interference and respect for sovereignty are still there, alongside the principles of the right of the Union to intervene in the "grave circumstances" listed above. Critics have also pointed out that the PSC's members have included countries that are not supportive of democratic practices and good governance, including Zimbabwe and Equatorial Guinea.

The PSC's founding document also notes that it will be supported by the AU's Commission, as well as a "Panel of the Wise, a Continental Early Warning System, and African Standby Force, and a Special Fund." Together these components are referred to as the African Peace and Security Architecture. The Panel is a five person body of highly respected Africans who have contributed to the "cause of peace, security, and development on the continent"; supported the PSC in conflict prevention; and has typically included former prime ministers and high-ranking government ministers. Each region is represented: Central Africa, Eastern Africa, Northern Africa, Southern Africa, and Western Africa. The first panel was appointed in 2007. The panel meets at least three times a year and produces reports for the PSC and chair of the commission.[12] To date, the African Standby Force is not functional, and it is unclear how active the other elements are.

RELATIONSHIP BETWEEN PSC AND THE UN SECURITY COUNCIL

The literature on regional peace organizations has shown that regional organizations can have more political authority and legitimacy than the UN, and can help the UN's own challenges with inadequate resources and cases where Security Council politics or hesitation can slow or stop possible action. Regional organizations can reduce the UN's burden of responsibility in responding to conflicts throughout the world.

The AU and its PSC have had a complex relationship with the United Nations. As noted in Chapter 11, UN Secretary-General Boutros Boutros-Ghali in *Agenda for Peace* emphasized the importance of increasing the role of regional organizations in addressing conflict, through steps to prevent conflict and to respond to it.

Both the Security Council and the PSC understand that given Africa's many conflict and security issues, it is important that both institutions play a role in addressing them. They know that the SC has primary responsibility for maintaining international peace and security, while the AU is a source of political authority in the region. During most years between 2002 and today, there has been at least one non-permanent member of the Security Council who is also on the PSC. Given the SC's primary position and the fact that the AU lacks sufficient financial and logistical resources, the partnership between the two institutions is an unequal one. One early and tricky aspect of the relationship was an ambiguity about whether the PSC needed UN Security Council authorization before authorizing a peace operation. The UN Charter requires that the UN Security Council endorse any use of force outside of self-defense, but the PSC Protocol was ambiguous on whether or not it requires Council authorization. As noted above, Article 16.1 states that the AU has "the primary responsibility for promoting peace, security and stability in Africa," which implies it can authorize interventions on its own. But Article 17.1 notes that the UN Security Council "has the primary responsibility for the maintenance of international peace and security." By 2005, however, the PSC publicly agreed that it would seek UN Security Council authorization of any of its enforcement actions.[13] And the AU and UN have developed a number of security coordination mechanisms since 2006.

Where the AU has major peace operations, it still depends on the UN and other donors for support.[14] In fact, 63 percent of all UN peace operations, more than 80 percent of the UN's peacekeeping budget, and close to 90 percent of all UN peacekeepers are in Africa.[15] Indeed, there are many more African peacekeepers in UN operations in Africa, than there are peacekeepers in AU operations. As an example, in 2012, there were almost 35,000 Africans serving in UN peace operations in Africa, compared with fewer than 20,000 servicing in AU missions.

Despite active collaboration, tension between the PSC and the Security Council has persisted. The AU was critical of the UN Security Council's 2005 referral of the situation in Darfur to the International Criminal Court's Chief Prosecutor for investigation and prosecution of war crimes and crimes against humanity. In 2009, the Court issued a warrant for the arrest of Sudanese president Omar al-Bashir. The AU later passed a resolution criticizing the ICC. In fact, this issue took a dramatic turn in 2015 at the African Union's Summit in Johannesburg, which South Africa's government allowed al-Bashir to attend. Despite South Africa's assurances that Bashir would be safe, the country's High Court ordered the government to detain him. The Sudanese president managed to slip away from the Summit and the country and return home without incident.[16] The AU and Security Council were also at odds on how to respond to the crisis in Libya in 2011. The AU supported a more diplomatic approach to convince Qaddafi to step down and cease the conflict. The Security Council instead authorized military action, which provided a mandate for NATO's intervention. Africa expert Alex de Waal argued that the AU was hurt by its inability to convince the broader community, other Africans, or Libyans that "it was a credible interlocutor for peace in Libya."[17]

Scholars Arthur Boutellis and Paul D. Williams have noted that collaboration has been most successful when the political interests of the UN Security Council and the AU's PSC are aligned and least successful when they are not.[18] A recent High-Level Independent Panel on United Nations Peace Operations calls for strengthening the strategic partnership between the UN and the AU, including having the UN provide more predictable financing to AU peace operations.

PSC'S MAJOR PEACE OPERATIONS

Since 2002, the PSC has led three major peace missions and has also been involved in a number of smaller missions. The major missions were in Burundi (AMIB, 2003–04), Darfur (AMIS, 2004–07), and Somalia (AMISOM, since 2007). The big three were structured to be bridging operations to prepare for larger UN peacekeeping missions.[19]

Burundi

Burundi took steps toward peace when the government-dominated party and leading Hutu rebels signed the Arusha Agreement for Peace and Reconciliation in 2000. Because other rebel Hutu factions boycotted the agreement, regional mediators sought to build a ceasefire agreement. AMIB was the first peace operation completely organized by the AU. The AU arrived before there was a formal ceasefire, which showed its willingness to engage in a peace enforcement mission. The UN would not get involved without a ceasefire. The AU operation consisted of around 3,000 troops that provided a measure of stability and paved the way for the UN's mission, United Nations Operation in Burundi (ONUB), which began on June 1, 2004. Among its activities, the AU force protected politicians who had joined the transitional government and helped to reintegrate former militia members into society.[20] AMIB's mission faced many challenges, including a lack of resources. Donors provided just $60 million of an estimated overall budget of $134 million. South Africa, one of the key contributors of AMIB's troops, ended up covering most of the costs. Gilbert Khadiagala has pointed out that while the lack of resources meant that AMIB could not do much to help with disarmament and demobilization, "its presence was important in increasing the level of confidence among parties in the transitional institutions and generating momentum for the return to normalcy."[21] ONUB's personnel initially consisted mainly of the AMIB forces, most of whom were "re-hatted," or absorbed into the larger UN force of around 5,500 personnel. Voters in Burundi approved a new constitution in February 2005 that institutionalized power sharing between the Hutu and Tutsi, and ONUB supervised a number of elections. The president asked ONUB to leave in 2006, although the UN still has had a presence in the country through an election observer mission and activities of the UN Peacebuilding Commission. While the AU's peacekeepers may have acquitted themselves well in this case, the country's situation did not have a happy ending. The president's desire to seek a third term, not allowed by the constitution, resulted in a coup attempt in May 2015 and fresh rounds of protests and violence.

Darfur

As noted in Chapter 3, the violent conflict in Darfur, which began in 2003, pitted government forces and a pro-government militia against two rebel movements and resulted in the slaughter, rape, and torture of hundreds of thousands of civilians by the government militias (called Janjaweed), the displacement of over two million people, and a major humanitarian crisis. The AU was a relevant player in the Darfur crisis in terms of its mediation and peacemaking efforts. AU Commission Chairperson, President Alpha Konaré, helped to organize and conclude a ceasefire in April 2004, and the initial deployment of the African Union Mission in Sudan (AMIS) followed soon after.[22] The AU was also involved in later rounds of peace talks and established in 2008 the AU High-Level Panel on Darfur to examine the conflict, consult with all relevant stakeholders, and make recommendations on how to promote reconciliation and healing.

AMIS did not succeed in its efforts. It began with a small ceasefire observer mission, but the ceasefire itself did not hold and was quickly violated by both the rebels and the army and militia. Its mandate was too narrow to allow it to do much in terms of implementing peace-building activities, and overall, the AU force was poorly equipped and under-resourced despite support from the UN, the European Union, NATO, and the governments of Japan and South Korea.[23] As scholar de Waal noted, "Its size and mandate were wholly incommensurate with the scale of the conflict and the demand for civilian protection."[24] The PSC was brand new and its Peace and Security Division had little experience in managing a complex operation. AMIS was strengthened by the end of 2005, with over 7,000 military personnel and civilian police. While the pace of killings declined significantly by late 2006, there was still no peace to keep. The UN Security Council in August 2006 called for a larger, better-equipped UN operation in Darfur. However, the Sudanese government insisted on keeping the "African character" of peacekeeping forces. The compromise was a new UN-AU Hybrid Mission in Darfur, which took over from AMIS on December 31, 2007, even in the absence of a working peace agreement.[25]

Somalia

The AU's operation in Somalia is a third example of deployment in the absence of a stable ceasefire. As detailed in Chapter 3, the country has suffered from civil war for almost two decades. Before the AU arrived, it had already seen a string of peacekeeping efforts, including the US-led multinational force and the two UN peacekeeping missions in the mid-1990s. The African Union Mission to Somalia (AMISOM) was created in January 2007 with a six-month mandate, authorized by the UN Security Council. It still exists and is now the longest standing and most complex peace operation the AU has ever undertaken. AMISOM's goals are to assist the government in stabilizing the country, to assist with the political reconciliation process (protect politicians), to facilitate the delivery of humanitarian aid, and to fight insurgents. It is multidimensional in the sense that it has military, policy, and civilian components. For four years, it was heavily focused on fighting to push al-Shabab Islamist militants and other anti-government forces out of Mogadishu and other parts of the country. Al-Shabab forces withdrew from central Mogadishu in August 2011, in what was seen as a major success for the AU mission.

As of 2015, the mission consisted of more than 22,000 troops, funded by the UN and other donors, with heavy support from the EU. Interestingly, the SC has supported AMISOM from assessed UN peacekeeping contributions, which is the first time the UN has funded a non-UN peace operation in this way. The funds are provided by a novel UN-AU mechanism, UN Support Office for AMISOM, which has offered a great deal of logistical support to AMISOM.[26] But the mission has been troubled in other respects. Expert Williams has argued that even 22,000 is simply not enough to control large sections of the country that are struggling with violence. The mission does not have sufficient air power and the ability to project firepower rapidly, which he argues is necessary to destroy al-Shabab's forces. AMISOM comprises forces from Uganda, Burundi, Djibouti, Kenya, and Ethiopia. Each contingent has its own commander, and they often do not work smoothly together.[27] AU troops in Somalia have also been accused by Human Rights Watch of raping and mistreating women and girls in Mogadishu.[28]

EVALUATION

It is not easy to evaluate the African Union's PSC and the peace operations it has launched. The literature on the topic is still very slim. Scholars are pessimistic about the PSC's ability to be effective in preventing, managing, and resolving conflicts given such constraints, but they also believe the PSC has a role to play in the region. Makinda and Okumu argued that without more resources from both AU member states and donors, there is simply no way for the PSC to handle complex security problems. They concluded that there is a "growing disillusionment about the AU's capacity to bring about rapid change."[29] Williams expressed the complexity of evaluating the PSC by saying it is suboptimal but still has an impact on the region's security dynamics. "It is reasonable to assume," he argued, "the security situation in Africa would probably have been worse without the PSC. To use a clichéd phrase, if the PSC didn't exist, it would be wise to invent it."[30] Heidi Hardt emphasized the importance of speedy response by peacekeepers, which can contribute to the effectiveness of a peace operation and save lives. In this area the PSC has done well and responds more quickly to crises than the European Union, with its more bureaucratic decision-making processes.[31] For NGOs like Human Rights Watch, sexual abuse and exploitation by AU peacekeepers is a terrible, serious problem that should result in the withdrawal of donor support if the relevant authorities are not taking appropriate measures to stop it.[32]

CONCLUSION

This chapter has examined the mixed performance of the PSC's peace operations. The AU's move from the principle of "non-interference" to "non-indifference" is a significant step forward. The mandate is a critical foundation for action, even if implementation is imperfect. The AU's peace operations are helpful in the sense that the peacekeeping burden in Africa is huge and too much for any one organization to handle on its own. The AU has responded where the UN could not or would not, and the AU can also respond more quickly. The AU's PSC might be far from an unmitigated success yet, but it is still a very young institution. One spot of good news is that there seems to be more recognition that the UN and AU can create ways of cooperating and coordinating. The UN has also provided assistance in training the PSC to also encourage more effective collaboration. The UN Office to the African Union set up at AU headquarters and the new Joint Task Force on Peace and Security, both set up in 2010, are also promising.[33]

However, Africa is still experiencing many violent conflicts, including those caused by terrorists and insurgents, and sometimes members of one AU state directly or indirectly support conflict in another state. Since 2000, for example, we have seen Sudan's People's Liberation Army receive support from Uganda, Eritrea, and Ethiopia; the Lord's Resistance Army in Uganda has received support from Sudan. Darfur rebels have received support from Chad, Eritrea, and Libya. Liberia has supported rebels in Sierra Leone, Guinea, and Côte d'Ivoire. Rebels in the Democratic Republic of Congo have received support from Uganda, Rwanda, and Burundi.[34] The list goes on. Fragile states in Africa are creating conditions for growth of violent extremists and terrorists, such as Boko Haram and al-Shabab. As the above examples show, the performance of its peace operations is mixed. The lack of resources is a very serious problem. The AU missions often do not have sufficient troops and lack equipment, logistical support, and advisory expertise. Quite often, the PSC's interventions have not received strong enough commitment from AU member states.

Even the AU's broader commitment to some of its new goals has been called into question. The current AU leader is Robert Mugabe, 91, the long-time dictator of Zimbabwe, a country suffering from corruption, graft, and political violence, where dissent is not tolerated and thousands of citizens have been tortured and murdered over the decades. And while the AU Commission strongly opposes coups that change the constitutional order, it hasn't tried to stop member-state presidents who seek to change political rules to stay office after their terms expire. Ultimately, the powerful ingredients of political will from member states, sufficient resources, and closer cooperation and consultation with the UN will be key to building a strong, more effective PSC.

BIBLIOGRAPHY

African Union. "Constitutive Act of the African Union." 2000.
———. "Peace and Security Council (PSC)." http://www.peaceau.org/en/page/38-peace-and-security-council.
Akokpari, John, Tim Murithi, and Angela Ndinga-Muvumba. "Introduction: Building an African Union for the 21st Century." In *The African Union and Its Institutions*, edited by John Akokpari, Angela Ndinga-Muvumba, and Timothy Murithi, 1–21. Auckland Park, South Africa: Fanele, 2008.
Bosco, David. "Omar Al-Bashir Just Made a Mockery of International Justice. Again." In *Voice: Foreign Policy*, 2015.
Boutellis, Arthur, and Paul D. Williams. "Peace Operations, the African Union, and the United Nations: Toward More Effective Partnerships." New York: International Peace Institute, April 2013.
Butcher, Tim. "Gaddafi Casts a Shadow over African Union." *The Telegraph*, July 8, 2002.

de Waal, Alex. "The African Union and the Libya Conflict of 2011." *Reinventing Peace* (blog): World Peace Foundation, December 19, 2012. https://sites.tufts.edu/reinventing-peace/2012/12/19/the-african-union-and-the-libya-conflict-of-2011/.

———. "Sudan: Darfur." In *Responding to Conflict in Africa: The United Nations and Regional Organizations*, edited by Jane Boulden, 283–306. New York: Palgrave Macmillan, 2013.

Hardt, Heidi. *Time to React: The Efficiency of International Organizations in Crisis Response.* New York: Oxford University Press, 2014.

Hellquist, Elin. "Regional Organizations and Sanctions against Members: Explaining the Different Trajectories of the African Union, the League of Arab States, and the Association of Southeast Asian Nations." edited by KFG. Berlin: Freie Universitat Berlin, January 2014.

High-Level Independent Panel on Peace Operations. "Uniting Our Strengths for Peace—Politics, Partnership and People." New York: United Nations, June 2015.

Human Rights Watch. "The Power These Men Have over Us: Sexual Exploitation and Abuse by African Union Forces in Somalia." New York: Human Rights Watch, 2014.

Khadiagala, Gilbert M. "Burundi, 2002–2012." In *Responding to Conflict in Africa: The United Nations and Regional Organizations*, edited by Jane Boulden, 101–19. New York: Palgrave Macmillan, 2013.

Makinda, Samuel M., and F. Wafula Okumu. *The African Union: Challenges of Globalization, Security, and Governance.* Routledge Global Institutions. New York: Routledge, 2008.

Maruf, Haran. "Al-Shabab Attacks Expose AMISOM Weaknesses." *Voice of America*, July 1, 2015.

Murithi, Tim. "Between Reactive and Proactive Interventionism: The African Union Peace and Security Council's Engagement in the Horn of Africa." *African Journal on Conflict Resolution* 12, no. 2 (2012): 87–110.

Mwanasali, Musifiky. "From Non-Interference to Non-Indifference: The Emerging Doctrine of Conflict Prevention in Africa." In *The African Union and Its Institutions* edited by John Akokpari, Tim Murithi, and Angela Ndinga-Muvumba, 41–61. Auckland Park, South Africa: Fanele, 2008.

Nathan, Laurie. "The African Union and Regional Organisations in Africa: Communities of Insecurity." *African Security Review* 19, no. 2 (2010): 106–13.

Williams, Paul D. "The Peace and Security Council of the African Union: Evaluating an Embryonic International Institution." *Journal of Modern African Studies* 47, no. 4 (2009): 603–26.

Notes

PREFACE

1. Claude Jr., Inis L. Swords into Plowshares: *The Problems and Progress of International Organization.* New York: Random House, 1956.

CHAPTER 1

1. Inis L. Claude, *Swords into Plowshares: The Problems and Progress of International Organization* (New York: Random House, 1956), 41.
2. See Joseph E. Stiglitz, *Globalization and Its Discontents*, 1st ed. (New York: W. W. Norton, 2002), 9; Claude, *Swords into Plowshares*, 41.
3. *Merriam-Webster Online Dictionary*, s.v. "govern" (2015), http://www.merriam-webster.com/dictionary/govern.
4. Pascal Lamy, "Global Governance: Getting us Where we all Want to go and Getting us There Together," *Global Policy* 1, no. 3 (2010).
5. National Intelligence Council and EU Institute of Security Studies, *Global Governance 2025: At a Critical Juncture* (Washington, DC: Office of the Director of National Intelligence, 2010).
6. Thomas G. Weiss and Ramesh Thakur, *Global Governance and the UN: An Unfinished Journey*, United Nations Intellectual History Project Series (Bloomington: Indiana University Press, 2010), 6–7.
7. Weiss and Thakur, *Global Governance,* 6–7.
8. Deborah D. Avant, Martha Finnemore, and Susan K. Sell, eds., *Who Governs the Globe?* (New York: Cambridge University Press, 2010), 1.
9. Avant, *Who Governs the Globe?,* 2–3.
10. Organizations with members from two states are bilateral rather than truly international.
11. Most people think of NGOs as nonprofit, nonreligious, and nonmilitary groups, although the distinctions do vary. This means that generally corporations and religious groups, for example, are not widely defined as NGOs, even if they are nongovernmental in nature.
12. Europa Publications Limited, "The Europa Directory of International Organizations" (London, U.K.: Routledge, 2005). The Yearbook (2005–06) also highlights factors that complicate clear definitions, including international agreements where one of the parties is another IO or agreements signed on behalf of states that may not "fully engage" the states in practice.
13. Peter M. Haas, Robert O. Keohane, and Marc A. Levy, *Institutions for the Earth: Sources of Effective International Environmental Protection* (Cambridge: MIT Press, 1993), 4–5.
14. Robert O Keohane, "International Institutions: Can Interdependence Work?," *Foreign Policy* 110 (1998), 82.
15. Stephen D. Krasner, "Structural Causes and Regime Consequences: Regimes as Intervening Variables," in *International Regimes*, ed. Stephen D. Krasner (Ithaca, NY: Cornell University Press, 1983), 2.
16. John Gerard Ruggie, *Multilateralism Matters: The Theory and Praxis of an Institutional Form*, New Directions in World Politics (New York: Columbia University Press, 1993), 573.
17. See Chapter 7 for discussion of the Bretton Woods system.
18. For a history of the development of IOs see Harold K. Jacobson, *Networks of Interdependence: International Organizations and the Global Political System*, 1st ed. (New York: Knopf, 1979), 10. He pointed out that the Delian League and the Hanseatic League may be seen as historical prototypes to the modern-day international organization, but they were isolated phenomena. The Delian League, 478–404 B.C., was a group of Greek city-states seeking military cooperation against common enemies. Athens was the dominant state. The Hanseatic League consisted of an alliance of German trading cities seeking to dominate trade on the Baltic Sea.
19. Jacobson, *Networks of Interdependence*, 33; Michael Wallace and J. David Singer, "Intergovernmental Organization in the Global System, 1815–1964: A Quantitative Description," *International Organization* 24, no. 2 (1970).
20. Jacobson, *Networks of Interdependence*, 33. Its founding members were France, Netherlands, and the German states of Baden, Bavaria, Hesse, Nassau, and Prussia.
21. Paul Weindling, *International Health Organisations and Movements, 1918–1939* (New York: Cambridge University Press, 1995), 5. "Cholera at Mecca," *The New York Times*, November 13, 1881; "Sanitary Reform at Last in Arabia's Holy Places," *The New York Times,* May 31, 1895.

22. Claude, *Swords into Plowshares*, 24.

23. Claude, *Swords into Plowshares,* 21.

24. Thomas G. Weiss, David P. Forsythe, and Roger A. Coate, *The United Nations and Changing World Politics*, 4th ed. (Boulder, CO: Westview Press, 2004), 5.

25. Akira Iriye, *Global Community: The Role of International Organizations in the Making of the Contemporary World* (Berkeley: University of California Press, 2002), 11.

26. Claude, *Swords into Plowshares*, 28.

27. League of Nations, "Covenant of the League of Nations," Article 12, http://avalon.law.yale.edu/20th_century/leagcov.asp.

28. Claude, *Swords into Plowshares*, 44.

29. Weiss, Forsythe, and Coate, *The United Nations*, 6.

30. Claude, *Swords into Plowshares*, 46. Wilson famously pleaded with the Senate and the nation in July 1919, asking "Dare we reject it and break the heart of the world?" but the Versailles Treaty that contained the League's Covenant failed by seven votes.

31. Paul Kennedy, *The Parliament of Man: The Past, Present, and Future of the United Nations* (New York: Random House, 2006), 24.

32. Union of International Associations, ed. *Yearbook of International Organizations 2014–2015* (Brussels, Belgium: Brill, 2014).

33. Stephan Ryan, *The United Nations and International Politics* (New York: Palgrave Macmillan, 2000): 1.

34. United Nations General Assembly, "Programme Budget for the Biennium 2014–2015, A/C.5/69/17" (January 14, 2015). http://www.un.org/en/ga/search/view_doc.asp?symbol = A/C.5/69/17.

35. United Nations, "Peacekeeping Fact Sheet: Fact Sheet as of 30 June 2015," http://www.un.org/en/peacekeeping/resources/statistics/factsheet.shtml.

36. World Trade Organization, "WTO Secretariat Budget for 2013–2014," https://www.wto.org/english/thewto_e/secre_e/budget_e.htm.

37. See Mark A. Pollack, *The Engines of European Integration: Delegation, Agency, and Agenda Setting in the EU* (New York: Oxford University Press, 2003).

38. Jessica T. Mathews, "Power Shift," *Foreign Affairs* 76, no. 1 (1997), 50.

39. These include US actions in Somalia, Bosnia, Haiti, Kosovo, and Afghanistan, among others. See Alexander Thompson, "Coercion Through IOs: The Security Council and the Logic of Information Transmission," *International Organization* 60, no. 1 (2006).

40. G. John Ikenberry, *After Victory: Institutions, Strategic Restraint, and the Rebuilding of Order After Major Wars* (Princeton, NJ: Princeton University Press, 2001).

41. John J. Mearsheimer, "The False Promise of International Institutions," *International Security* 19, no. 3 (1994).

42. Eastern European countries also had some concerns about future Russian aggression, but many studies have argued that the symbolic nature of NATO was more important than its strategic function.

43. Susan Strange, "Cave! Hic Dragones: A Critique of Regime Analysis," *International Organization* 36, no. 2 (1982): 484.

44. Jon C. Pevehouse, "Democratization, Credible Commitments, and Joining International Organizations," in *Locating the Proper Authorities: The Interaction of Domestic and International Institutions*, ed. Daniel W. Drezner (Ann Arbor: The University of Michigan Press, 2003).

45. Sir Brian Urquhart, interview by Harry Kreisler, "The United Nations after 9/11: Conversation with Sir Brian Urquhart," University of California Berkeley, February 23, 2004, http://globetrotter.berkeley.edu/people4/Urquhart/urquhart04-con0.html.

46. The World Bank, IMF, and the Organization for Economic Co-operation and Development, and, of course, various UN agencies, are among those IOs involved in developing the MDGs.

47. Cited in Brian Urquhart, *Hammarskjold*, 1st ed. (New York,: Knopf, 1972), 48.

CHAPTER 2

1. John Lewis Gaddis, "International Relations Theory and the End of the Cold War," *International Security* 17, no. 3 (1992/93): 6.

2. Robert W. Cox, "Social Forces, States and World Orders: Beyond International Relations Theory," in *Neorealism and Its Critics*, ed. Robert O. Keohane (New York: Columbia University Press, 1986), 204.

3. Inis L. Claude, *Swords into Plowshares: The Problems and Progress of International Organization* (New York: Random House, 1956), 3.

4. For different strands of this debate, see Jessica T. Mathews, "Power Shift," *Foreign Affairs* 76, no. 1 (1997); Miles Kahler and David A. Lake, *Governance in a Global Economy: Political Authority in Transition* (Princeton, NJ: Princeton University Press, 2003); Thomas L. Friedman, *The World Is Flat: A Brief History of the Twenty-First Century*, 1st ed. (New York: Farrar, Straus and Giroux, 2005).

5. Robert Jervis, "Realism in the Study of World Politics," *International Organization* 52, no. 4 (1998). See Jervis's discussion on factors shaping different research programs.

6. Claude, *Swords into Plowshares*, 7.

7. Lisa L. Martin and Beth A. Simmons, "Theories and Empirical Studies of International Institutions," *International Organization* 52, no. 4 (1998).

8. The journal, *International Organization*, was founded to "take definite action toward the dissemination of accurate information and informed comment on the manifold problems of international organization." Harvey H. Bundy, "An Introductory Note," *International Organization* 1, no. 1 (1947). In its first two decades, over half of each issue contained summaries of and documents from various UN and other agencies.

9. Martin and Simmons, "Theories and Empirical Studies," 732.

10. David Easton, "Introduction: The Current Meaning of Behavioralism in Political Science," in *The Limits of Behavioralism in Political Science: A Symposium Sponsored by the American Academy of Political and Social Science*, ed. James Clyde Charlesworth (Philadelphia, PA: American Academy of Political and Social Science, 1962).

11. Gabriel A. Almond and Stephen J. Genco, "Clouds, Clocks, and the Study of Politics," *World Politics* 29, no. 4 (1977): 498. The authors were also critical of behavioralism.

12. Robert E. Riggs et al., "Behavioralism in the Study of the United Nations," *World Politics: A Quarterly Journal of International Relations* 22, no. 2 (1970).

13. Brian Urquhart, "Looking for the Sheriff," *New York Review of Books,* 16 July 1998.

14. Urquhart, "Looking for the Sheriff."

15. Ernst B. Haas, *The Uniting of Europe: Political, Social, and Economic Forces, 1950-1957* (Stanford, CA: Stanford University Press, 1958).

16. Karl W. Deutsch, *Political Community and the North Atlantic Area: International Organization in the Light of Historical Experience*, Publications of the Center for Research on World Political Institutions (Princeton, NJ: Princeton University Press, 1957).

17. This was called the "Luxembourg Compromise" of 1966.

18. Ernst B. Haas, *The Uniting of Europe.* Philippe Schmitter, "A Revised Theory of European Integration," in Leon N. Lindberg and Stuart A. Scheingold, *Regional Integration: Theory and Research* (Cambridge, MA: Harvard University Press, 1971). Schmitter recognized that some of these categories were crude typologies.

19. Martin and Simmons, "Theories and Empirical Studies," 444.

20. Stephen D. Krasner, *International Regimes* (Ithaca, NY: Cornell University Press, 1983). The Krasner edited volume was a seminal study of regimes. Europeans have also been deeply involved in regime research. See Edward L. Miles, *Environmental Regime Effectiveness: Confronting Theory with Evidence* (Cambridge: MIT Press, 2002).

21. John Gerard Ruggie, "International Responses to Technology: Concepts and Trends," *International Organization* 29, no. 3 (1975). The term *international regimes* was introduced in the international relations literature by John Ruggie, in 1975.

22. John Gerard Ruggie, "International Responses to Technology: Concepts and Trends," *International Organization* 29, no. 3 (1975): 571.

23. See, for example, Robert O. Keohane, *After Hegemony: Cooperation and Discord in the World Political Economy* (Princeton, NJ: Princeton University Press, 1984); Kenneth A. Oye, *Cooperation Under Anarchy* (Princeton, NJ: Princeton University Press, 1986); Oran R. Young, *The Effectiveness of International Environmental Regimes: Causal Connections and Behavioral Mechanisms* (Cambridge: MIT Press, 1999); Oran R. Young, *Governance in World Affairs* (Ithaca, NY: Cornell University Press, 1999)

24. Susan Strange, "Cave! Hic Dragones: A Critique of Regime Analysis," *International Organization* 36, no. 2 (1982).

25. Strange, "Cave! Hic Dragones," p. 488. Her point in giving this example is that the notion of regime exaggerates a "static quality" of international arrangements that are actually very dynamic.

26. Early realists, writing in the ancient world, include Sun Tzu, writing over 2,000 years ago; Kautilya; and Thucydides. Before states existed, the emphasis was on kingdoms, empires, or republics seeking to maintain power.

27. This is a key difference between neorealists and classical realists, since human nature, will, and values played a role in the latters' theory. As Ruggie put it, Waltz "shed all aspects of the 'social texture' of international politics." John Gerard Ruggie, *Constructing the World Polity: Essays on International Institutionalization* (New York: Routledge, 1998), 7.

28. Kenneth N. Waltz, *Theory of International Politics*, 1st ed. (Boston, MA: McGraw-Hill, 1979), 65.

29. John J. Mearsheimer, "The False Promise of International Institutions," *International Security* 19, no. 3 (1994).

30. Hans J. Morgenthau, Kenneth W. Thompson, and W. David Clinton, *Politics Among Nations: The Struggle for Power and Peace*, 7th ed. (Boston, MA: McGraw-Hill Higher Education, 2006). Morgenthau cited as examples US Secretary of State Cordell Hull's 1943 declaration that the United Nations would end power politics, and British Minister of State Philip Noel-Baker's view in

1946 that the United Nations would "kill power politics."

31. The roots of functionalist theory go back to the 1950s to scholars like David Mitrany.

32. Keohane, *After Hegemony.*

33. Robert O. Keohane, *International Institutions and State Power: Essays in International Relations Theory* (Boulder, CO: Westview Press, 1989).

34. For a useful summary of the neorealist/neoliberal debate, see Randall L. Schweller and David Priess, "A Tale of Two Realisms: Expanding the Institutions Debate," *Mershon International Studies Review* 41 (1997): 1–32.

35. See Theda Skocpol, *States and Social Revolutions: A Comparative Analysis of France, Russia, and China* (New York: Cambridge University Press, 1979); Douglass C. North, *Structure and Change in Economic History*, 1st ed. (New York: Norton, 1981); Hugh Heclo, *Modern Social Policies in Britain and Sweden* (Cambridge, UK: Cambridge University Press, 1974).

36. Paul DiMaggio and Walter W. Powell, "Introduction," in *The New Institutionalism in Organizational Analysis*, ed. Walter W. Powell and Paul DiMaggio (Chicago, IL: University of Chicago Press, 1991), 1.

37. Kenneth A. Shepsle, "Studying Institutions: Some Lessons from the Rational Choice Approach," *Journal of Theoretical Politics* 1 (1989): 131–147.

38. Ronald H. Coase, "The Nature of the Firm," *Economica* 16 (1937). Also see Oliver E. Williamson, *Markets and Hierarchies, Analysis and Antitrust Implications: A Study in the Economics of Internal Organization* (New York: Free Press, 1975); Oliver E. Williamson, *The Economic Institutions of Capitalism: Firms, Markets, Relational Contracting* (New York: Free Press, 1985). A more specific definition of transaction costs is "the costs of deciding, planning, arranging, and negotiating the actions to be taken and the terms of exchange when two or more parties do business." From Paul Milgrom and John Roberts, "Bargaining Costs, Influence Costs and the Organization of Economic Activity," in *Perspectives on Positive Political Economy*, ed. James E. Alt and Kenneth A. Shepsle (Cambridge, UK: Cambridge University Press, 1990), 60. Economic historian and Nobel Prize winner Douglass North also applied arguments about transaction costs to his work on the history of political institutions and how they shape economic performance. See, for example, North, *Institutions, Institutional Change, and Economic Performance.*; Douglass C. North, *Structure and Change in Economic History* (New York: Norton, 1981).

39. The ideas have been around for hundreds of years. Adam Smith, for example, wrote in the 17th century about the divergent interests between the directors and proprietors of joint stock companies: "The directors of such companies . . . being the managers rather of other people's money than of their own, it cannot well be expected that they should watch over it with the same anxious vigilance with which the partners in a private (company) frequently watch over their own. . . . Negligence and profusion, therefore, must always prevails, more or less, in the management of the affairs of such a company." Adam Smith, *An Inquiry into the Nature and Causes of the Wealth of Nations*, Book 5, Chapter 1 (London: Printed for W. Strahan and T. Cadell, 1776).

40. Armen A. Alchian and Harold Demsetz, "Production, Information Costs, and Economic Organization," *The American Economic Review* 62, no. 5 (1972); Michael C. Jensen and William H. Meckling, "Theory of the Firm: Managerial Behavior, Agency Costs and Ownership Structure," *Journal of Financial Economics* 3, no. 4 (1976).

41. Mathew D. McCubbins, Roger G. Noll, and Barry R. Weingast, "Administrative Procedures as Instruments of Political Control," *Journal of Law, Economics, and Organizations* 3, no. 2 (1987); Matthew D. McCubbins, Roger G. Noll, and Barry R. Weingast, "Structure and Process, Politics and Policy: Administrative Arrangements and the Political Control of Agencies," *Virginia Law Review* 75 (1989); Kathleen Bawn, "Political Control Versus Expertise: Congressional Choice About Administrative Procedures," *American Political Science Review* 89, no. 1 (1995); D. Roderick Kiewiet and Mathew D. McCubbins, *The Logic of Delegation: Congressional Parties and the Appropriations Process* (Chicago, IL: University of Chicago Press, 1991).

42. Terry Moe, "The New Economics of Organization," *American Journal of Political Science* 28, no. 4 (1984); Terry Moe, "The Politics of Structural Choice: Toward a Theory of Public Bureaucracy," in *Organization Theory: From Chester Barnard to the Present and Beyond*, ed. Oliver E. Williamson (New York: Oxford University Press, 1990); Jean Tirole, "The Internal Organisation of Government," *Oxford Economic Papers* 46, no. 1 (1994).

43. Mark A. Pollack, *The Engines of European Integration: Delegation, Agency, and Agenda Setting in the EU* (New York: Oxford University Press, 2003); Jonas Talberg, "Delegation to Supranational Institutions: Why, How, and With What Consequences," *West European Politics* 25, no. 1 (2002); Torbjörn Bergman, "Delegation and Accountability in European Integration: Introduction," *Journal of Legislative Studies* 6, no. 1 (2000).

44. Tony Killick, "Principals, Agents and the Failings of Conditionality," *Journal of International Development* 9, no. 4 (1997); Mohsin S. Kahn and Suni Sharma,

"IMF Conditionality and Country Ownership of Adjustment Programs," *World Bank Research Observer* 18, no. 2 (2003).

45. This comes out of work by people like Anthony Downs, James Buchanan and Gordon Tullock, Mancur Olson, and Russell Hardin. See, for example, Anthony Downs, *An Economic Theory of Democracy* (New York: Harper, 1957); James M. Buchanan and Gordon Tullock, *The Calculus of Consent: Logical Foundations of Constitutional Democracy* (Indianapolis, IN: Liberty Fund Inc., 1957); Mancur Olson, *The Logic of Collective Action: Public Goods and the Theory of Groups* (Cambridge, MA: Harvard University Press, 1971).

46. John A. C. Conybeare, "International Organization and the Theory of Property Rights," *International Organization* 34, no. 3 (1980). Also see Roland Vaubel and Thomas D. Willett, *The Political Economy of International Organizations: A Public Choice Approach*, The Political Economy of Global Interdependence (Boulder, CO: Westview Press, 1991).

47. See, for example, Meyer and Rowan, "Institutionalized Organizations."; Powell and DiMaggio, *The New Institutionalism.*.

48. Peter A. Hall and Rosemary C.R. Taylor, "Political Science and the Three New Institutionalisms," *Political Studies* 4, no. 4 (1996): 947.

49. Martha Finnemore, "Norms, Culture, and World Politics: Insights from Sociology's Institutionalism," *International Organization* 50, no. 2 (1996). This is an excellent review of three books by sociological institutionalists and their applicability to the study of international relations.

50. Hall and Taylor, "Political Science"; Finnemore, "Norms, Culture, and World Politics."

51. The term was first used in international relations by Nicholas Onuf in his 1989 book, *World of Our Making: Rules and Rule in Social Theory and International Relations* (Columbia: University of South Carolina Press).

52. Martha Finnemore and Kathryn Sikkink, "Taking Stock: The Constructivist Research Program in International Relations and Comparative Politics," *Annual Review of Political Science* 4 (2001): 393. Also see Alexander Wendt, *Social Theory of International Politics* (New York: Cambridge University Press, 1999); Friedrich V. Kratochwil, *Rules, Norms, and Decisions: On the Conditions of Practical and Legal Reasoning in International Relations and Domestic Affairs* (New York: Cambridge University Press, 1989).

53. Finnemore and Sikkink, "Taking Stock," 394.

54. Margaret E. Keck and Kathryn Sikkink, *Activists Beyond Borders: Advocacy Networks in International Politics* (Ithaca, NY: Cornell University Press, 1998).

55. Michael N. Barnett and Martha Finnemore, "The Politics, Power, and Pathologies of International Organizations," *International Organization* 53, no. 4 (1999). This argument can also be found in Michael N. Barnett and Martha Finnemore, *Rules for the World: International Organizations in Global Politics* (Ithaca, NY: Cornell University Press, 2004).

56. Ruggie, *Constructing the World Polity: Essays on International Institutionalization*, 62.

57. Peter A. Hall, *Governing the Economy: The Politics of State Intervention in Britain and France* (New York: Oxford University Press, 1986), 19.

58. Hall and Taylor, "Political Science."

59. Paul Pierson, "The Path to European Integration: A Historical Institutionalist Perspective," *Comparative Political Studies* 29, no. 2 (1996). Also see Tanja A. Börzel, *States and Regions in the European Union* (New York: Cambridge University Press, 2002).

60. While this book focuses on mainstream theoretical orientations, there are also critical theorists, feminist theorists, Marxist theorists, and postmodern theorists who work in international relations, and some of them write about issues relating to international organizations. See, for example, work by Carolyn Hannan, "Feminist Strategies in International Organizations: The United Nations Context," in *Feminist Strategies in International Governance*, ed. Gülay Caglar, Elisabeth Prügl, and Susanne Zwingel (London: Routledge, 2013); Devaki Jain, *Women, Development, and the UN: A Sixty-Year Question for Equality and Justice* (Bloomington: Indiana University Press, 2005); Cox, "Social Forces, States and World Orders."; Richard K. Ashley, "The Poverty of Neorealism," *International Organization* 38, no. 2 (1984).

61. For more on this debate, see David A. Baldwin, *Neorealism and Neoliberalism: The Contemporary Debate* (New York: Columbia University Press, 1993); Lloyd Gruber, *Ruling the World: Power Politics and the Rise of Supranational Institutions* (Princeton, NJ: Princeton University Press, 2000). Rationalist approaches are also used within the broader field of IR to make very different arguments about state behavior, such as why it is difficult for states to cooperate and why and how cooperation can emerge, i.e., Waltz, *Theory of International Politics*; Robert M. Axelrod, *The Evolution of Cooperation* (New York: Basic Books, 1984). On rationalism and international relations see Miles Kahler, "Rationality in International Relations," *International Organization* 52, no. 4,

International Organization at Fifty: Exploration and Contestation in the Study of World Politics (1998).

62. Waltz, *Theory of International Politics*, 91. It is important to note that Waltz does not perfectly fit the rationalist model, in the sense that for him structure plays such an important role in shaping and constraining state behavior. See discussion in Kahler, "Rationality in International Relations."

63. Kenneth Waltz, interview by Harry Kreisler on February 10, 2003, "Theory and International Politics." *Conversations with History*, Institute of International Studies, U.C. Berkeley. globetrotter.berkeley.edu/people3/Waltz/waltz-con1.html (Accessed March 20, 2013).

64. Mearsheimer, "The False Promise of International Institutions," 7.

65. Mearsheimer, "The False Promise of International Institutions," 15. In terms of faulty logic, he argued that liberal institutionalists ignore the issue of relative gains, citing work such as Joseph M. Grieco, "Anarchy and the Limits of Cooperation: A Realist Critique of the Newest Liberal Institutionalism," *International Organization* 42, no. 3 (1988). Caring about how the pie is divided can make it harder for states to cooperate.

66. Robert O. Keohane and Lisa L Martin, "The Promise of Institutionalist Theory," *International Security* 20, no. 1 (1995): 47–48.

67. Keohane and Martin, "The Promise of Institutionalist Theory," 43–44.

68. See Gaddis, "International Relations Theory and the End of the Cold War." For a discussion of other factors influencing the rise of constructivist scholarship in IR, see Emanuel Adler, "Constructivism and International Relations," in *Handbook of International Relations*, ed. Walter Carlsnaes, Thomas Risse, and Beth A. Simmons (London: Sage, 2002).

69. Barnett and Finnemore, *Rules for the World*.

70. Barnett and Finnemore, *Rules for the World*, 8.

71. Barnett and Finnemore, *Rules for the World*, Chapter 5.

72. See for example, Samantha Power, *A Problem from Hell: America and the Age of Genocide* (New York: Basic Books, 2002); Michael N. Barnett, *Eyewitness to a Genocide: The United Nations and Rwanda* (Ithaca, NY: Cornell University Press, 2002).

73. For example, Daniel L. Nielson and Michael J. Tierney, "Delegation to International Organizations: Agency Theory and World Bank Environmental Reform," *International Organization* 57, no. 2 (2003).

74. Tamar L. Gutner, "Explaining the Gaps Between Mandate and Performance: Agency Theory and World Bank Environmental Reform," *Global Environmental Politics* 5, no. 2 (2005).

75. James Fearon and Alexander Wendt, "Rationalism v. Constructivism: A Skeptical View," in *Handbook of International Relations*, ed. Walter Carlsnaes, Thomas Risse, and Beth A. Simmons (London: Sage Publications, 2005), 53.

76. Fearon and Wendt, "Rationalism v. Constructivism," 59–60.

77. Songying Fang and Randall W. Stone, "International Organizations as Policy Advisors," *International Organization* 66, no. 4 (2012).

78. Joel E. Oestreich, *International Organizations as Self-Directed Actors: A Framework for Analysis*, Routledge Global Institutions Series (New York: Routledge, 2012).

79. Excellent examples include Shashi Tharoor, "Why America Still Needs the United Nations," *Foreign Affairs* 82, no. 5 (2003); Bruce Rich, *Mortgaging the Earth: The World Bank, Environmental Impoverishment, and the Crisis of Development* (Boston, MA: Beacon Press, 1994). One exception in the academic world is Thomas G. Weiss, David P. Forsythe, and Roger A. Coate, *The United Nations and Changing World Politics*, 4th ed. (Boulder, CO: Westview Press, 2004).

80. G. John Ikenberry, *After Victory: Institutions, Strategic Restraint, and the Rebuilding of Order after Major Wars* (Princeton, NJ: Princeton University Press, 2001).

81. Daniel W. Drezner, *Locating the Proper Authorities: The Interaction of Domestic and International Institutions* (Ann Arbor: The University of Michigan Press, 2003); Peter B. Evans, Harold K. Jacobson, and Robert D. Putnam, *Double-Edged Diplomacy: International Bargaining and Domestic Politics* (Berkeley: University of California Press, 1993); Helen V. Milner, *Interests, Institutions, and Information: Domestic Politics and International Relations* (Princeton, NJ: Princeton University Press, 1997).

82. Ngaire Woods, "Good Governance in International Organizations," *Global Governance* 5, no. 1 (1999); Ruth Grant and Robert O. Keohane, "Accountability and Abuses of Power in World Politics," *American Political Science Review* 99, no. 1 (2005).

83. Mathews, "Power Shift."

84. Clifford Bob, *The Marketing of Rebellion: Insurgents, Media, and International Activism* (New York: Cambridge University Press, 2005); Paul Kevin Wapner, *Environmental Activism and World Civic Politics*, Suny Series in International Environmental Policy and Theory (Albany: State University of New York Press, 1996); Michelle M. Betsill and Elisabeth Correll, eds., *NGO Diplomacy: The Influence of Nongovernmental Organizations in International Environmental Negotiations* (Cambridge: MIT Press, 2007).

85. Ernst B. Haas, *When Knowledge Is Power: Three Models of Change in International Organizations* (Berkeley: University of California Press, 1990).

86. Michael N. Barnett and Raymond Duvall, *Power in Global Governance* (New York: Cambridge University Press, 2005); Deborah D. Avant, Martha Finnemore, and Susan K. Sell, eds., *Who Governs the Globe* (New York: Cambridge University Press, 2010).

87. Bruce Rich, *Foreclosing the Future: The World Bank and the Politics of Environmental Destruction* (Washington, DC: Island Press, 2013).

88. Oran R. Young, *The Institutional Dimensions of Environmental Change: Fit, Interplay, and Scale* (Cambridge: MIT Press, 2002).

89. Olav Schram Stokke and Sebastian Oberthür, "Introduction: International Interaction in Global Environmental Change," in *Managing Institutional Complexity: Regime Interplay and Global Environmental Change*, ed. Sebastian Oberthür and Olav Schram Stokke (Cambridge: MIT Press, 2001).

90. Tamar Gutner, "When 'Doing Good' Does Not: The IMF and the Millennium Development Goals," in *Who Governs the Globe*, eds. Avant, Finnemore, and Sells, 266–291.

91. Kal Raustiala and David G. Victor, "The Regime Complex for Plant Genetic Resources," *International Organization* 58 (2004).

92. David P. Fidler, "The Challenges of Global Health Governance," in *International Institutions and Global Governance Program* (New York: Council on Foreign Relations, 2010).

93. Daniel W. Drezner, "The Power and Peril of International Regime Complexity," *Perspectives on Politics* 7, no. 1 (2009).

94. Susan K. Sell, "TRIPS Was Never Enough: Vertical Forum Shifting, FTAS, ACTA, and TPP," *Journal of Intellectual Property Law* 18, no. 447 (2011): 450.

95. Tamar Gutner and Alexander Thompson, "The Politics of IO Performance: A Framework," *Review of International Organizations* 5, no. 3 (2010): 233.

96. Allen Buchanan and Robert O. Keohane, "The Legitimacy of Global Governance Institutions," *Ethics and International Affairs* 20, no. 4 (2006).

97. Heidi Hardt, *Time to React: The Efficiency of International Organizations in Crisis Response* (New York: Oxford University Press, 2014), 2.

98. Hardt, *Time to React*, 4.

99. Linda G. Morra Imas and Ray C. Rist, *The Road to Results: Designing and Conducting Effective Development Evaluations* (Washington, DC: The World Bank, 2009), 16.

100. Morra Imas, *The Road to Results*, xv.

CHAPTER 3

1. Ralph Bunche, Nobel Lecture, 11 December 1950, University of Oslo.

2. United Nations Charter, Art. 24.1.

3. Thomas G. Weiss et al., *UN Voices: The Struggle for Development and Social Justice* (Bloomington: Indiana University Press, 2005), 3.

4. Cited in Linda M. Fasulo, *An Insider's Guide to the UN* (New Haven, CT: Yale University Press, 2004), 9.

5. James Traub, *The Best Intentions: Kofi Annan and the UN in the Era of American World Power*, 1st ed. (New York: Farrar, Straus and Giroux, 2006), 4.

6. Traub, *The Best Intentions*, 4.

7. Stanley Meisler, *United Nations: The First Fifty Years*, 1st ed. (New York: Atlantic Monthly Press, 1995), 3.

8. Stephen C. Schlesinger, *Act of Creation: The Founding of the United Nations* (Boulder, CO: Westview Press, 2003), 37; The Atlantic Charter (August, 1941).

9. Frank L. Kluckhohn, "War Pact Is Signed," *The New York Times*, January 3 1942; Townsend Hoopes and Douglas Brinkley, *FDR and the Creation of the U.N.* (New Haven, CT: Yale University Press, 1997).

10. Hoopes and Brinkley, *FDR and the Creation of the U.N.*, 46.

11. In fact, the first decision of Harry Truman's presidency was to make sure the White House announced that the San Francisco conference would continue as planned. Schlesinger, *Act of Creation*, 7.

12. Hilderbrand, cited in Schlesinger, 47.

13. Meisler, *United Nations*; Michael Mastanduno, "Economics and Security in Statecraft and Scholarship," *International Organization* 52, no. 4, International Organization at Fifty: Exploration and Contestation in the Study of World Politics (1998).

14. David L. Bosco, *Five to Rule Them All: The UN Security Council and the Making of the Modern World* (New York: Oxford University Press, 2009), 20.

15. Bosco, *Five to Rule Them All*, 25.

16. Schlesinger, *Act of Creation*, 50–51.

17. Stanley Meisler points out that some of the biggest disagreements that pitted the Soviets against the Americans and British were negotiated outside of these two conferences, at meetings in Yalta and Moscow. Meisler, *United Nations*, 2–3.

18. Schlesinger, *Act of Creation*, 121.

19. Excellent histories of the UN's birth include Hoopes and Brinkley, *FDR and the Creation of the U.N.*; Schlesinger, *Act of Creation*.

20. Lawrence E. Davies, "Historic Plenary Session Approves World Charter," *The New York Times*, June 26, 1945.

21. Davies, "Historic Plenary Session Approves World Charter."

22. Hoopes and Brinkley, *FDR and the Creation of the U.N.*, 115.
23. United Nations, "The Story of the United Nations Headquarters," http://www.un.org/wcm/webdav/site/visitors/shared/documents/pdfs/FS_UN%20Headquarters_History_English_Feb%202013.pdf.
24. United Nations Charter, Art. 1.
25. United Nations Charter, Art. 2.7.
26. Thomas G. Weiss, David P. Forsythe, and Roger A. Coate, *The United Nations and Changing World Politics*, 4th ed. (Boulder, CO: Westview Press, 2004), xxxix.
27. Traub, *The Best Intentions*, p. 4.
28. The 10 nonpermanent members consist of two from Africa, two from Asia, two from Latin America, one from Eastern Europe, two from Western Europe or *other* states.
29. United Nations Department of Public Information, "Middle East--Untso--Background," United Nations, http://www.un.org/Depts/dpko/missions/untso/background.html.
30. United Nations Information Service, "Looking Back/Moving Forward," http://www.unis.unvienna.org/unis/en/60yearsPK/index.html.
31. While the General Assembly was involved in condemning the Korean War, in fact, technically this was not done through the Uniting for Peace resolution because the item was removed from the Security Council agenda one day earlier. For more details see Keith S. Petersen, "The Uses of the Uniting for Peace Resolution," *International Organization* 13, no. 2 (Spring 1959).
32. General Assembly, "Resolution 997 (Es-I)," (1956).
33. Lester Pearson, who, at the time, was Canada's foreign minister, played a leading role in organizing this new peacekeeping operation and was awarded the 1957 Nobel Peace Prize for his efforts.
34. Lindsay Parrott, "U.N. Body Orders Study in Hungary," *The New York Times*, November 5, 1956.
35. M. J. Peterson, *The UN General Assembly* (New York: Routledge, 2006), 1.
36. GA sessions can contain over 1,000 participants, since each member state may have multiple delegates. The UN Charter specifies that each country can have up to five delegates, but the GA's own rule (25) permits up to five representatives, plus five alternates, and "as many advisers, technical advisers, experts and persons of similar status as may be required by the delegation." General Assembly, "Rules of Procedure," http://www.un.org/ga/ropga_delegt.shtml.
37. Kofi Annan, "In Larger Freedom: Toward Security, Development and Human Rights for All," (New York: United Nations, 2005), 158–64.
38. United Nations General Assembly, "Agenda of the Sixty-Ninth Session of the General Assembly," (New York: United Nations, September 19, 2014).
39. The regional allocation gives developing countries the majority on ECOSOC, which, like the General Assembly, has one vote per state: 14 seats go to African states, 11 to Asian, six to Eastern European, 10 to Latin American and Caribbean states, and 13 to Western European and "other" states.
40. Fasulo, *An Insider's Guide to the UN*, 155.
41. United Nations General Assembly, "Composition of the Secretariat: Staff Demographics," (New York: United Nations, 2012).
42. United Nations Charter, Art. 100.1.
43. Shashi Tharoor, ""The Most Impossible Job" Description," in *Secretary or General? The UN Secretary-General in World Politics*, ed. Simon Chesterman(New York: Cambridge University Press, 2007), 34. Tharoor worked in a variety of capacities at the UN, most recently as Under-Secretary-General for Communications and Public Information. He was one of the unsuccessful candidates to replace Kofi Annan.
44. Tharoor, "'The Most Impossible Job' Description," 33.
45. Brian Urquhart, "How to Fill a Job with No Description," *Foreign Affairs* 85, no. 5 (2006): 16.
46. Urquhart, "How to Fill a Job," 16.
47. Urquhart, "How to Fill a Job," 16.
48. Brian Urquhart, "The Evolution of the Secretary-General," in *Secretary or General? The UN Secretary-General in World Politics*, ed. Simon Chesterman (New York: Cambridge University Press, 2007), 23.
49. Samantha Power, *Chasing the Flame: Sergio Vieira De Mello and the Fight to Save the World* (New York: Penguin, 2008), 239.
50. Michael Ignatieff, "The Confessions of Kofi Annan," *The New York Review of Books* LIX, no. 19 (2012).
51. "Iraq War Illegal, Says Annan," *BBC News*, September 16, 2004.
52. Tharoor, "'The Most Impossible Job' Description," 42.
53. Joseph Loconte, "The U.N. Sex Scandal," *The Weekly Standard*, January 3, 2005.
54. Paul A Volker, Richard J. Goldstone, and Mark Pieth, "Independent Inquiry Committee into the United Nations Oil-for-Food Programme," (New York: United Nations, 2005). Annan's son, Kojo Annan, was also involved, since he worked for a company that received a contract through the program. Kofi Annan was criticized by the report for not being more aggressive in examining the relationship between this company and the United Nations, but he was not accused of influencing the contract. See Warren Hoge, "Panel Says Annan Didn't Intervene in Iraq Contract," *The New York Times*, March 30, 2005.
55. Maria Newmann, "Ban Ki-Moon," *The New York Times*, September 26, 2007.

56. Warren Hoge, "U.N. Chief Is Assuaging Doubts About Leadership," *The New York Times*, February 19, 2007.

57. "In New Report, Ban Outlines Measures to Strengthen UN Peace Operations, Tackle Abuse," *UN News Centre*, September 11, 2015.

58. Simon Chesterman, "Introduction: Secretary or General?," in *Secretary or General? The UN Secretary-General in World Politics*, ed. Simon Chesterman (New York: Cambridge University Press, 2007), 3.

59. International Court of Justice, "Members of the Court," http://www.icj-cij.org/court/index.php?p1 = 1&p2 = 2& PHPSESSID = 8ab362b09042424317d7145e2ace59ac. Judges include three from Africa, two from Latin America and the Caribbean, three from Asia, five from Western Europe and other states, and two from Eastern Europe. This is the same distribution as members of the Security Council, and the Court has always included judges from the Security Council's P-5 countries.

60. International Court of Justice, "Members of the Court."

61. Howard N. Meyer, *The World Court in Action: Judging among the Nations* (Lanham, MD: Rowman & Littlefield Publishers, 2002), 88.

62. James Crawford and Tom Grant, "International Court of Justice," in *The Oxford Handbook on the United Nations*, ed. Thomas G. Weiss and Sam Daws (New York: Oxford University Press, 2007), 196.

63. United Nations Department of Public Information, "The International Court of Justice," (New York: United Nations, 2000), 27–28.

64. Crawford and Grant, "International Court of Justice," 203; United Nations Department of Public Information, "The International Court of Justice."

65. Roger Cohen, "U.S. Execution of German Stirs Anger," *The New York Times*, March 5, 1999; International Court of Justice, "The Lagrand Case (Germany V. United States of America): Summary of Order," (Netherlands: International Court of Justice, 1999). The Court urged the United States to delay the second of the two executions until it could rule. Arizona's officials conceded that they did not observe the Vienna Convention, which would have advised the brothers they had a right to consular assistance at their trial, but the state went forward with the execution.

66. Ralph Wilde, "Trusteeship Council," in *The Oxford Handbook on the United Nations*, ed. Thomas G. Weiss and Sam Daws (New York: Oxford University Press, 2007), 155.

67. See for example Julie Mertus, *The United Nations and Human Rights: A Guide for a New Era* (New York: Routledge, 2005); Joel E. Oestreich, *Power and Principle: Human Rights Programming in International Organizations* (Washington, DC: Georgetown University Press, 2007).

68. Brian Urquhart, "Looking for the Sheriff," *New York Review of Books* (1998).

69. Weiss, Forsythe, and Coate, *The United Nations*, 4th ed., 52–53.

70. "Excerpts from the Debate in the U.N. Security Council," *The New York Times*, August 22, 1968.

71. Peterson, *The UN General Assembly*, 45–46.

72. Edward C. Luck, *Mixed Messages: American Politics and International Organization, 1919–1999* (Washington, DC: Brookings Institution Press, 1999), 107.

73. Luck, *Mixed Messages*, 108.

74. Gerald R. Ford, "President Gerald R. Ford's Address to the 29th Session of the General Assembly of the United Nations" (1974).

75. Cited in Luck, *Mixed Messages*, 114.

76. The United States rejoined ILO three years after withdrawing, and it rejoined UNESCO in 2003.

77. United Nations, "Post Cold-War Surge," United Nations, http://www.un.org/en/peacekeeping/operations/surge.shtml.

78. Boutros Boutros-Ghali, "An Agenda for Peace: Preventive Diplomacy, Peacemaking and Peace-Keeping" (New York: United Nations, 1992).

79. Ban Ki-moon, "'Poorest of the Poor' Lagging Amid 'Uneven' Progress on Millennium Development Goals, Secretary-General Tells Economic and Social Council Launch of Report," news release, July 7, 2011, http://www.un.org/press/en/2011/sgsm13694.doc.htm.

80. Office of the High Commissioner for Human Rights, "United Nations Human Rights," United Nations, http://www.ohchr.org/en/issues/pages/whatare humanrights.aspx.

81. Paul Kennedy, *The Parliament of Man: The Past, Present, and Future of the United Nations* (New York: Random House, 2006), 181.

82. Anne Marie Clark, *Diplomacy of Conscience* (Princeton, NJ: Princeton University Press, 2001), 4.

83. Thomas G. Weiss et al., *The United Nations and Changing World Politics*, 7th ed. (Boulder, CO: Westview Press, 2014), 163.

84. Thomas G. Weiss, *What's Wrong with the United Nations and How to Fix It*, 2nd ed. (Malden, MA: Polity, 2012), 41.

85. James Traub, "U.N. Human Rights Council Condemns Actual Human Rights Abusers!," *Foreign Policy*, June 1, 2012. foreignpolicy.com/2012/06/01/u-n-human-rights-council-condemns-actual-human-rights-abusers/.

86. Michael W. Doyle and Nicholas Sambanis, *Making War and Building Peace: United Nations Peace Operations* (Princeton, NJ: Princeton University Press, 2006), 14.

87. Boutros-Ghali, "An Agenda for Peace."

88. Kofi Annan, "Report of the Secretary-General Pursuant to General Assembly Resolution 53/35: The Fall of Srebrenica," (New York: United Nations, 1999), 7.

89. Lise Morjé Howard, *UN Peacekeeping in Civil Wars* (New York: Cambridge University Press, 2008), 44–45.

90. Annan, "The Fall of Srebrenica," 6.

91. John Francis Murphy, *The United States and the Rule of Law in International Affairs* (Cambridge, UK: Cambridge University Press, 2004), 185.

92. Thomas G. Weiss et al., *The United Nations and Changing World Politics*, 6th ed. (Boulder, CO: Westview Press, 2010), 67.

93. Meisler, *The First Fifty Years*, 297.

94. Howard, *UN Peacekeeping in Civil Wars*, 23.

95. Howard, *UN Peacekeeping in Civil Wars*, 27–28. See also Meisler, *The First Fifty Years*; Ken Rutherford, *Humanitarianism under Fire: The US and UN Intervention in Somalia* (Sterling, VA: Kumarian Press, 2008).

96. Traub, *The Best Intentions*, 38.

97. Howard, *UN Peacekeeping in Civil Wars*, 52–87.

98. Tommie Sue Montgomery, "Getting to Peace in El Salvador: The Roles of the United Nations Secretariat and ONUSAL," *Journal of Interamerican Studies and World Affairs* 37, no. 4 (1995): 161.

99. Alexander Thompson, *Channels of Power: The UN Security Council and U.S. Statecraft in Iraq* (Ithaca, NY: Cornell University Press, 2009).

100. Lakhdar Brahimi, "Report of the Panel on United Nations Peace Operations," (New York: United Nations, 2000).

101. Brahimi, "Report of the Panel," x.

102. William J. Durch et al., "The Brahimi Report and the Future of UN Peace Operations," (Washington, DC: The Henry L. Stimson Center, 2003).

103. Kosovo was a case where the UN condemned the persecution and killing of ethnic Albanians by Serbian military forces in a province of Serbia, but was unwilling to authorize action and instead NATO launched a bombing campaign without UN authorization.

104. Gareth Evans and Mohamed Sahnoun, et al., "The Responsibility to Protect: Report of the International Commission on Intervention and State Sovereignty," (Ottawa, Canada: International Development Research Centre, 2001).

105. Evans and Sahnoun, et al., "Responsibility to Protect."

106. Annan, "In Larger Freedom," 35.

107. See United States Government Accountability Office, "Darfur Crisis: Death Estimates Demonstrate Severity of Crisis, but Their Accuracy and Credibility Could Be Enhanced," US Government Accountability Office, http://purl.access.gpo.gov/GPO/LPS77420. Most studies calculate between 100,000 and 400,000 have died. It is challenging to collect precise data, given the conditions.

108. Gerard Prunier, *Darfur: The Ambiguous Genocide* (Ithaca, NY: Cornell University Press, 2005), 140.

109. Prunier, *Darfur*, 142.

110. High-Level Independent Panel on Peace Operations, "Uniting Our Strengths for Peace - Politics, Partnership and People," (New York: United Nations, 2015).

111. UNSC Resolution 1973 (March 17, 2011).

112. Alex J. Bellamy, "The Responsibility to Protect—Five Years On," *Ethics & International Affairs* 24, no. 2 (2010).

113. High-Level Independent Panel on Peace Operations, "Uniting Our Strengths," 5.

114. In addition to the works discussed here, see also Paul F. Diehl, *International Peacekeeping, Perspectives on Security* (Baltimore, MD: Johns Hopkins University Press, 1993); Roland Paris, *At War's End: Building Peace after Civil Conflict* (Cambridge, UK: Cambridge University Press, 2004).

115. Howard, *UN Peacekeeping in Civil Wars*.

116. Virginia Page Fortna, *Does Peacekeeping Work? Shaping Belligerents' Choices after Civil War* (Princeton, NJ: Princeton University Press, 2008).

117. Michael Lipson, "Performance under Ambiguity: International Organization Performance in UN Peacekeeping " *Review of International Organizations* 5, no. 3 (2010).

118. Jesse Helms, "Saving the U.N.: A Challenge to the Next Secretary-General," *Foreign Affairs* 75, no. 5 (1996): 2.

119. Madeline K. Albright, "United Nations," *Foreign Policy* (2003): 16

CHAPTER 4

1. Michael N. Barnett, *Eyewitness to a Genocide: The United Nations and Rwanda* (Ithaca, NY: Cornell University Press, 2002), 1.

2. Central Intelligence Agency, "Rwanda," CIA, https://www.cia.gov/library/publications/the-world-factbook/geos/rw.html#People.

3. Barnett, *Eyewitness to a Genocide,* 51–52; Romeo Dallaire, *Shake Hands with the Devil: The Failure of Humanity in Rwanda*, with Brent Beardsley (New York: Carroll & Graf, 2004), 47.

4. United Nations, "Report of the Independent Inquiry into the Actions of the United Nations During the 1994 Genocide in Rwanda," (New York: United Nations, 1999), 8.

5. Michael Dobbs, "Warnings of Catastrophe" in *National Security Archive Electronic Briefing Book* (Washington, DC: National Security Archive, 2014).

6. Alan J. Kuperman, *The Limits of Humanitarian Intervention: Genocide in Rwanda* (Washington, DC: Brookings Institution Press, 2001), 15–16.
7. Dallaire, *Shake Hands with the Devil*, 462.
8. Dallaire, *Shake Hands with the Devil*, 229; Barnett, *Eyewitness to a Genocide*, 98.
9. Dallaire, *Shake Hands with the Devil*, 142.
10. Romeo Dallaire, Fax to BARIL/DPKO/UNATIONS, New York, January 11, 1994. http://www.pbs.org/wgbh/pages/frontline/shows/evil/warning/cable.html.
11. United Nations, "1994 Genocide in Rwanda," 11–12. Booh Booh was the former foreign minister of Cameroon. Incidentally, Habyarimana never followed up with the information he was given on January 12.
12. Barnett, *Eyewitness to a Genocide* 98–99.
13. Dallaire, *Shake Hands with the Devil*, 284.
14. Barnett, *Eyewitness to a Genocide*, 102; Paul Lewis, "Security Council Votes to Cut Rwanda Peacekeeping Force," *The New York Times*, April 22, 1994.
15. United Nations, "1994 Genocide in Rwanda," 19–20.
16. Barnett, *Eyewitness to a Genocide*, 105–06.
17. Quoted in Greg Barker, "Ghosts of Rwanda," in *Frontline* (2004). A HERC is a Hercules military transport aircraft.
18. United Nations, "1994 Genocide in Rwanda," 22.
19. Kuperman, *The Limits of Humanitarian Intervention*, 20.
20. Dallaire later had a nervous breakdown and attempted suicide: Today, recovered, he remains one of the most impassioned and eloquent speakers on the genocide and tells his poignant story in the book, *Shake Hands with the Devil*.
21. Samantha Power, *A Problem from Hell: America and the Age of Genocide* (New York: Basic Books, 2002), 368.
22. United Nations, "1994 Genocide in Rwanda," 18–19.
23. United Nations, "1994 Genocide in Rwanda," 27.
24. Barnett, *Eyewitness to a Genocide*, 148.
25. Barnett, *Eyewitness to a Genocide*, 149.
26. Human Rights Watch, "Leave None to Tell the Story," (New York: Human Rights Watch, 1999), 24.
27. Dallaire, *Shake Hands with the Devil*, 434.
28. Dallaire, *Shake Hands with the Devil*, 474.
29. Human Rights Watch, "Leave None to Tell the Story."
30. Raymond Bonner, "Panic Kills 30—Refugee Total at 1 Million," *The New York Times*, July 18, 1994.
31. Cited in Kuperman *The Limits of Humanitarian Intervention*, 2.
32. Bill Clinton, "Remarks by the President to Genocide Survivors, Assistance Workers, and U.S. And Rwanda Government Officials," (Washington, DC: Office of the Press Secretary, 1998).

33. Human Rights Watch, "Ten Years Later," (New York, 2004).
34. Samantha Power, "Bystanders to Genocide," *The Atlantic Monthly* (2001).
35. Power, "Bystanders to Genocide."
36. Power, *A Problem from Hell*, 340–41.
37. *A Problem from Hell*, 364.
38. *A Problem from Hell*, xviii.
39. Power, "Bystanders to Genocide." The convention calls on signatories to prevent and punish this crime.
40. Cited in Power, "Bystanders to Genocide," 96–97.
41. Power, *A Problem from Hell*, 358.
42. Barnett, *Eyewitness to a Genocide*, 15.
43. United Nations, "1994 Genocide in Rwanda," 27.
44. Kuperman, *The Limits of Humanitarian Intervention*; Alan Kuperman, "Rwanda in Retrospect," *Foreign Affairs* (2000).
45. A number of military experts, as well as Dallaire, have said that 5,000 experienced soldiers could have averted the genocide.
46. Kuperman, *The Limits of Humanitarian Intervention*, 88.
47. Kuperman, "Rwanda in Retrospect," 117.
48. Barnett had a special vantage point from which to write his book; he was a political officer at the US Mission to the United Nations during the Rwandan genocide, on a fellowship that allows academics to spend a year in government service.
49. Barnett, *Eyewitness to a Genocide*, 175.
50. Barnett, *Eyewitness to a Genocide*, 159–60.
51. Barnett, *Eyewitness to a Genocide*, 4.
52. Barnett, *Eyewitness to a Genocide*, 177.
53. United Nations, "1994 Genocide in Rwanda," 3.

CHAPTER 5

1. The World Bank commonly refers to the International Bank for Reconstruction and Development (IBRD) with 188 members and the International Development Association (IDA) with 173 members.
2. See, Ernst B. Haas, *When Knowledge Is Power: Three Models of Change in International Organizations* (Berkeley: University of California Press, 1990).
3. Jim Yong Kim et al., "Sickness Amidst Recovery: Public Debt and Private Suffering in Peru," in *Dying for Growth: Global Inequality and the Health of the Poor*, ed. Jim Yong Kim et al. (Monroe, ME: Common Courage Press, 2000), 142.
4. See, for example, Kevin Danaher, *10 Reasons to Abolish the IMF & World Bank*, 2nd edition ed. (New York: Seven Stories Press, 2004).

5. Sebastian Mallaby, *The World's Banker: A Story of Failed States, Financial Crises, and the Wealth and Poverty of Nations* (New York: Penguin Press, 2004), 4.

6. "New Development Bank," http://ndbbrics.org.

7. Walter W. Haines, "Keynes, White, and History," *The Quarterly Journal of Economics* 58, no. 1 (1943).

8. Haines, "Keynes, White, and History," 125–27.

9. Jochen Kraske, *Bankers with a Mission: The Presidents of the World Bank, 1946–91* (New York: Oxford University Press, 1996), 13; D. E. Moggridge, *Maynard Keynes: An Economist's Biography* (New York: Routledge, 1992), 727.

10. Edward S. Mason and Robert E. Asher, *The World Bank since Bretton Woods* (Washington, DC: Brookings Institution, 1973), 14–15.

11. Morgenthau was engaged in an internal battle with the State Department, which was developing its own proposal. In getting Roosevelt's approval, Rich concludes "The U.S. Treasury had won the turf war of the century, and the State Department has been trying to regain influence in international economic affairs ever since." Bruce Rich, *Mortgaging the Earth: The World Bank, Environmental Impoverishment, and the Crisis of Development* (Boston, MA: Beacon Press, 1994), 52.

12. Quoted in Moggridge, *Maynard Keynes*, 727.

13. John H. Crider, "Monetary Parley Called for July 1," *The New York Times*, May 27, 1944. When asked at a news conference if the press could attend the Bretton Woods conference, President Roosevelt quipped that they could, provided they don't sleep with the delegates. There was at least one unusual delegate, as well. According to the Bank's history, one "gentleman who, having been swept up into an evening discussion in the delegate's suite, listened intently, said little, and, when asked to which delegation he belonged, replied, 'None. I am the Arthur Murray instructor.'" According to the World Bank, "The governments represented were: Australia, Belgium, Bolivia, Brazil, Canada, Chile, China, Colombia, Costa Rica, Cuba, Czechoslovakia, Dominican Republic, Ecuador, Egypt, El Salvador, Ethiopia, France, Greece, Guatemala, Haiti, Honduras, Iceland, India, Iran, Iraq, Liberia, Luxembourg, Mexico, The Netherlands, New Zealand, Nicaragua, Norway, Panama, Paraguay, Peru, Philippines, Poland, South Africa, USSR, United Kingdom, United States, Uruguay, Venezuela, Yugoslavia." World Bank, "Bretton Woods Conference," http://web.worldbank.org/WBSITE/EXTERNAL/EXTABOUTUS/EXTARCHIVES/0,,contentMDK:64054691 ~ menuPK:64319211 ~ pagePK:36726 ~ piPK:36092 ~ theSitePK:29506,00.html.

14. Kraske, *Bankers with a Mission*, 16.

15. Mason and Asher, *The World Bank since Bretton Woods*, 11.

16. Georges Theunis, "Report of Commission II (International Bank for Reconstruction and Development) to the Executive Plenary Session, July 21, 1944," in *Proceedings and Documents of the United Nations Monetary and Financial Conference* (Washington, DC: United States Government Printing Office, 1944), 1101.

17. Mason and Asher, *The World Bank since Bretton Woods*, 53.

18. Mason and Asher, *The World Bank since Bretton Woods*, 53, 54.

19. World Bank, "Pages from World Bank History: Richard Demuth," January 24, 2003, http://web.worldbank.org/WBSITE/EXTERNAL/EXTABOUTUS/EXTARCHIVES/0,contentMDK:20087352 ~ pagePK:36726 ~ piPK:36092 ~ theSitePK:29506,00.html.

20. In particular, the Bank's Article V ("Organization and Management") is very similar to Articles XII and XIII of the fund.

21. Jacques Pollack, "The World Bank and the IMF: A Changing Relationship," in *The World Bank: Its First Half Century*, ed. Devesh Kapur, John P. Lewis, and Richard Webb (Washington, DC: The Brookings Institution, 1997), 473.

22. Today, as is discussed below, the broader World Bank Group consists of four arms—the IBRD, the International Development Association, International Finance Corporation (IFC), and Multilateral Investment Guarantee Agency, and each technically has its own board, but the boards of the IBRD, IFC, and IDA consist of the same members. This chapter mainly focuses on the IBRD.

23. Mason and Asher, *The World Bank since Bretton Woods*, 40.

24. International Bank for Reconstruction and Development, "Second Annual Report," (Washington, DC: International Bank for Reconstruction and Development, 1947), 36.

25. Daniel W. Drezner, "The System Worked: Global Economic Governance During the Great Recession," *World Politics* 66, no. 1 (2014): 144.

26. Kraske, *Bankers with a Mission*, 28–29.

27. Kraske, *Bankers with a Mission*, 67; United Nations General Assembly, "Agreement between the United Nations and the International Monetary Fund," (New York: United Nations, 1947).

28. Katherine Marshall, *The World Bank: From Reconstruction to Development to Equity* (New York: Routledge, 2008), 35.

29. Kraske, *Bankers with a Mission*, 67.

30. World Bank, "World Bank Group Strategy," (Washington, DC: World Bank, 2013).

31. World Bank, "Annual Report 2013," (Washington, DC: World Bank, 2013), 9.

32. The Bank's president, John McCloy, was in favor of the Marshall Plan, and testified in support of it, even though he knew it would end the Bank's work in European reconstruction. McCloy left the Bank in 1949 to become the United States' high commissioner to Germany.

33. "The World Bank's First Loan May 9, 1947," World Bank, http://web.worldbank.org/WBSITE/EXTERNAL/ EXTABOUTUS/EXTARCHIVES/0,,contentMDK:2003570 4 ~ pagePK:36726 ~ piPK:36092 ~ menuPK:56273 ~ theSitePK:29506,00.html.

34. Richard H. Demuth, the Assistant to the World Bank's Vice President in 1947, is quoted in Chuck Ziegler, "The World Bank's First Loan May 9, 1947," (Washington, DC: World Bank), http://web.worldbank .org/WBSITE/EXTERNAL/EXTABOUTUS/EXTARCHIVES /0,,contentMDK:20035704 ~ pagePK:36726 ~ piPK:36 092 ~ menuPK:56273 ~ theSitePK:29506,00.html.

35. Kraske, *Bankers with a Mission*, 59–60.

36. International Bank for Reconstruction and Development, "Fifth Annual Report to the Board of Governors 1949–1950," (Washington, DC: World Bank, 1950), 50–51.

37. International Bank for Reconstruction and Development, "Fifth Annual Report," 5.

38. Kraske, *Bankers with a Mission*, 165. McNamara became president of Ford the day after John F. Kennedy was elected president, and Kennedy quickly tapped McNamara to be his defense secretary.

39. Nicholas Stern and Francisco Ferreira, "The World Bank as 'Intellectual Actor,'" in *The World Bank: Its First Half Century*, ed. Devesh Kapur, John P. Lewis, and Richard Webb (Washington, DC: The Brookings Institution, 1997), 534–35.

40. Rich, *Mortgaging the Earth*, 81.

41. Mallaby, *The World's Banker*, 35.

42. Robert S. McNamara, "Address to the Board of Governors," (Washington, DC: International Bank for Reconstruction and Development, 1973).

43. McNamara, "Address to the Board of Governors."

44. James Huttlinger, "Robert S. McNamara, at the World Bank Group: A Chronology of Significant Events," (Washington, DC: World Bank, 2003).

45. Rich, *Mortgaging the Earth*, 84.

46. Tamar L. Gutner, *Banking on the Environment: Multilateral Development Banks and Their Environmental Performance in Central and Eastern Europe* (Cambridge: MIT Press, 2002), 51–53.

47. Rich, *Mortgaging the Earth*, 86.

48. Rich, *Mortgaging the Earth*, 88–89.

49. Mallaby, *The World's Banker*, 36.

50. Warren C. Baum, interview with Robert W. Oliver, World Bank Group Archives Oral History Program, July

23, 1986, quoted in Jochen Kraske, *Bankers with a Mission: The Presidents of the World Bank, 1946–91* (New York: Oxford University Press), 13.

51. Jeffry A. Frieden, *Global Capitalism: Its Fall and Rise in the Twentieth Century*, 1st ed. (New York: W.W. Norton, 2006), 374

52. Frieden, *Global Capitalism*.

53. Stern and Ferreira, "The World Bank as 'Intellectual Actor,'" 539–42.

54. Willi A. Wapenhans, "Efficiency and Effectiveness: Is the World Bank Group Well Prepared for the Task Ahead?," ed. Bretton Woods Commission (Washington, DC: Bretton Woods Commission, 1994), C-293.

55. Mallaby, *The World's Banker*, 44–45.

56. Country Economics Department, "Adjustment Lending: An Evaluation of Ten Years of Experience," in *Policy and Research Series* (Washington, DC: World Bank, 1988), 1.

57. In 1988, for example, just under one quarter of total Bank loans were in the form of adjustment lending. In highly indebted countries, the share was 37.3 percent of lending. See Country Economics Department, "Adjustment Lending," 10–11.

58. Ngaire Woods, *The Globalizers: The IMF, the World Bank, and Their Borrowers* (Ithaca, NY: Cornell University Press, 2006), 51; World Bank, "Annual Report 1989," (Washington, DC: World Bank, 1989), 96.

59. Woods, *The Globalizers*, 53.

60. See, for example, William Easterly, "What Did Structural Adjustment Adjust? The Association of Policies and Growth with Repeated IMF and World Bank Adjustment Loans," *Journal of Development Economics* 76 (2005).

61. Stern and Ferreira, "The World Bank as 'Intellectual Actor.'"

62. Mallaby, *The World's Banker*, 44–46.

63. See, for example, Tamar Gutner, "The Political Economy of Food Subsidy Reform: The Case of Egypt," *Food Policy* 27 (2002).

64. Portfolio Management Task Force, "Effective Implementation: Key to Development Impact," (Washington, DC: World Bank, 1992), ii.

65. Quality Assurance Group, "Portfolio Improvement Program: Draft Reviews of Sector Portfolio and Lending Investments," (Washington, DC: World Bank, 1997).

66. "Fifty Years Is Enough: US Network for Global Economic Justice,"

67. Mallaby, *The World's Banker*, 63.

68. Mallaby, *The World's Banker*.

69. Cited in Mallaby, *The World's Banker*, 111.

70. David A. Phillips, *Reforming the World Bank: Twenty Years of Trial—and Error* (New York: Cambridge University Press, 2009), 58–61.

71. Mallaby, *The World's Banker*, 113–14.
72. Bruce Rich, "The World Bank under James Wolfensohn," in *Reinventing the World Bank*, ed. Jonathan R. Pincus and Jeffrey A. Winters (Ithaca, NY: Cornell University Press, 2002), 34, 47–48.
73. For details, see Gutner, *Banking on the Environment: Multilateral Development Banks and Their Environmental Performance in Central and Eastern Europe*, 88–92; Phillips, *Reforming the World Bank*, 60–63.
74. The report is known as the Meltzer Commission Report, after its chair, Professor Allan Meltzer of Carnegie-Mellon University. See Allan (Chairman) Meltzer, "Report of the International Financial Institution Advisory Commission," (Washington, DC: 2000).
75. Rich, "The World Bank under James Wolfensohn," 26.
76. Stephen Fidler, "Who's Minding the Bank?," *Foreign Policy* September/October (2001): 40.
77. United Nations, "The Millennium Development Goals Report 2005," (New York: United Nations, 2005).
78. Alan Beattie and Edward Alden, "Shareholders' Dismay at Lack of Consultation," *Financial Times*, March 16, 2005.
79. This issue received more publicity after Wolkowitz's departure, when former US Federal Reserve Chairman Paul A. Volcker issued a report after investigating the anti-corruption agency of the World Bank. The report concluded that the Bank's anti-corruption agency, the Institutional Integrity Department, was doing an important job, fairly well, but needed some tweaks in how it was set up and reported to the Bank president. The report also argued that Bank staff should stop resisting the work of this agency. See Paul A. Volcker et al., "Independent Panel Review of the World Bank Group Department of Institutional Integrity," (Washington, DC 2007).
80. Paul Wolfowitz, "An Outsider's Fate," *The Economist*, May 19, 2007.
81. See also Vice President and Corporate Secretary, "Second Report of the Ad Hoc Group," (Washington, DC: World Bank, 2007).
82. "Zoellick's Clean-up Duty," *The Wall Street Journal*, May 31, 2007.
83. Steven R. Weisman, "Deal is Offered for Chief's Exit at World Bank," *The New York Times*, May 8, 2007.
84. Robert B. Zoellick, "Why We Still Need the World Bank," *Foreign Affairs* 91, no. 2 (2012).
85. Matthew S. Winters, "The World Bank and the Global Financial Crisis: The Reemergence of Lending to Middle-Income Countries," *Whitehead Journal of Diplomacy and International Relations* 12, no. 2 (2011).

86. World Bank, "Annual Report 2012," (Washington, DC: The World Bank, 2012), 22.
87. Robin Harding, "Man on a Mission: World Bank," *Financial Times*, April 8, 2014.
88. See Independent Evaluation Group, "The Matrix System at Work: An Evaluation of the World Bank's Organizational Effectiveness," (Washington, DC: World bank, 2012).
89. Laurie Garrett and Scott Rosenstein, "Missed Opportunities: Governance of Global Infectious Diseases," *Harvard International Review* 27, no. 1 (2005): 66.
90. Jessica Einhorn, "The World Bank's Mission Creep," *Foreign Affairs,* September/October (2001): 22.
91. Mallaby, *The World's Banker*, 6–7.
92. Bruce Rich, *Foreclosing the Future: The World Bank and the Politics of Environmental Destruction* (Washington, DC: Island Press, 2013), 13.
93. Daniel L. Nielson and Michael J. Tierney, "Delegation to International Organizations: Agency Theory and World Bank Environmental Reform," *International Organization* 57, no. 2 (2003).
94. Tamar L. Gutner, "Explaining the Gaps between Mandate and Performance: Agency Theory and World Bank Environmental Reform," *Global Environmental Politics* 5, no. 2 (2005).
95. Tamar L. Gutner, "Explaining the Gaps between Mandate and Performance: Agency Theory and World Bank Environmental Reform," *Global Environmental Politics* 5, no. 2 (2005): 22–23.
96. Fidler, "Who's Minding the Bank?," 41.
97. Catherine Weaver, *Hypocrisy Trap: The World Bank and the Poverty of Reform* (Princeton, NJ: Princeton University Press, 2008), 19.
98. Weaver, *Hypocrisy Trap*, 6.
99. Marshall, *The World Bank*, 12.
100. Devesh Kapur, John P. Lewis, and Richard C. Webb, "Introduction," in *The World Bank: Its First Half Century*, ed. Devesh Kapur, John P. Lewis, and Richard C. Webb (Washington, DC: Brookings Institution, 1997).

CHAPTER 6

1. See Robert Wade, "Greening the Bank: The Struggle over the Environment, 1970–1995," in *The World Bank: Its First Half Century*, ed. Devesh Kapur, John P. Lewis, and Richard Webb (Washington, DC: Brookings Institution Press, 1997); Catherine Weaver, *Hypocrisy Trap: The World Bank and the Poverty of Reform* (Princeton, NJ: Princeton University Press, 2008).
2. The G8 countries are France, Germany, Italy, the United Kingdom, Japan, the United States, Canada,

and Russia. This is the smaller group of powerful nations that excludes emerging powers.

3. World Bank, "Annual Report 2013," (Washington, DC: World Bank, 2013), 3.

4. See, for example, "World Bank Climate Funds: 'A Huge Leap Backwards,'" *Bretton Woods Project*, Update no. 60 (2008), http://www.brettonwoodsproject.org/art-560997.

5. Bruce Rich, "Foreclosing the Future: Coal, Climate and Public International Finance," (Washington, DC: Environmental Defense Fund, 2009).

6. Independent Evaluation Group, "Environmental Sustainability: An Evaluation of World Bank Group Support," (Washington, DC: World Bank, 2008).

7. Jennifer Clapp and Peter Dauvergne, *Paths to a Green World: The Political Economy of the Global Environment* (Cambridge: MIT Press, 2005), 56.

8. Wade, "Greening the Bank," 623.

9. United Nations Environment Programme, "Declaration of the United Nations Conference on the Human Environment," (1972).

10. J. A. G. van Gils, "Modelling of Accidental Spills as a Tool for River Management" (paper presented at the Chemical Spills and Emergency Management at Sea, Amsterdam, Netherlands, 1988).

11. World Commission on Environment and Development, *Our Common Future* (New York: Oxford University Press, 1987), Chapter 1.

12. World Commission on Environment and Development, *Our Common Future*.

13. World Bank, "World Development Report 1992: Development and the Environment," (Washington, DC: World Bank, 1992).

14. Jennifer Clapp and Peter Dauvergne, *Paths to a Green World: The Political Economy of the Global Environment* (Cambridge: MIT Press, 2005), 64.

15. Clapp and Dauvergne, *Paths to a Green World*, 65–66.

16. World Bank, "Restructuring Paper on a Proposed Restructuring of the Efficient Lighting and Appliances Project to the United Mexican States Approved on November 23, 2010," (Washington, DC: World bank, 2012). The project included grant financing from the Global Environmental Facility.

17. Independent Evaluation Group, "Environmental Sustainability."

18. This section draws heavily on Tamar L. Gutner, *Banking on the Environment: Multilateral Development Banks and Their Environmental Performance in Central and Eastern Europe* (Cambridge: MIT Press, 2002).

19. Wade, "Greening the Bank," 623.

20. Wade, "Greening the Bank," 621.

21. Bruce Rich, *Mortgaging the Earth: The World Bank, Environmental Impoverishment, and the Crisis of Development* (Boston, MA: Beacon Press, 1994), 114.

22. World Bank, "Loan Agreement, Northwest Region Development Program—First Phase, between Federative Republic of Brazil and International Bank for Reconstruction and Development," Loan Number 2061 (Washington, DC: World Bank, 1981).

23. Rich, *Mortgaging the Earth*, 27–29.

24. Wade, "Greening the Bank," 662.

25. Rich, *Mortgaging the Earth*, 34–35.

26. Rich, *Mortgaging the Earth*.

27. Rich, *Mortgaging the Earth*, 35–37.

28. World Bank, "Mainstreaming the Environment: The World Bank Group and the Environment since the Rio Earth Summit," (Washington, DC: World Bank, 1995), 119–20.

29. World Bank, "Mainstreaming the Environment," 4.

30. Sanjeev Khagram, *Dams and Development: Transnational Struggles for Water and Power* (Ithaca, NY: Cornell University Press, 2004), 2.

31. Wade, "Greening the Bank," 688–94.

32. Wade, "Greening the Bank," 696.

33. Rich, *Mortgaging the Earth*, 150.

34. Dana Clark, Jonathan Fox, and Kay Treakle, *Demanding Accountability: Civil Society Claims and the World Bank Inspection Panel* (Lanham, MD: Rowman & Littlefield Publishing, 2003), 3.

35. Bradford Morse and Thomas Berger, "Sardar Sarovar: Report of the Independent Review," (Ottawa, Canada: Resources for the Future, Inc., 1992), xx.

36. Morse and Berger, "Sardar Sarovar," 226.

37. Rich, *Mortgaging the Earth*, 302.

38. World Bank, "Effective Implementation: Key to Development Impact," (Washington, DC: World Bank, 1991), ii.

39. Ken Conca, *Governing Water: Contentious Transnational Politics and Global Institution Building* (Cambridge: MIT Press, 2006), 191–93.

40. Conca, *Governing Water*, 198.

41. Conca, *Governing Water*.

42. Conca, *Governing Water*, 204–05.

43. World Bank, "Making Sustainable Commitments: An Environmental Strategy for the World Bank," (Washington, DC: World Bank, 2001).

44. World Bank, "Toward a Green, Clean, and Resilient World for All: A World Bank Group Environmental Strategy 2012–2022," (Washington, DC: World Bank, 2012).

45. World Bank, "Development and Climate Change: A Strategic Framework for the World Bank Group," (Washington: DC, 2008).

46. Bruce Rich, *Foreclosing the Future: The World Bank and the Politics of Environmental Destruction* (Washington, DC: Island Press, 2013), 142.

47. By "industrialized countries" I refer to the Annex I countries under the United Nations Framework Convention on Climate Change, which includes industrialized countries, the EU, and "economies in transition," which include Russia and other countries in the former Soviet bloc.
48. World Bank, "Annual Report 2013," 12.
49. Independent Evaluation Group, "Annual Review of Development Effectiveness: Achieving Sustainable Development," (Washington, DC: World Bank, 2009), 50.
50. Independent Evaluation Group, "Annual Review of Development Effectiveness," 57.
51. Independent Evaluation Group, "Results and Performance of the World Bank Group 2013," (Washington, DC: World Bank, 2014), xii.
52. Heike Mainhardt-Gibbs, "World Bank Energy Sector Lending: Encouraging the World's Addiction to Fossil Fuels," (Washington, DC: Bank Information Center, 2009).
53. Rich, "Coal, Climate and Public International Finance," 13–14.
54. Rich, *Foreclosing the Future*.
55. Rich, *Foreclosing the Future*, 145.
56. World Bank, "Making Sustainable Commitments," xix.
57. World Bank, "Promoting Environmental Sustainability in Development: An Evaluation of the World Bank's Performance," (Washington, DC: World Bank, 2002), vii.
58. World Bank, "Promoting Environmental Sustainability in Development, 19.
59. Independent Evaluation Group, "Environmental Sustainability: An Evaluation of World Bank Group Support," xviii.
60. Independent Evaluation Group, "Environmental Sustainability."
61. Independent Evaluation Group, "Environmental Sustainability," xix.
62. Independent Evaluation Group. "Environmental Sustainability," xx.
63. Independent Evaluation Group, "Annual Review of Development Effectiveness," xvii.
64. Kenneth Chomitz, Dinara Akhmetova, and Stephen Hutton, "Adapting to Climate Change: Assessing the World Bank Group Experience," (Washington, DC: Independent Evaluation Group, 2013).
65. Daniel L. Nielson and Michael J. Tierney, "Delegation to International Organizations: Agency Theory and World Bank Environmental Reform," *International Organization* 57, no. 2 (2003).
66. Tamar L. Gutner, "Explaining the Gaps between Mandate and Performance: Agency Theory and World Bank Environmental Reform," *Global Environmental Politics* 5, no. 2 (2005); Tamar Gutner, "World Bank Environmental Reform: Revisiting Lessons from Agency Theory," *International Organization* 59 (2005). For their reply, see Daniel L. Nielson and Michael J. Tierney, "Theory, Data, and Hypothesis Testing: World Bank Environmental Reform Redux."
67. Susan Park, *World Bank Group Interactions with Environmentalists: Changing International Organisation Identities* (Manchester, UK: Manchester University Press, 2010).
68. Michael Goldman, *Imperial Nature: The World Bank and Struggles for Social Justice in the Age of Globalization* (New Haven, CT: Yale University Press, 2005).
69. Wade, "Greening the Bank."
70. Rich, *The World Bank and the Politics of Environmental Destruction*.
71. Gutner, "Explaining the Gaps," 21–23.
72. Gutner, *Banking on the Environment*.
73. World Bank, "Toward a Green, Clean, and Resilient World for All," 87–88.

CHAPTER 7

1. Devesh Kapur, "The IMF: A Cure or a Curse?," *Foreign Policy* 111 (1998): 115.
2. Moises Naim, "The FP Interview: A Talk with Michel Camdessus About God, Globalization, and His Years Running the IMF," *Foreign Policy* 120 (September-October 2000): 36.
3. SDR stands for "Special Drawing Right." It was created to be an international reserve asset, and it is also the IMF's unit of account. IMF member states can exchange SDRs for hard currencies like the dollar or yen, through voluntary trading with another member state. Members receive SDRs based on their standing in the IMF. Today, it is based on a basket of currencies that include the US dollar, the Euro, the Japanese yen, and the British pound. For more information, see IMF, "Special Drawing Rights (SDRs)," www.imf.org/external/np/exr/facts/sdr.htm.
4. IMF, "The IMF at a Glance," International Monetary Fund, http://www.imf.org/external/np/exr/facts/glance.htm.
5. J. Lawrence Broz and Jeffry A. Frieden, "The Political Economy of Exchange Rates," in *The Oxford Handbook of Political Economy*, ed. Barry R. Weingast and Donald A. Wittman (New York: Oxford University Press, 2006), 587.
6. Other types of "beggar-thy-neighbor" policies include tariffs and quotas on imports.
7. Jeffry A. Frieden, *Global Capitalism: Its Fall and Rise in the Twentieth Century*, 1st ed. (New York: W.W. Norton, 2006), 7.

8. Frieden, *Global Capitalism*, 257.

9. Paul Blustein, *The Chastening: Inside the Crisis That Rocked the Global Financial System and Humbled the IMF* (New York: Public Affairs, 2001), 22.

10. Blustein, *The Chastening*.

11. IMF, "IMF Conditionality," www.imf.org/external/np/exr/facts/conditio.htm.

12. For an excellent account of conditionality, see Erica R. Gould, *Money Talks: The International Monetary Fund, Conditionality, and Supplementary Financiers* (Stanford, CA: Stanford University Press, 2006).

13. Graham R. Bird, *The IMF and the Future: Issues and Options Facing the Fund* (New York: Routledge, 2003), 7.

14. Kapur, "The IMF: A Cure or a Curse?," 123.

15. See IMF, "Special Drawing Rights (SDRS)."

16. Randall W. Stone, "IMF Governance and Financial Crises with Systemic Importance," in *Studies of IMF Governance: A Compendium*, ed. Ruben Lamdany and Leonardo Martinez-Diaz (Washington, DC: International Monetary Fund, 2009).

17. IMF, "Fund Facilities," http://www.imf.org/external/np/exr/faq/facilitiesfaqs.htm.

18. More specifically, a member receives 250 basic votes, plus one extra vote for each 100,000 SDR of quota.

19. Vreeland, *The International Monetary Fund*, 19.

20. J. Keith Horsefield, *The International Monetary Fund, 1945–1965; Twenty Years of International Monetary Cooperation*, vol. I (Washington, DC: International Monetary Fund, 1969), 200–02.

21. Frieden, *Global Capitalism*, 340.

22. The speech is available on YouTube, https://www.youtube.com/watch?v = iRzr1QU6K1o.

23. Frieden, *Global Capitalism*, 341. Between December 1971 and March 1973, the Group of Ten (G10) industrial countries agreed to a new arrangement of fixed exchange rates vis-à-vis the dollar, but it collapsed due to continued pressure against the dollar. See James M. Boughton, *Silent Revolution: The International Monetary Fund, 1979–1989* (Washington, DC: International Monetary Fund, 2001), 16–17.

24. Alfred E. Eckes, *A Search for Solvency: Bretton Woods and the International Monetary System, 1941–1971* (Austin: University of Texas Press, 1975). Quoted in Frieden, *Global Capitalism*, 342.

25. Norman K. Humphreys, *Historical Dictionary of the International Monetary Fund*, 2nd ed. (Lanham, MD: Scarecrow Press, 1999), 21.

26. Boughton, *Silent Revolution*, 293. The US resources included $1 billion from the US Energy Department, $1 billion from the Exchange Stabilization Fund, and $1 billion from the Department of Agriculture's Commodity Credit Corporation.

27. On the roots of the crisis, see William R. Cline, *International Debt: Systemic Risk and Policy Response* (Cambridge: MIT Press, 1984).

28. Boughton, *Silent Revolution*, 288.

29. Timothy Curry, *History of the Eighties—Lessons for the Future*, vol. 1 (Washington, DC: FDIC, 1997), 191.

30. The Fund offered to give Mexico $1.3 billion in 1983 and similar amounts in the subsequent two years, which would leave a gap of $7 billion. Official creditors could be expected to provide around $2 billion, so de Larosière asked the banks for $5 billion in new loans. Boughton, *Silent Revolution*, 307.

31. Boughton, *Silent Revolution*, 277.

32. Ngaire Woods, *The Globalizers: The IMF, the World Bank, and Their Borrowers* (Ithaca, NY: Cornell University Press, 2006), 48.

33. Boughton, *Silent Revolution*, 274.

34. Many banks were able to swap their loan balances for what were called *Brady Bonds*, or bonds with reduced principal or interest, but with the benefit of a government guarantee.

35. Ian Vasquez, "The Brady Plan and Market-Based Solutions to Debt Crises," *Cato Journal* 16, no. 2 (1996): 236.

36. Joseph E. Stiglitz, *Globalization and Its Discontents*, 1st ed. (New York: W. W. Norton, 2002), 89.

37. David Folkerts-Landau, Donald J. Mathieson, and Garry J. Schinasi, eds., *International Capital Markets: Developments, Prospects, and Key Policy Issues* (Washington, DC: International Monetary Fund, 1997), 28.

38. Blustein, *The Chastening*, 54.

39. Martin Feldstein, "Refocusing the IMF," *Foreign Affairs* 77, no. 2 (1998).

40. Blustein, *The Chastening*, 62.

41. Thomas L. Friedman, *The Lexus and the Olive Tree* (Thorndike, ME: Thorndike Press, 1999).

42. Stiglitz, *Globalization and Its Discontents*, 95.

43. Steven Radelet and Jeffrey Sachs, "The East Asian Financial Crisis: Diagnosis, Remedies, Prospects," in Harvard Institute for International Development, 1998, 28.

44. Blustein, *The Chastening*, 214.

45. Blustein, *The Chastening*, 106–08.

46. Blustein, *The Chastening*, 147–49.

47. Blustein, *The Chastening*, 181.

48. Blustein, *The Chastening*, 202.

49. Joseph E. Stiglitz, "The Insider," *The New Republic*, April 17, 2000.

50. Naim, "The FP Interview," 37–38.

51. Feldstein, "Refocusing the IMF."

52. Feldstein, "Refocusing the IMF."

53. Feldstein, "Refocusing the IMF."

54. Kapur, "The IMF: A Cure or a Curse?."

55. Alan Meltzer (Chairman), "Report of the International Financial Institutional Advisory Commission," (Washington, DC: 2000).

56. Meltzer, "Advisory Commission," 4.

57. Blustein, *The Chastening*, 10.

58. Blustein, *The Chastening*, 9. The G7 nations are Canada, France, Germany, Italy, Japan, the United Kingdom, and the United States.

59. Kenneth Rogoff, "The IMF Strikes Back," *Foreign Policy* 134 (2003).

60. Rogoff, "The IMF Strikes Back."

61. Vreeland, *The International Monetary Fund*, 85.

62. Vreeland, *The International Monetary Fund*, 86–91.

63. Vreeland, *The International Monetary Fund*, Chapter 5.

64. Michael N. Barnett and Martha Finnemore, *Rules for the World: International Organizations in Global Politics* (Ithaca, NY: Cornell University Press, 2004), 63–66.

65. William Russell Easterly, *The White Man's Burden: Why the West's Efforts to Aid the Rest Have Done So Much Ill and So Little Good* (New York: Penguin Press, 2006), 4. This particular book by Easterly is not a scholarly tome, but rather a book intended for a more general audience. Easterly worked for many years as a World Bank economist.

66. Stiglitz, *Globalization and Its Discontents*, 24.

67. See Carmen M. Reinhart and Kenneth S. Rogoff, *This Time Is Different: Eight Centuries of Financial Folly* (Princeton, NJ: Princeton University Press, 2009).

CHAPTER 8

1. World Bank, "Annual Report 2009," (Washington, DC: World Bank, 2009), 12; World Bank, "Annual Report 2010," (Washington, DC: World Bank, 2010).

2. Cited in David Wessel, "Top Economists Rethink Post-Crisis Policy; Old Remedies Not Helpful for Spurring Growth, Preventing Calamity," *The Wall Street Journal*, November 13, 2013.

3. World Bank "Annual Report 2009," 13; World Bank "Annual Report 2010," 10.

4. International Monetary Fund. "Annual Report 2014." Washington, DC: International Monetary Fund, 2014, Appendix II.1.

5. International Monetary Fund, "Initial Lessons of the Crisis," (Washington, DC: International Monetary Fund, February 6).

6. Robert R. Callis, and Melissa Kresin, "US Census Bureau News: Residential Vacancies and Homeownership in the Third Quarter 2013," (Washington, DC: US Department of Commerce, 2013), 5.

7. US Securities and Exchange Commission, "SEC Enforcement Actions: Addressing Misconduct That Led to or Arose from the Financial Crisis," US Securities and Exchange Commission, http://www.sec.gov/spotlight/enf-actions-fc.shtml.

8. International Monetary Fund, "Global Financial Stability Report" (Washington, DC: International Monetary Fund, 2008).

9. "Lessons of the Fall," *The Economist*, October 18, 2007.

10. The story has a happier ending when it was split in two and the bank part was sold to Virgin Money in 2012.

11. Patrick Kingsley, "Financial Crisis: Timeline," *The Guardian*, August 7, 2012. http://www.theguardian.com/business/2012/aug/07/credit-crunch-boom-bust-timeline.

12. Eric Dash, "Citigroup Profit Fell 57% in Third Quarter," *The New York Times*, October 15, 2007.

13. "Crash Course," *The Economist*, September 7, 2013.

14. "Crash Course," *The Economist*.

15. A year earlier, Bear Stearns was trading at $170 per share. Andrew Ross Sorkin, "JP Morgan Pays $2 a Share for Bear Stearns," *The New York Times*, March 17, 2008.

16. This was a good deal for the Fed, which was repaid in full that Monday morning, March 17, with almost $4 million in interest. See Board of Governors of the Federal Reserve System, "Bear Stearns, JPMorgan Chase, and Maiden Lane Llc," US Federal Reserve, http://www.federalreserve.gov/newsevents/reform_bearstearns.htm.

17. Board of Governors of the Federal Reserve System, "Bear Sterns."

18. Henry M. Paulson, *On the Brink: Inside the Race to Stop the Collapse of the Global Financial System*, 1st ed. (New York: Business Plus, 2010).

19. James R. Hagerty, Ruth Simon, and Damian Paletta, "U.S. Seizes Mortgage Giants," *The Wall Street Journal*, September 8, 2008.

20. Paulson, *On the Brink*.

21. Federal Housing Finance Agency Office of Inspector General, "A Brief History of the Housing Government-Sponsored Enterprises," (Washington, DC: Federal Housing Finance Agency Office of Inspector General, 2013), 3.

22. Paulson, *On the Brink*.

23. Bill Saporito, "Freddie Mac and Fannie Mae Shareholders," *Time*, November 3, 2008.

24. Federal Housing Finance Agency Office of Inspector General "A Brief History," 6.

25. Carrick Mollenkamp et al., "Lehman Files for Bankruptcy, Merrill Sold, AIG Seeks Cash," *The Wall Street Journal*, September 16, 2008.

26. Paulson, *On the Brink*.

27. Matthew Karnitschnig et al., "U.S. to Take over AIG in $85 Billion Bailout; Credit Dries Up," *The Wall Street Journal*, September 16, 2008.

28. Karnitschnig et al., "U.S. to Take over AIG."

29. "The World This Week," *The Economist*, September 20, 2008. AIG, by the way, received an additional $30 billion loan from the US government in March 2009, under TARP.

30. Paulson, *On the Brink*.

31. "The World This Week."

32. This was TARP, or Troubled Asset Relief Program. The program included the government buying distressed mortgage assets.

33. In the end, Latin America saw a relatively small 2 percent decline in GDP in 2009. East Asian market experienced sharper declines but fiscal stimulus packages in many of its countries helped them to rebound. See Stephan Haggard, "Politics in Hard Times Revisited: The 2008–09 Financial Crisis in Emerging Markets," in *Politics in the New Hard Times: The Great Recession in Comparative Perspective*, ed. Miles Kahler and David A. Lake (Ithaca, NY: Cornell University Press, 2013).

34. Independent Evaluation Office, "IMF Performance in the Run-up to the Financial and Economic Crisis: IMF Surveillance in 2004–07," 4.

35. Joseph P. Joyce, *The IMF and Global Financial Crises: Phoenix Rising?* (New York: Cambridge University Press, 2013), 153.

36. International Monetary Fund, "Initial Lessons of the Crisis."

37. Independent Evaluation Office, "IMF Performance in the Run-up to the Financial and Economic Crisis: IMF Surveillance in 2004–07," (Washington, DC: International Monetary Fund, 2011), 1.

38. International Monetary Fund, "IMF Management and Staff Respond to the Report by the Independent Evaluation Office on IMF Performance on the Run-up to the Financial and Economic Crisis," (Washington, DC: International Monetary Fund, 2011).

39. Carmen M. Reinhart and Kenneth S. Rogoff, *This Time Is Different: Eight Centuries of Financial Folly* (Princeton, NJ: Princeton University Press, 2009): 214.

40. Paul Krugman, "Why Weren't Alarm Bells Ringing?," *The New York Review of Books*, October 23, 2014.

41. International Monetary Fund, "IMF Executive Board Approves 12.3 Billion Euro Stand-by Arrangement for Hungary," International Monetary Fund, http://www .imf.org/external/np/sec/pr/2008/pr08275.htm.

42. Joyce, *The IMF and Global Financial Crises*, 170.

43. The G20 consisted of 19 countries (Argentina, Australia, Brazil, Canada, China, France, Germany, India, Indonesia, Italy, Japan, Republic of Korea, Mexico, Russia, Saudi Arabia, South Africa, Turkey, United Kingdom, and United States) and the European Union, represented by the European Central Bank and the president of the European Council. The meeting was a little awkward in the sense that took place in the middle of a US presidential transition. Bush was on his way out, but Obama was not yet in office.

44. Yoko Nishikawa, "Japan to Offer IMF up to $100 Billion from Fx Reserves," *Reuters*, November 13, 2008.

45. International Monetary Fund, "Annual Report 2009," (Washington, DC: International Monetary Fund, 2009), 27.

46. Richard Samans, Klaus Schwab, and Mark Mallock-Brown, "Running the World, after the Crash," *Foreign Policy* (January 3, 2011).

47. See for example Colin I. Bradford, Johannes F. Linn, and Paul Martin, "Global Governance Breakthrough: The G20 Summit and the Future Agenda," in *Policy Brief #168* (Washington, DC: The Brookings Institution, 2008).

48. "Be Bold," *The Economist*, April 2, 2009.

49. International Monetary Fund, "Lending by the IMF," International Monetary Fund, http://www.imf.org/ external/about/lending.htm.

50. International Monetary Fund, "London Summit-Leader's Statement," (Washington, DC: International Monetary Fund, 2009); Joyce, *The IMF and Global Financial Crises*, 175.

51. The FSF was created following the 1997 to 1998 Asian financial crisis with a goal of promoting international financial stability. Its small secretariat was based at the Bank for International Settlements in Basel, Switzerland. Its members included bankers and finance officials from the US, Japan, Germany, UK, France, Italy, Canada, Australia, Netherlands, Hong Kong, and Singapore; international financial institutions; central bank experts; and the European Central Bank. It has made recommendations calling for private banks to be better prepared for crisis while endorsing self-regulation in some areas.

52. International Monetary Fund, "London Summit-Leader's Statement."

53. Frieden et al., "After the Fall," 26–27.

54. Annual report says 66.7 billion SDRs. Currency units for SDR for April 2009 is $1.50/SDR, so this is my conversion.

55. "East Asian Ministers Working to Expand Currency Deals," *The New York Times*, May 4, 2008. This was also called the Chiang Mai initiative, renamed Chiang Mai Initiative Multilateralization, which grew to over $240 billion by 2012.

56. Martin A. Weiss, "International Monetary Fund: Background and Issues for Congress," (Washington, DC: Congressional Research Service, 2013), 19.

57. Kenneth S. Rogoff, "After the Scandal, More of the Same at the I.M.F.," *The New York Times*, June 15, 2011.

58. International Monetary Fund, "2014 Triennial Surveillance Review—Overview Paper," (Washington, D.C.: International Monetary Fund, 2014).

59. International Monetary Fund, "Annual Report 2011,"(Washington, DC: International Monetary Fund, 2011), 37.

60. John B. Taylor, "Obama and the IMF Are Unhappy with Congress? Good; the International Monetary Fund Needs to Get Its House in Order before Washington Green-Lights More Money," *The Wall Street Journal*, February 13, 2014.

61. Frieden et al., "After the Fall," 1–2.

62. Naazneen Barma, Ely Ratner, and Steven Weber, "The Mythical Liberal Order," *The National Interest* 124 (2013).

63. Ian Bremmer and Nouriel Roubini, "A G-Zero World," *Foreign Affairs* 90, no. 2 (2011).

64. Barry Eichengreen, "Out of the Box Thoughts About the International Financial Architecture," in *IMF Working Paper* (Washington, DC: International Monetary Fund, 2009).

65. Ruben Lamdany and Sanjay Dhar, "IMF Response to the Financial and Economic Crisis," (Washington, DC: Independent Evaluation Office, 2014).

66. Joyce, *The IMF and Global Financial Crises*, 177.

67. Daniel W. Drezner, "The System Worked: Global Economic Governance During the Great Recession," *World Politics* 66, no. 1 (2014).

68. Eric Helleiner, "Reregulation and Fragmentation in International Financial Governance," *Global Governance* 15, no. 1 (2009).

CHAPTER 9

1. OECD, "Global Value Chains: Preliminary Evidence and Policy Issues," (Paris: OECD, 2011), 40.

2. Moises Naim, "Lori's War," *Foreign Policy*, no. 118 (April 1, 2000): 22.

3. Adam Smith, *An Inquiry into the Nature and Causes of the Wealth of Nations* (London: Printed for W. Strahan and T. Cadell, 1776), book 1, chapter 2.

4. Smith, *An Inquiry into the Nature*.

5. "International Trade Statistics " (Geneva, Switzerland: World Trade Organization, 2010).

6. World Trade Organization, "World Trade Report 2014," (Geneva, Switzerland: World Trade Organization, 2014), 18–19.

7. See for example Edward A. Gargan, "Bound to Looms by Poverty and Fear, Boys in India Make a Few Men Rich," *The New York Times* 1992.

8. World Trade Organization, "World Trade Report 2014," 34.

9. Paul Collier, *The Bottom Billion: Why the Poorest Countries Are Failing and What Can Be Done About It* (New York: Oxford University Press, 2007), 81.

10. Miles Kahler and David A. Lake, "Globalization and Governance," in *Governance in a Global Economy*, ed. Miles Kahler and David A. Lake (Princeton, NJ: Princeton University Press, 2003), 3.

11. Douglas A. Irwin, "Trade and Globalization," in *Globalization: What's New?*, ed. Michael M. Weinstein (New York: Columbia University Press, 2005), 26.

12. Mike Moore, "In Praise of the Future," (Geneva, Switzerland: WTO, 2000), at http://www.wto.org/english/news_e/spmm_e/spmm34_e.htm.

13. Cited in Jeffrey J. Schott, ed., *The WTO After Seattle* (Washington, DC: Institute for International Economics, 2000): xiv

14. Free traders are critical of policies or regulations that harm trade, but support government policies that encourage trade, like contract enforcement and property rights.

15. For a good explanation, see Robert Gilpin and Jean M. Gilpin, *The Political Economy of International Relations* (Princeton, NJ: Princeton University Press, 1987), 26–31.

16. Peter B. Kenen, *The International Economy* (Englewood Cliffs, NJ: Prentice Hall, 1985), 44, 47. Ricardo's model assumed the two countries have a fixed supply of labor and both the wine and cloth industries require a fixed number of workers to produce a unit of output. Portugal's advantage reflected technology that allows fewer workers to produce a unit of output.

17. Jeffry A. Frieden, *Global Capitalism: Its Fall and Rise in the Twentieth Century*, 1st ed. (New York: W.W. Norton, 2006), 2.

18. Helen V. Milner, "International Trade," in *Handbook of International Relations*, ed. Walter Carlsnaes, Thomas Risse, and Beth A. Simmons (London: Sage, 2003), 451.

19. The term was coined by Joseph Schumpeter in his 1942 book, *Capitalism, Socialism and Democracy*.

20. John Howard Jackson, *The World Trade Organization: Constitution and Jurisprudence* (London: Royal Institute of International Affairs, 1998), 15.

21. Frieden, *Global Capitalism*, 256.

22. Frieden, *Global Capitalism*, 256.

23. World Trade Organization, "The General Agreement on Tariffs and Trade (GATT 1947)," (Geneva, Switzerland: World Trade Organization) http://www.wto.org/english/docs_e/legal_e/gatt47_01_e.htm. The founding states were: Australia, Belgium, Brazil, Burma, Canada, Ceylon, Chile, China, Cuba, Czechoslovakia, France, India, Lebanon, Luxembourg, Netherlands, New Zealand, Norway, Pakistan, Southern Rhodesia, Syria, South Africa, United Kingdom, and United States.

24. Jackson, *The World Trade Organization*, 12–13.

25. Anne O. Krueger, "Introduction," in *The WTO as an International Organization*, ed. Anne O. Krueger (Chicago, IL: Chicago University Press, 1998), 5.

26. Jackson, *The World Trade Organization*, 37.
27. Carolyn Rhodes, *Reciprocity, U.S. Trade Policy, and the GATT Regime* (Ithaca, NY: Cornell University Press, 1993), 8, 80–81.
28. Jagdish N. Bhagwati, *Termites in the Trading System: How Preferential Agreements Undermine Free Trade* (New York: Oxford University Press, 2008).
29. See Sikina Jinnah, "Overlap Management in the World Trade Organization: Secretariat Influence on Trade-Environment Politics," *Global Environmental Politics* 10, no. 2 (2010); Manfred Elsig, "The World Trade Organization at Work: Performance in a Member-Driven Milieu," *Review of International Organizations* 5, no. 3 (2010).
30. World Trade Organization, "Understanding the WTO," (Geneva, Switzerland: World Trade Organization, 2010), 15.
31. World Trade Organization, "Understanding the WTO," 11.
32. Krueger, "Introduction," 6.
33. US Office of Technology Assessment, "Trade and the Environment: Conflicts and Opportunities," (Washington, DC: Government Printing Office, 1992), 61.
34. The GATT, incidentally, did have rules pertaining to NTBs. For example, Article VI set rules on antidumping and countervailing duties.
35. World Trade Organization, "Understanding the WTO," 17.
36. Alan Riding, "109 Nations Sign Trade Agreement," *The New York Times*, April 16, 1994.
37. Paul Blustein, *Misadventures of the Most Favored Nations: Clashing Egos, Inflated Ambitions, and the Great Shambles of the World Trade System*, 1st ed. (New York: PublicAffairs, 2009), 47.
38. World Trade Organization, "The Uruguay Round," http://www.wto.org/english/thewto_e/whatis_e/tif_e/fact5_e.htm.
39. Riding, "109 Nations Sign Trade Agreement."
40. Krueger, "Introduction," 1.
41. Blustein, *Misadventures of the Most Favored Nations*, 31.
42. World Trade Organization, "Understanding the WTO," 107.
43. Kent Jones, *The Doha Blues: Institutional Crisis and Reform in the WTO* (New York: Oxford University Press, 2010), 22.
44. John H. Barton et al., *The Evolution of the Trade Regime: Politics, Law, and Economics of the GATT and the WTO* (Princeton, NJ: Princeton University Press, 2006), 2.
45. Lloyd Gruber, *Ruling the World: Power Politics and the Rise of Supranational Institutions* (Princeton, NJ:

Princeton University Press, 2000); Gregory Shaffer, "Power, Governance, and the WTO: A Comparative Institutional Approach," in *Power in Global Governance*, ed. Michael Barnett and Raymond Duvall (New York: Cambridge Universitiy Press, 2005).
46. Cited in Blustein, *Misadventures of the Most Favored Nations*, 18.
47. All the various councils consist of all member states. The plurilaterals, by contrast, are not signed by all members.
48. World Trade Organization, "Overview of the WTO Secretariat," (Geneva, Switzerland: World Trade Organization) http://www.wto.org/english/thewto_e/secre_e/intro_e.htm.
49. Frank Biermann et al., "Studying the Influence of International Bureaucracies: A Conceptual Framework," in *Managers of Global Change: The Influence of International Environmental Bureaucracies*, ed. Frank Biermann and Bernd Siebenhüner (Cambridge: MIT Press, 2009), 47–49.
50. Jinnah, "Overlap Management."
51. Susan Esserman and Robert Howse, "The WTO on Trial," *Foreign Affairs* 82, no. 1 (2003).
52. David A. Lake, "Rightful Rules: Authority, Order, and the Foundations of Global Governance," *International Studies Quarterly* 54, no. 3 (2010): 602.
53. Barton et al., *The Evolution of the Trade Regime*, 71.
54. Esserman and Howse, "The WTO on Trial."
55. Barton et al., *The Evolution of the Trade Regime*.
56. World Trade Organization, "Chronological List of Disputes Cases," (Geneva, Switzerland: World Trade Organization) http://www.wto.org/english/tratop_e/dispu_e/dispu_status_e.htm.
57. Christina L. Davis, *Why Adjudicate? Enforcing Trade Rules in the WTO* (Princeton NJ: Princeton University Press, 2012), 8.
58. World Trade Organization, "Understanding the WTO," 56.
59. Davis, *Why Adjudicate?*, 18.
60. Gary P. Sampson, "Overview," in *The Role of the World Trade Organization in Global Governance*, ed. Gary P. Sampson (Tokyo: United Nations University Press, 2001), 3.
61. Davis, *Why Adjudicate?*, 9.
62. "The Price of Tariffs," *The Wall Street Journal*, July 15, 2003; "Bush's Steel Opening," *The Wall Street Journal*, November 5, 2003.
63. "Bush's Steel Opening."
64. Peter Wonacott and Scott Miller, "China Weights Tariffs on U.S. Goods," *The Wall Street Journal*, November 21, 2003, A11.
65. Shaffer, "Power, Governance, and the WTO," 137.
66. Shaffer, "Power, Governance, and the WTO," 136.
67. The big march on November 30 was sponsored by groups that included Direct Action Network, Global

Exchange, Earth First, Ruckus Society, National Lawyers Guild, Seattle Green Party, and others. The sea turtles were part of a large group sponsored by Friends of the Earth, Sierra Club, Humane Society, and Animal Welfare Institute.

68. WTO History Project, "NGO Attendees-2," Seattle: University of Washington, http://depts.washington.edu/wtohist/orgs.htm.
69. See "After Seattle: A Global Disaster," *The Economist*, December 11, 1999; Rorden Wilkinson, *The WTO: Crisis and the Governance of Global Trade* (New York: Routledge, 2006).
70. Elsig, "The World Trade Organization at Work."
71. "Ministerial Declaration," in *WT/MIN (01)/Dec/1* (Geneva, Switzerland: Doha WTO Ministerial, 2001).
72. Joseph Kahn, "Amid Trade Agenda Talks, Sharpened Focus on Rich-Poor Disputes," *The New York Times*, November 1, 2001, C1.
73. Blustein, *Misadventures of the Most Favored Nations*, 12–13.
74. Kent Jones, *The Doha Blues*, 3–5.
75. Gary Clyde Hufbauer, Jeffrey J. Schott, and Woan Foong Wong, *Figuring out the Doha Round* (Washington, DC: Peterson Institute for International Economics, 2010), 2.
76. Alan Beattie, "Economic Gloom Puts Free Trade at Risk: News Analysis," *Financial Times*, June 14, 2012.
77. Sudeep Reddy and Alex Frangos, "Trade Slows around World—Declining Growth in Exports Dims Prospects for U.S. Economy; Europe Cuts Imports," *The Wall Street Journal*, October 1, 2012.
78. Reddy and Frangos, "Trade Slows around World."
79. L. Fulponi, M. Shearer, and J. Almeida, "Regional Trade Agreements: Treatment of Agriculture," *OECD Food, Agriculture and Fisheries Working Papers* (2011): 11.
80. Howard Schneider, "On Asia Trip, Obama Presses Economic Counter to China," *The Washington Post*, November 19, 2012.
81. Fulponi, Shearer, and Almeida, "Regional Trade Agreements," 9.
82. Kerry A. Chase, "Multilateralism Compromised: The Mysterious Origins of GATT Article XXIV," *World Trade Review* (2006).
83. Bhagwati, *Termites in the Trading System*, 20–23, 26–29.
84. C. Fred Bergsten, "Open Regionalism," in *Working Paper 97-3* (Washington, DC: Peterson Institute for International Economics, 1997).
85. Bhagwati, *Termites in the Trading System*.
86. Bhagwati, *Termites in the Trading System*, 63. He fondly calls this a "spaghetti bowl" phenomenon.
87. Pascal Lamy, "Multilateral and Bilateral Trade Agreements: Friends or Foes?," (New York: Annual Memorial Silver Lecture, Columbia University, 2006).

88. Bergsten, "Open Regionalism."
89. See, for example, Andreas Dür, "EU Trade Policy as Protection for Exporters: The Agreements with Mexico and Chile," *Journal Common Market Studies* 45, no. 4 (2007).
90. Fulponi, Shearer, and Almeida, "Regional Trade Agreements," 9.
91. David Dollar, "Globalization, Poverty, and Inequality," in *Globalization: What's New?*, ed. Michael M. Weinstein (New York: Columbia University Press, 2005), 124.
92. Jean-Pierre Chauffour and Jean-Christophe Maur, "Beyond Market Access," in *Preferential Trade Agreement Policies for Development* ed. Jean-Pierre Chauffour and Jean-Christophe Maur (Washington, DC: The World Bank, 2011), 17.
93. Bernard Hoekman, "North-South Preferential Trade Agreements," in *Preferential Trade Agreement Policies for Development* ed. Jean-Pierre Chauffour and Jean Christophe Maur (Washington, DC: The World Bank, 2011).
94. Dani Rodrik, "Globalization for Whom?," *Harvard Magazine* (July-August 2002).
95. Claire Jones, "Emerging Markets Exports to Drive Growth," *Financial Times*, February 27, 2013.
96. Patrick F. J. Macrory, Arthur E. Appleton, and Michael G. Plummer, eds., *The World Trade Organization: Legal, Economic, and Political Analysis* (New York: Springer, 2005), 10.
97. Jeffrey D. Sachs, *The End of Poverty* (New York: The Penguin Press, 2005), 281–82.
98. Jennifer Clapp, "WTO Agriculture Negotiations: Implications for the Global South," *Third World Quarterly* 27, no. 4 (2006).
99. See, for example, Joanne Gowa and Soo Yeon Kom, "An Exclusive Country Club: The Effects of GATT 1950–94," *World Politics* 57 (2005).
100. Davis, *Why Adjudicate?*; Peter Rosendorff and Helen Milner, "The Optimal Design of International Trade Institutions: Uncertainty and Escape," *International Organization* 55, no. 4 (2001).
101. Richard Baldwin, "Multilateralizing Regionalism: Spaghetti Bowls as Building Blocs on the Path to Global Free Trade," *World Economy* 29, no. 11 (2006).
102. Jinnah, "Overlap Management."
103. See Barton et al., *The Evolution of the Trade Regime.*; Wilkinson, *The WTO*.
104. Susan K. Sell, *Private Power, Public Law: The Globalization of Intellectual Property Rights* (New York: Cambridge University Press, 2003).
105. For a succinct literature review, see Barton et al., *The Evolution of the Trade Regime*, 22–25.

106. Wilkinson, *The WTO*.
107. Mark A. Pollack and Gregory C. Shaffer, *When Cooperation Fails: The International Law and Politics of Genetically Modified Foods*, 1st ed. (New York: Oxford University Press, 2009).
108. Blustein, *Misadventures of the Most Favored Nations*, ix.
109. Wilkinson, *The WTO*, 4–5.

CHAPTER 10

1. Susan K. Sell, "TRIPS-Plus Free Trade Agreement and Access to Medicines," *Liverpool Law Review*, no. 28 (2007): 41.
2. HIV/AIDS stands for human immunodeficiency virus/ acquired immune deficiency syndrome.
3. World Health Organization, "Tuberculosis: WHO Global Tuberculosis Report 2014," http://www.who .int/tb/publications/factsheet_global.pdf; UNAIDS fact sheet 2013.
4. UNAIDS, "UNAIDS Report Shows That 19 Million of the 35 Million People Living with HIV Today Do Not Know That They Have the Virus," http://www .unaids.org/en/resources/presscentre/pressrelease-andstatementarchive/2014/july/20140716prgap report/.
5. Abbott Laboratories chairman comment, cited in Adrian Flint, *HIV/AIDS in Sub-Saharan Africa: Politics, Aid and Globalization* (New York: Palgrave Macmillan, 2011), 157.
6. Flint, *HIV/AIDS in Sub-Saharan Africa*, 146.
7. Margaret Chan, "Opening Remarks: Creating Synergies between Intellectual Property Rights and Public Health," World Trade Organization, http:// www.wto.org/english/tratop_e/trips_e/techsymp_ july10_e/techsymp_july10_e.htm#chan.
8. "Report of the Ebola Interim Assessment Panel," (Geneva, Switzerland: World Health Organization, 2015).
9. David P. Fidler, "The Challenges of Global Health Governance," in *International Institutions and Global Governance Program* (New York: Council on Foreign Relations, 2010), 5.
10. Fidler, "The Challenges of Global Health Governance," 4.
11. Chan, "Opening Remarks."
12. Ethan B. Kapstein and Joshua W. Busby, *AIDS Drugs for All: Social Movements and Market Transformations* (New York: Cambridge University Press, 2013).
13. Laurence R. Helfer, "Regime Shifting: The TRIPS Agreement and New Dynamics of International Intellectual Property Lawmaking," *Yale Journal of International Law* 29, no. 1 (2004): 2.
14. John H. Barton, "TRIPS and the Global Pharmaceutical Market," *Health Affairs* 23, no. 2 (2004).
15. Flint, *HIV/AIDS in Sub-Saharan Africa*, 152.
16. See John Odell and Susan K. Sell, "Reframing the Issue: The WTO Coalition on Intellectual Property and Public Health 2001," in *Negotiating Trade: Developing Countries in the WTO and NAFTA*, ed. John Odell (New York: Cambridge University Press, 2006).
17. Barton, "TRIPS and the Global Pharmaceutical Market."
18. Barton, "TRIPS and the Global Pharmaceutical Market."
19. Before a person or company asks for a compulsory license, they are supposed to attempt to negotiate a voluntary license with the patent holder. CRS report.
20. TRIPS agreement, Article 31. http://www.wto.org/ english/docs_e/legal_e/27-trips_01_e.htm
21. Jagdish Bhagwati, "Patent Protection Does Not Belong with WTO," *Financial Times*, February 20, 2001.
22. United Nations Development Programme, "Making Global Trade Work for People," (New York: Earthscan, 2003).
23. Kapstein and Busby, *AIDS Drugs for All*.
24. Flint, *HIV/AIDS in Sub-Saharan Africa*, 147.
25. G8 Information Centre, "G8 Communique Okinawa 2000," http://www.g8.utoronto.ca/summit/2000okinawa/ finalcom.htm.
26. United Nations, "Millennium Development Goals and Beyond 2015," (New York: United Nations, 2014).
27. Richard G. Marlink and Alison G. Kotin, *Global AIDS Crisis: A Reference Handbook* (Santa Barbara, CA: ABC-CLIO, 2004).
28. Helen Cooper, Rachel Zimmerman, and Laurie McGinley, "Patents Pending: AIDS Epidemic Traps Drugs Firms in a Vise: Treatment Vs. Profits—Suit in South Africa Seeks to Block Generic Copies," *The Wall Street Journal*, March 2, 2001.
29. The story did not actually end there, though. South African President Thabo Mbeki had, in 2000, questioned whether HIV caused AIDS and he had doubts about the ARV drugs. Right after the drug companies dropped their suit in April 2001, South Africa's health minister told journalists that the country was not actually in a hurry to use ARV drugs, arguing that the medications might be too dangerous and still too expensive. She recommended a focus on government-backed nutrition program and other forms of treatment. See Robert Block, "South Africa May Reject Use of AIDS Drugs—Having Beaten Back Lawsuit, Pretoria Now Is Hedging on Antiretroviral Agents," *The Wall Street Journal*, April 20, 2001.
30. Oxfam International, "GSK Breaks with Industry Ranks to Improve Access to Medicines," http://www .oxfam.org/en/pressroom/pressreleases/2009-02-17/ gsk-breaks-industry-ranks-improve-access-medicines; Block, "South Africa May Reject Use of AIDS Drugs."

31. Ian F. Fergusson, "The WTO, Intellectual Property Rights, and the Access to Medicines Controversy," in *CRS Report for Congress* (Washington, DC: Congressional Research Service, 2006), 3.

32. Flint, *HIV/AIDS in Sub-Saharan Africa*, 163.

33. Fergusson, "Access to Medicines Controversy," 6.

34. Susan K. Sell, "TRIPS Was Never Enough: Vertical Forum Shifting, FTAS, ACTA, and TPP," *Journal of Intellectual Property Law* 18, no. 447 (2011): 453.

35. Kelley Lee, Devi Sridhar, and Mayur Patel, "Bridging the Divide: Global Governance of Trade and Health," *Lancet* 373, no. 9661 (2009): 417–18.

36. WTO, "Decision Removes Final Patent Obstacles to Cheap Drug Imports," (Geneva, Switzerland: WTO, 2003).

37. Flint, *HIV/AIDS in Sub-Saharan Africa*, 165.

38. PEPFAR, "Executive Summary of PEPFAR's Strategy," United States President's Emergency Plan for AIDS Relief, http://www.pepfar.gov/about/strategy/document/133244.htm.

39. Marilyn Chase, "Clinton Foundation, Unitaid Strike Deals on Price Cuts for AIDS Drugs," *The Wall Street Journal*, April 29, 2008.

40. World Bank, "World Bank and HIV/AIDS: The Facts," http://www.worldbank.org/en/topic/hivandaids/brief/world-bank-and-hivaids-the-facts.

41. World Bank, "World Bank and HIV/AIDS.".

42. World Health Organization, "Tuberculosis," (Geneva, Switzerland: World Health Organization. http://www.who.int/mediacentre/factsheets/fs104/en/.

43. World Health Organization. "Tuberculosis."

44. World Health Organization, "World Malaria Report 2013," (Geneva, Switzerland: World Health Organization, 2013), v. Out of the deaths caused by malaria in 2012, most were children under five years old in Africa.

45. Lee, Sridhar, and Patel, "Bridging the Divide," 419.

46. Francis Gurry, "Opening Remarks: Creating Synergies between Intellectual Property Rights and Public Health" (paper presented at the WHO-WIPO-WTO Joint Technical Symposium, Geneva, July 16, 2010). They call their relationship "trilateral cooperation."

47. Jeremy R. Youde, *Global Health Governance* (Malden, MA: Polity Press, 2012), 8.

48. This is due, in part, to the higher percentage of older people in low and middle income countries. See WTO, WIPO, WHO, "Promoting Access to Medical Technologies and Innovation: Intersections between Public Health, Intellectual Property and Trade," (Geneva, Switzerland: WTO, WIPO, WHO, 2013), 25.

49. Martin Friede et al., "WHO Initiative to Increase Global and Equitable Access to Influenza Vaccine in the Event of a Pandemic: Supporting Developing Country Production Capacity through Technology Transfer," *Vaccine* 20S (2011), A4.

50. Friede et al., "WHO Initiative," A4. WHO would have the ability to provide sublicenses of this technology, which was developed by the Institute of Experimental Medicine in St. Petersburg, Russia.

51. K. Saini, N. Saini, and A. Baldi, "Impact of Anti-Counterfeiting Trade Agreement on Pharma Sector: A Global Perspective," *Journal of Current Pharmaceutical Research* 6, no. 1 (2011).

52. Olivia Solon, "Acta La Vista, Baby! European Parliament Rejects Controversial Trade Agreement," *Wired*, July 4, 2012.

53. Sell, "TRIPS Was Never Enough," 456.

54. Fidler, "The Challenges of Global Health Governance," 12.

55. Fidler, "The Challenges of Global Health Governance," 3.

56. Helfer, "Regime Shifting," 6.

57. Sell, "TRIPS Was Never Enough."

58. Kapstein and Busby. *AIDS Drugs for All: Social Movements and Market Transformations*.

59. Pascal Lamy, "Coherence between Health, Intellectual Property and Trade Key to Access to Medicines" (Geneva, Switzerland: World Trade Organization, 2013).

CHAPTER 11

1. Union of International Associations, ed., *Yearbook of International Organizations 2014–2015* (Brussels, Belgium: Brill, 2014): Figure 2.1. http://ybio.brillonline.com.proxyau.wrlc.org/sites/brill.uia.org/files/pdf/v5/2014/2_1.pdf. Interestingly, the Yearbook shows the number of such organizations peaked at 296 in 1985, and then declined to a low of 166 in 2002, before climbing back to the current level. This number is likely lower than the actual number of such organizations, since the Yearbook's data does not include region banks or courts.

2. See Edward D. Mansfield and Helen V. Milner, "The New Wave of Regionalism," *International Organization* 53, no. 3 (1999): 590; Bruce M. Russett, "International Regions and the International System," in *Regional Politics and World Order*, ed. Richard A. Falk and Saul H. Mendlovitz (San Francisco, CA: W. H. Freeman & Co. Ltd., 1973).

3. Thomas G. Weiss, David P. Forsythe, Roger A. Coate, and Kelly-Kate Pease, *The United Nations and Changing World Politics*, Westview Press, 2010, sixth edition.

4. Peter J. Katzenstein, *A World of Regions* (Ithaca, NY: Cornell University Press): 6–11.

5. Heidi Hardt, *Time to React: The Efficiency of International Organizations in Crisis Response* (New York: Oxford University Press, 2014), 1.

6. Delegation of the European Union to the United States, "What is the European Union?," (Washington, DC: Delegation of the European Union to the United States) http://www.euintheus.org/who-we-are/what-is-the-european-union/

7. Vivien A. Schmidt, "The European Union: Democratic Legitimacy in a Regional State?" *Journal of Common Market Studies*, 42, no. 5 (2004): 975–997; Alberta Sbragia, "Thinking about the European Future: The Uses of Comparison," in *Euro-Politics: Institutions and Policymaking in the 'New' European Community,* Alberta M. Sbragia, ed. (Washington, DC: The Brookings Institution, 1992); James A. Caporaso, "The European Union and Forms of State: Westphalian, Regulatory or Post-Modern?" *Journal of Common Market Studies*, 34, no. 1 (2008: 29–52).

8. Jon C. Pevehouse, "With a Little Help from My Friends? Regional Organizations and the Consolidation of Democracy," *American Journal of Political Science* 46, no. 3 (July 2002): 611–626.

9. Miles Kahler, "Regional Institutions in an Era of Globalization and Crisis," in *Integrating Regions: Asia in Comparative Context*, ed. Miles Kahler and Andrew MacIntyre (Stanford, CA: Stanford University Press, 2013).

10. The Czech Republic, Hungary, and Poland joined in 1999; Bulgaria, Estonia, Latvia, Lithuania, Romania, Slovakia, and Slovenia joined in 2004; and Albania and Croatia joined in 2009.

11. Barack Obama, "Remarks by President Obama and NATO Secretary-General Rasmussen before Meeting," White House Office of the Press Secretary http://www.whitehouse.gov/the-press-office/2014/03/26/remarks-president-obama-and-nato-secretary-general-rasmussen-meeting.

12. James M. Goldgeier, "The Future of NATO," (New York: Council on Foreign Relations, 2010).

13. Twenty-eight of its 47 members are also members of the EU.

14. Kahler, "Regional Institutions in an Era of Globalization and Crisis," 3.

15. There is an Islamic Development Bank, based in Saudi Arabia, but its 56 member states include many in Africa and Central Asia, as well as Albania, Malaysia, and Bangladesh.

16. Ramesh Thakur and Luk Van Langenhove, "Enhancing Global Governance through Regional Integration," *Global Governance* 12, no. 3.

17. Katzenstein, *A World of Regions*, 22.

18. Boutros Boutros-Ghali, "An Agenda for Peace: Preventive Diplomacy, Peacemaking and Peace-Keeping," (New York: United Nations, 1992).

19. Thakur and Van Langenhove, "Enhancing Global Governance through Regional Integration," 236–37.

20. Miles Kahler, *International Institutions and the Political Economy of Integration* (Washington, DC: The Brookings Institution): 83–83.

21. Elizabeth E. Bomberg, John Peterson, and Richard Corbett, *The European Union: How Does It Work?*, 3rd ed., The New European Union Series (Oxford, UK: Oxford University Press, 2012), 4.

22. European Union, "Living in the EU." http://europa.eu/about-eu/facts-figures/living/index_en.htm

23. Robert Schuman, "The Schuman Declaration," (1950). http://europa.eu/about-eu/basic-information/symbols/europe-day/schuman-declaration/index_en.htm.

24. European Union, "EU Treaties," http://europa.eu/eu-law/decision-making/treaties/index_en.htm.

25. The ECSC, Euratom, and EEC were formally combined in 1967 and together were known as the European Communities, or European Community (EC).

26. Michelle Egan and Maria Helena Guimaraes, "Compliance in the Single Market," *Business and Politics* 14, no. 4 (2012).

27. Europa, "Treaty of Lisbon," http://europa.eu/lisbon_treaty/glance/index_en.htm

28. Matthias Matthijs and R. Daniel Kelemen, "Europe Reborn: How to Save the European Union from Irrelevance," *Foreign Affairs* (January/February, 2015).

29. In 2013, for example, it lent €7.7 billion to nonmember states. European Investment Bank, "Financial Report 2013," 3. http://www.eib.europa.eu/attachments/general/reports/fr2013en.pdf.

30. Mark A. Pollack, *The Engines of European Integration: Delegation, Agency, and Agenda Setting in the EU* (New York: Oxford University Press, 2003); Maria Green Cowles and Stephanie Curtis, "Developments in European Integration Theory: The EU as 'Other,'" in *Developments in the European Union 2*, ed. Maria Green Cowles and Desmond Dinan (New York: Palgrave MacMillan, 2004).

31. The Council also has some executive responsibilities.

32. European Parliament at your Service, "European Citizen's Initiative," http://www.europarl.europa.eu/aboutparliament/en/001eb38200/European-citizens%27-initiative.html.

33. The approval process for the president and commission members is a good example of how confusing some EU processes are. According to the EU's website, the candidate for President of the Commission is proposed to the European Parliament by the European Council, which decides by qualified majority and taking into account, which the elections to the European Parliament.

The Commission President is then elected by the European Parliament by a majority of its component members (which corresponds to at least 376 out of 751 votes). Following this election, the President-elect selects the 27 other members of the Commission on the basis of the suggestions made by member states. The final list of Commissioners-designate has then to be agreed between the President-elect and the Council. The Commission as a whole needs the Parliament's consent. Prior to this, Commissioners-designate are assessed by the European Parliament committees.

Seven of the members are vice presidents. See European Commission, "About the European Commission," http://ec.europa.eu/about/index_en.htm.

34. Sometimes the EU Council is confused with the European Council, which is a meeting of EU leaders around four times a year to discuss big political priorities for the Union, which ends up producing a great deal of legislation. There is also a Council of Europe, which is actually not an EU institution. This Council of Europe, based in Strasbourg, is a human rights organization, whose membership includes EU members as well as 19 other countries. These states have signed the European Convention on Human Rights, which seeks to protect human rights, democracy, and the rule of law.

35. Miles Kahler, "Economic Crisis and Global Governance: The Stability of a Globalized World," in *Politics in the New Hard Times: The Great Recession in Comparative Perspective*, ed. Miles Kahler and David A. Lake (Ithaca, NY: Cornell University Press, 2013), 41.

36. Jean Pisani-Ferry, *The Euro Crisis and Its Aftermath* (New York: Oxford University Press, 2011), xi.

37. John Authers, *Europe's Financial Crisis: Short Guide to How the Euro Fell into Crisis, and the Consequences for the World*, 1st ed. (Upper Saddle River, NJ: FT Press, 2013), 2.

38. It was later revised higher.

39. Helena Smith, "Strikes Hit Greece as Debt Crisis Grows," *The Guardian US,* December 17, 2009. http://www.theguardian.com/business/2009/dec/17/greece-protests-strikes-debt-crisis.

40. "Eurozone Approves Massive Greece Bail-Out," *BBC News*, May 2, 2010.

41. International Monetary Fund, "Greece: Ex Post Evaluation of Exceptional Access under the 2010 Stand-by Arrangement," in *IMF Country Report No. 13/156* (Washington, DC: International Monetary Fund, 2013).

42. International Monetary Fund, "Greece."

43. The Irish government decided to guarantee the debts of its banks after Lehman's collapse, but Irish banks had deep problems and the country had its own property bubble. The fact that the country had also enjoyed healthy economic growth ahead of the crisis was not enough to keep it out of trouble. Portugal, meanwhile, had experienced slow growth in previous years.

44. Authers, *Europe's Financial Crisis*, 101.

45. Randall Henning, *Tangled Governance: Regime Complexity, the Troika, and the Euro Crisis,* manuscript, American University.

46. Miles Kahler and David A. Lake, "Introduction," in *Politics in the New Hard Times: The Great Recession in Comparative Perspective*, ed. Miles Kahler and David A. Lake (Ithaca, NY: Cornell University Press, 2013), 5.

47. John Peterson, "Policy Networks," in *European Integration Theory*, ed. Antje Wiener and Thomas Diez (New York: Oxford University Press, 2009).

48. Matthijs and Kelemen, "Europe Reborn."

49. See Henning, *Tangled Governance*.

50. International Monetary Fund, "Greece."

CHAPTER 12

1. Morocco is not a member, given its opposition to membership of the Sahrawi Arab Democratic Republic (Western Sahara). The Central African Republic's membership is currently suspended, given that it is essentially a failed state in the midst of civic and religious violence since a 2013 coup ousted its president, who was later sanctioned by the UN Security council for pushing the country to the brink of catastrophe.

2. John Akokpari, Tim Murithi, and Angela Ndinga-Muvumba, "Introduction: Building an African Union for the 21st Century," in *The African Union and Its Institutions*, ed. John Akokpari, Angela Ndinga-Muvumba, and Timothy Murithi (Auckland Park, South Africa: Fanele, 2008).

3. African Union, "Constitutive Act of the African Union,"(2000).

4. Elin Hellquist, "Regional Organizations and Sanctions against Members: Explaining the Different Trajectories of the African Union, the League of Arab States, and the Association of Southeast Asian Nations," ed. KFG (Berlin: Freie Universitat Berlin, 2014).

5. Heidi Hardt, *Time to React: The Efficiency of International Organizations in Crisis Response* (New York: Oxford University Press, 2014).

6. Samuel M. Makinda and F. Wafula Okumu, *The African Union: Challenges of Globalization, Security, and Governance*, Routledge Global Institutions (New York: Routledge, 2008): 12.

7. Tim Butcher, "Gaddafi Casts a Shadow over African Union," *The Telegraph*, July 8, 2002.

8. Paul D. Williams, "The Peace and Security Council of the African Union: Evaluating an Embryonic International Institution," *Journal of Modern African Studies* 47, no. 4 (2009): 606.

9. Butcher, "Gaddafi Casts a Shadow over African Union."

10. Musifiky Mwanasali, "From Non-Interference to Non-Indifference: The Emerging Doctrine of Conflict Prevention in Africa," in *The African Union and Its Institutions* ed. John Akokpari, Tim Murithi, and Angela Ndinga-Muvumba (Auckland Park, South Africa: Fanele, 2008).

11. African Union, "Peace and Security Council (PSC)," http://www.peaceau.org/en/page/38-peace-and-security-council.

12. See http://www.peaceau.org/en/resource/93-organ-panel-of-the-wise for a list of the Panel's reports and communiqués.

13. Williams, "The Peace and Security Council of the African Union," 611.

14. Arthur Boutellis and Paul D. Williams, "Peace Operations, the African Union, and the United Nations: Toward More Effective Partnerships," (New York: International Peace Institute, 2013).

15. High-Level Independent Panel on Peace Operations, "Uniting Our Strengths for Peace—Politics, Partnership and People," (New York: United Nations, June 2015).

16. David Bosco, "Omar Al-Bashir Just Made a Mockery of International Justice. Again," in Voice: *Foreign Policy*, June 16, 2015, http://foreignpolicy.com/2015/06/16/bashir-sudan-south-africa-mugabe/.

17. Alex de Waal, "The African Union and the Libya Conflict of 2011," in *Reinventing Peace* (blog), World Peace Foundation December 19, 2012, https://sites.tufts.edu/reinventingpeace/2012/12/19/the-african-union-and-the-libya-conflict-of-2011/.

18. Boutellis and Williams, "Peace Operations, the African Union, and the United Nations."

19. Boutellis and Williams, "Peace Operations, the African Union, and the United Nations," 10.

20. Tim Murithi, "Between Reactive and Proactive Interventionism: The African Union Peace and Security Council's Engagement in the Horn of Africa," *African Journal on Conflict Resolution* 12, no. 2 (2012).

21. Gilbert M. Khadiagala, "Burundi, 2002–2012," in *Responding to Conflict in Africa: The United Nations and Regional Organizations*, ed. Jane Boulden (New York: Palgrave Macmillan, 2013).

22. Alex de Waal, "Sudan: Darfur," in *Responding to Conflict in Africa: The United Nations and Regional Organizations*, ed. Jane Boulden (New York: Palgrave Macmillan, 2013).

23. Tim Murithi, "Between Reactive and Proactive Interventionism."

24. de Waal, "Sudan: Darfur," 288.

25. Boutellis and Williams, "Peace Operations, the African Union, and the United Nations," 12.

26. Boutellis and Williams, "Peace Operations, the African Union, and the United Nations," 12.

27. Haran Maruf, "Al-Shabab Attacks Expose AMISOM Weaknesses," *Voice of America,* July 1, 2015.

28. Human Rights Watch, "The Power These Men Have over Us: Sexual Exploitation and Abuse by African Union Forces in Somalia," (United States: Human Rights Watch, 2014).

29. Samuel M. Makinda and F. Wafula Okumu, *The African Union.*

30. Williams, "The Peace and Security Council of the African Union," 622.

31. Hardt, *Time to React.*

32. Human Rights Watch, "The Power These Men Have over Us."

33. Boutellis and Williams, "Peace Operations, the African Union, and the United Nations," 4–5.

34. Laurie Nathan, "The African Union and Regional Organisations in Africa: Communities of Insecurity," *African Security Review* 19, no. 2 (2010).

Index

About the Author

Tamar Gutner is Associate Professor of International Relations at American University's School of International Service (SIS). She received her PhD in political science from the Massachusetts Institute of Technology, and an MA in international relations from the School of Advanced International Studies at the Johns Hopkins University. She is the author of *Banking on the Environment: Multilateral Development Banks and Their Environmental Performance in Central and Eastern Europe* (MIT Press, 2002) and has written journal articles and book chapters on international organizations, with an emphasis on evaluating their performance. Dr. Gutner also served as an associate dean and the director of two master's degree programs at SIS. Before becoming an academic, she was a financial journalist with AP-Dow Jones.